H E I N E M A N N G E O G R A P H Y

The Human Environment

Series Editor

Bob Digby Lecturer in Education/Geography, Brunel University, London

Authors

Bob Digby Lecturer in Education/Geography, Brunel University, London

Sue Bermingham Head of Humanities, Royton and Crompton School, Oldham and PGCE Tutor, University of Manchester

Graham Butt Lecturer in Geography Education, University of Birmingham

Peter Capener Education Co-ordinator, Centre for Sustainable Energy, Bristol

Linda King Teacher of Geography/Leisure and Tourism, Industry Links Co-ordinator, Royton and Crompton School, Oldham

Graham Ranger Geography and Environmental Education Adviser, Derbyshire

Roger Robinson Development Education Centre, Birmingham, and School of Education, University of Birmingham

Celia Tidmarsh Lecturer in Geography, Bridgwater College, Somerset

Heinemann

Heinemann Educational Publishers
a division of Heinemann Publishers (Oxford) Ltd
Halley Court, Jordan Hill, Oxford OX2 8EJ

MADRID ATHENS PARIS FLORENCE PRAGUE WARSAW
PORTSMOUTH CHICAGO SAO PAULO
SINGAPORE TOKYO MELBOURNE AUCKLAND
IBADAN GABORONE JOHANNESBURG

First published 1996

00 99 98 97
10 9 8 7 6 5 4 3

ISBN 0 435 35226 1

Designed and typeset by Pentacor plc,
High Wycombe, Bucks (*Russell Horton*)

Illustrations by Brian Aldred, Arcana, Stefan Chabluk,
Tracy Hawkett, Russell Horton, Kevin Jones Associates,
Kathy Lacey, Sandra Storey.

Index compiled by Dr F. E. Merrett, member of the Society
of Indexers

Cover design by MCC
Printed in Spain by Mateu Cromo Artes Graficas SA

Acknowledgements

The authors and publishers would like to thank the following
for permission to use photographs/copyright material:

Avmark Aviation Economist, diagram 'Battle of the hubs'
p. 145; Bangkok Post Publishing Co., extracts from 'NHA tackle
"eye sore"' p. 56, rental advertisement p. 57; *The Big Issue*, quote
Bernard McGee (issue 108) p. 125; Birmingham Metronews, Ben
Taylor 'Fear of no-go zone in Brum' p. 123; Blackwell Publishers,
extract J. Seabrook *The Leisure Society* p. 125; BMJ Publishing
Group, table 'Symptoms reported from visitors...' BMJ 1990; 303
by Barlarhan et al. p. 206; Bord Failte [Irish Tourist Board]
extract *Islands of Ireland* p. 128; Cartoonist and Writers
Syndicate, cartoon by EWK p.158; Christian Aid, 'Escalator'
cartoon by Polyp p. 108; *The Daily Telegraph*, articles Malcolm
Smith 'Willow set to become a power in the land' (21/1/95)
p. 246, Jonathan Petre 'Compensation for opencast mining
needs review' (24/4/91) p. 99 reproduced by permission of Ewan
McNaughton Associates; Development Education Centre
(Birmingham), extracts 'Elizabeth' from *Land and Life*, 1995
p. 99, 'Peter' from *Beyond the Backyard* 193, p. 99 extract and
map from Delta Electronics Inc. from *The Money Machine* p. 151
and 'Interview with Kanishka' from *The Money Machine* 1994
p. 153; *The Ecologist*, Agriculture House, Bath Road, Sturminster
Newton, Devon, DT10 1DU, article 'Dragons in Distress: Crisis
and Conflict in Asia's Miracle Economics' published in 1990 by
the Institute for Food and Development Policy (Food First) 145
Ninth Street, San Francisco, USA, p. 155; *The Financial Times*,
extracts 'd' and 'e' (9/11/93) p. 89, Rich and Moony 'South
Crofty tin mine wins its fight for life' (6/8/94) p. 185, 'Chinese
tin exports rattle a fragile market' (12/8/94) p. 187, Aviane
Genillard 'Too much of a good thing' (23/6/93) p. 223, Stefan

Wagstyl 'An Indian tale of two extremes' (30/3/94) p. 230,
Damian Fraser 'Finding a dustbin for corruption' (27/4/94)
p. 230, D. Lascellas & H. Simonian 'Radioactive waste rules may
tighten' (28/2/95) p. 232, Emiko Terazona 'Mixed welcome
awaits nuclear cargo' (25/4/95) p. 232, 'MPs back wind farms
for Wales' (21/7/94) p. 243, 'Wind farms win public support'
(21/7/94) p. 243, 'Curb wind farms says tourist board' p. 243;
The Guardian, articles 'a' (23/7/93) 'b' and 'c' (7/9/93) p. 89,
Simon Beavis 'Rover sell-off irks Japanese' p. 123, 'A quiet word
is no longer sufficient' (28/11/92) p. 123, 'Crust of a wave'
(13/5/94) p. 164, 'Hidden agenda to boost opencast coal'
(23/10/92) p. 169, John Vidal 'The waste colonialists' (14/2/92)
p. 228; ICAO Journal, graph p. 142; *The Independent*, extracts
Mary Fagan 'Samsung venture means 3000 jobs for Teeside'
(18/10/94) p. 152, 'Vortex of debt and despair' p. 173, Geoffry
Lear 'Britain's dirty beaches make you sick' (30/1/94) p. 207, '
St Ives pumping station' p. 209; © International Institute for
Environment and Development, tables p. 80, extract p. 84,
quotes p. 200; Jessica Kingsley Publishers, tables 'Age structure
1960-88' p. 61, 'Household size and composition' p. 61, from
International Perspectives in Urban Studies, 'Estimates of total
urban and rural population' p. 62; Kings Cross Railway Lands
Group, article 'Kings Cross Carrion' p. 71, maps p. 72; Moon
Publications Inc., extract 'Requiem for a city' from *Thailand
Handbook* p. 47; *New Internationalist*, extracts Charles Secrett
'The Last Frontier', June 1988, p. 239; © reproduced by
permission of *New Scientist*, article p. 101; Fred Pearce 'Human
lives shrugged off in flood plan' (11/5/91) p.199; The *Observer*,
article Michael Prestage 'Cornish miners on a cliff edge as pits
die' (30/1/94) p. 180; Ordnance Survey © Crown Copyright
reproduced with the permission of the Controller of HMSO,
maps pp. 209, 244; Reuters, article 'Britain still dirty man of
Europe' (1/2/94) p. 176; Routledge, maps from T. H. Elkins and
B. Hofmeister, *Berlin* p. 35; Royal Geographical Society, figure by
Ellger from *The Geographical Journal*, Vol.158, 1992:42 p. 34;
South West Water plc for their kind permission to reproduce
the map p. 208 and brochure extract p. 211; Thomas Nelson &
Sons Ltd, extract D. Waugh 'Urban model of a city in an ELDC'
from *Geography an Integrated Approach* p. 24; © Times
Newspapers Limited, 1992, article Michael McCathy 'Toxic leak
threatens shellfish' (17/1/92) p. 183; Universal Press Pty Ltd,
map p. 91.

Photocredits
Aerofilms 3.9, 5.9, 5.25, 6.14; Arcaid/David Churchill 3.21;
Aspect Picture Library/Kim Naylor 1.18, 1.19, 3.32b; Associated
Press 1.5, 1.26; Bangladesh Space Research and Remote Sending
Organization 9.5; *Bangkok Post* 2.38; Bob Digby Intro. 1.1, Intro.
1.2, Intro. 1.5, 2.32, 2.33, 2.35, 2.36; J. Allan Cash Intro. 1.6,
2.10, 10.7a, 11.3b; Courtesy of Ecogen Limited 11.19a, 11.19b;
Environmental Picture Library/Pierre Gleizes 7.20, Martin Bond
10.24, Nigel Rolston 8.29, Guy Van Jaaij 10.5a; ETSU Intro. 3.2;
Robert Harding Picture Library 1.4, 1.13b, 8.31b; Hutchison
Library/S Lloyd 3.36; Courtesy of Jewellery Quarter Discovery
Centre/Birmingham City Council 5.10; Lucy Kirkham/DEC 6.6,
6.9; Network Photographers/W Kunz 1.9, Denis Doran 2.12,
Paul Lowe 2.23; Courtesy of Olympic Co-Ordination Authority
(Sydney) Intro. 2.1; Panos Pictures/Jon Spaull 3.32a, Trygve
Bølstad 9.9; Jaspar Pleydell-Bouverie 10.14; Rex Features 9.6;
Roger Robinson 4.2, 5.7a, 5.7b, 5.8a, 5.8b, 6.10, 6.13, 7.2b,
7.10; David Stanton 7.15; Still Pictures/Mark Edwards 2.34, 4.3;
David Hoffman 8.1; South American Pictures 11.10; Courtesy of
3PR 6.14; Telegraph Colour Library/Dilip Mehta 1.16;
Trip/Dinodia Picture Agency 1.17a, 1.20; Ullstein
Bilderdienst/Hans Peter Frentz 2.11.

The publishers have made every effort to trace the copyright
holders, but if they have inadvertently overlooked any, they
will be pleased to make the necessary arrangements at the first
opportunity.

Contents

Throughout this book you will find:

Theory boxes which explain geographical processes (e.g. page 15)
Technique boxes which explain geographical techniques (e.g. page 16)

Activities to help you explore and understand geographical ideas (on green tints e.g. page 57)
Section summaries which list key ideas and are useful for revision (e.g. page 163)

1

The challenge of urbanization

Hong Kong – a challenge for the 21st century

Figure 1 is a photograph taken from a plane approaching Hong Kong, at the point where the city and Hong Kong Island come into sight. It is a breathtaking view, and prepares travellers to Hong Kong for the spectacular sights they will see when they land and travel into the city. The country's culture – a mix of Chinese, West European, South-East Asian, Japanese, and US – means that it is a melting pot of ideas and different ways of life.

What is Hong Kong like?

Hong Kong is first and foremost a Chinese environment, even though it has been ruled directly from the UK as a British colony since 1897. British visitors may be surprised that relatively few people speak English and 82 per cent of the population speak Chinese in the Cantonese dialect – yet why should they do otherwise? Its 1994 population of 5.8 million people was predominantly Chinese, many having migrated to Hong Kong. Figure 2 shows the cultural mix at street level. The language may be Cantonese, but the advertisements, cars, and consumer goods on sale make this a commercial city with all the signs of a booming economy.

▼ **Figure 1** Aerial view of Hong Kong.

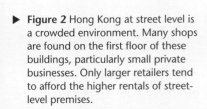

► **Figure 2** Hong Kong at street level is a crowded environment. Many shops are found on the first floor of these buildings, particularly small private businesses. Only larger retailers tend to afford the higher rentals of street-level premises.

You can see from Figure 3 that Hong Kong is about 55 km from east to west and about 40 km from north to south. This makes it similar in size to west Yorkshire or Greater London. Much of this area is water, with a land area of only 1059 km². It is a country consisting of three main areas, each shown on Figure 3:

- Hong Kong
- Kowloon
- New Territories.

The name Hong Kong is now used to include the island of Hong Kong and Kowloon. As Figure 4 shows, the built-up area of Hong Kong is quite small, and most of the area is taken up by the New Territories. These are lands which divide the urban area from the border with China. The population density of the whole country is about 5500 people per km², making Hong Kong the second most densely populated country in the world. Macau, only 30 km away, is the most densely populated country in the world. The population density in Hong Kong is not evenly distributed, however. The New Territories are relatively less dense (2000 people per km²) compared with the remarkable density of the city itself which is over 30 000 people per km². This is changing, however, as newer towns are constructed around the edge of Kowloon and urban development occurs towards the Chinese border.

Hong Kong's Gross Domestic Product (GDP) is one of the highest in South-East Asia, at over US $13 000 in 1991. GDP is a measure of a country's wealth. In South-East Asia only Japan and Singapore have higher GDPs. Hong Kong's GDP is growing at nearly 6 per cent annually, at a time when most of the countries of the EU are struggling to maintain a 2 to 3 per cent annual increase. This GDP is not distributed evenly. Chinese families who have moved to Hong Kong in the last decade often work for low wages and live in small, cheap flats of one room, while Hong Kong's business and professional classes live in some of South-East Asia's most expensive property. Large apartments in some of the high-rise blocks shown in Figure 5 may cost HK $50 000 (about £4000) in rental per month.

◄ **Figure 3** The location of Hong Kong.

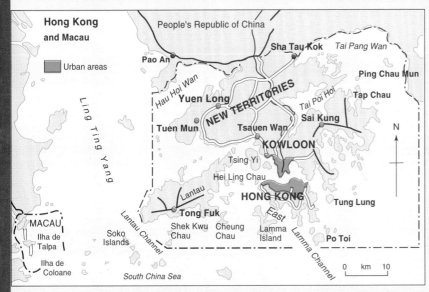

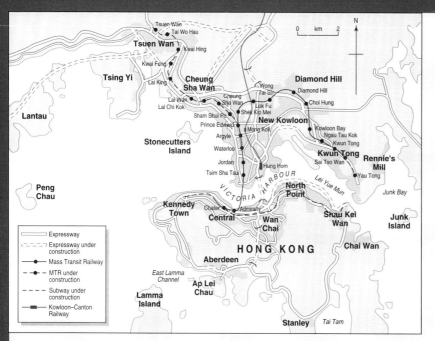

▲ **Figure 4** The urban area of Hong Kong Island and Kowloon.

▲ **Figure 5** High-rise apartment blocks on Victoria Island overlooking Hong Kong harbour. These apartments are among the most expensive in the world. Many Asian cities have similar developments of very expensive accommodation, which contrasts with the living conditions of the poorest members of the urban population.

How is Hong Kong changing?

In 1997, Hong Kong will cease to be ruled from the UK and will revert to Chinese rule. This poses all kinds of questions. Why will it change? What effects will Chinese rule have upon Hong Kong socially and economically? Who will gain? Who will lose?

In groups of three to four, brainstorm possible reactions
a) in China
b) in the UK
to Chinese rule of Hong Kong.
Are these positive (in favour of the change), or negative (against it)?

Why will it change?

Having been under UK rule for almost a century with a lease arrangement between the UK and China, Hong Kong will face political change in 1997 as it ceases to be ruled by a Governor. Hong Kong's population has only recently, in 1991, elected its own government, and most governing power lies in the hands of unelected officials. However, China's government is not elected, and it is possible that the people of Hong Kong will face direct rule from Beijing, the capital of China. China in the 1980s and 1990s has a low image in the world as a poor protector of human rights, and many people fear Chinese rule.

What social effects will Chinese rule have?

Hong Kong is an attractive place to outsiders.

- Its high GDP gives it an image of wealth.
- Nine years of schooling are guaranteed to all residents.
- The infant mortality rate is one of the lowest in the world, at less than 6 per 1000 births.
- Life expectancy is over 80 years for a baby born in 1994.
- Literacy rates are high, at about 90 per cent.

Hong Kong has all the characteristics of a country with a high standard of living. In many ways it resembles an economically more developed country (EMDC) more than an economically less developed country (ELDC).

China, across the border, has a record of human rights that has been criticized for many years, and it does not allow free movement outside its borders. Other countries in South-East Asia such as Kampuchea have suffered governments which have records of mass killings and which have not tolerated political beliefs other than their own. Hong Kong's border controls are severe, and until 1997 there will be strict controls on the number of people who can migrate there. Some people settle illegally in Hong Kong, while others have sought refugee status, arriving as 'boat people' from other countries in South-East Asia such as Kampuchea.

The pressure to migrate to Hong Kong is strong, and the contrast between Hong Kong and China is acute. That Hong Kong is wealthier than China is supported by the following contrasts.

- Rate of GDP – China's per capita GDP is US $370.
- Infant mortality rates in China of 29 per 1000 births – low by ELDC standards but high compared with Hong Kong.
- Life expectancy in China of 69 years.
- 38 per cent of Chinese women and 27 per cent of Chinese men are illiterate.

One of the questions facing both Hong Kong and China is whether rules about migration will change. There are – admittedly wild – estimates that without enforced border controls, Hong Kong's population could be 40 million by the year 2010.

What economic effects will Chinese rule have?

It is clear from the attitude of the Chinese government that it will benefit from regaining Hong Kong. Hong Kong has Asia's second most important financial market after Tokyo, containing a Stock Exchange, headquarters of banks, and overseas investors. It is in Beijing's interest to maintain the huge flow of money into Hong Kong which this provides. Does Hong Kong stand to gain? Already there is evidence that manufacturing companies are finding China a cheaper country in which to employ people, and are moving there to reduce costs. Will Hong Kong actually lose employment when control switches to Beijing? The evidence from elsewhere in the world is that manufacturing is moving to the cheaper ELDCs of the world, leaving EMDCs as providers of services and finance rather than manufacturing.

1 Draw graphs to show social and economic contrasts between Hong Kong and China.

2 What could be the effects on Hong Kong of a massive increase in migration from China? Consider housing, services, and employment.

What challenges of urbanization face Hong Kong?

This section of the book considers the challenge of urbanization.

- In what ways is urbanization a challenge?
- How do changes in Hong Kong match those occurring elsewhere?

Read the theory box below to find out what is meant by the term 'urbanization'.

What is urbanization?

Urbanization refers to the increasing numbers of people who live in cities. During the 20th century, the number of people living in cities has increased, as has the percentage that they occupy in the population as a whole. This change has been different depending on which part of the world you are in. In the EMDCs, urban populations were already high in 1900, having increased during the industrial revolution of the 19th century. In ELDCs, however, the change has been remarkable. Chapter 3 shows how, in 1980, most of the world's largest cities were in the EMDCs. Since then the populations of those cities have barely changed, or have even declined slightly. The world's largest cities are now almost entirely in the ELDCs. São Paulo, Shanghai, Calcutta, Buenos Aires, Rio de Janeiro, and Seoul are among the top ten largest cities, soon to be joined in the mid-1990s by Bombay and Beijing. Cities such as New York, London, Paris, and Los Angeles have been displaced from the top ten during the 1990s.

Why is urbanization a challenge?

The challenges are partly caused by unpredictable events. You will have seen that much of what has been written about Hong Kong here is speculative. Until the leadership alters, it is difficult to predict what changes the new rule of Hong Kong will bring. Similarly, it is difficult to know exactly what changes urbanization will create. Imagine the challenges that would face a population of 40 million in Hong Kong. This is the kind of population issue that Mexico City will face over the next 15 years. Bangkok, discussed in Chapter 2, will double its population in less than 20 years. How can cities cope?

The effects of rapid population growth will be social, economic, and environmental.

- *Social effects* describe the impacts on people and the way they live.
- *Economic effects* describe the impacts on jobs, services, and how the economy copes with its population.
- *Environmental effects* describe the impacts on urban and rural environments.

Urban environments are at stake because about one-third of the extra people in urban areas are migrants, moving from rural and smaller urban areas to the large cities. Often, migrants are much poorer than the urban population as a whole, so they put a strain on housing, services, and employment. Figure 6 shows the poverty experienced by many in Hong Kong. Poverty usually causes a deterioration of the urban environment and indicates a failure of society to cope. Rural environments also suffer as more land is absorbed into cities and the cities spread outwards.

In this section you will be asked to consider what changes are occurring in urban areas, and how they deal with change.

- What causes the change?
- Who stands to gain?
- Who stands to lose?

It is unlikely that those living in the Hong Kong apartments shown in Figure 5 will suffer from a change of government in 1997. Any growth or change in Hong Kong is likely to affect the most disadvantaged who, as Chapter 3 shows, have become poorer during the 1980s and 1990s. The challenge of urbanization is one of the biggest challenges facing the 21st century – how to cope with growing inequality.

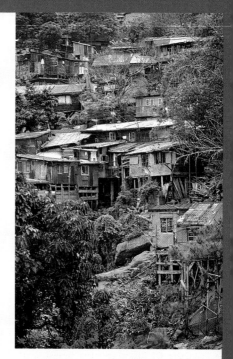

▲ **Figure 6** Housing for some of Hong Kong's less well-off population.

1 Divide into pairs.
   a) Find the world's largest cities in an atlas, using the population symbols shown for cities.
   b) Select one of the world's largest cities in an EMDC such as New York, London, Paris, or Los Angeles, and one of the largest cities in an ELDC.
2 Using atlases, news articles (including CD-ROM), geography textbooks, and your library resources, identify:
   a) what changes have been taking place
   b) why they are taking place
   c) what effects these changes are having socially, economically, and environmentally
   d) who stands to gain from the changes
   e) who stands to lose from the changes.

1 The changing face of cities

Studying cities – an introduction to urban geography

Towns and cities represent our successes and our failings as people on Earth. Urban areas are built by people and therefore shaped by us. Globally, more and more people are choosing to live in urban areas. Cities are the centres of social interaction, where people, their culture, and economic activity are brought together.

If you have visited cities like Manchester or London, or know about cities such as Cairo, São Paulo, Paris, or Hong Kong, you will know how congested urban areas can be. Old and new buildings, architecture of various periods, different languages and cultures, people of all ages and backgrounds exist side by side. Cities are alive with noise and bustle, and show evidence of constant change. Some people are bewildered by it and hate it – others find order or excitement in the confusion.

Geographers suggest that cities have a pattern to their layout. *People* are the reason why towns and cities exist, and are the driving force behind change in cities. Have you considered what gives a city its personality? Is it the buildings, the people, or something else? Answers to these questions will become clearer as you ask and answer questions about cities. The theory box below lists questions for you to consider when studying urban areas.

Enquiry in Geography

Enquiry is a means of learning. Enquiry questions help you to focus your ideas and give a purpose to your research and findings. These are questions to consider when studying urban areas:

- *What* changes are taking place? Land use, function, importance, buildings, density, type, morphology, infrastructure, layout, size, townscape, etc.

- *Where* are changes taking place? Spatially (city centre/CBD, fringe of the city)? How wide is the change? Is it occurring to the same extent in all areas?

- *When* do changes occur? Over what timescale? What is the rate of change, period of growth, or decline?

- *Why* are changes taking place? Economic, social, political, environmental issues, causes behind growth and decline, policies of renewal and redevelopment.

- *Who* causes the change? Who are the decision-makers? Public or private sector, central or local government? Market influences, protest groups, developers, external influences?

- What are the *impacts*? Economic, environmental, political, social implications, development versus conservation, inequalities in access and opportunities, changes in the quality of life.

- How are changes *managed*? Are they sustainable? Can they be integrated with others?

- What is the *future*? Evaluate changes and consider *alternatives*.

Classifying urban land use

Figure 1.1 shows a means of classifying what we see around us in cities – that is, land use. Urban fieldwork often involves looking at how land is used, recording it, and classifying it.

1 Arable land	Cereals, root crops, legumes, fodder crops, industrial crops, fallow
2 Horticulture and orchards	Allotments, nurseries, market gardens, flowers, fruit, hops, etc.
3 Grass (including parkland with scattered trees)	Only natural grasslands – excludes tended open space and public parks
4 Heathland and bog	Natural rough land
5 Woodland and shrubland	Coppices and shrubland with a canopy greater than 50%
6 Inland rocks and screes	Areas where more than 50% of the surface is covered by rock
7 Wetland and water	Lakes, reservoirs, ponds, rivers, canals
8 Coastal features	Beaches, salt marshes, and dunes
9 Quarries and other extractive industries	Not to include construction sites – see item 19
10 Agricultural buildings	Barns, stables, kennels, etc. but not farmhouses or cottages
11 Transport routes and features	Roads, railways, canals, stations, port facilities, airfields, etc.
12 Discontinuously built land – residential	Housing where gardens comprise more than 50% of the ground
13 Continuously built land – residential	Housing where gardens comprise less than 50% of the ground
14 Commercial buildings and areas	Private businesses, warehousing, open-air stockpiles, etc.
15 Industrial buildings and areas	Factories, workshops, and public utilities, e.g. sewerage, power stations, etc.
16 Public institutions	Schools, hospitals, council offices, etc. and their grounds
17 Tended open space	Public parks, designated public gardens, etc.
18 Waste land, derelict land, and derelict buildings	Only areas where it is clear that no use is imminent or planned
19 Land in transition	Construction sites, earth-moving operations, etc.
20 Miscellaneous	Land not apparently covered by any of the above

▶ **Figure 1.1** An urban land use classification scheme.

This is just one method of recording land use. Another method may be better for your local urban area. Remember that geographers may not have the time to map an entire city, and can get the same result by selecting a sample, or using a transect. A transect survey maps land use along a line which you follow through the built-up area from one part of a city to another. See Figure 1.2.

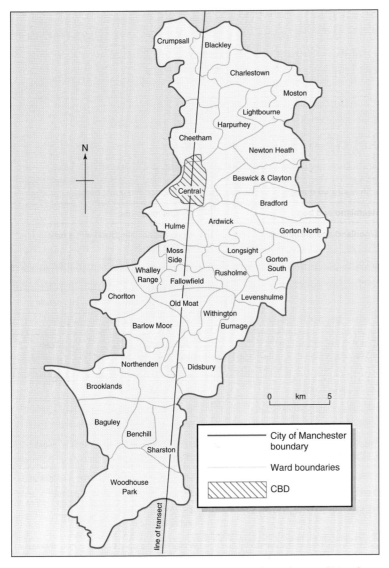

▲ **Figure 1.2 (a)** Transect surveys. An urban transect through part of Manchester.

▲ **Figure 1.2 (b)** A student's work.

Chicago

'No city in America has a stronger notion of itself, a fiercer sense of its own identity . . .' (Richard Conniff)

When fieldwork and research are completed, geographers look at patterns that emerge, and from there develop theories about why these patterns exist. This chapter investigates some of the theories about how and why cities change, with particular reference to Chicago, where many early theories about cities were developed.

Where is Chicago? What is it like?
How did it get like that?

You can gain access to a great deal of information to help you answer these questions by using the Internet. Figure 1.3 shows the kind of information that is available on Chicago.

Altitude:	176m above sea-level
Population:	2 768 483
Births (1993):	57 323
Deaths (1993):	24 826
Area:	571km²
Lake front:	46km of shoreline
Average temperature in 1993:	9.1 °C
Warmest day (27 August 1993):	34.4 °C
Coldest day (24 February 1993):	−20.6 °C
Snowfall:	1010mm
Precipitation:	1078mm

▲ **Figure 1.3** Internet information on Chicago, May 1995.

▼ **Figure 1.4** Chicago's CBD, showing The Loop – an elevated railway encircling the CBD.

Using an atlas

1 Find out the longitude and latitude of Chicago.

2 What is the time difference between Chicago and the UK?

3 Use thematic maps to find out the climate type, climatic features in winter and summer, and vegetation in and around Chicago.

4 Describe Chicago's location and distance from other US cities.

The *Chicago Travel Guide* says that Chicago: 'owes its origin to four Frenchmen in a canoe who, in 1679, paddled up the Chicago river and set up a trading post on its banks. The name derives from an Illinois Indian word *checagou* meaning "wild onion" or "strong and great".'

The city became important as a port linking the Great Lakes with the Mississippi river. Its trade increased to the east when the Erie Canal was opened in 1825, and the railway in the 1850s. Industries, for example steel, lumbering, and meat processing, grew around these transport links.

By 1900, thousands of Europeans were emigrating to Chicago, attracted by work opportunities there. The first steel-framework skyscraper was built in 1884. Elevated railway lines gave the CBD its name, The Loop, in the 1890s. The Loop has now expanded beyond these traditional limits. People began to move out to the suburbs at the turn of the century and there has been continued growth and movement outwards from the centre.

How and why has Chicago changed during the 20th century?

Since 1900, population growth rates have slowed down. In 1929, the stock market crashed and halted all major building work. Large-scale building did not start again until the election of Richard J. Daley as Mayor in 1955. Daley pursued a policy of urban renewal but could not prevent the continued migration of people out to the suburbs from downtown Chicago.

Chicago's manufacturing is diverse, and includes electrical machinery, paper, printing, chemicals, furniture, food processing, and confectionery, including Wrigley's Spearmint Chewing Gum. The largest manufacturing industry is still iron and steel. In the 1980s, Chicago was the USA's main steelmaking centre supplying car manufacturers in Detroit, like General Motors and Ford. It leads the country in the production of telephone equipment. Its O'Hare International Airport is the busiest in the world, and its harbour is the largest on the Great Lakes. The city is also a centre for research, with a number of universities.

Since 1960, over half of manufacturing employment has been lost and in the 1990s manufacturing only accounts for around 20 per cent of all jobs in the city. A growing tertiary – or service – sector has compensated for some of these losses. Financial services employ many people who have an education and qualifications. But one-third of Chicago's adults are illiterate and whilst some find employment in the service sector as waiters and cleaners, 17 per cent depend on state benefits. Despite this, Chicago is still seen as a city of opportunity. The philosophy is that determination to achieve has the best chance of meeting with success, if it is supported by hard work. Chicago's social radicalism – by US standards – is demonstrated by the election in Chicago of the first female mayor in 1979 and the first black mayor in 1983.

In the 1980s, US $10 billion were invested in new buildings. Chicago is the second largest US city after Los Angeles in terms of area, and the third largest city by population after New York and Los Angeles. It has three of the USA's tallest buildings: the Sears Tower (Figure 1.5) is 443 metres (1454 feet) high, and is the world's tallest building.

◀ ▲ **Figure 1.5** Sears Tower, Chicago.

Geographical theories for studying cities

Now you know more about Chicago, the next part of the enquiry looks at some of the theories that help to explain urban change. The Burgess concentric model is one of the most commonly used urban theory models. This enquiry sequence explores the following questions.

- Who was Burgess?
- What is the concentric model?
- How are zones identified?
- Did Burgess's model fit Chicago in the 1920s?
- What are the criticisms of the concentric model?
- Can the concentric model be used to explain today's cities?
- What alternative models exist?

Draw a time-line of events showing Chicago's history and development.

In pairs, consider whose ideas you find useful in explaining aspects of society. What kind of people are they – politicians, musicians, teachers, writers, media personalities?

Who was Burgess?

Burgess was a sociologist who used ideas and theories from late 19th century thinkers such as Durkheim, Marx, Engels, and Weber. Known as 'the founding fathers of urban sociology', they believed that communities would collapse with increasing industrialization. Their ideas were taught at the University of Chicago between 1916 and 1940, when Burgess was there.

What is the concentric model?

Park and Burgess developed a theory of human ecology, based on Charles Darwin's theory of survival of the fittest. In 1831, Darwin set off on an expedition around the world to study coastlines, flora, and fauna. His theory was developed after he read Malthus' *An Essay on the Principle of Population* (1798). Darwin concluded that certain species would be better able to survive than others, under particular environmental conditions. Over time, these conditions would change and the species would invade a new area in order to survive, allowing other species to move into the first area. At first, the most powerful would occupy the prime sites. Over time, the desirability of areas would change and new parts would be invaded.

Burgess adapted these ideas to explain Chicago's development. Many critics believe that this view of how cities change has racist implications.

How are zones identified?

Burgess continued working on the Darwinist approach to urban processes. He published his ideas in *The City* in 1925. He based his study on Chicago and the USA, and developed the concentric zone model. He argued that different types of functions competed with each other for limited space in the city, so certain functions – those with most money – became dominant in particular areas.

His model contains five concentric functional zones (Figure 1.6). These are based on differences in land use and culture in Chicago.

- At the centre is the central business district (CBD) of offices, financial services, shops, and entertainment.
- The zone of transition is where migrant communities lived on arriving in Chicago. Increased prosperity allowed them to move out – hence the transitional nature of the population.
- Lower-quality housing was to be found in Zone 3.
- Higher-quality housing was found in Zone 4.
- The ability of businesses to pay high costs automatically allowed them to survive in the most competitive place – the CBD. This is explained in the theory box on 'Bid-rent curves' opposite.

Make your own annotated copy of Figure 1.6. Explain how the five zones become separated.

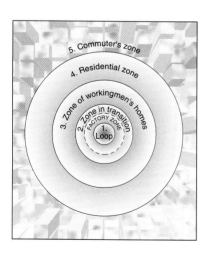

▲ **Figure 1.6** The Burgess concentric zone model.

Bid-rent curves

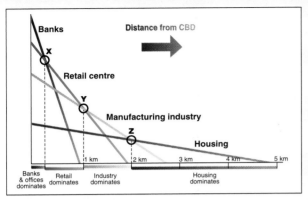

▲ **Figure 1.7** Bid-rent curves.
(a) Bid-rent lines for four different users.

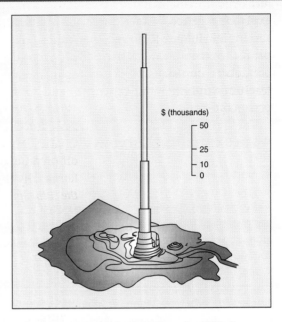

▶ (b) Land values in Topeka, Kansas, USA. Notice how although the CBD stands out in terms of rents, other minor centres stand out too. These might be local retail areas, industrial or science parks, or desirable suburbs.

The Burgess concentric zone model is based on a simple idea: that some areas of the city are more desirable than others. This affects people's willingness to pay high or low land prices. It costs much the same to build a house or office in one place as it does in another, so the cost of land affects whether a building is valuable or not.

The single factor that affects land value is its accessibility. Accessibility is determined by transport routes. Routes usually converge on city centres, making them the most accessible parts of a city, so they become the most desirable.

Those who are most able to pay usually pay the highest prices in competition with each other. Compare, for example, residents, industrialists, and office or retail developers. Individual residents are least able to afford high prices. Industrialists usually want large areas of land, so although they are wealthier than individual residents, they are restricted to places where land is plentiful. However, office and retail developers are usually able to pay much higher prices for smaller amounts of land. The ability of different groups to pay high costs is shown in Figure 1.7a, and is known as a bid-rent curve – that is, what users are willing to pay for their rents.

Figure 1.7a shows the following features.

• Office and retail developers are willing to pay highest prices but only for land they most want. A bank requires less space than a retail centre. It is

willing to pay to be in the heart of a CBD. Its theoretical bid-rent is high, but falls rapidly away from the CBD. At point X on Figure 1.7a, its price is outbid by a retail centre, which in turn is able to outbid other competing land uses. Point X is close to the city centre. Hence demand is highest at the city centre, but falls off rapidly with distance.

• Industrial users may be more flexible. Their demand for accessibility and land enables them to outbid residential users, but only to outbid banks and retail centres at certain points – point Y on Figure 1.7a, 1km from the city centre.

• Between Y and Z on Figure 1.7a, industrialists are able to outbid other users. At Z, the desirability of land for industry has fallen, so housing is now able to outbid all other users.

This is the theory behind all concentric circle models – outbidding of one land use by another. The pattern of land use shows a progression from the city centre: banks, retail, industry, and housing.

Bid-rent theory also explains variation in prices between different places. Your own home area will show differences in house prices between places that may be very close physically. This is simply a reflection of what people are willing to pay, and is shown in Figure 1.7b, based on the city of Topeka in Kansas, USA.

Within city zones and across their boundaries, Burgess identified areas where a particular ethnic or social group concentrated. These areas lead to ethnic segregation, breaking up different communities. Burgess believed that other factors break up the concentric pattern. High ground is often more desirable or a more marketable location, making the land expensive, and so it is used for high-value housing. As the town grows, groups improve their economic status, move away from the ghettos and the inner-city zones, and are absorbed into the settlement's population. This idea is based on the scientific theory of invasion, succession, and equilibrium, which follows from Darwin's theory.

Approximation surveys

Figure 1.6 uses a land use mapping technique called an approximation survey. A city is divided into areas, and each area is classified depending on what is being studied, for example land use, function, social group, age of buildings, etc. As a result of fieldwork, you may find that a small area of a city contains a variety of buildings of different ages – Victorian, Edwardian, etc. Approximation allows you to make a judgement of its general age based on the majority of buildings. In Figure 1.8, census data have been used to map the majority population.

Draw a grid onto a local street map of your chosen settlement. For your fieldwork, stand approximately in the centre of each grid square and make a visual summary of the area. Use colours or shading for different categories, to plot your results as you move from square to square. This method gives a quick overall impression of the place.

Where census data are used to map social or economic patterns, select from the data the majority population, or a minority above a certain percentage.

Identifying ethnic neighbourhoods

Burgess identified ethnic neighbourhoods as they appeared on the map in 1925 (Figure 1.11). Today, on the 1990s map, 87 ethnic neighbourhoods can still be identified in Chicago. These are popular places to experience different cultures or to be reminded of one's own, with over 6000 different ethnic restaurants (see Figure 1.8). The Illinois Bureau of Tourism promotes this feature of Chicago as a selling point, as it 'enriches the city with its cuisine, customs, folk festivals and parades'. Forty-one per cent of Chicago's people are African-American and they form the largest group in the south of the city, in neighbourhoods such as Englewood, Grand Boulevard, Chatham, Roseland, and Garfield Park, west of The Loop. The northern areas of Chicago are not dominated by a single ethnic group – so the north of the city has ethnic integration which the Burgess model did not take into account.

Richard Conniff describes how the grid system of streets means that anyone from the city can learn the location of places easily. Knowing someone's address, then, 'can also reveal where your grandparents come from, how much money you have and what colour your skin is'. Such neighbourhoods exist in cities in the UK, such as China Town in Manchester, and the Muslim community in Manningham, Bradford, where 90 per cent of the Muslim population come from just a few villages in Pakistan or Kashmir.

An advantage of neighbourhoods is that they provide an ideal

▼ **Figure 1.8** Chicago's ethnic mosaic.

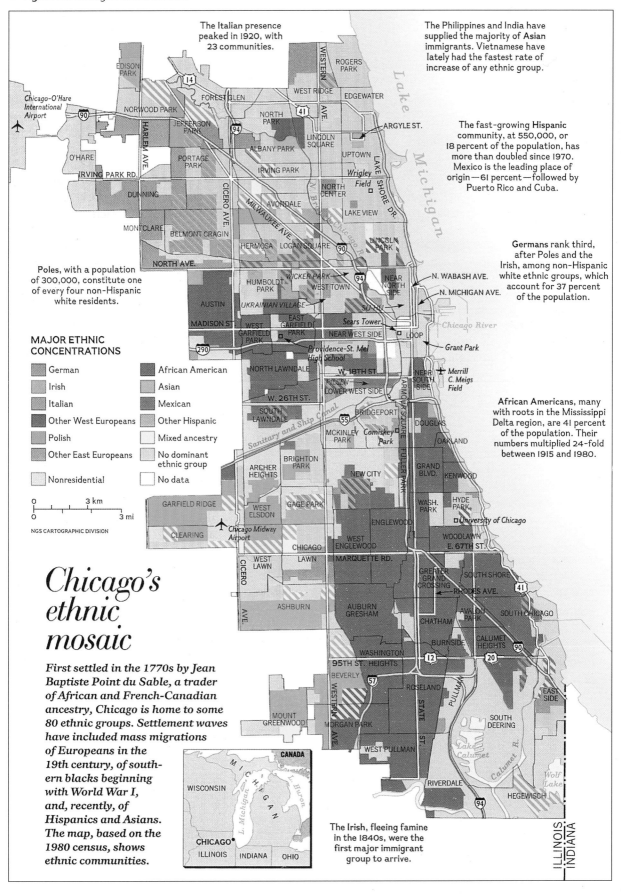

The Italian presence peaked in 1920, with 23 communities.

The Philippines and India have supplied the majority of **Asian** immigrants. Vietnamese have lately had the fastest rate of increase of any ethnic group.

The fast-growing **Hispanic** community, at 550,000, or 18 percent of the population, has more than doubled since 1970. Mexico is the leading place of origin—61 percent—followed by Puerto Rico and Cuba.

Poles, with a population of 300,000, constitute one of every four non-Hispanic white residents.

Germans rank third, after Poles and the Irish, among non-Hispanic white ethnic groups, which account for 37 percent of the population.

MAJOR ETHNIC CONCENTRATIONS

- German
- Irish
- Italian
- Other West Europeans
- Polish
- Other East Europeans
- Nonresidential
- African American
- Asian
- Mexican
- Other Hispanic
- Mixed ancestry
- No dominant ethnic group
- No data

0 — 3 km
0 — 3 mi

NGS CARTOGRAPHIC DIVISION

African Americans, many with roots in the Mississippi Delta region, are 41 percent of the population. Their numbers multiplied 24-fold between 1915 and 1980.

Chicago's ethnic mosaic

First settled in the 1770s by Jean Baptiste Point du Sable, a trader of African and French-Canadian ancestry, Chicago is home to some 80 ethnic groups. Settlement waves have included mass migrations of Europeans in the 19th century, of southern blacks beginning with World War I, and, recently, of Hispanics and Asians. The map, based on the 1980 census, shows ethnic communities.

The **Irish**, fleeing famine in the 1840s, were the first major immigrant group to arrive.

▲ **Figure 1.9** An African-American neighbourhood in Chicago.

transition zone for immigrants seeking employment in an unfamiliar environment. Those who moved here in earlier years temporarily provide services and support for those who follow. Language, religion, and food become established within a small community and support all members through a period of settling in. Once the city becomes a familiar home, people usually move out to new and different things. This movement is similar to the Darwin theory used by Park and Burgess.

Today, Chicago has around 10 000 immigrants arriving each year, mainly from Asia. The USA has far more applicants for migration than it can manage. Investigate the immigration policy for the USA, and find out how the demand for a Green Card is managed. The US Embassy is a possible source of information, and also the Internet.

One disadvantage of this initial 'invasion' of the neighbourhood is the clash between old and new. The difference between the level of economic development in the home country, and the gradual adoption of American values and attitudes, may lead to conflicting values and attitudes within families and between existing and more recent migrants in a neighbourhood. Traditional family networks break down as younger members adapt to the mobility of life in the USA, moving away for employment and leaving older family members behind. More recent migrants benefit from education, and are more able to take up professional positions.

Issues of segregation

Neighbourhoods lead to segregation – or geographical separation – of different ethnic groups. The search for security and community sometimes produces rivalries. A classic film of interest to any geographer is *West Side Story*, which is based on the story of Romeo and Juliet, and describes rivalry between ethnic gangs in the Upper East Side of New York during the 1950s. People have a great sense of identity within their own area and see it as separate from those outside.

Segregation takes place as a result of two processes:

- *Voluntary segregation* – this refers to the ways in which people select a particular area in which to live. This may include a wish to be with those who speak the same language, or follow the same religion. It is therefore a conscious process.
- *Involuntary segregation* – migrants in Chicago, particularly African-Americans, have faced many difficulties, such as in finding work. They encounter racism, through prejudice and discrimination. Often they earn far less than white people, and Chapter 5 shows that similar groups in the UK suffer much higher unemployment. Low wages force such groups to adopt the cheapest and poorest housing. Identification of a person's address by postcode may lead to refusal of credit. Such groups become segregated into areas with long waiting lists for housing, and demand for property enables unscrupulous private landlords to take advantage of high rents for poor property. This is involuntary segregation – it is beyond the control of the group that suffers.

Continual discouragement and difficulties may eventually lead to a lack of expectation. Resentment of racism, and rebellion against both the values of the ethnic culture and of the USA, may create disaffection. Invasion of communities by opportunist drug dealers, and the chance for a few to make money from trafficking, make worse the problems of gang warfare and crime. Policing policies against crime often antagonize many people who are otherwise uninvolved.

The role of education
Yet where Chicago's traditional belief exists, of great expectations for those who try, even the most disadvantaged groups seem to find success.

Conniff (1991) found this in the achievements of the Providence–St Mel school. The High School has 530 students who are all black. When President Reagan visited the school, the CIA took extra boxes along for confiscated weapons but they returned empty. By comparison, at another school nearby there were two shootings in a week. The headteacher of the Providence–St Mel school has never seen his students as an underclass and tells all the students that each will win college admission. On entry to the school, most students are low achievers, in the bottom 45 per cent of US student attainment. When they leave, most are in the 72nd percentile (for an explanation, read the technique box below).

Averages and percentiles

Percentiles are used to find out where something occurs within a distribution. For instance, Providence–St Mel school says that its students when they enter the school are in the bottom 45 per cent of US student attainment. This could be expressed as the 45th percentile – that is, 55 per cent of students achieve a higher level than they do. By graduation, students are, on average, in the 72nd percentile – that is, only 28 per cent of students achieve above them.

Figure 1.10 shows the normal distribution curve for any group of people or objects.

- *The mean* – this is the average, found by adding the total for the group, and then dividing by the number in the group.
- *The standard deviation from the mean* – this is the amount within which you can expect most items to fall within a group. Car manufacturers often advertise the average figures of fuel consumption for a particular model. Some cars have better fuel

consumption and are above the mean, some have poorer fuel consumption and are below the mean. The majority of cars are within a certain range of the mean. Using the graph, 68 per cent of cars have fuel consumption close to the mean. Only 2.25 per cent have a very low fuel consumption, and only 2.25 per cent have high fuel consumption.

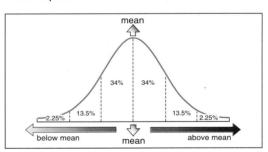

▲ **Figure 1.10** A normal distribution curve based on car fuel consumption.

Did Burgess's model fit Chicago in the 1920s?
The Burgess model sparked further research, and it is still widely studied today. His theory was a generalization based on studies of one North American city in the 1920s. Some academics then did not agree with his view of a city as a natural unit, with its own social laws, and believed that *individuals* shape cities and their zones.

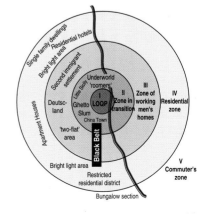

▶ **Figure 1.11** Burgess's 1925 map of urban areas. Compare this with Burgess's concentric zone model (Figure 1.6).

What are the criticisms of the concentric model?

Critics of the model believe that it has little value for explaining current urban patterns because cities have changed. They argue that Chicago is unique because of its historical and cultural background, so the model cannot be applied to other cities. Recent studies show little evidence of sharp boundaries between various zones. In pre-industrial cities of ELDCs, such as India or Bangladesh, higher-income groups are likely to be found at the centre, and low-income groups on the edges, in shanty town areas. (This is shown in Bombay later in this chapter.) There are also influential agencies within society which control urban development, for example government planners, local councils, and private developers, all of whom may limit Burgess's process of invasion and succession. This is especially true of Chicago and other cities, where in the 1980s and 1990s inner-city regeneration has changed many of the perceptions of inner cities.

Can the concentric model be used to explain today's cities?

Study the quotes in Figure 1.12 from Burgess's work in 1925. Draw a two-column table. In column A, copy each quote. In column B, write your own assessment of how well each quote fits a city that you know well.

'Problems that alarm and bewilder us [such] as divorce, delinquency, and social unrest, are to be found in their most acute forms in our largest [American] cities.'

'The Metropolitan area . . . is coming to be defined by . . . transportation that enables a business man to live in a suburb of Chicago and to work in The Loop, and his wife to shop at Marshall Fields and attend Grand Opera in the auditorium.'

'[There is a] tendency of each inner zone to extend its area by the invasion of the next outer zone . . . all five zones [of the model] were [once found in] . . . the present business district.'

'Neither Chicago nor any other city fits perfectly . . . this ideal scheme. Complications are introduced by the lake front, the Chicago river, railroad lines, historical factors in the location of industry, the . . . resistance of communities to invasion, etc.'

'. . . there is the natural tendency for local and outside transportation to converge in the CBD.'

'In the downtown (CBD) section of every large city we expect to find department stores, skyscraper office buildings, railroad stations, great hotels, theatres, art museum, and the city hall . . . the economic, cultural, and political life centres here.'

'More recently [1925] sub-business centres have grown up in outlying zones.'

'The area of deterioration . . . of stationary or declining population, is also one of regeneration . . .'

'The highest land values in [the city] are at the point of greatest mobility in the city . . . in The Loop (the CBD).'

▲ **Figure 1.12** Quotes from Burgess's work.

What alternative models exist?

Models are theoretical land use patterns and they simplify the real world. The Hoyt sector model (1939) and the Harris and Ullman multiple nuclei model (1945) both show alternative patterns of land use to those suggested by Burgess. All three models show a segregation of land uses. These ideas are explained in the theory box.

Other models of urban development

Hoyt's model

The Hoyt model (1939) considers direction as well as distance. Figure 1.13a considers direction and desirability of land, as well as distance. Hoyt found that cities rarely contain identical land use within the same radial zones, but vary, with industry and housing found together. 'Wedges' of residential land use grow out from the centre, with higher-value housing in the most attractive location. Hoyt assumed that cities vary in landscape and relief, and desirable areas would develop, such as the northern lakeside of Chicago (Figure 1.13b). High-income earners are likely to want (and are able to afford) to live here, and are unlikely to choose a location close to industry, near noxious smells or noise. Once the industrial area is defined – usually along transport links – it influences the location of other zones which have to fit around it.

Cheapest housing is usually found in the less popular, less marketable areas. These areas may be adversely affected by industrial noise or fumes, and are occupied by low-income earners. However, they benefit from low transport costs to and from work. In Chicago, for example, cheaper housing and heavy industry were located to the south. This is similar to Hoyt's sector model. Industry benefited from a nearby labour supply and needed cheap land. Residents nearby benefited from job opportunities.

Harris and Ullman's model

Another urban theory is Harris and Ullman's multiple nuclei model (1945). This theory was developed later, and in response to criticisms of the others, so is more complex. Harris and Ullman saw the CBD as just one nucleus for development because only some land uses can afford the high rents of a city-centre location. Elsewhere, suburban shopping centres or nearby villages may be absorbed into the growing, larger settlement, and these form nuclei for further development. Burgess had found evidence of sub-business centres in outlying zones. Cities develop from a number of points, therefore, rather than from a single point as suggested by other models. Each nucleus grows until it merges with others, producing a larger urban area.

▼ **Figure 1.13(a)** The Hoyt sector model.

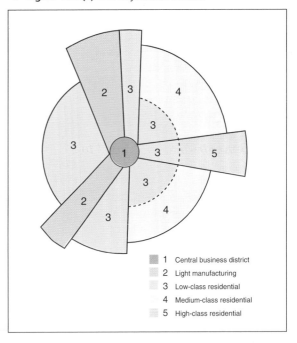

1 Central business district
2 Light manufacturing
3 Low-class residential
4 Medium-class residential
5 High-class residential

(b) Chicago's northern lakeside area. Hoyt identified affluent urban 'sectors' such as this one.

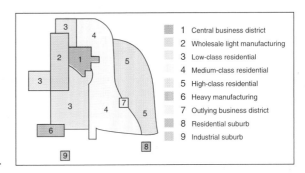

1 Central business district
2 Wholesale light manufacturing
3 Low-class residential
4 Medium-class residential
5 High-class residential
6 Heavy manufacturing
7 Outlying business district
8 Residential suburb
9 Industrial suburb

▶ **Figure 1.14** The Harris and Ullman multiple nuclei model.

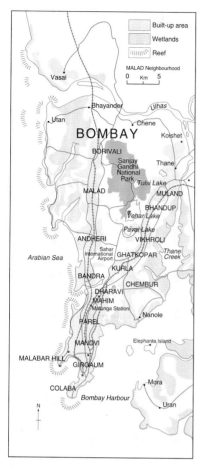

▲ **Figure 1.15** Bombay.

Bombay

In this part of the chapter we look at a city in an ELDC – Bombay. Culturally, socially, economically, and politically, India is very different from the USA.

Carry out the following geographical enquiry about Bombay.

- What is it? Where is it?
- What is it like?
- How did it get like this?
- How and why is it changing?
- What are the implications of change?

Use a variety of sources of information, e.g. atlases, CD-ROM, Internet, textbooks, journals, video.

Background history

The city of Bombay was founded on seven islands. In 1534 it was taken over by the Portuguese, who named the area Bom Bahia (Good Bay). In 1664, India became a British colony. In the 19th century land reclamation schemes turned the area into a single island by draining wetlands. On one side, the island is separated from the mainland by the Vasai Creek. The Arabian Sea lies to the west and the south (see Figure 1.15). In the 1830s, steamships were developed and Bombay became a port and manufacturing centre because of its large, natural harbour. It now extends to the mainland.

The city is built on volcanic rocks, which have created fertile black soils used for growing cotton. It is one of India's largest textile manufacturing centres. Over half of its factory workers are employed in cotton textiles. Other textile manufacturing includes silk, synthetic fibres, bleaching, and dyeing. Bombay's industries also include bicycle manufacture, printing, glassware, and pharmaceuticals. It is a centre for research and education, there is an atomic research centre, the University of Bombay, the Institute of Technology, and the National Centre for Software Technology, which links education and research worldwide by Ernet, which allows direct access to the Internet.

People and movement

The city receives migrants by the hundred each day. Many arrive by train. Over half of its 1991 population of 12 570 000 live on the streets or in slums and survive by begging.

Investigate how the census is carried out in the UK. How frequently is it updated? How is it carried out? How long does it take? How reliable is it? How reliable would it be in a city like Bombay, where many people live on the streets and hundreds are arriving each day? How would you estimate numbers who arrive each day in a place?

Bombay is incredibly crowded. Sixty-seven per cent of Bombay's population live on Bombay Island. Trains run in and out of the Victoria Terminus every two minutes – they are loaded to well over their legal capacity (Figure 1.16). Bombay has one of the highest population densities in the world. The overall population density for Bombay is 580 people per square kilometre. However, Dharavi, to the east of Mahim Bay, is known as Asia's largest slum – here 230 000 people live in less than one square kilometre. Most of the newest arrivals are from rural villages. Rural areas suffer poverty because here there are large numbers of landless people, and subsistence farmers who work plots that are too small to provide a reasonable income.

▲ **Figure 1.16** Journey to work in Bombay – a crowded environment.

Read the technique box on population densities. Choose an appropriate technique to represent the densities of India, Bombay, and Dharavi, and suggest reasons for the differences between them.

Population densities

Population density is used to show average densities of people in an area. It can be done by country, as here, or by city, or by part of a city. It is calculated by dividing the number of people living in an area by the size of the area – usually in square kilometres. Below are population density figures per km² for a selection of countries.

India	291
UK	238
USA	27
Japan	328
Australia	2.2
Hong Kong	5860
Brazil	18

1 Draw seven squares, each 2 x 2cm.

2 Represent population densities by dots in each square, 1 dot = 10 people.

3 Each dot in each square should be identical, and spaced equally from all others.

Migration – breaking from tradition?

People move to a city like Bombay for a variety of reasons – to take up a university place, perhaps, or to join a brother or sister already living there, to search for medical treatment, or simply to seek a new and better life. Bombay is the most cosmopolitan of the cities in India, offering great religious diversity – Hindus (over 50 per cent), Muslims, Christians, Parsees, Buddhists, and Jains. City lifestyles often contrast with the traditional views held by families and their religion. Some see life in Bombay as a way of escaping the control of the family and religious practice. Career women in Bombay enjoy more freedom than elsewhere in India. They can drive their own car, live on their own, marry their choice of partner rather than that of their family, and are subject to relatively less harassment. The education system allows children to be educated in ten different languages.

However, there are tensions and violence, partly created by cultural diversity. Riots in December 1992 began with a Muslim response to the destruction by Hindus of a 16th-century mosque in Ayodhya. Hindus believe that the mosque was built on the sacred birthplace of the god Rama. The following month the Hindu-led riots broke out which culminated in bombings in March 1993. Over 1000 people were killed, and the city's economy lost hundreds of millions of rupees in damage and loss of business.

Identifying different areas of Bombay

Bombay has contrasting areas or zones, just as Chicago does. The theory box below shows an urban model of cities in ELDCs. One similarity between the two cities is the existence of a CBD. Bombay has problems of gang rivalry, particularly over land and property. With such shortages of space, land prices are very high, with prime-site properties in the city among the most expensive in the world. High prices are caused by a shortage of property and a shortage of land because the city is built on an island. A wealthy financier may pay over £1 million for a flat in the city. The skyline is full of skyscrapers because of these prices, and many of these are occupied by overseas companies which are prepared to pay to be close to the CBD.

Urban models for cities in the ELDCs

Figure 1.17a shows Bombay's CBD skyline. The existence of a CBD is one of many similarities between cities in EMDCs and ELDCs. However, there are many differences too. Figure 1.17b shows a model for a city in an ELDC based on Brazil. The term *favelas* is used for squatter settlements on the edge of the city. Different names are used for similar settlements around the world – *pueblos jovenes* in Lima (Peru), *bustees* in Calcutta, for example. However, their location is similar, on the outskirts of large cities where land is cheapest. Harrassment of squatters is common where land is in demand in the CBD, and squatters are forced to move further away from the centre.

The rapid growth of cities in ELDCs has meant that recent expansion has taken place on the edges, leaving older and more expensive property close to the centre. Mixed in with this are high-rise blocks of expensive apartments close to the CBD, as for example in Hong Kong (see the introduction to this section) and in Bangkok (see Chapter 2).

▼ **Figure 1.17** Cities in ELDCs.

(a) Bombay's CBD skyline.

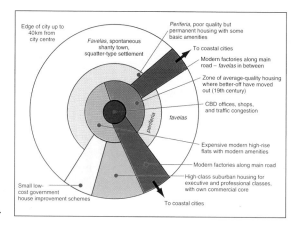

(b) Urban model of a city in an ELDC, based on Brazil.

1 Identify similarities between the model in Figure 1.17b, and those of Burgess, Hoyt, and Harris and Ullman for cities in EMDCs.

2 Identify features that make cities in ELDCs unique.

Development in Bombay is also affected by environmental groups. Father D'Britto, a Roman Catholic priest, leads marches to protest against further destruction of arable land in Vasai, to the north. Apartment blocks built on the land have provided much-needed housing. However, housing has placed more pressure on nearby water supplies. As more people now use the wells, salinity levels have increased and in some cases the wells have dried up completely.

Bombay cannot meet the demands of its growing population for amenities. Dharavi is the biggest slum area and has one standpipe for every 200 families. It is one of the better slum areas to live in. In 1981, there was 0.4ha of open land for every 3000 people, including grassy areas in the middle of traffic roundabouts. Pressure on land and amenities is increasing, because the population is growing rapidly.

▲ **Figure 1.18** Crowded island environments in Bombay.

Opportunity and diversity

As in Chicago, people succeed even in the most deprived communities. One example is the Koli fishing community, one of the oldest communities on the island of Bombay. Their catch is used to produce the famous Bombay duck (fried pieces of dried fish). As the city grew, the group became sandwiched between office blocks and apartments, in the CBD and along the shoreline. The Koli people succeeded in halting the Back Bay land reclamation project, by going to court. The proposed scheme would have prevented them fishing, by limiting their access to the water. The land would have been used for offices and apartments. The group was given 8500m² of land, which allowed them to continue fishing in the same way, although the government has prevented new migrants from joining the community.

The Dabbawallah

Religious diversity creates both problems and opportunities. When Bombay was smaller, people were able to walk home for lunch but now some have to travel 50km from home to work. Many workers have to leave their homes before 7 am because traffic is congested and slow. The Dabbawallah were created for this very reason. 'Dabbawallah' is the name given to people who provide a unique and efficient delivery service. They are officially known as the 'Union of Tiffin Box Suppliers'. Each Dabbawallah collects around 40 aluminium containers from workers' homes, with a special meal inside, prepared by the family. Each container is addressed with the district, office block, and floor of its recipient. Most Dabbawallah are unable to read and use a form of hieroglyphics. Without the Dabbawallah, those preparing the meal would have to get up before dawn to have lunch ready in time for when the worker leaves.

The carriers are taken to the nearest railway station and sorted into various office districts. Trays of containers are then carried on the Dabbawallah's heads as they board trains to take them to the city centre. Each worker therefore receives a meal matching the dietary requirements of their religion. In the afternoon, the Dabbawallah picks up the empty carriers and returns them home, to be used again. This economic opportunity has developed out of the supply of cheap labour.

▶ **Figure 1.19** The Dabbawallah.

▲ **Figure 1.20** New housing development in Bombay.

Select *one* of these essay titles:

- What similarities and differences do you see between Bombay and Chicago?

- Using the information in this chapter, and further reading, how useful do you think urban models are in understanding how cities develop?

Planning a New Bombay

In 1981, the City and Industrial Development Corporation (CIDCO) of Maharashtra planned a New Bombay, in 20 satellite towns, to be located on the mainland. It was hoped that the New Bombay would reduce congestion and pollution in the city, because a new harbour could handle goods intended for places outside Bombay. Vashi was one of the new townships in this plan. Vashi was to provide homes for 10 000 families, mainly employed in the petroleum, chemical, and cement industries. Although homes still had only one room of 14m^2, with a tap inside and a toilet outside, they were attractive to those living in slums such as Dharavi. Within the first year, the development had attracted 12 500 people from Bombay Island.

Facing the future

On 23 April 1995, the UK *Observer* newspaper reported that from 1 May 1995, Bombay would be known in India as Mumbai, after a Hindu goddess. Hindu extremists Shiv Sena had taken control of the local government after elections in March 1995. Riots between Muslims and Hindus began once again. Muslims have been asked to prove their Indian citizenship. An anti-Muslim campaign has been pursued under Shiv Sena's authority: 70 000 Muslims have been removed from the electoral role until they can prove they are Indian citizens. Persecution has led to Muslims taking refuge in certain neighbourhoods, which are becoming Muslim ghettos. Divisions are increasing, and Muslims only feel safe within their own communities. Hindus and Muslims seem unable to mix, and a compromise is difficult.

Kobe

Kobe is on the island of Honshu in Japan and lies roughly in the middle of the island (Figure 1.21). The main urban area lies between the Rokko mountain range and the coast. The city is a linear shape 2–4km wide, following the coast for 30 km to the east and west. Its has been shaped by the physical landscape, just as Chicago was affected by Lake Michigan, and Bombay by its island location. The Rokko mountains are prone to landslides. In the mid-1990s Kobe was reshaped by an even greater natural phenomenon – an earthquake.

Land use zoning in Kobe is clear (Figure 1.22). The port lies by the water's edge, and the industrial area is further inland but parallel to the coastline. Residential areas are on high land overlooking the coast. The settlement grew around the harbour in the 13th century, as trade with China and other Asian countries prospered. Industrialization overseas in the late 19th century expanded trade, and population grew as employment opportunities developed. Figure 1.23 shows Kobe's population growth. Between 1889 and 1939 the population grew from 134000 to 1 million, and Kobe was one of Japan's six largest cities by 1939. The Second World War had a devastating effect on the city, and by 1945 the population had fallen to 400 000. Planning and industrialization have restored the city's economy and in January 1991 the population was 1 479 888.

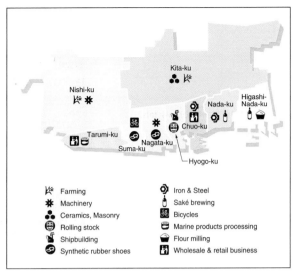

▲ **Figure 1.22** Land use in the suburbs of Kobe.

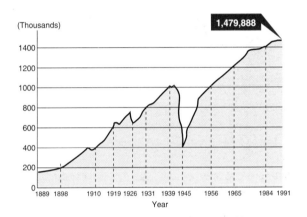

▲ **Figure 1.23** Population growth in Kobe, 1889–91.

The port is very important in Kobe's economy. It has attracted industries such as steelmaking, shipbuilding, shipping, and foodstuffs. As Japan has a shortage of raw materials, the industries are close to the port to reduce transport costs. Daihatsu and Mitsubishi are located in Kobe. The city is a traditional centre for brewing saké – Kobe saké is considered to be one of the best.

Population density along the coast is 6788 people per km². As the city has grown, surrounding farmland has been threatened by urban land uses. Local farmers supply fruit, milk, vegetables, and beef. The sea has always provided an important part of the Japanese diet.

◀ **Figure 1.21** Kobe.

1 Draw a table with three columns, A, B, and C. In A, list the five aims of Kobe's development plan. In B, score from 0 to 5 how well you think Chicago meets these aims. In C, score how well you think Bombay meets these aims. Add a score for each city.

2 Justify your scores.

3 In pairs, identify two examples of how each of the five aims of Kobe's plan might work.

4 How much do you agree with the aims of the Kobe plan? How big a job is it to achieve them?

Kobe had a development plan before the major earthquakes in 1994–95 devastated sections of the city. By 2001 Kobe should have become 'the city with a human face', following a plan which gave great importance to the natural environment. The plan had five main points:

● Human Environment City – harmony between humans and nature

● International and Information City – economic activities closely linked to the life and culture of the citizens

● City of Civic Culture – provides citizens with the joy of creation in their daily lives

● Human Welfare City – citizens live in affluent circumstances and lead worthwhile lives

● People-based City – where every citizen takes a part in creating a better city.

The Kobe earthquakes, 1994–95

In December 1994 and January 1995, a series of earthquakes struck Kobe. The information in Figures 1.24 and 1.25 comes from news reports and the Internet. (Try to obtain updated information, using CD-ROM and the Internet.)

▼ **Figure 1.24** News reports on the Kobe earthquake.

Japan picked up the pieces yesterday following three strong earthquakes in fourteen hours.

Seismologists warned of worse tremors to come.

(a) From the *Financial Times*, 28 December 1994.

The Japanese community in Britain spent yesterday trying to contact relatives and friends as they watched footage of the devastation on television. . . Rescue teams fought fires and searched for the dead and missing throughout last night after the earthquake disaster that Japan thought could never happen killed 1800 people and injured more than 6330. The 'quake which struck at 5.46 am measured 7.2 on the Richter scale and was Japan's worst for almost 50 years. . . The tremors destroyed or damaged more than 12 000 buildings and twisted road and rail links throughout the region, particularly in Kobe, a city of 1.4 million people about 450km west of Tokyo. Gas and water supplies were cut and transport and telecommunication links were paralyzed. Kansai International Airport, opened recently on reclaimed land off Osaka, continued to function but there were several delays. . . Yesterday's 'quake, measured by seismologists as magnitude 7.2, was worse only because its epicentre lay under a densely populated area. The earlier 'quakes – magnitude 7.5 on 28 December, 6.7 on New Year's Day, 6.9 on 7 January – were all off the eastern coast of north Honshu and caused only a few fatalities . . . The death toll may rise, as about a thousand people were still missing in freezing temperatures last night, and more than 6000 were injured. Water supplies were cut, hindering efforts to contain fires that still burned into the night.

(b) From *The Times*, 18 January 1995.

'There are a lot of wooden houses in my neighbourhood. Now they are destroyed without pity. Soon it got lighter and I could see my surroundings. Some went mad. I went to hospital with my grandmother who was rescued from a heap of rubble – her finger was tearing off. We got to hospital. It was hell on earth. A man bleeding from his head, a child – purplish maybe from suffocation. It was filled with people. My grandmother was disinfected, that's all. Her injury was not serious compared with others. My grandmother's house and my grandfather's house, both were burned down. We couldn't get out anything. The town I liked had changed in a moment. I was sad. Now I live in one of the refuges and I get scared during the night. I want to see Kobe rebuilt again soon.' Yasuyo Morita (17 years)

'We don't have gas and water yet. So I go to the river to take water for toilet everyday since the earthquake.' Hiromi Tsukamoto (17 years)

'I'm very tired of life these days. I'm not so busy every day but I feel stress. I want to alleviate stress soon. But there aren't places where we can play and relax in Kobe. Come back those happy days.' Mio Nakajima (17 years)

'The saddest thing for me was I lost my favourite friend. Buildings can be rebuilt again. Life . . . no more.' Misa Hamaguchi (17 years)

'This earthquake brought us a lot of sad things, but I found one thing that is good for me. Very beautiful night sky came back to us, I think. It may be because chemical plants were forced to stop working.' Mio Nagamoto (17 years)

▲ **Figure 1.25** Quotes from the Internet: eye-witness accounts of the Kobe earthquake, by Akatsukayama High School students.

◄ **Figure 1.26** Devastation following the Kobe earthquake, December 1994/January 1995.

Rebuilding a city – a decision-making exercise

Form groups of three or four. Assume the role of advisers, and report on how Kobe should be redeveloped. Take into account the Kobe development plan outlined on page 28.

1 Identify the problems that have arisen as a result of the earthquake.

2 Produce your own plan for Kobe. Suggest
   a) Short-term changes which relieve the immediate problems.
   b) Long-term changes which make use of the opportunity to re-organize the city.
   c) Priorities for action.

3 Justify your plans and present them on display for the people of Kobe at the next round of local district meetings.

Ideas for further study

You have studied three cities in three countries, and theories on why and how cities change. Now complete a study of your local town or nearest city.

1 Map land use in the settlement. Use techniques described in this chapter, and the 'official' land use classification code (Figure 1.1). A colour key may make it easier to identify patterns.

2 Discuss how closely the settlement fits Burgess's model, and other models.

3 Suggest reasons why the settlement does not fit any model perfectly.

Summary

- Cities, although complex, can more easily be understood using urban models.
- Cities develop as a result of:
  – economic processes, which determine land use patterns
  – social processes such as segregation
  – administrative processes such as planning.
- Cities reflect societies in the way that they demonstrate issues of social justice.
- Urban areas are diverse socially, economically, and environmentally – such diversity creates advantages and problems.
- Urban planning attempts to manage some of the challenges presented by cities.

References and further reading

R. Conniff, 'Welcome to the neighbourhood', *National Geographic* Vol.179 No.5 May 1991, pp.50–77.

J. McCarry, 'Bombay. India's capital of hope', *National Geographic* Vol.187 No.3 March 1995, pp.42–67.

R. E. Park, E. W. Burgess and R. D. McKenzie, *The City*, University of Chicago Press, 1925.

S. Warn and C. Bottomley, *Towns and Cities*, Arnold Wheaton, 1987.

This chapter looks closely at Berlin and Bangkok. Both are changing rapidly and illustrate some of the ideas from Chapter 1 about how cities develop and change. Berlin is changing as a result of German reunification, and Bangkok because of a rapid growth in population.

Berlin – divided past, united future?

Berlin is described in *Germany – The Rough Guide* as:

'. . . like no other city in Europe, or, indeed, the world. For over a century its political climate has either mirrored or determined what has happened in the rest of Europe; heart of the Prussian kingdom, economic and cultural centre of the Weimar Republic, and, in the final days of Nazi Germany, the headquarters of Hitler's Third Reich, it is a weather vane of European history. After the war, the world's two most powerful military systems stood face-to-face here, sharing the spoils of a city split by . . . the Berlin Wall. As the Wall fell in 1989, Berlin was once again pushed to the forefront of world events.'

Until 1990 Berlin was a divided city 'locked' within the state of East Germany (Figure 2.1). Politically part of West Germany, West Berlin was located inside East Germany, a separate country inside the communist 'Iron Curtain'. Capitalist and communist worlds existed on either side of the boundary which separated Germany into two countries. East Berlin was divided from West Berlin by the Berlin Wall, and was itself the capital of East Germany.

Reunification created a united Germany in 1990. The decision to re-establish a united Berlin as the capital provides a unique study of urban change under different political and economic conditions.

▼ **Figure 2.1** Berlin's location within Germany before 1990. The border between the former East and West Germany is shown. Notice Berlin's location deep within the former East Germany, even though the West of the city was politically part of West Germany.

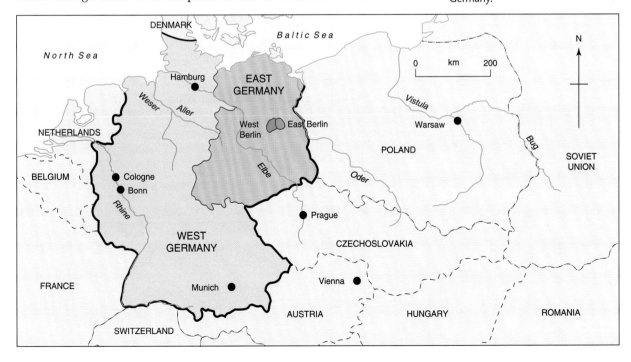

Berlin will soon regain from Bonn its status as capital of Germany. Given its location in the 'depressed' eastern half of Germany the future commercial success of Berlin is important, and the city is already attracting new businesses. The scale of necessary urban redevelopment is huge: restoring architectural sites, constructing government buildings, and renewing housing, retailing, and industry. Berlin has also always possessed a distinct cultural, political, administrative, musical, and academic function, which it is keen to enhance in the coming years.

This part of the chapter explores the following questions:

- How has Berlin been affected by its past?
- What changes have been brought about by reunification?
- How will people's lives be affected by these changes?

How has Berlin been affected by its past?

The Second World War caused the destruction of much of Berlin's infrastructure. Germany was occupied by the Allies – the USA, the former Soviet Union, Britain, and France – in 1945 and Berlin became 'landlocked' within Soviet-controlled East Germany. It was divided into four Allied occupation sector (Figure 2.2). Each of the Allies received a share of the city, with the historic city centre of Berlin Mitte governed by the Soviets in East Berlin. In 1961, this part became separated from the rest by the famous Berlin Wall. East Berlin became the capital of East Germany whilst West Berlin developed as an isolated part of West Germany, its capital functions having been relocated to Bonn.

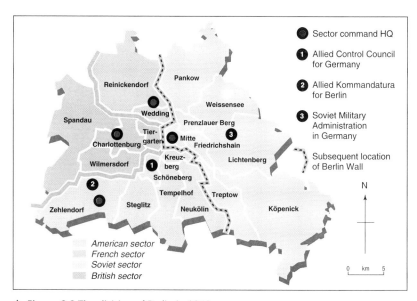

▲ **Figure 2.2** The division of Berlin in 1945.

For 45 years West Berliners lived in an 'island' community physically separate from, but politically and economically part of, West Germany 175km away. The bulk of West Berlin's trade was with West Germany. Like West Germany it received an influx of migrant labour from southern and south-eastern Europe, especially Turkey, during the economic booms of the 1960s and early '70s. Immigrants replaced the labour force from East Berlin who were prevented from working in the western half of the city by the Berlin Wall, which was built in 1961 to halt the drain of predominantly young professional people from East to West Berlin.

During 1989 many East Germans left their country via Hungary and Czechoslovakia, which had recently adopted more liberal communist regimes. In Berlin many protested for civil rights. On 9 November 1989, East Germany removed border controls along the Berlin Wall. Thousands of East Berliners flooded into the West to be greeted by West Berliners (Figure 2.3). The two city governments set up new border crossings and re-opened U Bahn (underground) stations in East Berlin that had been closed for 30 years. The divided city had become physically united again.

Figure 2.3 describes the freedom that Berliners felt, but raises questions about whether the fall of the Berlin Wall was beneficial to everyone.

1 List and discuss some of the possible disadvantages of the Wall's removal. Who might gain or lose the most?

2 What might be the short-term and long-term problems of unifying a city like Berlin?

Berlin's urban structure before 1945

In order to help understand the present-day appearance and form of Berlin we need to look at how far the city 'fits' geographical models of urban growth and land use. Three models of urban structure – the Burgess concentric model, the Hoyt sector model, and the Harris and Ullman multiple nuclei model – are described in Chapter 1. Study these carefully. Berlin does not conform exactly to any one of these, but contains:

- concentric 'growth rings'
- sectors of contrasting economic activities and status
- a number of subsidiary nuclei.

Wartime damage, capitalist and communist influences, and post-war reconstruction have all complicated the structure of the city.

Every German can tell you where he or she was on the night of 9 November 1989, when the news spread that the Berlin Wall was open. I remember sitting in front of our TV with my friends, drinking champagne and watching speechless, stunned, and happy as young Berliners climbed up the wall and cheered to the crowd. It is one of those events that, like the assassination of John F. Kennedy, is permanently branded on the memory of a nation.

The euphoric mood that prevailed directly after the fall of the Berlin Wall, however, has vanished. Three years after the country was officially reunited, on 3 October 1990, emotions about unification, especially among Easterners, are mixed. Whereas the political and bureaucratic structures of West Germany were quickly introduced into the former East Germany, the economic and psychological gap has yet to be overcome. For the average West German, unification has meant an increased tax burden, as state resources are siphoned off to support and modernize eastern Germany. For East Germans, nearly every aspect of their lives has changed. People are still happy about their newly won political freedom, but there remains a lot of anger over the past. Moreover, unification has meant a huge surge in unemployment, and many East Germans, long used to a cradle-to-grave welfare system (where everyone was guaranteed a job), are struggling to cope with the demands of a free-market economy. The number of homeless in both East and West has increased considerably, and panhandlers [beggars] are now a common sight in the bigger cities.

▲ **Figure 2.3** The fall of the Wall – from *Germany on the Loose.*

Berlin consists of an urban core, an area encircling it known as the Wilhelmian ring, and an outer zone.

The urban core

The central core of Berlin was developed around the site of a medieval city. Until 1939 this area contained shops, offices, warehouses, and workshops, and a 'zone in transition' from which people were moving to find better accommodation.

Concentric urban development grew from the core, each phase of growth marked by a 'fringe' where industries or activities needing space were forced to locate away from the crowded centre. Major routeways, such as the Kurfurstendamm and Unter den Linden, helped to create sectors of different land use.

The Wilhelmian ring

The second concentric zone is the Wilhelmian ring (see Figure 2.4), mainly built during the 1860s and '70s. It covers the districts of Friedrichshain, Kreuzberg, Wedding, and the inner areas of Schöneberg, Wilmersdorf, Charlottenburg, Neukölln, Prenzlauer Berg, and Lichtenberg.

The Wilhelmian ring contains large, five-storey apartment buildings with interior courts, radial roads, and few open spaces. Small industries and schools developed within the courts where land rents were low. These are now inner-city dwellings of working-class Berliners and immigrant populations, with high residential densities of up to 1000 people per hectare.

Look at the three urban models in Chapter 1, and at Figure 2.5. Do Berlin's structure and land use pattern in 1940 fit these models?

▼ **Figure 2.4** Berlin's urban area.

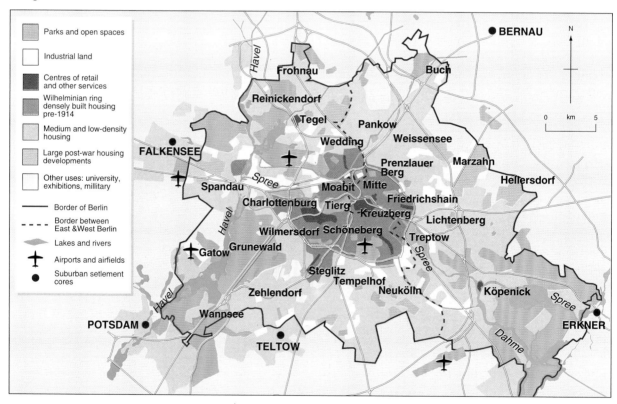

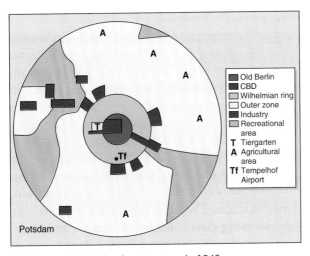

Legend:
- Old Berlin
- CBD
- Wilhelmian ring
- Outer zone
- Industry
- Recreational area
- **T** Tiergarten
- **A** Agricultural area
- **Tf** Tempelhof Airport

Potsdam

▲ **Figure 2.5** Berlin's urban structure in 1940.

Although this area appears to fit the model of concentric circles of growth, within this circle there are also sectors. Heavy industry moved out to the edge of the city in the 19th century on to sites besides the river Spree or along rail routes, thus creating industrial sectors. Meanwhile, the western side of the Wilhelmian ring saw the development of higher-quality housing and commercial land uses along the Kurfurstendamm, the present location for up-market retailing, entertainment, cafés, and restaurants.

The outer zone
Outer Berlin (see Figure 2.4) was typified by forests, lakes, agricultural land, and lower-density settlement. Separate residential areas and villages developed, and were incorporated into the city by suburbanization. High-quality housing, open spaces, museums, and academic land uses are found here. Beyond are villages and 'garden suburbs'.

Outer areas of Berlin grew between 1918 and 1939, when modern apartment buildings were constructed by housing associations. These were provided with a planned 'municipal social' mix of parks, cinemas, swimming pools, schools, and utilities.

1945 – one city destroyed, two cities rebuilt
The theory box on page 156 explains the differences between communism and capitalism. Read this, as it helps to understand some of the changes that took place within East and West

Berlin after 1945. Three processes altered Berlin after 1945.

- Central Berlin was badly affected by war damage. Rubble was used in rebuilding the city, or bulldozed into landscaped tips. Central city retailing, offices, and businesses were abandoned.
- Many functions of Berlin had to be duplicated in West Berlin after the city's division in 1945, as the town hall, university, library, museums, and administrative areas were all located in East Berlin. West Berlin created a new city government, a Free University, museums, and a concert hall. City functions gradually transferred to the Zoo Station area, which became a focus for transport, shops, offices, banks, the Stock Exchange, tourism, hotels, entertainment, and services – in other words, the CBD.
- In contrast, East Berlin was developing as a capital city. Its central location within the communist state of East Germany made it an obvious choice as an administrative centre, with government institutions, embassies, museums, and educational institutions.

In East Berlin the city centre was redeveloped as a traffic-free area, with four major squares for political rallies and cultural assemblies. The functions of a communist capital city were planned, with headquarters of state industries, display space for cultural and political propaganda, embassies for other communist states, and tourism functions. Retailing was limited, and was usually incorporated into residential areas. In East Berlin many government buildings were abandoned, as the new capital administered a smaller state than pre-war Germany.

1 What might have been the priorities for Berlin's urban planners before the Second World War with respect to industry, housing, and recreation?
2 Read through the changes that took place in Berlin after 1945. How did the urban structure of Berlin change after the city was divided?

What changes have been brought about by reunification?

Since Berlin became part of a unified Germany, there have been many changes. Here we look at how industry, the economy, land values, housing, the population, and services are facing change.

Industry

Industry in West Berlin

By 1945, West Berlin had lost 23 per cent of its production capacity from wartime destruction, and 53 per cent as Soviets dismantled plant to take to the Soviet Union. Fortunately its manufacturing industry has largely recovered. Traditional West Berlin industries of electrical goods, machinery, foodstuffs, sweets, and tobacco have remained for over 40 years. However, there are a number of issues facing companies.

- Lack of space has meant that few new industrial sites have been developed. Companies have transferred to other cities in Germany and some de-industrialization is occuring now that the city is reunited. Manufacturing will probably transfer from expensive city sites either to suburban or rural 'greenfield' locations, or to emerging economies within the developing world.

- Technological changes, recession, and rationalization in the 1970s and '80s have each had an effect. In West Berlin, 50 per cent of employment in the electrical industry was lost, compared with only 15 per cent in the rest of West Germany. With a narrowing industrial base, rising unemployment, and a lack of specialist workers, Berlin's industrial problems are becoming worse.

Lack of space in West Berlin meant that many industries redeveloped on existing rather than on greenfield sites after 1945. What advantages and disadvantages would this create for industry, employees, local residents, and the environment?

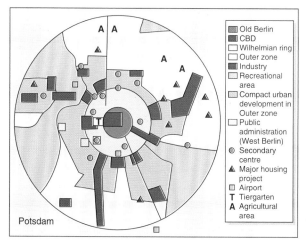

▲ **Figure 2.6** Berlin's urban structure in 1987.

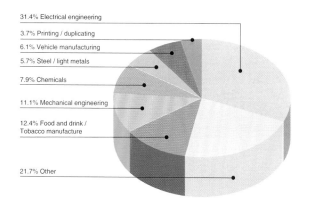

31.4% Electrical engineering

3.7% Printing / duplicating

6.1% Vehicle manufacturing

5.7% Steel / light metals

7.9% Chemicals

11.1% Mechanical engineering

12.4% Food and drink / Tobacco manufacture

21.7% Other

▲ **Figure 2.7** Industrial employment by sector in Berlin.

Industry in East Berlin

In East Berlin, the communists created new industrial areas on the outskirts of the city during the 1980s. There are now three major industrial areas (Figure 2.6) within Marzahn, Lichtenberg, and Weissensee, conveniently located for workers who live nearby. However, much of Germany's industry is now duplicated. With high staffing rates, and the removal of employment protection which was previously assured by the communist government, 500 000 East Berlin workers now face redundancy or retraining.

1 Use an annotated diagram to show the changes to industry in both West and East Berlin.

2 Why was industry in East Berlin able to move to greenfield sites before 1990, while industry in West Berlin was not able to make this move?

Berlin's economy

With reunification, Berlin has found itself at the centre of major economic change. Since 1990 Berlin has attracted 400 new companies, 180 large-scale investment projects totalling DM37 billion (£16 billion), and created 130 000 new jobs.

It seems on the face of it that economic growth has been rapid. However, West and East Berlin have experienced problems.

In spite of subsidies from the West German government for manufacturing and transport, tax reductions for residents, and urban renewal, investment in West Berlin fell behind that of other West German cities. Its ageing manufacturing industry is struggling now that financial support has been removed. It therefore has many barely profitable factories, whose future is at risk. The workforce is underqualified, because of the 'brain drain' of graduates to the West before 1989.

In East Berlin the combining of German currencies in 1990 created a 'hard cash' economy which East Berlin industries were unused to. This still presents difficulties. The East Berliners were accustomed to a centrally planned market without competition. Under the free market, industries will either go bankrupt, unless they are supported by grants from the German government, or will be purchased cheaply by companies from western Germany, or Western Europe. Investment in manufacturing in Eastern Germany is low. Changing state-owned industries into private businesses is not easy: ownership is unclear, and industrial practices are dated or inefficient. The future for East Berlin's low-skill, mass production manufacturing industries is not bright.

Population: 3.5 million

Workforce: 1.4 million

Manufacturing industry 200 000

Retailing 230 000

Services 750 000

Other 320 000

Annual GDP: DM120 billion (4.5% of Germany's GDP, and greater than the annual GDP of Ireland, Greece, or Portugal).

▲ **Figure 2.8** Berlin's economic factfile.

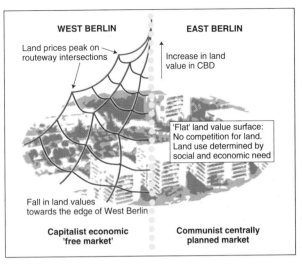

▲ **Figure 2.9** Urban land value surfaces.

Land values and rents

Variations in land values and rents in capitalist cities are caused by different demands for sites throughout the city. They have a strong influence on the urban form. You can read more about this in Chapter 1 on page 15. Figure 2.9 shows such theoretical land values. West Berlin is typical of capitalist cities – land values peak at the most accessible points, such as local route intersections. East Berlin had an even land value surface, typical of communist urban planning. Here land use was determined in theory by economic and social need, and not market value created by competition.

Re-introduction of land pricing in East Berlin has meant competition for sites for the first time since 1945. This is causing a change of land use, as offices and shops bid higher prices for land occupied by state housing or industry. After 1990, there was a rush for office and retail space in the city. Competition for space has affected both residential and retailing property markets where price rises have not yet been controlled. Rents have risen 600 per cent for shops and commercial premises in Kreuzberg, because of its close proximity to the new central core of Berlin.

Why would
a) East Berlin and
b) West Berlin
each be affected by rising land values now? You need to consider different reasons for each.

▲ **Figure 2.10** Karl Marx Allee.

Housing

In West Berlin, three phases have been seen in housing. Initially, the policy was to repair and later rebuild the apartment blocks which had been damaged. Subsequently, major housing projects were completed in the 1960s and 1970s on the outskirts of West Berlin, each accommodating 50 000 to 60 000 people. These served a dual purpose: to remove slums on the rural urban fringe, and to rehouse inner-city residents from cleared areas. But they also caused commuting problems, and early schemes suffered from poor planning, with little or no provision of shops, schools, play areas, or services. Finally, 'urban infill' was introduced, using spaces within inner-city areas. This avoided the use of scarce land and meant that inner-city residents could stay where they had always lived. Socially disadvantaged occupants – the old, unemployed, sick, single-parent families, and immigrants – are unwilling to move out of rented apartments to more expensive dwellings in new housing schemes. Planners moved to a policy of 'repairs before modernization, and modernization before renewal', maintaining inner-city housing by protectionist policies and rent controls which were only removed just before the fall of the Wall.

In East Berlin there were also three different periods of development. Land here was state owned. There was also a close relationship between residential and industrial land uses, social equality of housing, and public transportation. Land use was determined on the basis of need rather than profit. In the first wave of development, blocks of flats were built in the 1950s, similar to those in West Berlin, along routes such as Karl Marx Allee. Built as the first 'socialist' street in Berlin, Karl Marx Allee is 80 metres wide: at significant locations towers, statues, and fountains were planned. These developments contained the first shops and restaurants to be built after the war, and relocated functions well away from the previous CBD.

However, such schemes were expensive to construct and would not meet all of East Berlin's housing needs. The second process, therefore, involved large-scale construction of prefabricated housing in the old centre of East Berlin. This is quite different from CBD land use in capitalist cities, which edges out most residential development. Residential populations within some parts of the centre of East Berlin have increased, unlike capitalist cities where populations have fallen. Finally, in the 1970s, large outer-city projects such as the one shown in Figure 2.11 at Marzahn were built for over 100 000 residents, near workplaces to prevent commuting, or with access to S Bahn (surface rail link) stations. The schemes were designed to encourage a social mix of people all paying a low rent, usually only 5 per cent of a

▼ **Figure 2.11** Marzahn.

family's income.

Housing issues facing the new city

Severe housing shortages have been created by the numbers of people moving into Berlin. Key features of Berlin's housing market are as follows:

- Most of Berlin's 1.8 million dwellings are rented.
- Ownership rates are low – 11 per cent in the west of the city, and a fraction of this in the east.
- There is a high percentage – 45 per cent – of single-person households.
- As many as 10 000 new dwellings are needed before the year 2000 to keep pace with demand, as well as schools, services and hospitals.
- Thousands of apartments lie empty in East Berlin because they need repair (Figure 2.12).
- Improvement is delayed by repossession claims made by East Berliners on property taken away under communist rule. None of these properties can be sold until claims are legally resolved.
- The cost of providing new housing is huge – an estimated DM17 billion (£7.5 billion) over the next 20 years – whilst renovation of pre-war housing could cost a further DM10 billion (£4.5 billion) during the period 1995–2005.

1 In groups of three or four, suggest a plan for resolving Berlin's housing shortage and state the kinds of housing needed.

2 Which issues could the Berlin city authorities solve, and which would require federal help?

▼ **Figure 2.13** Changes in housing in Berlin, 1970–90.

Year	West Berlin	East Berlin
1971	1 024 600	463 720
1981	1 110 378	518 548
1985	1 139 682	567 816
1988	–	618 887
1989	–	631 338
1990	1 079 039	–

(a) Number of dwellings in West and East Berlin, 1971–90.

Year	Rooms per dwelling	Square metres per dwelling
1975	3.28	68.0
1980	3.92	86.4
1985	4.28	90.1
1990	4.41	–

(b) Change in housing stock: Berlin, 1975–90.

Year	Square metres per inhabitant
1971	24.1
1981	27.0
1985	28.3
1988	29.8
1989	30.4

(c) Change in housing stock: Berlin, 1971–89.

	West Berlin			East Berlin		
Year	Total	Inner city	Outer city	Total	Inner city	Outer city
1970	2115.3	954.6	1160.7	1085.4	431.9	653.5
1975	2004.3	831.9	1172.4	1098.2	422.5	675.7
1980	1896.2	767.1	1129.1	1152.5	405.7	746.8
1985	1860.1	747.0	1113.1	1215.6	365.5	850.1
1990	2158.0	902.2	1255.8	1275.7	331.0	944.7

West Berlin inner city = Wedding, Tiergarten, Charlottenburg, Wilmersdorf, Schöneberg, Kreuzberg
East Berlin inner city = Mitte, Prenzlauer Berg, Friedrichshain.

(d) Population (in thousands) of West and East Berlin, 1970–90.

3 Look at Figure 2.13 which shows housing and population change in West and East Berlin 1970–90. What changes took place during this period?

◀ **Figure 2.12** Disused apartments in East Berlin.

1 Using Figure 2.13, copy and complete the facing table to show the contrasts between West and East Berlin in 1985. What contrasts are revealed?

2 With reference to Figure 2.4, and using suitable techniques, show what seem to you to have been the most significant changes in housing. Justify the techniques you have chosen.

3 Compare Figures 2.15 and 2.16. What do they reveal about the distribution of the population born overseas who live in West Berlin? Why do you think the population might be distributed in this way?

	West Berlin	East Berlin
Population Number of dwellings Average number of people per dwelling		

Population

During the period to 2010 the population of the Brandenburg region surrounding Berlin will increase by some 1 million people, of whom one-third will choose to live in Berlin. This will raise the city's population to its pre-war size. The Berlin conurbation is currently the second largest in Germany, rivalled only by the old industrial heartland of the Rhine Ruhr with its population of around 12 million people.

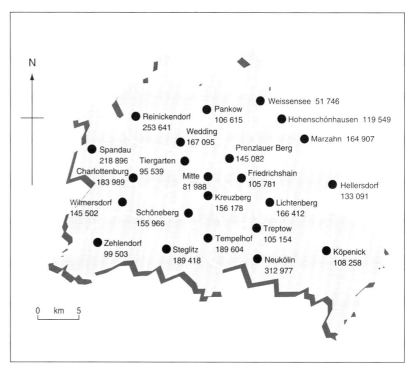

▲ **Figure 2.14** Berlin's boroughs and their population (December 1992).

Berlin's population of 3.5 million includes 11 per cent who are officially classified as 'born overseas', a proportion that is substantially lower than in many other German cities (Frankfurt 23.4 per cent, Munich 21 per cent, Stuttgart 20 per cent, Hamburg 11.8 per cent). The immigrant population, located almost entirely within West Berlin, is segregated – that is, different socio-economic groups live in different parts of the city. This is the same as in most other West European cities.

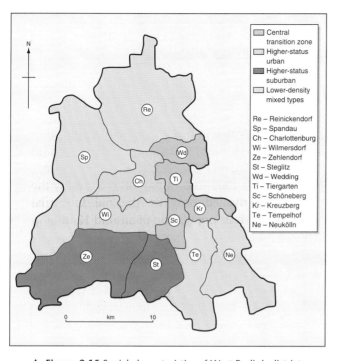

▲ **Figure 2.15** Social characteristics of West Berlin's districts.

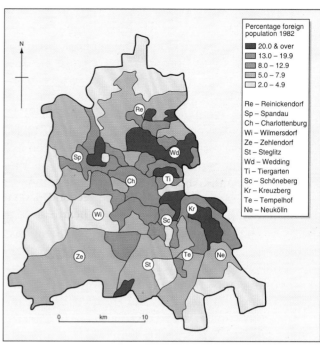

▲ **Figure 2.16** Percentage of West Berliners born overseas.

Dispersion diagrams

Figures 2.15 and 2.16 show types of maps known as choropleth maps which use densities of shading, grouped into categories.

How are categories decided? Figure 2.17 shows a dispersion diagram. It is used when you wish to see a range of values – for example, unemployment figures or the percentage of people in different districts who own a car. A vertical line is drawn, and scaled between the lowest and highest values. Examination grades can be decided by ranging all the marks from 0 to 100 in this way.

On Figure 2.17, a scale has been drawn between 0 and 50, and each value is plotted against it. 31 values have been plotted, ranging from 4 to 43.

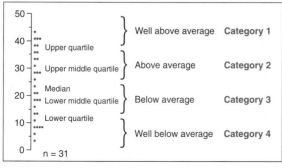

▲ **Figure 2.17** A dispersion diagram.

Data can be analysed by asking these questions:

1 What is the *mean*? The mean is the average figure for the 31 values, reached by adding all the values and dividing by 31.

2 What is the *median*? The median is the middle value in the sequence – in this case, the middle of 31 values would be the sixteenth.

3 What is the *range of values*? Here it would be 39 – from 4 (the lowest) to 43 (the highest).

4 What are the different 'quartiles'? A quartile is one-quarter of the number of values – one-quarter of 31 is about 8. Each quartile is grouped into a set of 8 values. Reading from the highest value, the first 8 extend from 43 to 36, and are known as the 'upper quartile'. The next highest are the 'upper middle quartile', then the 'lower middle quartile', and finally the 'lower quartile'.

In Geography quartiles are generally used to provide categories. As Figure 2.17 shows, the four categories 1–4 can be used when deciding how to shade a map. Occasionally, five categories may be more appropriate, so 'quintiles' (groups of five categories) replace 'quartiles'.

Population issues in West Berlin

Turks, by far the largest percentage of the overseas-born population (Figure 2.18), came to Berlin in the 1960s to fill job vacancies created by East Berliners being removed from the employment market following the building of the Berlin Wall. Like other immigrant populations they tend to work in low-income, semi-skilled or unskilled jobs. Seventy-five per cent of the Turkish population live in low-rent property in the Wilhelmian ring (predominantly in Kreuzberg and Wedding). In terms of size of population, Berlin is now the fifth largest 'Turkish' city in the world!

As the growth of the German economy has slowed, and the costs of reunification have risen, some Germans have become increasingly resentful of immigrants, whom they believe limit their own job opportunities. At its most extreme the emergent neo-Nazi movement has targeted workers' hostels, Turkish families, and minority immigrant groups for physical attack.

In response, German immigration officials have changed immigration laws to make it harder for immigrants to settle in Germany and gain German citizenship. Critics believe that this gives in to right-wing pressure without solving a growing domestic problem. There is a similar backlash against reunification by some former West Germans who resent the financial drain on both their personal and national economies of subsidizing the employment, services, and infrastructure of the former East Germany. For instance, a reunification 'tax' of DM80 per month has been imposed on each taxpayer in order to pay the costs of unifying the countries.

Population issues in East Berlin

East Berlin is unusual among European cities in that its population increased from 1.19 million in 1950 to 1.28 million in 1991, a rise which was due more to inward migration than natural increase (Figure 2.19). It is the only region within East Germany to show such an increase; the population of East Germany declined over the same period from 18.4 to 16.4 million. Socialist planning aimed to relocate people into cities, which contrasted strongly with large West European cities where there has been 'natural' out-migration and suburbanization. East Berlin was attractive because it offered opportunities for personal advancement – through gaining power, rather than money – and as a cultural, employment, and academic centre. Unlike West Berlin it has few marked socio-spatial contrasts, for the distribution of housing is not determined by a person's income or ability to pay.

Services

One of the greatest differences between East and West Berlin is in the size and distribution of retail and consumer services. Within West Berlin the capitalist past has ensured the development of a distinct CBD (Figure 2.20) centred around the Kurfurstendamm, Zoo Station, and Tauentzienstrasse, with sub-centres at Charlottenburg, Steglitz, Neukölln, Wedding, and Spandau (Figure 2.19). This contrasts with the lack of centralized retailing in East Berlin, though this is now changing. The loss of CBD functions in East Berlin was almost total. Communist East Berlin had no need for banks, so the banking quarter around Behrenstrasse disappeared and markets became residential areas.

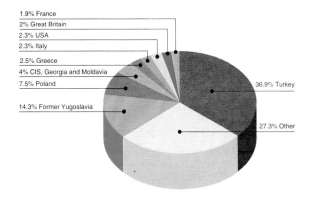

▲ **Figure 2.18** Overseas-born population in Berlin by country of origin.

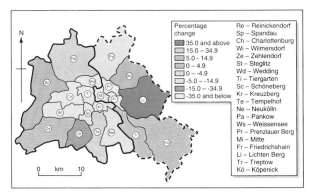

▲ **Figure 2.19** Berlin's population change, 1939–81.

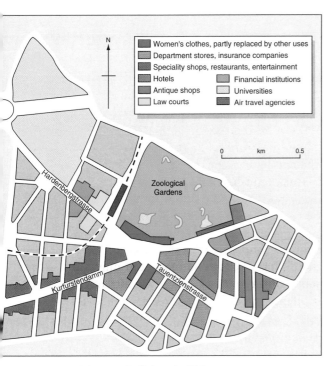

▲ **Figure 2.20** West Berlin's main CBD.

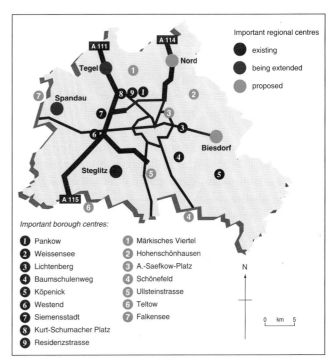

▲ **Figure 2.21** Distribution of retail and service centres outside the inner city.

How will people's lives be affected by changes?

In 1993 the Mayor of Berlin described the city as the 'workshop of German unity'. How will it achieve this function for itself and for the local, regional, and national populations?

Is there enough employment for everyone?

For some East Berliners, reunification has brought advantages. More than 110 000 East Berliners, and 55 000 from the surrounding region, have found new jobs in West Berlin since 1989. However, a further 200 000 originally employed by the East German government – 30 per cent of East Berlin's employees – have either lost, or face losing, their job. Economic union brought the two halves of Berlin and Germany together, but created employment problems. The loss of East European markets has cut manufacturing employment in the East by 67 per cent, increasing competition for jobs in the West.

1 Only 50% of Berlin's 'unemployed' are actually 'out of work' (Figure 2.22). Why are unemployment figures often disputed?

2 How seriously do you think the German government considers the problem of unemployment at this time?

Moving the state capital to Berlin will see a 'two-way' migration of jobs: 12 000 jobs will transfer from Bonn to Berlin, but 9000 will move out to Bonn, or to other German states. Regaining capital status is important to Berlin's employment market, as industries and businesses may now relocate their headquarters to the capital. Already Daimler Benz and Sony are moving their European headquarters to Berlin to exploit new markets in eastern Europe.

1 In spite of two different political, economic, and social systems, East and West Berlin are, in some respects, similar. What are these similarities? Have they occurred for similar reasons?

2 What are the most striking differences between East and West Berlin's post-war development?

▼ **Figure 2.22** Unemployment in Berlin.

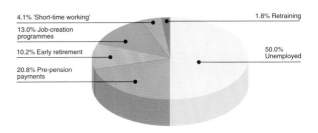

4.1% 'Short-time working'
13.0% Job-creation programmes
10.2% Early retirement
20.8% Pre-pension payments
1.8% Retraining
50.0% Unemployed

The problem of East Berlin

There are structural, economic, and psychological problems resulting from 40 years of division. East Berlin has the worst of the city's problems: its infrastructure is inadequate, and the majority of its industries have suffered years of under-investment. These industries exist today on the very margins of profitability, as inefficient and outdated plants. Commercial and domestic buildings in the East are collapsing, public services are inadequate, and the environment has been badly neglected. In short, East Berlin lacks many of the facilities and services of a modern, west European city. However, its people have great expectations, and will judge the success of reunification on the changes that are made.

What will the 'new Berlin' look like?

Planning the inner city

Problems created by years of independent planning and administration are apparent when comparing East and West Berlin. Two different political philosophies had a profound influence on the landscape. Well-known landmarks of Berlin, such as the Brandenburg Gate, became incorporated into its boundaries when Berlin was divided. Now they are once again central features of the new capital. New office blocks are planned for Potsdamer Platz by Sony Europe and Daimler Benz, with residential development for over 2000 people. Mitte will become the heart of the new city for the next millennium, with the re-introduction of government, retailing, residential, cultural, and educational functions.

The strip of undeveloped and derelict land along the line of the former Berlin Wall will have to be carefully planned, for it now lies at the centre of the reunited capital.

Since reunification, planners have worked hard at organizing Berlin's future. A land-use plan for the entire city now exists which includes a focus on landscaping. Major architectural changes are under way, with a new scheme for the previously blighted Spreebogen (Spree Bend), an island which will become the location for Germany's new parliament buildings.

Urban sprawl

With reunification, urban sprawl is developing as Berlin expands into the Brandenburg countryside. The city's planning authorities have received applications for 40 golf courses and 27 Disneyland-type theme parks around the edge of Berlin. Suburbanization is also putting pressure on the fringes: the more affluent people who are capable of moving outwards are doing so, leaving the less privileged to remain in the inner city. If this continues without planning, Berlin faces a future in which its population will become more socially divided, with increasing segregation of the poor, immigrant, and disadvantaged groups in the Wilhelmian ring. Maintaining the social mix of the former huge housing projects of East Berlin will also prove difficult.

Look at Figure 2.23. In pairs, decide how the derelict land along the route of the former Berlin Wall should be used. Share ideas with other pairs, and write a report of about 500 words, justifying your ideas.

▶ **Figure 2.23** Derelict land along the former Berlin Wall.

Regional planning

Many expect the former West Berlin to be the economic 'engine' that will drive future development in the Brandenburg region. This assumption has certain dangers. East Germany's former citizens look to West Berlin as the supplier of jobs and income.

The need is for 'growth poles' – centres outside Berlin which can supply jobs, goods, and services without the need to rely on Berlin.

The creation of a special region would aid planning. For instance, a variety of centres outside Berlin are to develop their retailing and housing – often along existing U and S Bahn lines – to encourage the use of public transport rather than cars.

Owing to a shortage of space within Berlin, economic activities are bound to spread into the surrounding region. Restructuring the Brandenburg region will be complicated. Excluding Berlin, the region is economically backward and only has 2.6 million people, barely 75 per cent of the population of Berlin. Berlin is therefore not only being reunited, but gaining regional functions to stimulate industrial regrowth in other towns which lie in a belt around the city.

How will reunification be judged?

Reunification is only a means to an end. Success will finally be gauged by whether the people of both East and West Berlin, and Germany, feel content and secure in their new lives. This depends on their feelings about job opportunities, leisure, housing, and future prospects. Here there is a 'gap' between residents of the former East Berlin and West Berlin, and standards of living for all need to be raised to those of the West. Only if this is achieved can all Germans feel accepted and valued.

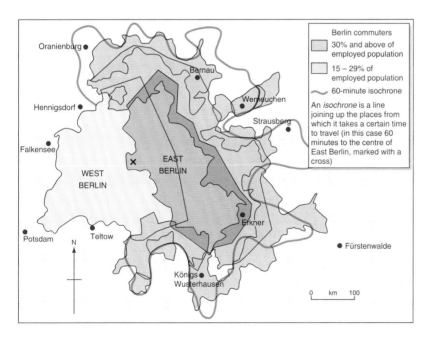

Look at Figure 2.24. Suggest how the commuter field might now be different, several years after Berlin's reunification.

◀ **Figure 2.24** The East Berlin commuter field before reunification.

▶ **Figure 2.25** Opinion poll taken in 1990 on what East and West Berliners thought about each other.

West Berliners (total sample 1505)		East Berliners (total sample 1353)	
% who had visited 'the East'	74	% who had visited 'the West'	97
% who had visited East Germany and East Berlin	43	% who had visited West Germany and West Berlin	46
% who had visited East Berlin only	22	% who had visited West Berlin only	50
% who had visited East Germany only	9	% who had visited West Germany only	1
1 What positive impressions did you gain of East Berlin?		**1 What positive impressions did you gain of West Berlin?**	
● Beautiful landscape	20%	● Wide selection of department stores	42%
● Friendly people	18%		
● Magnificent buildings	15%	● Orderliness and cleanliness	31%
(52% were 'broadly positive' towards East Berlin.)		(90% were 'broadly positive' towards West Berlin.)	
2 What negative impressions did you gain of East Berlin?		**2 What negative impressions did you gain of West Berlin?**	
● Deterioration of buildings	15%	Beggars and homeless	29%
● Empty stores	14%		
● Stench	13%		
● Dirt	12%		
(44% were 'broadly negative' towards East Berlin.)		(7% were 'broadly negative' towards West Berlin.)	
3 Which of the following are *better* in West Berlin compared with East Berlin?		**3 Which of the following are *better* in East Berlin compared with West Berlin?**	
● Environmental protection	96%	● Environmental protection	10%
● Industry	91%	● Industry	12%
● Science and technology	88%	● Science and technology	23%
● Health services	88%	● Health services	34%
● Public transport	78%	● Public transport	21%
● Leisure opportunities	73%	● Leisure opportunities	40%
● Adult education	67%	● Adult education	51%
● Job security	62%	● Job security	50%
● Art and theatre	57%	● Art and theatre	48%
● Equal opportunities for women	52%	● Equal opportunities for women	72%
● Protection against crime	52%	● Protection against crime	42%
● Housing	48%	● Housing	49%
● Sport	36%	● Sport	76%

1 Look at Figure 2.25. What can you tell about the attitudes of each group, or about the impressions they had gained? Do any of the results surprise you?

2 If a similar poll were taken today, do you think these attitudes would have changed?

3 In pairs, decide how, in ten years' time, people might judge the success of reunification using a similar questionnaire. What questions might be asked?

Bangkok – a dying city or a thriving city?

Bangkok, the capital city of Thailand, exists in a state of near-crisis. Its development has, until recently, been largely unplanned. This has resulted in a primate city (a city whose size dominates the whole country) of almost 9.5 million inhabitants lying in the Chao Phraya river basin in the central region of Thailand. The problems that the city faces each day are monumental – with a huge city centre, surrounded by sprawling suburbs, it contains almost 80 per cent of the country's vehicles. As a result Bangkok regularly grinds to a halt during 'rush hours' that can last all day. Journey times of three hours between the centre of Bangkok and the airport are common.

However, the city generates almost 50 per cent of the nation's GDP, processes 95 per cent of its trade, and its citizens have an average per capita income that is twice that of other Thai people. Many Thais see Bangkok as providing opportunities to improve their circumstances, and, like many people living in major cities, live with the problems. The purpose of this study is to assess Bangkok's most pressing needs and consider how these might be met.

REQUIEM FOR A CITY

Once known as the Venice of the East, modern Bangkok is now a city in crisis. Economic boomtimes have transformed the once-charming town into an environmental horror show where street-level pollution has long since passed international danger levels, waterways not filled with concrete are clogged with garbage, and rush-hour traffic grinds to a complete standstill. One out of five residents lives in illegal slums with no piped water or electricity. Residential pollution, the unregulated dumping of dangerous chemicals and fertilizers, and a complete lack of oxygen have killed the Chao Phraya river. Each day, Bangkok produces 5400 tonnes of garbage but only 4200 tonnes are collected; the remainder is dumped on street corners or in the waterways. Construction of artesian wells and high-rise buildings on soft soil is sinking the low-lying city under sea level, a horrifying prospect that may become reality within a single generation.

But it is the horrendous traffic that typifies what is most frightening in the City of Angels. Bangkok's traffic crisis – almost certainly the worst in the world – is the result of government inaction and unwillingness to make tough decisions. The problem is that most cities throughout the world use 20–25 per cent of their surface area for streets, but in Bangkok it's only 6 per cent. The city's 1.5 million cars will double in number in just seven years, but road surface is expected to increase by only 10 per cent. The gridwork of roads found in all major international cities has never been constructed in Bangkok. Instead, city authorities have allowed Bangkok to grow without any form of urban planning, depending on the self-interest of private investors rather than the controlling force of government policy.

The result is world-class traffic jams. According to the Traffic Committee, the average speed during rush hours has dropped to under 4km per hour; people walk at 4km per hour. The remainder of the day, traffic moves at just 7km per hour. When Dr Sumet Jumsai, the nation's foremost authority on architecture and urban planning, was asked about Bangkok, he said, 'It's irreversible destruction. The city is dying.'

▲ **Figure 2.26** Requiem for a city – one person's view of Bangkok.

Can the city survive?

Read Figure 2.26, then work in pairs.

1 a) Identify all the problems that Bangkok faces.
  b) Discuss which of the problems should be priorities for planners and which should not.

2 a) Brainstorm actions which you think the planners of Bangkok could take to deal with each problem.
  b) Compare your list of proposed actions with those of another pair. Have you common ideas?
  c) Make a list of obstacles that might hinder your possible solutions.

3 To what extent does Figure 2.26 provide a balanced view of the city?

Urbanization and economic growth in Thailand

Since 1953, Thailand has experienced substantial economic growth. In Figure 2.27 this growth is measured in terms of gross domestic product (GDP). You should refer to Chapter 4 for a discussion of GDP and its meaning; it is widely used as a measure of a country's income from goods and services.

By 1994, economic growth in Thailand was still 8.4 per cent annually, at a time when the majority of EMDCs were slowly emerging from recession. Between 1970 and 1980, exports grew at an average yearly rate of 10.3 per cent, increasing during the period 1980–92 to 14.7 per cent.

Growth in output from the industrial and service sectors has been more rapid than growth in employment, so that each person on average is producing more at work now than they were. This means that there is an increase in productivity per worker, whose taxes have helped to finance ambitious social and economic development programmes recently introduced by the newly-democratic Thai government.

However, this is a recent development in Thailand. Much of the country's economic growth has been achieved through a forcible military government keeping a firm (and undemocratic) hand on the country. Economic development has taken place as large multinational companies have established factories, attracted by the low wages paid in Thailand. Economic growth has been achieved, but at the price of human rights and welfare.

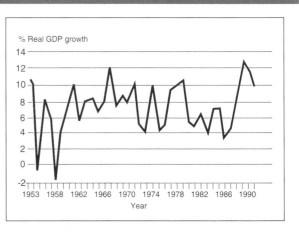

▲ **Figure 2.27** Thailand's recent growth in GDP.

Kader Industrial

Kader Industrial is a Hong Kong-owned multinational company, a toy manufacturer which makes, among other products, Bart Simpson dolls and models. Attracted to Thailand by cheap wages, the company has enjoyed huge growth. However, this growth has been achieved at a price. The company had been accused for years of ignoring safety and employment regulations. On 10 May 1993 Asia's worst factory fire at Kader's partly-owned subsidiary company killed 189 workers, most of whom were young women, and 500 others were injured. Initially the company denied responsibility, though eventually paid compensation of $8000 to the families of each of those who were killed.

How has Bangkok grown?

In 1960, American consultants were invited by the Thai government to produce a structure plan for Bangkok for the 1990s. This 'Greater Bangkok Plan 2533 (1990)' was the first attempt to map, plan, and restructure the city for the future. It estimated that the city would have a population of 4.5 million in 1990 (in fact it had 9 million), and suggested solutions to the city's growing transport problems, as follows:

- industrial and residential zoning (Figure 2.28)
- government introduction of planning for the city so that pressures on space could be resolved.

Neither of these strategies was adopted. Now people in Bangkok are forced to accept urban sprawl.

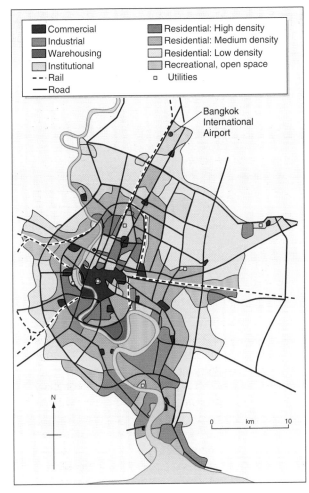

▲ **Figure 2.28** Bangkok's planned land use for 1990.

Study Figure 2.28. Which of the urban models described on page 21 seems to fit Bangkok?

▼ **Figure 2.29** Population of Bangkok, 1780–2000.

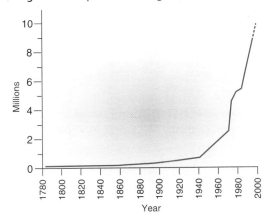

All the indications are that the Bangkok Metropolitan Region (BMR) will continue to grow (Figure 2.29). The city now contains almost half of Thailand's 21 per cent urban population, and estimates are that it will increase further to 11 million people by the year 2000. Bangkok is already one of the fourteen largest cities in the world, and some 23 times larger than Thailand's second city of Chiang Mai.

Bangkok's dominance of Thailand also extends to its political, economic, and cultural influence. Some people believe that primate cities like Bangkok are parasitic, preying on the rest of the country to extract wealth and prevent the growth of regional centres. High economic costs caused by traffic congestion and transport systems, negative environmental impacts, and rising land prices have now all become acute. Untouched they could cripple Bangkok and stifle developments in the regions, although currently businesses still find the city a profitable place in which to locate.

One of the problems is that growth has been unequal. The BMR has had its rapid expansion partly restricted by planning measures which have tried to decentralize growth and encourage industrial location elsewhere. Even so, it remains Thailand's largest economic and employment region. Current national plans have attempted to balance economic growth in urban and rural areas. Figure 2.30 shows how regional growth areas have been planned by the Thai government to absorb some of Bangkok's economic activities, and accommodate rural migrants.

Why has Bangkok grown?

Bangkok's population growth is based on three factors:

1 Natural increase – Thailand's birth rate in 1994 was 20 per 1000 people, and its death rate 6 per 1000 people.
2 In-migration – from the countryside and from other urban areas, of people attracted by economic prospects in the city.
3 Official 'expansion' of the city's administrative boundaries.

In 1994, Bangkok's population was about 9.5 million, increasing by about 3.5 per cent each year, a rate of growth that is likely to double the population in 20 years. Of the increased number of people each year, about 30 per cent are migrants and 70 per cent are a result of natural increase.

1 Use a spreadsheet to calculate the population now, and in ten years' time.

2 Produce graphs to illustrate the increase.

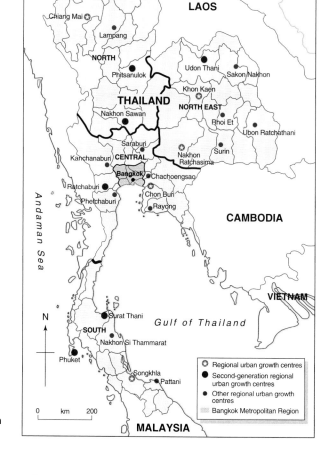

▶ **Figure 2.30** Regional urban growth centres in South-East Asia.

Migration has increased since the 1960s partly because successive governments have improved road links to the capital, and also because Bangkok seems (and is) much wealthier than other regions.

What is Bangkok like?

The growth of Bangkok has produced a huge urban sprawl over an area of 7639km². Although it may look chaotic, and shows how unplanned cities can develop, it has been divided up into four different administrative planning areas (Figure 2.31):

- the central area
- the suburban area
- the industrial area
- the Outer Bangkok Metropolitan Region.

The central area

The central area of 147km² consists of twelve metropolitan districts. Its total population is currently 3.3 million, with a high population density of 23 000/km² (see Figure 2.32) and increasing traffic congestion. This area has numerous problems. Public transport is inadequate – expressway construction has actually increased traffic congestion rather than helped to ease it – and the road system regularly fails, particularly when flooding causes a sudden traffic standstill in the centre. In the tropical monsoon climate this happens quite often. In the old business quarter buildings are decaying and pollution is extreme. Short-term plans have tried to encourage the private sector to maintain or rehabilitate decaying CBD areas, and to construct two or three medium-sized parks on vacant public land in the centre.

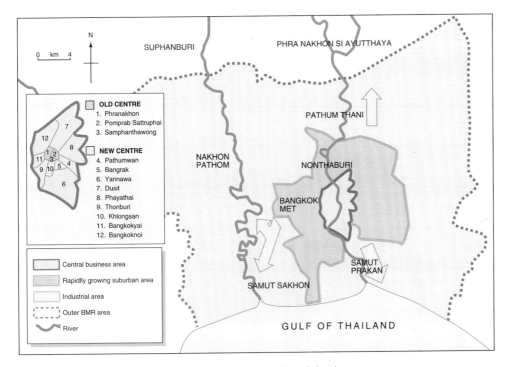

OLD CENTRE
1. Phranakhon
2. Pomprab Sattruphai
3. Samphanthawong

NEW CENTRE
4. Pathumwan
5. Bangrak
6. Yannawa
7. Dusit
8. Phayathai
9. Thonburi
10. Khlongsan
11. Bangkokyai
12. Bangkoknoi

Central business area

Rapidlly growing suburban area

Industrial area

Outer BMR area

River

▲ **Figure 2.31** Areas for planning Bangkok's future growth and development.

▼ **Figure 2.32** High-density building in central Bangkok.

The suburban area

The suburban area of 1065km² consists of eight metropolitan districts and three districts of Nonthaburi province. Its total population is 3.3 million, and its population density is 3100/km². This is a rapidly growing area with expanding residential, business, industrial, and commercial facilities. Figure 2.33 shows a peripheral settlement on the edge of Bangkok. Its new appearance is typical of such developments which surround the central area and spread along main arterial roads. The suburban area has a high population growth rate, but lack of planning results in a disorderly mix of commercial, industrial, service, and residential buildings amongst agricultural areas. Low-lying land is often vacant or under-used, with few connecting roads and poor provision of services. Groundwater is over-used, causing subsidence, and much of the area is increasingly susceptible to serious flooding.

▲ **Figure 2.33** A recent development on the periphery of Bangkok.

The industrial area

The industrial area of 75km² consists of specific industrial sites and estates in Samut Prakan, Pathum Thani, Samut Sakhon, and Nakhon Pathom provinces, all shown in Figure 2.31. These areas are rapidly expanding with population growth rates averaging 4 per cent each year. Industry is found in two main locations.

- The 'old' industrial area in Samut Prakan province, where the number of factories has recently increased rapidly. This has created demands on services, water supply, and infrastructure, resulting in deep well water extraction, land subsidence, and environmental pollution.
- The 'new' industrial area to the north in Pathum Thani province.

Agricultural land in both of these areas is now rapidly declining, whilst public water supply and workers' housing are in short supply.

The Outer Bangkok Metropolitan Region

The Outer Bangkok Metropolitan Region of 6352 km² consists of small regional towns and self-sufficient agricultural areas. The population is 1.27 million, with a low population density of 220/km². Main and secondary roads are in poor condition, with few connecting roads to create a proper network. There are major disagreements concerning whose responsibility it is to supply water to the population.

1 Using Figures 2.31, 2.32, 2.33, and the details in this section, draw an annotated map of the key features of the Bangkok Metropolitan Region.

2 To what extent do the problems you identified at the start of this study of Bangkok seem to be true?

What are the key issues for Bangkok?

Bangkok's growth and its variety of environments have created a range of issues.

1 Investment is needed in restructuring the urban transport network, for flood protection, and for better water supplies and housing. The major aim is to reduce congestion in the CBD and to plan for more efficient land use in the suburbs, thereby creating more work locally.

2 The 500 000 low-income urban poor and slum dwellers in the Bangkok Metropolitan Region (BMR) need special help. The official figure for the number of poor in Bangkok is almost certainly an underestimate. It excludes many 'mini' squatter settlements and the real figure may be almost a quarter of all Bangkok's population. House building, slum upgrades, improvement of basic services, and assured security of land tenure are all essential. Action needs to be based on community projects, and there is a need for occupational training and compulsory education amongst low-income groups. This would have to be done by central or city governments, using income derived from taxation.

3 Capital is needed for improvements to public services. Private businesses could in fact provide more money than either central or local government. Institutions using public services could pay more realistic rates for these, and rely less on government subsidies. This would free the government to direct money at the needs of the poor.

Identifying priorities for Bangkok

Democratic governments usually wish to be re-elected! The need for action to deal with Bangkok's problems is becoming clear to the Thai government. Four major programmes are agreed for the BMR:

- transport and traffic improvement
- water supply and flood protection
- housing development and slum upgrading
- development programmes for low-income groups.

Transport and traffic improvement

Traffic congestion in Bangkok is amongst the worst in the world (Figure 2.34). Congestion is made worse by poor planning and inadequate funding. At least five government agencies, which rarely co-ordinate their work, are responsible for Bangkok's roads. Investment in road improvements is low, and often based on expensive foreign loans. Bangkok has one of the lowest proportions of road surface to total area of any major city (around 6 per cent compared with London's 22 per cent and New York's 24 per cent), which makes seasonal flooding and subsidence even more of a problem. Journey

▲ **Figure 2.34** Traffic congestion in Bangkok.

▲ **Figure 2.35** River ferry in Bangkok. The cost of traffic congestion in Bangkok makes little sense when car ownership is beyond the means of most people. Ferries charge very little – 1baht (about 2.5p) is the usual fare.

times of three hours between the centre of Bangkok and the airport are common. Now a new elevated highway has been opened between central Bangkok and Don Muang Airport. Its effect so far has been to transfer congestion onto the elevated section.

However, there are positive features. Figure 2.35 shows one of the many passenger ferries and river taxis along the Chao Phraya river, which carry hundreds of thousands of people every day. The density of the canal network in Bangkok (canals are known there as *klongs*) is a resource that has great potential for moving people and goods.

Since the late 1980s, a number of ideas have been researched:

- extending the tolls on the two expressways to vehicles entering the CBD
- building an elevated highway between Don Muang Airport and the city centre
- restricting private vehicle access to the centre
- encouraging the development of a mass transit rail system, reducing traffic congestion, and improving average traffic speeds
- improving public transport services
- providing segregated bus lanes on selected routes
- reintroducing privatization and competition in the bus industry.

Water supply and flood protection

Water supply creates a variety of problems for the city of Bangkok. As settled areas of the city expand, demand for water grows. In 1987 the water supply system covered 475km^2 and catered for 4.78 million people (remember that Bangkok has double this number of people). Recent plans should expand this system to cover 610km^2 for 5.8 million people, but this will still only provide water for just over half the city's population.

Dependence on groundwater sources creates an additional problem of land subsidence and, as a result, a growing risk of more frequent and intense flooding. Newly developed areas of the city covering 500km^2 in the northern and eastern suburbs (Huai Khwang, Bang Kapi, Min Buri, Lat Krabang, and Phra Kanong districts) experience the worst problems, where land subsidence is 10cm per year. The city centre subsides by some 5–10cm each year. Public and private groundwater use is to be restricted by raising prices for water, whilst construction will be prevented on 240km^2 of land which is at most risk of subsidence.

In industrial areas the aim is to extend surface water supply systems from the Chao Phraya river and also to increase fees for the use of artesian wells in areas where a public water supply is available.

Form groups of three or four.

1 For each of the options listed above, discuss and list in a table its advantages and disadvantages, including any advice you would offer from your own knowledge of such proposals from elsewhere.

2 Based on this list, identify what you consider to be suitable and unsuitable proposals. Do any possibilities seem to have been overlooked within the options listed here?

3 Would you recommend public or private development of water resources for Bangkok? Justify your answer.

Housing development and slum upgrading

Provision of basic services and housing does not currently extend to the urban poor. The population officially classified by the government as 'poor' has declined from 11 per cent of the Bangkok population in 1976 to between 5 and 6 per cent, although almost 20 per cent still live in overcrowded conditions and require social service provision. The number of poor – as opposed to the percentage – is rising. Administration of relief is one of Bangkok's major problems – there is rarely any co-ordination of schemes, many public projects lack adequate financial plans, and very little gets done. Living in poverty and without public planning or finance, most people in the poorer socio-economic groups are squatters.

Bangkok's squatter settlements are rarely illegal, unlike those in many cities in ELDCs. As in many cities in ELDCs, however, squatter settlements vary. Study the three photographs in Figure 2.36. Two-thirds of housing is on privately owned land, and landlords extract rents from tenants. Those living on public land or land in the CBD are at risk of eviction as demand for industrial, commercial, and private residential space increases, especially in the city centre. Figure 2.36a is the view from a hotel in central Bangkok. Typically, squatter settlements of this type are short-lived: very high-density open-plan buildings, with roofs (in this case) made from large advertising boards. Squatters here are living in the heart of the CBD. Many people in such squatter settlements live in appalling conditions.

However, it is wrong to see all of Bangkok's settlements in this light. Many squatters live in permanent 'slums of hope' with a good income, in a stable community, with 'middle-class' aspirations, and owning a range of luxury goods. Figure 2.36b is almost stereotypically a squatter house. It is permanent, has services provided, and there are visible indications of pride and hope. It is located, with thousands of others, along one of Bangkok's *klongs*. In all respects life goes on here for people just as it does in residential areas in most cities – Figure 2.36c shows the local riverside shop.

▼ **Figure 2.36** Three views of squatter settlements.

(a) View from a hotel window in the centre of Bangkok.

(b) and (c) Riverside settlements along the Chao Phraya river.

Since the 1980s, official concern for squatter residents has increased. The media have raised public awareness, championing cases of poverty and poor living conditions, and have pressurized the government into taking action. The city government is also acutely aware that it must take action, or risk not being re-elected. Occasionally events catch up with the city government – see Figure 2.38. The World Bank and the International Monetary Fund (IMF) were due to hold a conference in Bangkok in October 1991. The squatters shown in Figure 2.38 lived close to the expressway exit near the location of the conference. These squatters were removed to another site, loaned money and given materials to create a permanent settlement. Others in less sensitive areas have been less fortunate.

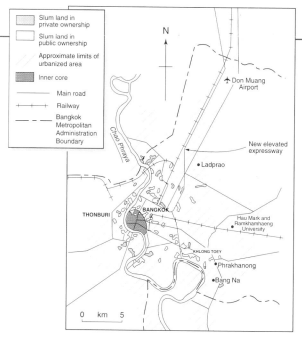

▲ **Figure 2.37** Slum and squatter settlements in Bangkok.

1 Describe the location of the slum areas shown in Figure 2.37.

2 Explain the pattern of these areas.

3 Are there lessons to be learned from what is described in Figure 2.38? How appropriate does the government's provision for these squatters seem to be now?

4 Explain the reluctance of squatters to move.

▼ **Figure 2.38** From the *Bangkok Post*, 4 August 1991.

NHA tackles 'eye-sore' by relocating slum dwellers

The National Housing Authority yesterday began removing slum communities from around the Sirikit National Convention Centre, the venue for the World Bank-IMF meeting in October.

Under the Interior Ministry plan, two communities, Duang Phitak and Khlong Phai Singto, must be resettled, but a new site is ready only for the Duang Phitak community. Part of its slum was removed yesterday on 25 trucks provided by the NHA, the First Region Army, the Bangkok Metropolitan Administration, the Expressway and Rapid Transit Authority, and the Public Welfare Department, according to an NHA statement. The community, near an expressway exit on Rama IV Road, is expected to be fully resettled on 27 rai in Rom Klao community, Lat Krabang, by early September.

The cleared land will become a temporary street linking Rama IV Road to Sukhumvit Road to ease traffic problems.

About 420 Duang Phitak dwellers reportedly sought relocation, but only 297 were allowed to move.

Apart from construction materials totalling 40 000 baht, each resettled family will be allocated a filled plot more than 17 square wah at a cost of 32 130 baht. This can be paid off at 510 baht per month for 10 years, or 435 baht per month for 15 years.

In the 1980s, some of the past problems of underfunding of housing projects were alleviated with the support of the World Bank. Now plans for the construction of 22 000 housing units, and the upgrading of a further 20 000 for low-income groups, are under way with the support of the private sector and the Government Housing Bank. The private sector has been attracted by a package of tax reductions linked to projects for the poor. However, the perennial problems of a lack of available land, and squatter communities preferring to stay where they are, still remain.

More serious in the long term is the cost of rented property. Bangkok now ranks with Singapore and Hong Kong as one of the world's most expensive cities for property to buy or rent. Figure 2.39 shows a selection of properties for rent in the *Bangkok Post*.

Currently Bangkok's central slums at Bangkok Noi, Bangkok Yai, Dusit, and Yan Nawa are being upgraded. Housing is also being developed for middle and high-income groups in the centre, to prevent commuting and alleviate transport problems. New suggestions for squatter 'land sharing', where land is divided between squatters and landowners, have sometimes proved successful where there are conflicting claims for land.

Development programmes for low-income groups

Residential and social services in Bangkok are better than those elsewhere in Thailand, although the processing of domestic sewage is still a huge problem. Only 2 per cent of the city's population is connected to a sewerage system, and most people use cesspits and septic tanks, resulting in sanitation and health problems.

Communities are forming self-help groups and taking part in government initiatives to improve education and training. Medical care, nutrition, and childcare schemes are also under way.

Conclusion – a dying city or an exciting city?

Consider the following passage from J. Rigg's book, *Southeast Asia: A region in transition*.

'The cities of South East Asia make a visitor most acutely aware of the poverty and disparities that continue to exist in the region. For it is in urban areas that the contrast between wealth and poverty, and luxury and squalor, are most obvious. Squatter settlements exist alongside modern, fully air-conditioned office blocks. BMW and Mercedes Benz cars crowd the streets, as do beggars, prostitutes, and child workers. At the same time, the problems of congestion, inadequate housing, and pollution seem almost intolerable and the cities on the verge of collapse.'

Bangkok is a city with enormous issues to face up to yet, for many, it is an economic life-line, a city with immense life and excitement, and great character. Its economic growth within South-East Asia, and its potential for greater growth still, will continue for many years yet. Is this compatible with a lifestyle that promotes the wealth of a few and leaves many in poverty?

Residential For Rent

Paholyothin	: Garden Home Village Townhouse, 3 Br ฿ 25,000/M
Paholyothin	: House, 3-4 Br, Pool ฿ 25- 45,000/M
Ratchada	: 3 Br attached House, Garden 10 min From Central Plaza ฿ 45,000/M
Srinakarin	: Ake Pai Rin Village New House ฿ 55,000/M
Soi Lang Suan	: Townhouse 3 St., 3 Br, 35 wah^2 ฿ 65,000/M
Wireless Rd.	: Townhouse beside IMPERIAL Hotel, W/Security ฿ 65,000/M
Sukhumvit 26	: 3 Br New Apt, 360 m^2/ unit/FL., W/Pool
Sukhumvit 39	: 3 Br Big House, 300 wah^2 ฿ 70,000/M
Sukhumvit 62	: Big House, W/Yard, 3 Br ฿ 65,000/M
Nang Lingee Rd	: 3Br Apt, 5 min From Height Way ฿ 45,000/M

'CPM' T.235-6600,235-7580-5 ext.6160/6407
Leave msg. 152 x150086

Exquisite House For Rent in Pratumwan area

Brand-new house with small garden; European owner.
Large living, separate dining, fully equipped western kitchen, 3 bedrooms with marble bathrooms, study, spacious built-in closets/-dressing area, 7 split aircons, spacious tiled porch and terrace, carpark.
Rent Baht 60,000 neg. - for appt. to view

Call Pranee 216-7509 or Jennifer 391-0559 before 11:00 AM. or after 3:00 PM.

▲ **Figure 2.39** Monthly rentals in Bangkok. Currencies are in Thai baht: 1 baht = 2.5p, 40 baht = £1.

1 Look back over the section on Bangkok. How far do you agree with Jonathan Rigg's assessment of South-East Asian cities, in relation to Bangkok? Is it a city 'on the verge of collapse', or are there more positive features?

2 Are the issues facing Bangkok those that face cities generally, or are they only typical of cities in ELDCs?

Ideas for further study

1 Compare and contrast the development of Berlin since 1990 with the development of another city from another EMDC. Consider not only the city itself, but also the region it serves.
2 Themes in this study have included social segregation, inner-city redevelopment, out-migration, and in-migration. Carry out a study of one of these themes in another city in an EMDC.
3 Many cities in ELDCs face similar issues to those facing Bangkok. Find out about self-help schemes, and other projects designed to improve housing quantity and quality. How effective are different schemes? Which schemes appear genuinely to improve the lives of the poor?

Summary

- Cities are the result of many historical processes, evidence of which is clear in the buildings and their layout at the present time.
- Cities develop functions such as industry, finance, and administration. These change as political philosophies change.
- The reunification of Germany has created many social and economic costs.
- Cities cannot be divorced from the regions in which they exist.
- Change often leads to conflicting issues, and different choices.
- The pace of change in ELDCs has created acute difficulties with respect to transport, housing, service provision, industrial location, and pollution.
- Most cities in ELDCs are experiencing a rapid growth in population. Those in East Asia are also experiencing huge economic growth.
- Urban blight and poverty can be made worse by a lack of co-ordinated planning, ineffectual controls on land use, restricted funds, and an unwillingness by governments to take action until problems become crises.
- Issues that arise as cities expand can be solved by careful planning.

References and further reading

'Unmasked – the East Asian economic miracle', *New Internationalist*, January 1995.

R. Hudson, 'Changes in Eastern Europe', *Geography Review*, November 1994.

J. Rigg, *Southeast Asia : A region in transition*, Routledge, 1991.

A. Ryder, 'Polish Cities – central places and socialist planning', *Geography Review*, March 1991.

How sustainable are cities?

Global urbanization

Chapters 1 and 2 include case studies of different cities to show how issues affect people, and how geographers can aid an understanding of these issues. Urbanization is a global process, because it is happening everywhere. It varies throughout the world, both spatially and in terms of when it occurs. This chapter explores the differences between urbanization in the economically more developed countries (the EMDCs) and in the economically less developed countries (the ELDCs).

Urban trends in the EMDCs

In his lengthy book *The History of the City*, historian Leonardo Benevelo concludes that the world's best urban model is the Ancient Greek city, or *polis*. He describes the *polis* as having the qualities that all cities should have – they are dynamic but stable, in balance with nature, and grow manageably even after reaching a large size. He writes:

'It is for these qualities . . . that the Greek city has always been, and will remain, a valid model for all other urban developments.'

Today's cities hardly match their well-planned Greek predecessors. They provide little that benefits nature, and do little to offer stability for their residents. Cities of the ELDCs in the less developed South are mushrooming in size, so much so that the rank order of largest cities shown in Figure 3.1 changed completely between 1950 and 1980, and will alter again by 2000. ELDC city populations are increasing so rapidly that to plot their growth in population requires logarithmic paper – see the techniques box on page 60. Meanwhile, in the EMDCs of the developed North, populations of cities and urban regions have changed significantly in the last 50 years, and the pace of change is unlikely to slacken yet.

City	1950 (million)	City	1980 (million)	City	2000 (million)
New York	12.3	Tokyo	16.9	*Mexico City*	25.6
London	8.7	New York	15.6	*São Paulo*	22.1
Tokyo	6.7	*Mexico City*	14.5	Tokyo	19.0
Paris	5.4	*São Paulo*	12.1	*Shanghai*	17.0
Shanghai	5.3	*Shanghai*	11.7	New York	16.8
Buenos Aires	5.0	*Buenos Aires*	9.9	*Calcutta*	15.7
Chicago	4.9	Los Angeles	9.5	*Bombay*	15.4
Moscow	4.8	*Calcutta*	9.0	*Beijing*	14.0
Calcutta	4.4	*Beijing*	9.0	Los Angeles	13.9
Los Angeles	4.0	*Rio de Janeiro*	8.8	*Jakarta*	13.7

◀ **Figure 3.1** The population of the world's ten largest metropolitan areas in 1950 and 1980, and projections for 2000. ELDC cities are given in *italics*.

Rates of growth – using logarithmic graphs

ELDC urban populations are growing so rapidly that it is difficult to make predictions about their future size. Figure 3.2a shows a population line graph which has become so steep that it would prove difficult to interpret. For such purposes, ordinary graph paper is unsuitable, and logarithmic paper may be needed. It is used in plotting figures with a range of values too large to be shown with a linear scale in any meaningful way.

There are two types of logarithmic graph paper.

● With one logarithmic and one linear scale – this is called **semi-log** or **log/linear** paper (Figure 3.2b). This can be used where dates are shown normally against a logarithmic vertical scale.

● With both scales logarithmic – this is **log/log** paper (Figure 3.2c). This is used when plotting two sets of data which both vary widely, such as Gross GDP and energy consumption.

Ordinary graph paper is used for graphs which increase by the same number on the scale, for example 10, 20, 30, 40, etc. Logarithmic scales increase by multiples of ten: 1, 10, 100, 1000, 10 000, etc. The base line for a logarithmic graph is never zero. It works back, where necessary, towards zero by divisions of ten: 0.1, 0.01, 0.001, etc. The number of cycles required depends on the range of the data.

▼ **Figure 3.2** Different ways of presenting graphs.

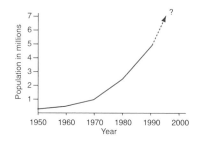

(a) A simple graph.

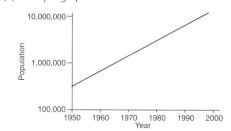

(b) On semi-log paper.

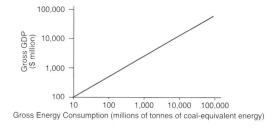

(c) On log/log paper.

In simple terms, changes are of two types.

1 *The distribution of population* Nowhere is this more clear than the change that has taken place between city populations and city regions. While the trend globally is for city populations to increase, in fact most cities in the EMDCs are declining. This is because the definition of cities is changing. Boundaries have remained in place, while city areas have increased. Lower densities of population, resulting from garden suburbs, planning restrictions, and retention of open spaces through the protection of green belts, have increased the space occupied by cities, while the number of people left in the cities themselves has fallen. City regions have increased in size, however. Revolutions in long-distance commuting, motorway travel, and technology that allows people to work at home or flexibly between different places, have all encouraged people to live and work away from cities. However, most people prefer to retain easy access to cities. Within 100km of London, the population of south-east England has risen while that of London itself has fallen.

2 *The composition of the population* This includes age structure (or the numbers in each age group), socio-economic and income group, and ethnic background. Changes have been society-wide, and therefore affect most places. However, impacts have been different according to the cultural differences and the effects of selective migration. Newcastle upon Tyne, for example, has few ethnic minorities, while Bradford 160km away has a substantial number of people from different ethnic groups.

Population terminology

Many different words and phrases describe population and urban growth.

Ageing populations As life expectancy increases with improved health care and standards of living, the percentage of those in older age groups increases. Together with smaller family sizes, this has created a population that is increasingly ageing.

Household type 'Traditional' family households of two adults plus children are less common. Many forms of living arrangements and lifestyles have resulted from:
- Divorce, which has increased the number of families with one adult rather than two.
- Increased freedom in many societies, which allows young people to establish their own homes (in the UK, for example, an 18-year-old can buy a house).
- Attitudes towards co-habitation – people are more tolerant of living arrangements between people of the same sex and opposite sexes.
- Elderly people are encouraged to live independently.

Average household size Households make demands on space: to house 100 single people requires four times the number of dwellings as 100 people living in four-person units. Populations may therefore remain static, while demand for housing actually increases.

Socio-economic group This is where a person or group fits into the social and economic status of a population. It is usually related to income group.

Ethnicity This refers to a group's or a person's cultural background, such as language, or religion.

Demographic structure This is the percentage of each sex and age group in a population. Ageing populations require more single-person dwellings than those consisting of people with families.

Selective migration Migration is the movement of people from place to place. It is selective in that some age and gender groups are more likely to migrate than others. In ELDCs, this group tends to be young (20–35 years old) males.

Fertility rate This is an indicator of the number of likely births. It is an index of the number of live births in a year, divided by the number of women aged between 15 and 49. Higher indices tend to be found in ELDCs, and lower indices in countries with declining birth rates such as EMDCs and some South-East Asian countries.

The geographical effects on cities are now being felt. Most of these changes create a demand for more flexible, and smaller, accommodation. For example, in Chapter 2 we saw that 45 per cent of Berlin's population now live in single-person dwellings.

▼ **Figure 3.3** Percentage age structure for selected European countries, 1960–88.

Country	0–14 years old		65 years and over	
	c.1960	c.1988	c.1960	c.1988
Austria	22.9	17.5	13.0	15.0
Belgium	23.8	18.3	12.2	14.4
Denmark	25.1	17.3	10.6	15.6
France	26.4	20.2	11.6	13.8
Germany (West)	21.7	14.7	11.0	15.2
Greece	26.7	20.0	8.2	13.6
Italy	24.7	17.8	9.5	13.8
Netherlands	30.3	18.5	9.0	12.5
Norway	25.8	18.9	11.1	16.2
Portugal	29.2	22.1	8.0	12.6
Sweden	21.9	18.0	12.0	18.0
UK	23.0	18.9	11.9	15.5

▼ **Figure 3.4** Household size and composition in selected European countries.

Country	Average no. persons/ household		One-person households (%)		Households without children (%)	One-parent families*
	c.1960	c.1980	c.1970	c.1980	c.1980	c.1980
Austria	3.1	2.8	1	26	n.a.	11.8
Belgium	3.0	2.7	19	23	64.0	9.6
Denmark	2.9	2.4	21	29	64.5	11.4
France	3.1	2.9	20	25	61.4	6.1
Germany (West)	2.9	2.5	25	3	67.0	9.4
Greece	4.1	3.8	11	15	54.5	n.a.
Ireland	4.0	3.9	14	17	49.1	12.6
Italy	3.6	3.3	13	18	58.4	10.5
Netherlands	3.6	2.9	17	22	62.4	8.1
Norway	3.1	2.7	17	28	n.a.	7.1
Portugal	3.9	2.9	27	28	48.9	n.a.
Sweden	2.8	2.3	25	33	n.a.	n.a.
UK	3.1	2.7	18	22	64.5	11.5

* as percentage of family households only   n.a. = not available

1 Referring to Figures 3.1, 3.3, and 3.4, write three paragraphs that highlight trends in urbanization in the EMDCs in recent decades. Refer to specific examples and use the following headings: City growth, Age structure, Household size and composition.

2 Explain how trends in city growth, age structure, and household size and composition are linked in ELDCs.

Urbanization in the ELDCs

While populations of cities in EMDCs have declined, those of ELDCs have increased markedly. Chapter 2 has shown that the population of Bangkok is increasing by about 3.5 per cent a year, a rate of growth that is likely to double the population in 20 years. This is the result of natural increase and of rural–urban migration. Migration is believed to account for 30 per cent of the increase in a city's population.

In many ELDCs, economic conditions have deteriorated in the 1990s. Economic decline and the world debt crisis have made life harder for most countries. Governments have cut back on welfare expenditure, leading to the view of the political right that private bodies can provide at least as well for people as government can. The ability of private businesses to supply services will always be limited to those who are most able to pay. The poor are often left to fend for themselves.

The debt crisis and recession of the early 1990s have probably had a greater impact on urban areas than on rural areas. Between 1970 and 1985, the numbers of people living in urban poverty rose faster than the numbers of rural poor in every region (Figure 3.5). Policies to improve agricultural productivity, to reduce protection of loss-making industries, to reduce subsidies for public services, and to reduce public expenditure, have had major consequences for urban residents in countries like Brazil, Mexico, Côte d'Ivoire, Morocco, and the Philippines. Prices of food, water, energy, and housing have increased, while real wages have fallen with inflation and unemployment. The rural sector has gained as farmers begin to receive higher producer prices, and urban residents benefit less from government subsidies on food.

▶ **Figure 3.5** Estimates of total, urban, and rural populations living in absolute poverty, 1970–85.

	% people living in absolute poverty		Millions of people living in absolute poverty		Percentage change 1970–85
	1970	1985	1970	1985	
Developing countries					
Total	52	44	944	1156	+22
Rural	59	49	767	850	+11
Urban	35	32	177	306	+73
Africa					
Total	46	49	166	273	+64
Rural	50	58	140	226	+61
Urban	32	29	26	47	+81
Asia					
Total	56	43	662	737	+11
Rural	61	47	552	567	+3
Urban	42	34	110	170	+55
Latin America					
Total	40	36	116	146	+26
Rural	62	45	75	57	−24
Urban	25	32	41	89	+117

The debt crisis

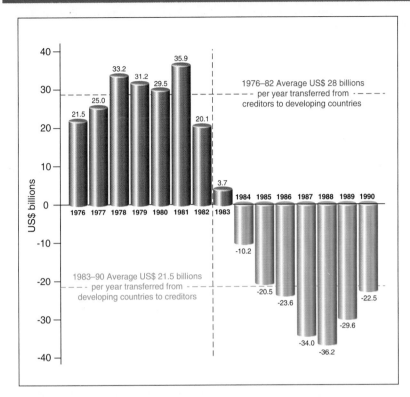

1976–82 Average US$ 28 billions per year transferred from creditors to developing countries

1983–90 Average US$ 21.5 billions per year transferred from developing countries to creditors

▲ **Figure 3.6** Net transfers to developing countries on long-term loans, 1976–90.

The total debt owed by developing countries to other countries increased from US $100 billion in 1970 to around US $1350 billion in 1990. Figure 3.6 shows an annual transfer of almost US $30 billion in long-term loans to developing countries. This in turn became an annual transfer of interest payments in the opposite direction of over US $20 million. Suddenly, the interest payments on outstanding loans, and annual repayments of capital, far exceeded any new loans. The total in net payments from developing countries has been calculated at US $242 billion between 1983 and 1989. The cause of this turnaround was the combination, in the early 1980s, of increased interest rates and reduced new lending. It is little wonder that the countries of the South cannot move on from this position.

The urban revolution: an overview

By the year 2010, for the first time ever, more people will live in towns and cities than in the countryside. This constitutes a revolution, and it is happening mainly in the ELDCs. It took London's population 130 years to rise from 1 million to 8 million. By contrast, Mexico City rose from 1 million to 20 million in less than 50 years.

The urban challenge for the 21st century is to improve the quality of life for urban dwellers by creating cities that are 'sustainable' – that is, using resources in a way that replaces them for future generations. Transport congestion, pollution, and sanitation systems are likely to break down as mega-cities grow. However, urban issues are as vital in EMDCs as they are in ELDCs. The next part of this chapter looks at case studies of urban change, and highlights some of the challenges ahead.

1 a) Using the proportional bar technique that is shown on Figure 3.7 and an atlas, draw a similar world map to show the world's largest cities in the year 2000.

b) Describe and attempt to explain the changes you have mapped.

2 Why could generalized population density shading on a map be a misleading way to show population density?

3 Summarize the recent trends in urban growth in ELDCs.

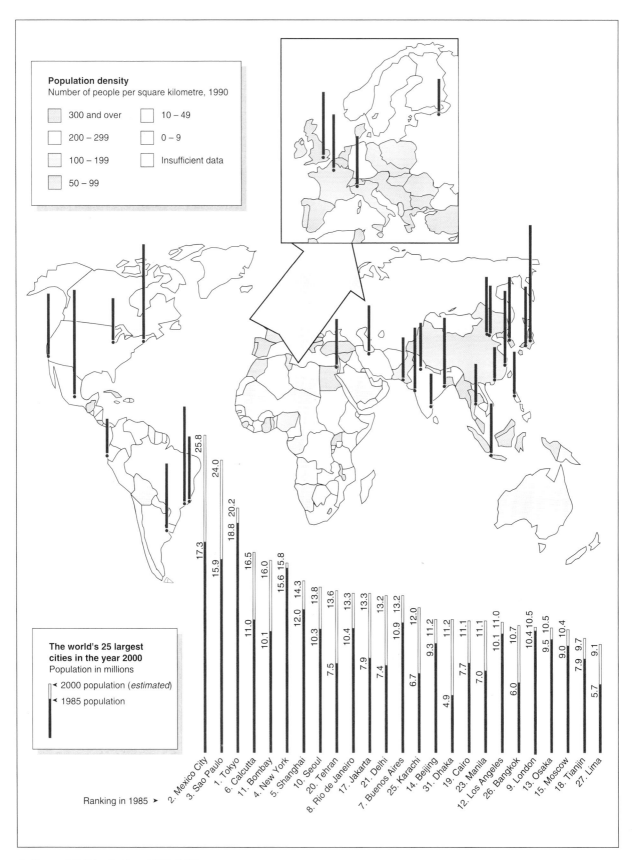

▲ **Figure 3.7** Urbanization, 1985–2000.

Urban renewal and development

Here we look at two possible redevelopments in London: the area around King's Cross and St Pancras stations, and No.1 Poultry in the heart of the City of London. In Chapter 2 a framework of questions is offered for enquiry. The enquiry framework for exploring urban change at King's Cross is as follows.

- What is this area like?
- How did it get like this?
- What is going to happen here?

All change at King's Cross

King's Cross is one of the major rail termini in central London. However, the transfer of much of the capital's goods and passenger traffic from rail to road since 1945 has left land vacant and derelict in a city that has one of the world's major financial markets and the most expensive land in the country and even in the world. How should it be used?

What is this area like?

The King's Cross area consists of derelict land that is awaiting redevelopment. The area known as the Railway Lands to the north and west of King's Cross and St Pancras stations has suffered economically since the decline of goods marshalling by rail in the area.

▼ **Figure 3.8** King's Cross Station, London.

The issue is typical of many parts of London, in terms of the threat to the environment. Since the abolition of the Greater London Council in 1986, London has had no single council or body to oversee development or manage the environment. Decision-making processes affecting the city are taken by undemocratic, government-appointed bodies known as 'quangos'. London has, until recently, maintained a reputation for being a comfortable place to live and work in. But these qualities appear to be under threat. Most of all, there are inner-city areas, such as the Railway Lands near to King's Cross and St Pancras Stations shown in Figure 3.11, which pose special challenges for the city.

Sustainable urban development

A sustainable city may be defined as one in which current resource decisions do not compromise the quality of life of future generations. Here are some possible indicators for a sustainable city.

- An effective transport system, which helps to keep cars off the roads and maintain good air quality.
- Affordable housing and rents, within reach of everybody.
- A mix of land uses, for example work and housing, which would avoid long-distance commuting.
- A good infrastructure – services such as hospitals, roads, schools.
- Other good quality-of-life indicators, such as parks and green spaces.

Features of cities which act against a sustainable future include anything that is environmentally destructive – for example traffic pollution – or that is short-term, and uses high energy-consuming materials, whose futures are finite.

How did it get like this?

Recent trends in urban planning are well illustrated by what is happening at King's Cross. As the time-line in Figure 3.12 shows, it is symptomatic of what has happened to London. The current proposals for the development of a 54ha site of former railway land to the north of the two stations (see Figure 3.11), raise questions about how major urban developments should be paid for and who benefits most from them. The area demonstrates the impact that the transport revolution of the 19th century has had on London. Two passenger stations survive in this area – St Pancras and King's Cross – and two railway hotels (the Midland Grand and the Great Northern). The Regent's Canal to the north of the stations represents an earlier revolution in inland transport. Nearby, goods depots were established when the railways arrived.

1 Give examples of each of the five criteria for a sustainable city listed in the theory box, and explain how they would help to make urban areas sustainable.

2 To what extent do they apply to your nearest town or city?

3 What sources of evidence might you look for to justify your answer to question 2?

4 What are the main issues which prevent sustainable lifestyles in your urban centre?

5 Identify three actions that would make your local urban centre more sustainable.

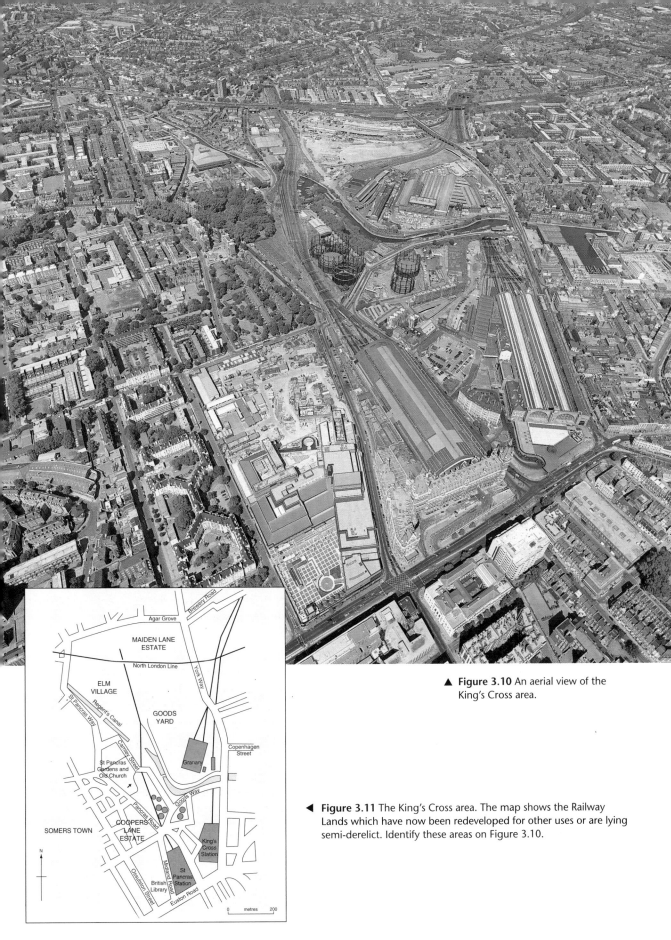

▲ **Figure 3.10** An aerial view of the King's Cross area.

◄ **Figure 3.11** The King's Cross area. The map shows the Railway Lands which have now been redeveloped for other uses or are lying semi-derelict. Identify these areas on Figure 3.10.

Map labels:
Agar Grove
Brewery Road
MAIDEN LANE ESTATE
North London Line
York Way
ELM VILLAGE
St Pancras Way
Regent's Canal
GOODS YARD
Camley Street
Copenhagen Street
Granary
St Pancras Gardens and Old Church
Goods Way
Pancras Road
SOMERS TOWN
COOPERS LANE ESTATE
King's Cross Station
Midland Road
N
Ossulston Street
St Pancras Station
British Library
Euston Road

0   metres   200

All Change at KING'S CROSS

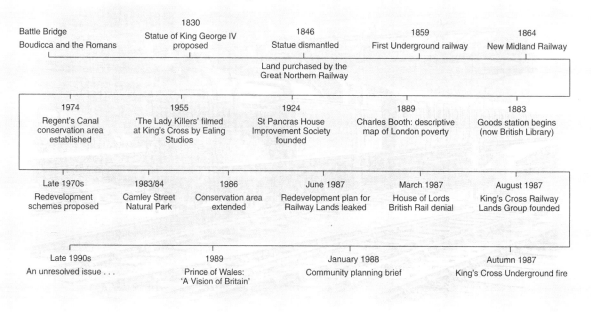

1830		1846	1859	1864
Battle Bridge	Statue of King George IV	Statue dismantled	First Underground railway	New Midland Railway
Boudicca and the Romans	proposed			

Land purchased by the
Great Northern Railway

| 1974 | 1955 | 1924 | 1889 | 1883 |
| Regent's Canal conservation area established | 'The Lady Killers' filmed at King's Cross by Ealing Studios | St Pancras House Improvement Society founded | Charles Booth: descriptive map of London poverty | Goods station begins (now British Library) |

| Late 1970s | 1983/84 | 1986 | June 1987 | March 1987 | August 1987 |
| Redevelopment schemes proposed | Camley Street Natural Park | Conservation area extended | Redevelopment plan for Railway Lands leaked | House of Lords British Rail denial | King's Cross Railway Lands Group founded |

| Late 1990s | 1989 | January 1988 | Autumn 1987 |
| An unresolved issue . . . | Prince of Wales: 'A Vision of Britain' | Community planning brief | King's Cross Underground fire |

▲ **Figure 3.12** Some of the main events in the history of King's Cross/St Pancras.

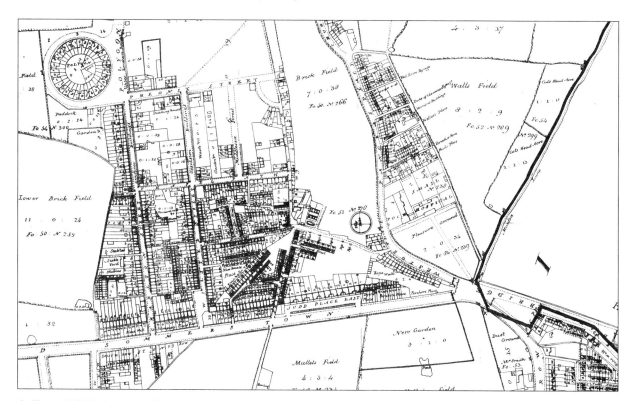

▲ **Figure 3.13** St Pancras parish, by J. Tompson, published about 1800. The Smallpox Hospital is on the site of King's Cross Station.

What is going to happen here?

Competition for space is important in an urban area. Space in an urban area can be divided into two broad categories:

- exchange space (homes, shops, workplaces, parks, community facilities, etc.)
- movement space (roads, car parks, railway tracks, pavements, etc.) used as a means of getting to exchange space.

Increasing the amount of movement space means transforming space from exchange space to movement space.

To transform transport systems by building a new road or a rail terminal usually requires removing residential and community facilities. This raises certain questions.

- Who makes the decisions for land use changes?
- Where does the power lie in the decision-making processes?
- Who are the gainers and the losers?

Behind King's Cross and St Pancras stations lies an enormous area of neglected land. This has been created as a result of the decline of manufacturing and of freight transport, which have suffered as economic recession and competition with roads have eroded traditional rail freight markets. The problem is how to generate change that is beneficial socially, economically, and environmentally.

In summer 1987, British Rail presented a plan for the 54ha of King's Cross Railway Lands. In size and scope it was a major plan: building would be on a 14ha site, with another 32ha of land available for future development. The result would have been a huge development of multi-storey office blocks and a sub-surface railway station – the Channel Tunnel Rail Link (CTRL) terminus. However, this would not amount to 54ha of building. Further proposals include the following.

- 15ha – 28 per cent of the total area – of open space, to include a new central park, tree-lined avenues and walkways, and the Regent's Canal.
- 14.5ha – 27 per cent of the area – to be given to offices.
- 7ha – 13 per cent of the area – to be developed as housing. The developers argue that this shows a commitment to creating a new 'living' district for London.

The proposals are contentious because they involve questions about how space should be used in cities. Union Rail, a company owned by British Rail, carried out a consultation exercise about possible options for the development of the King's Cross–St Pancras area.

Many local people felt that for British Rail to carry out such an exercise about a proposal for which it was in favour, would lead only to conclusions that would suit British Rail. The response of people in the area was to set up an umbrella organization, 'The King's Cross Railway Lands Group' (KXRLG). The Group was concerned with the proposal, and with decision-making processes which, they claimed, failed to provide a forum for the views of local people.

Movement space ☐   Exchange space ■

▲ **Figure 3.14** How increasing movement space erodes exchange space. This forces the city to expand to compensate for lost exchange opportunities.

1 Use an overlay with Figure 3.10 to produce a land use map. Identify industrial sites, main residential areas, transport centres, and other uses.
2 Place a second overlay over your map drawn from Figure 3.10. Map the movement and exchange space.
3 What is the percentage of each land use type?
4 Use an overlay and squared paper placed over Figure 3.13 to calculate movement and exchange space and to make a general comparison with the year 1800.
5 What can you conclude about urban change in the last two centuries?

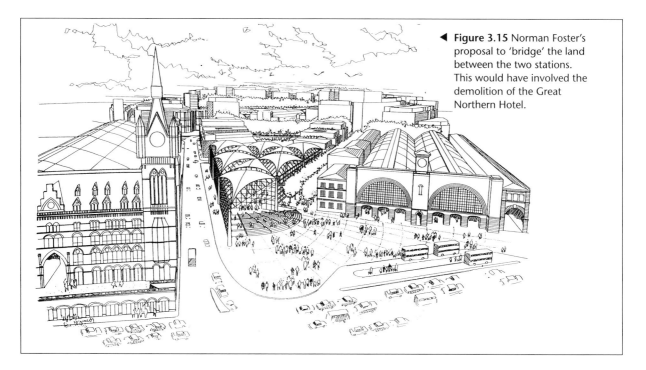

◀ **Figure 3.15** Norman Foster's proposal to 'bridge' the land between the two stations. This would have involved the demolition of the Great Northern Hotel.

1 Review the five criteria for sustainable development in cities on page 66. Consider each of the KXRLG's proposals and say how well each fits the criteria.

2 Study each of the documents in Figures 3.16 and 3.17. Work in pairs.

a) What assumptions are made by the writers of each document?

b) Identify what you see as strengths and weaknesses in each document.

c) How could the results from residents who completed the LRC document be used by the developers to 'block' a protest?

Their starting point was the establishment of some of their own local proposals.

● Under King's Cross station is the wrong place for the CTRL.
● The office-dominated scheme for the Railway Lands should be rejected.
● The major land use here should be low-cost housing, providing at least 1850 units of 'socially affordable' housing.
● Local people and local businesses want, and expect, to stay and prosper in and around the Railway Lands.
● Any development should produce a real increase in the number of jobs appropriate for local people in light and general industries.
● Any development should look to make good deficiencies in local community facilities.
● As far as possible, listed and historic buildings should be preserved.
● Any development should improve the physical links between the local communities.
● All new development should be of a good quality, designed and managed to secure the sustainable integration of the area's elements.
● Any new development should ensure that there is maximum local involvement and control.

There have been two processes of consultation. The London Regeneration Consortium (LRC), the original choice by British Rail as developers of the site, produced the questionnaire in Figure 3.16 to seek the opinions of local people. The KXRLG had a different style of consultation, publishing the *King's Cross Carrion*, a campaign newsletter (Figure 3.17).

◀ **Figure 3.16** LRC consultation exercise.

Tell us what you think

As developers of the King's Cross site, we at the London Regeneration Consortium are keen to hear your views on the development.

(1) My views on the development are:

(2) I would especially like the development to contain:

King's Cross Carrion

Petitioning Parliament

By the time you read this the Channel Tunnel Rail Link Bill may have had its second reading. We should have until mid-February to deposit petitions, which means they will have to be written and decisions on who is going to present them to Parliament taken well before this.

A Parliamentary petition is not your usual petition, i.e. a statement followed by a string of signatures. It is a somewhat archaic document with a beginning and end in 'OLDE ENGLISHE'. However, the teeth are in the middle and that is the part that counts. If you are affected by the Bill you have a right to petition. In broad terms this means you must show in what way the Bill affects you. Some obvious examples are the dust, noise, heavy goods vehicles in residential areas, and the disruption caused by a massive building site in your area. You may be going to lose your home,

business, or place of work. The road closures and sewer works will cause more disruption.

What is less obvious is that the effects of the road closures and road widening and straightening will affect traffic miles away in both Camden and Islington. There are dramatic effects on listed buildings, conservation areas, Camley Street Park, and the canal. Dumping Kent commuters here will drastically affect the once good public transport services in the area. They can barely cope now, so what will it be like then? There are plenty of good solid grounds for petitioning. So let's use them!

Camden have started the ball rolling with a series of meetings for local people in Somers Town, King's Cross, and Maiden Lane, supported by the Railways Lands Group. Islington and the Cally Rail Group are looking at the way UR wants to take the track out of tunnel in Islington and onto the Railway Lands.

In January the Railway Lands Group are organizing petitioning surgeries where we will have available information on how you are likely to be affected, how to petition, and model petitions for you to use. We will have word-processing facilities available so that once you know how you are affected we can give you your petition in its proper form ready for you to sign. These surgeries have been advertised locally and we hope you can make one of them.

The three surgeries are all 6.30–8.00 pm:

- 9 January at Coopers Lane Tenants Hall
- 16 January at Maiden Lane Community Centre
- 23 January at Holy Cross Church, Cromer Street.

If you don't manage to make any of these, or you want to arrange a special session for you or your group, please ring the office.

▲ **Figure 3.17** From *King's Cross Carrion*, The Quarterly Journal of the King's Cross Railway Lands Group, January 1995

1 Assess the three sets of priorities in Figure 3.20 against the five criteria for sustainable urban development in the theory box on page 66.

2 How does each measure up?

3 Discuss why other criteria may be influential in shaping urban change.

4 Look at the extract from the *King's Cross Carrion*. To what extent are local people involved in the decision-making process?

The KXRLG was successful in contesting the passage through Parliament of the original Bill produced by British Rail. The result was the Channel Tunnel Rail Link Bill passing through Parliament in 1995, with over 1000 petitions raised against it from the 71km route of the link to the Tunnel. Sixty were concerned with St Pancras and the impacts of the development on local people. Nine MPs on the Select Committee heard evidence from the petitioners. The battle for Kings Cross-St Pancras had sharpened, with the KXRLG on one side, and the government and Union Rail on the other.

A number of plans have been put forward at various times for the development of this site. There are three versions: one from Sir Norman Foster (see Figure 3.15), one showing some priorities from the KXRLG (see Figure 3.18), and one from Alan Baxter Associates (see Figure 3.19), commissioned by Camden Council. Figure 3.20 shows some of the key differences between these plans.

The Select Committee's outcome is crucial – follow what happens in the next few years. A positive vote means that the government can go ahead with compulsory land purchase and Foster's scheme. The Baxter initiative and that of the KXRLG are designed to get the government to think again about the shape of future development.

▼ **Figure 3.18** The route of the Channel Tunnel Rail Link, in a document produced by the KXRLG.

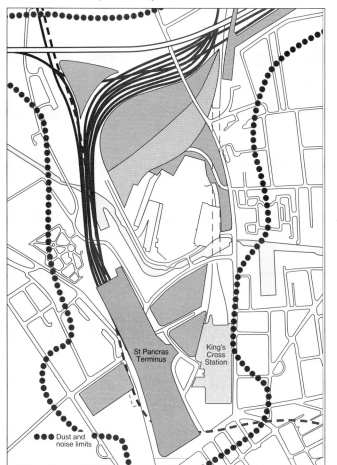

▼ **Figure 3.19** KXRLG revised plan put forward by Alan Baxter Associates.

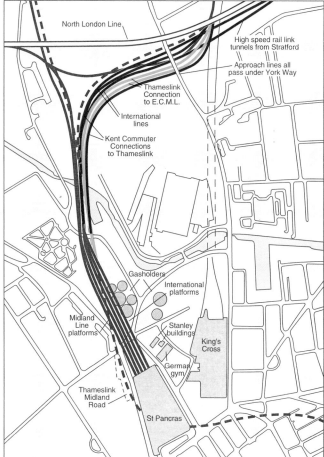

FOSTER	BAXTER	KXRLG
<ul><li>a radical rethink of the area</li><li>sees the area currently as 'an urban black hole'</li><li>the starting point is a large park surrounded by offices</li><li>some say Foster's plan is more radical and in keeping with the urban vision of the Victorians</li><li>tuck all services underground, such as railway lines, underground pipes, tubes, and tracks, canals, water basins, industrial buildings, and cap them with a park</li><li>the design of the park means the removal of some Victorian buildings but not their destruction</li><li>houses for 5000 people will surround the park</li><li>buildings designed by Europe's finest modern architects</li></ul>	<ul><li>celebrates the railway</li><li>a reworking of the old London</li><li>an organic or traditional redevelopment of a run-down triangle of Victorian London</li><li>retain street layout where possible</li><li>widen pavements and realign junctions for greater pedestrian safety</li><li>maximize and integrate new housing development</li></ul>	<ul><li>all proposals to be worked up with full consultation including with taxi operators, local community groups, groups concerned with people with disabilities</li><li>pedestrians and public transport will take priority, not private transport</li><li>look at what existing bus routes can survive, what minibuses will be needed, and other service arrangements necessary</li><li>provision for car parking will be minimized and only local traffic will be allowed in residential and community areas</li></ul>

▲ **Figure 3.20** Differences between three proposals for the Railway Lands.

No.1 Poultry – changing fashion?

No.1 Poultry is in the heart of the City of London (see Figure 3.22). The site has been at the centre of a 35-year running debate about urban redevelopment. It comprises a group of listed buildings in an urban conservation area. The key issues are these.

- Should this group of listed buildings be knocked down?
- Should a prime site in the City of London be knocked down for commercial gain? If so, what sort of development should result?

The story began in 1962 when the young developer Peter Palumbo asked the 76-year-old architect Mies van der Rohe to design a scheme for the site. A time-line for the site is shown in Figure 3.23. The issue is still unresolved, although redevelopment has begun.

▲ **Figure 3.21** No.1 Poultry – ripe for redevelopment?

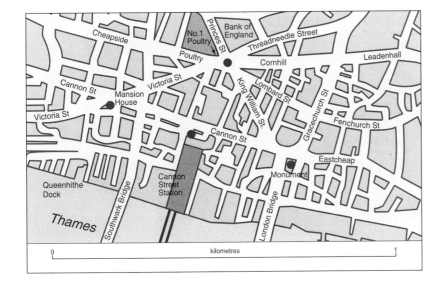

◀ **Figure 3.22** A key site – Poultry in the City of London.

▼ **Figure 3.23** Time-line to show the various plans for No.1 Poultry.

1962 – the 26-year-old Palumbo approaches the 76-year-old Mies van der Rohe to design a scheme for Mansion House Square, a 2.4ha site which he begins to assemble.

1968 – the proposals go on show at the Royal Exchange, and a poll of visitors favours them.

1969 – planning approval is obtained in principle, subject to Palumbo getting control of the whole site so that he can carry out the complete development. Mies van der Rohe dies.

1982 – the City Corporation changes its mind and unanimously rejects the scheme after Palumbo has spent 20 years buying up 12 out of 13 freeholds, and 345 of 348 leaseholds.

1984 – the three-month public inquiry pits the pro-Palumbo architectural establishment (Lubetkin, Summerson, Manser, Rogers, Foster, Stirling, and others) against the planners (City and Greater London Council) and the conservationists. At Hampton Court the Prince of Wales labels the design 'another giant glass stump better suited to downtown Chicago than the City of London'.

1985 – inquiry inspector Stephen Marks' report lies on Patrick Jenkin's desk with a recommendation to turn down the scheme. The Environment Secretary ponders what to do. Mrs Thatcher thinks about it too . . .

1986 – planning application for a scheme by James Stirling is submitted for approval.

1989 – Palumbo (now Lord Palumbo) wins fight to pull down No.1 Poultry and build a replacement scheme designed by James Stirling.

Tastes and fashions change . . .

1994 – Lord Palumbo pays £2 million for excavation of site expected by English Heritage to reveal important Roman remains.

1995 – redevelopment begins.

What are the priorities in redevelopment?

Discuss each of the following factors, and rank them in priority order for re-developing the site.

- Blend with existing style of architecture.
- Retain ancient street pattern where possible.
- Increase the range of business functions in the area.
- Match the height of the surrounding buildings.
- Make a new national architectural contribution.
- Involve local people in the decision-making process.
- Secure the maximum economic return from the site.
- Offer community services which are needed.

The story of the site

Read Figure 3.23, which shows how ideas have changed about this site. The developer, Peter Palumbo, had a vision to build a world-class development in London, to help the city to rival Tokyo and New York as a financial centre. The architect, Mies van der Rohe, developed a scheme in 1962 (see Figure 3.24), which was approved in principle by the city. The developer tried to buy the site, but this took 20 years! During that time, tastes changed. The city rejected the plan. The developer appealed and the appeal went to public inquiry. Planners and the public no longer wanted a tower block. Powerful groups pressed for conservation in the area. The developer employed a new architect, James Stirling (Mies van der Rohe is now dead), and an alternative design was approved, with conditions. It has yet to be built.

HRH The Prince of Wales in his 'A Vision of Britain, a personal view of architecture', talks about this site:

'A subject of two monumental public enquiries is the Mappin & Webb site in a conservation area at the heart of the City. There are plans to pull it down and replace it with a building which, I think, looks rather like an old 1930s wireless. But why pull down one of the few remaining bits of the Victorian city, including no fewer than eight listed buildings, at all? What on earth is the point of having conservation areas if we are going to disregard them? . . . J. and J. Belcher's Mappin & Webb building, with its fine Flemish curved tower, is one of the City's best examples of Victorian commercial architecture.'

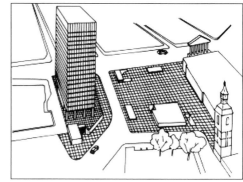

▶ **Figure 3.24** The Mies van der Rohe scheme, 1962.

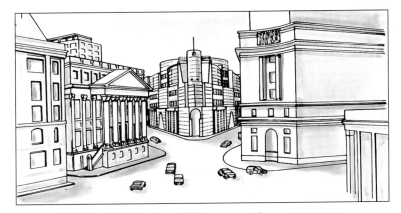

▲ **Figure 3.25** An alternative from SAVE, a conservation pressure group.

Look at Figures 3.24 and 3.25 and the photograph in Figure 3.21.

1 Give your views on each.

2 Explain how tastes in urban redevelopment have changed.

The public inquiry process

A public inquiry is not a law court. An inquiry is held when the local planning authority and a developer cannot agree on the outcome of a planning application. It is held before the Secretary of State or her/his representative, who makes a judgement. Public inquiries usually involve major developments. There are about 3000 each year. They have two purposes in law:

● to give citizens a statutory right to be heard, in support of their objections
● to ensure that the Minister is better informed of the facts of the case.

Each inquiry is given 'terms of reference' – that is, a specific brief to work to, which avoids over-lengthy investigations into issues that may not be relevant. It does however have legal powers, such as the power to make its final decision legally binding. At the end of the process, a decision is made (see Figure 3.26).

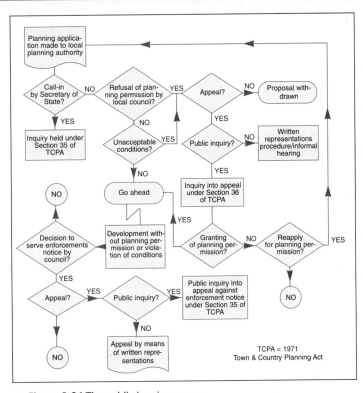

▲ **Figure 3.26** The public inquiry process.

1 Find out about the last planning issue to go to a public inquiry in your nearest urban area.
2 Trace its development through the flow chart shown on Figure 3.26 to see how it got to public inquiry.
3 Who were the key players in the inquiry? Summarize their positions.
4 What was the outcome? Who held the power in the decision-making process?

Produce a table summarizing each of the views expressed at the public inquiry into the Mies scheme. Use these column headings.

- Main views or ideas expressed
- Values being promoted
- What power or influence is held by the person (or people)
- Reasons for views held
- For or against the scheme

The public inquiry for No.1 Poultry

On 1 May 1984, the public inquiry opened into Peter Palumbo's proposal to replace a group of 19th-century buildings. His scheme had been refused planning permission by the City Corporation in September 1982. If this ruling had been reversed, and a major City conservation area containing listed buildings radically rebuilt, the conservation trend of the previous 20 years would have been reversed. This inquiry was really about a debate on the direction that architecture should take in the early 21st century.

Many of the issues raised during the inquiry were of more than local interest. The debate touched on the acceptability of modern design in historic urban settlements. Some of the evidence presented by key witnesses at the inquiry is set out below.

'The subject matter of the inquiry is not ultimately, nor simply, about architecture, but about the quality of the City as a whole and the urban design criteria that are applied to maintain and enhance that quality.'

▲ **Figure 3.27** Statement made by Roy Worskett, Bath's former chief architect, at the public inquiry during 1984.

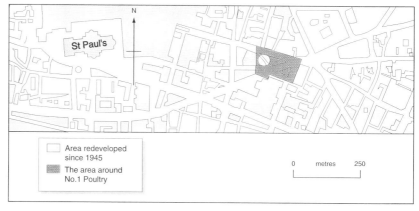

▲ **Figure 3.28** Redevelopment in the City of London since 1945.

Figure 3.28 shows the amount of redevelopment in the City since the end of the Second World War. Some of this is as a result of bomb damage, but much is as a result of commercial pressure. Some people feel that if what is left of the character of the City is to be maintained, there must be a point at which new development is unacceptable.

The character of the City of London is made up of five major elements:

- the medieval layout of small roads and lanes
- the effect of Victorian roads driven in part across the medieval layout
- the central cross-city route of Cheapside and Poultry – the biggest road in the medieval city
- the presence of small, sometimes hidden, courtyards and churchyards, and the three main public spaces associated with focal points of activity (around St Paul's, the Guildhall, and the Royal Exchange)
- the presence of individual buildings and groups of buildings, many of them Victorian and Edwardian.

Within the area of the proposal, all these elements are found, and all are threatened.

Witness Peter Carter, the project architect for the Mies building.

'Often when the Mies project is discussed, the three components of its design – the office building, the shopping forum, and the public square – are treated as if they were totally separate and unrelated in any way. This was not the intention of the design. From his earliest studies, Mies took account of the fact that the site is surrounded by a number of the City's visually strongest buildings. He also concluded that if the design was to respond to the fact that the site is at the very hub of the City's pedestrian movement – both at street level and immediately below – then the office building should be to the west of the site, where its structure would be free from entanglement with the existing underground tunnels and pedestrian concourses. Having positioned the office building, Mies' next logical step was to realign Queen Victoria Street along the front of the building because this would result in a considerable improvement on the present hazardous situation for pedestrians here, and would also provide an open space for public use of about 45 x 60m next to the Mansion House.'

▲ **Figure 3.29** Statement made by Peter Carter at the public inquiry during 1984.

Witness Geoffrey Broadbent, the then head of Portsmouth Polytechnic School of Architecture, gave evidence for 'SAVE', a conservation-minded pressure group. He argued that Mies is both unsound in his details and a threat to the health and happiness of office workers.

'I am not, by nature, a conservationist, nor am I a committed modernist. My concern is with building performance, with the health, welfare, and well-being of building users. In comparing buildings, I like to use a five-function model, according to which: any building is a container for human activities; it is an environment filter; it is a cultural symbol; it is a capital investment; and it has an impact on the environment.

'Here I want to concentrate on the fit of the spaces to activities. The "free flowing" spaces in the Mies building, to allow for changes in use, were a strength cited by Peter Carter, an earlier witness. Yet openness often means that different functions interfere with each other, visually and acoustically. A lot of people need privacy for their work. Recent German research suggests that open planning causes stress in various ways, including lack of privacy, exposure to constant disturbance, and the inability of individuals to control their own work environments.'

▲ **Figure 3.30** Statement made by Geoffrey Broadbent at the public inquiry during 1984.

Although the 1984 inquiry decided against the Mies van der Rohe development, the developer Peter Palumbo finally succeeded with a modified planning permission for the site. The City's longest-running planning battle was finally decided in the House of Lords in February 1991, nearly 25 years after the original submission. This was after a saga of 'near obsession, bad faith, Royal intervention, change of architect, public inquiries, and legal appearances which would make a worthy subject for a grand opera.' The successful combination was one of Peter (now Lord) Palumbo, at the time of the success Chair of the Arts Council, and James Stirling, the new architect. The site remains undeveloped to this day . . . and it is still a live issue.

A healthy city

This section investigates some of the issues linked to quality of life in cities, and their sustainability. Two cities – São Paulo in Brazil, and Surabaya in Indonesia – are drawn from ELDCs, since it is here that urban processes will be at the forefront of thinking as numbers of people rise sharply.

Households and environments in São Paulo

The city of São Paulo, with a population of almost 10 million inhabitants, is at the centre of what is called Greater São Paulo, which had 15.4 million inhabitants in 1991. In the 1980s, the population of Greater São Paulo grew at an average annual rate of 1.7 per cent. The central city grew at 1 per cent, while the 37 outer municipalities grew at an average of 3.1 per cent.

What is the cause of the much lower growth rate in central São Paulo? The reasons are complex and include the world economic crisis, the development of other economic growth poles, and increases in urban land prices. The economic recession and debt crisis in Brazil have slowed the rate of in-migration over the last decade, and out-migration of people back to their original region has increased. Census data for 1991 suggest that most population growth in the 1980s was in the suburban districts, whilst central districts declined in population.

The total fertility rate of the population fell from 3.5 in the 1970s to 2.1 in the 1980s. The number of people per dwelling fell from 4.0 in the 1970s to 3.5 in the 1980s. In the 1980s, 25 per cent of the occupied population worked in the industrial sector, while 70 per cent worked in services, reflecting a high proportion of informal economic activity.

The 1980s have come to be known as the 'lost decade' in Latin America, as most countries suffered serious economic decline after decades of relatively high growth. The statistics showed greater poverty in São Paulo, as incomes froze, inflation rose, and recession and unemployment hit hard, making pockets of urban poverty more widespread. In-migration and land occupation by squatters in the city's suburban areas slowed, but poverty and in-migration increased the proportion of people living in the *favelas* (squatter areas) from 1 per cent in 1973 to 8 per cent – or 820 000 people – by 1990. This is less than the population in semi-permanent houses, which increased from 1.7 million in 1980 to 3 million in 1990; 28 per cent of the population is now housed in such buildings.

Most of the city's population live in housing of inadequate environmental quality. In 1995, there were 4.3 million people living in semi-permanent houses and *favelas*, and 2.5 million in semi-permanent precarious self-built houses as squatters on illegal plots. According to the 1987 census of *favelas*, there are 592 of these in the municipal area of São Paulo, most with a small number of household

▲ **Figure 3.31** The position of São Paulo in Brazil.

▼ **Figure 3.32** Two images of São Paulo.

(a) A squatter settlement.

(b) A mix of semi-permanent and permanent housing.

units. Very few (0.8 per cent) are in the central city area. Urban expansion now faces environmental barriers. There is almost no land suited to urban occupation in the city, and urban growth is taking place on sites that are not suitable for residential occupation. The quality of life is under threat.

Researching quality of life

Recent research on quality of life was published by Pedro Jacobi in 1994. Over 1000 households in different *favelas* in São Paulo were asked about:

- their perceptions about services and their quality
- their dwelling and housing conditions
- sanitation links and conditions
- links between living conditions and health, as they perceived it
- how they saw environmental problems, and types of action needed to solve them
- their awareness about improving their quality of life.

The results are shown in Figures 3.33 and 3.34.

Refer to the urban models you encountered in Chapter 1.

1 How far does this recent research on São Paulo agree with the land use pattern of any of the models?

2 Why are there differences?

1 What links can you see between the main problems in a neighbourhood and the provision of infrastructure and services?

2 Write a profile of two contrasting socio-economic groups.

3 How far does the research challenge the view that there is a large gap between the 'haves' and the 'have nots' in this ELDC?

4 Draw up a table with four columns and three rows. In the left column, list the three problems of:

- the disposal of large quantities of solid waste
- air pollution control
- land degradation.

For the remaining columns use the heads: Technical strategies, Political strategies, Environmental education strategies. Complete the table, showing the actions you think are necessary for dealing with these problems.

Socio-economic stratum / Environmental issue	Stratum I	Stratum II	Stratum III	Stratum IV	Stratum V	Stratum VI	Total
1 Water quality	9.8	5.1	3.1	6.6	7.8	10.6	6.5
2 Pollution of rivers	2.4	1.5	5.7	8.2	5.2	7.1	5.7
3 Floods	2.4	1.3	7.4	11.2	3.9	3.5	6.1
4 Sewage	0.0	0.0	1.7	7.1	10.8	14.2	6.6
5 Solid waste	2.4	3.8	3.9	5.1	2.6	4.4	3.8
6 Air pollution	24.4	31.6	15.3	16.3	5.2	3.5	13.3
7 Noise pollution	24.4	16.5	3.9	1.5	1.3	4.4	4.8
8 Lack of green areas	2.4	13.9	10.5	7.7	7.8	4.4	8.3
9 Hillside instability	0.0	0.0	0.9	0.0	0.9	1.8	0.7
10 Traffic	7.3	2.5	7.4	3.1	0.9	1.8	3.6
11 Lack of public transport	0.0	2.5	5.7	3.6	8.2	11.5	6.1
12 Lack of day care centres	2.4	8.9	5.7	6.6	3.9	7.1	5.7
13 Lack of schools	0.0	0.0	6.1	1.0	3.0	0.9	2.7
14 Lack of health services	0.0	5.1	12.2	7.7	14.7	10.6	10.4
15 Violence	19.5	3.8	9.2	12.2	21.1	8.0	12.8
16 Lack of public lighting	0.0	0.0	0.4	1.0	0.9	1.8	0.8
17 Lack of electricity	0.0	1.3	0.0	0.0	0.0	0.9	0.2
18 Other	2.4	2.5	0.9	1.0	2.2	3.5	1.8

▲ **Figure 3.33** The main problems in São Paulo.

Infrastructure and services	Stratum I	Stratum II	Stratum III	Stratum IV	Stratum V	Stratum VI	Total
Paved roads and sidewalks	90.4	96.6	83.1	73.2	58.6	60.5	73.6
Public water supply	94.2	97.7	94.9	96.2	91.6	93.5	94.4
Public sewerage system	92.3	97.7	80.9	73.2	60.2	58.1	73.3
Public lighting	94.2	98.9	94.5	92.5	86.1	84.7	91.1
Electricity	94.2	97.7	97.1	95.8	89.6	94.3	94.5
Solid waste collection	92.3	97.7	93.3	87.7	87.6	89.3	90.5
Total households sampled	52	87	272	213	251	125	1000

▲ **Figure 3.34** Provision of basic infrastructure and services in São Paulo.

Research is useful when it leads to policy changes by decision-makers. In São Paulo, the environmental degradation has led to risks to human health from water provision and sewage services. These result from:

- the disposal of large quantities of solid waste
- air pollution control
- land degradation.

The management of environmental risks is a technical, political, and environmental education problem. Technical expertise is necessary to be able to deal with the problems; politicians have to be persuaded to act; and people generally have to be educated for environmental care.

Marginal urban settlements in Indonesia – a problem or an opportunity?

Here we look at what are called the 'marginal settlements' in Surabaya, Indonesia. The most common characteristics of marginal settlements are that:

- they are located on marginal, or poor, land
- they are in a substandard physical condition
- their inhabitants earn a very low income
- they are not served by urban services
- they are perceived by those in power as an eyesore.

However, these criteria are not always adequate. They are too generalized. Here, we will propose a more appropriate definition of such settlements, which are known locally as *pemukiman kumuh*.

▼ **Figure 3.36** Indonesian street scene.

▲ **Figure 3.35** Location of the three largest cities in Indonesia.

Urbanization in Indonesia

Surabaya is one of the three largest cities in Indonesia (Figure 3.37). While most of the poorer groups of people in the city do not live in marginal settlements – only about 1 per cent of Surabaya's people do – in a city of over 2 million, this represents 20 000 people. These areas have the added disadvantage that they have failed to attract the attention of government investment for housing improvement.

The Central Bureau of Statistics for Indonesia has recently released some figures on the country's poor. According to their figures, the percentage of poor people has declined from 40.1 per cent in 1976 to 17.4 per cent in 1987. As the population of Indonesia is about 170 million, the absolute figure is about 30 million poor people – more than the population of many Western countries. One-third of the poor (about 9.7 million) live in the cities. But this depends on how you define the term 'poor'.

Enter the data from Figure 3.37 onto a spreadsheet.

1 Draw graphs to show the rate of population growth in these cities.

2 What is the percentage rate of growth in each case since 1920?

3 Project the population for each city to the year 2000, based on rates of growth since 1970.

4 Describe the rate of growth this century in the largest cities of Indonesia.

Year	Jakarta	Surabaya	Medan
1905	173 000	150 000	–
1920	253 818	192 190	45 248
1930	435 184	341 675	76 584
1961	2 973 152	1 007 945	479 098
1971	4 579 052	1 556 255	635 562
1980	6 503 449	2 027 913	1 378 955
1988	8 803 725	2 457 393	1 876 412

▲ **Figure 3.37** Population of the three largest cities in Indonesia.

Indonesia is placed 108th in the HDI ranking. The lowest-earning 40 per cent of households have only 21.2 per cent of Indonesia's wealth; 17 per cent of Indonesia's people live in absolute poverty (20 per cent of people in urban areas, 16 per cent of people in rural areas); 65 per cent of the urban population have access to water, 40 per cent to sanitation services.

Surabaya

Surabaya is one of the largest and oldest cities in Indonesia. It has been built up through the agglomeration of existing villages. It is the capital city of the most populated province (East Java) representing 0.6 per cent of the area but 6.7 per cent of its population. Its population of 2 096 599 in an area of 291.8km^2 is growing. To the people of East Java, the city represents the chance of improvement, so there is in-migration from the villages. Housing for poorer groups is 'informal' – known as *kampungs*, which are urban suburbs surrounding the fringes of Surabaya. Other settlements include the fringe villages around the city.

Measuring human development

The Human Development Index (HDI) was introduced in the first *Human Development Report* of 1990. This report argued that the real purpose of development should be to enlarge people's choices. The HDI was introduced as a yardstick of human progress. It uses indicators of purchasing power, education, and health, and gives a broader measure of development than GDP. There is no automatic link between income and quality of life. Some countries, such as Chile, Tanzania, and Uruguay, have done well in distributing GDP. Their Human Development rank position is well above their per capita GDP rank position. In other countries, for example in Algeria, the United Arab Emirates, and Angola, the opposite is the case.

The *Human Development Report* defines 'poor' as being below the poverty line, or 'the income level below which a minimum nutritionally adequate diet plus essential non-food requirements are not affordable'.

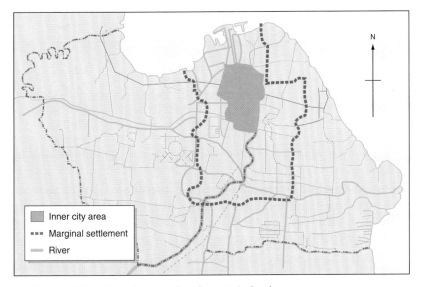

▲ **Figure 3.38** Location of marginal settlements in Surabaya.

Look at the profiles of kampungs and fringe villages.

1 Identify the characteristics of each type of settlement, and the urban problems.

2 What needs to be done to improve the quality of life in each case?

Kampungs and fringe villages

Kampungs house more than 67 per cent of people in the city's built-up area. They are found in all parts of the city from the CBD to the urban periphery. Most have developed from rural villages to 'urban villages'. Nearly a quarter were created by squatters, mainly in the post-war period when incoming migrants could not find space in the original kampungs. Although they are mainly residential areas, some informal businesses are based there.

'Fringe villages' have grown in importance for low-income families, because improved transport has made them more accessible. Densities are lower than in kampungs and housing is usually cheaper here. The many improvements that have taken place in urban Indonesia – asphalted streets, flood protection, cleaner environments, construction of shopping malls and plazas – have by-passed both types of marginal settlement.

Four types of marginal settlement

The criteria for classifying marginal settlements in Surabaya are their degree of security, their physical condition, their accessibility, and their purchase price. They can then be assessed on the basis of whether or not they should be formally recognized as a part of the city – paying taxes and in return receiving services. This process is known as 'regularization'.

Average family size:	4
% of family heads with no formal education:	19.8
% of family heads employed:	95
% of households with more than one source of income:	33
% of households earning below subsistence level:	36
% of family income used for housing:	9.2
% of family income used for food:	72
% who assist their neighbours' daily needs:	34
% who have received friends or relatives since arriving in Surabaya:	45
% with services, such as piped water, electricity, schools:	0

▲ **Figure 3.39** Data about marginal settlements in Surabaya.

1 a) Identify and summarize the problems facing the residents of marginal settlements.
  b) Place the problems in order of priority and justify your order.
  c) For each priority, justify two actions which could be taken to resolve them.

2 For two cities – one in an EMDC and the other in an ELDC – identify problems that make those cities 'unsustainable'. How could they be improved, and by whom?

Four types of marginal settlement are recognized.

Type 1 In fair physical condition with the possibility of future regularization
The main problem is that these settlements are on illegal land. Physical conditions are better than in most existing low-income settlements, including those provided by public housing programmes.

Type 2 In good physical condition but need special adjustments prior to regularization
These are on land reserved for future expansion of public services such as railways and water purification plants. Some are very long-established, for example those on land belonging to the port authority and on land reserved for drainage reservoirs. Most settlers pay rent to the respective agencies.

Type 3 In poor condition with almost no chance of proper rehabilitation or improvement
These are usually on 'illegal' land, with some physical improvement but on land that cannot be regularized. This includes land situated below high-tension electricity cables, low-lying river beds, and land beside railway tracks.

Type 4 In very poor condition with no possibility of any assistance
In these settlements there is no chance of regularization or improvement. They include land under bridges, or pavements where hawkers sleep as well as sell their goods. This type is the cheapest and the best located but presents the biggest problems for local authorities.

Our respondent arrived in Surabaya at the age of 7, in 1958. By the age of 12 he was already helping his father to collect and recycle second-hand goods from house to house. At the age of 19 he married and went to live with his parents-in-law. Two years later his wife quarrelled with her brothers and they left the house, she to live temporarily with his parents, and he in the cemetery.

A friend invited him to work with him, but later accused him of cheating, and he was jailed. When he was released in 1982, his family refused to have him back, but his mother-in-law allowed him to build his own shack next to her house near the railroad track.

At last he has the opportunity to live peacefully, and he earns a living as a garbage recyclist, although he has to work day and night. Both of his children are now at elementary school, in a kampung next to the marginal settlement.

▲ **Figure 3.40** Profile of a marginal settlement inhabitant.

Ideas for further study

1 In 1992, the Rio Summit produced Local Agenda 21, a strategy requiring local councils or bodies to develop in sustainable ways. How has your local council responded in managing transport, housing, or employment?

2 Assess the response of your local city council to Local Agenda 21, and evaluate this against needs as they are perceived by people in the local area.

3 Investigate the sustainability of urban planning in your local area. Look at transport strategies (public/private transport, pedestrianization, traffic calming), housing (suburban growth, cost of housing), employment (job opportunities, by job type/age/gender).

4 Use data from UNICEF or similar organizations to produce quality-of-life indices for different countries. Use publications such as *The New Internationalist* to help you explain contrasts that you find.

Summary

- Global urbanization continues to increase rapidly.
- Urban areas in ELDCs show little sign of reduced rates of growth in population. Meanwhile, there is counter-urbanization in EMDCs.
- In spite of counter-urbanization, cities in EMDCs continue to make great demands on space. The challenge of urbanization there is to decide how space should be used, and who should make those decisions.
- Taken together, the challenges of urbanization are global, and cannot be blamed on just the ELDCs or EMDCs.
- Many aspects of urban life and development are unsustainable in their present form – transport congestion, demands on space, unemployment and poverty, and environmental degradation all threaten the future abilities of people to support themselves.
- To combat such lifestyles, planning is essential. The challenge is whether decision-makers involve those likely to be affected by their decisions.

References and further reading

D. Engwicht, *Towards an Eco-City – Calming the Traffic*, Envirobook, 1992.

M. Fisher and U. Owen, *Whose Cities?* Penguin, 1991.

H. Sherlock, *Cities are Good for Us*, Paladin, 1991.

Streetwise, the magazine of Places for People (The National Association for Urban Studies).

The challenge of urbanization: Summary

In this section you have learned about challenges facing people living in urban areas. The table below shows you how these studies are linked to the requirements of the syllabus you are studying. Your examiners who will be setting the examination papers on the topics in this book will use the summary points below.

Key ideas	Explanation	Examples
1 Definition of urbanization	Characteristics of urban areas. Functions of urban settlements.	• Hong Kong, Chicago, Berlin, Bangkok, London • Chicago – zones, Berlin – changing functions
2 The cycle of urbanization, suburbanization counter-urbanization, and reurbanization has major impacts	A study of the issues arising for societies, e.g. demographic, economic, social, environmental, and political impacts.	• The growth of Chicago, Berlin and London in EMDCs • The growth of Bombay, Bangkok, Surabaya and São Paulo in ELDCs
	Urbanization in EMDCs occurred during the 19th century and has had effects for the 20th and 21st centuries. In ELDCs it is recent and has effects, e.g. – suburbanization and sprawl; – counter-urbanization; – reurbanization through inner city redevelopment; – millionaire cities.	• Berlin, Bangkok, Surabaya • Berlin and Chicago • London • Bangkok and Bombay
3 There is a national and global hierarchy of cities with some cities showing primacy	At national, continental, and global scales, cities have significant roles. This results in the development of special functions and demands on space.	• A study of an EMDC city to show change – Chicago, Berlin, London
	The dominance of a settlement over the economic and social life of an ELDC.	• A study of an ELDC city to show its importance in that country – Bangkok
4 The structure of cities changes as they grow and decline	Cities are dynamic.	• Urban land use models in different cities – Chicago and Bangkok
	Urban landscapes respond differently to change, and reflect this in their function and structure.	• Case studies to show how change in urban areas, and its effects on people, is politically and economically determined – Berlin, London, São Paulo, Surabaya
5 The functions of urban areas are dynamic and change in time and space	Towns and cities act as centres for housing, shopping, industry, residential, and commercial activity.	• Models of human activity in all cities studied
	Renewal and redevelopment, change from the industrial to the service city, the growth of recreation, tourism, and conservation.	• Economic growth in cities (e.g. change in London and Berlin, growth of industry in Bangkok), and decline (e.g. issues of decline in East Berlin)
	Issues surrounding areas of redevelopment and renewal, contrasted with areas of conservation.	• Berlin, London
	Changing CBDs.	• Berlin, London
	The changing rural-urban fringe.	• Berlin, ELDC cities
6 The quality of life in cities	Social justice and access to goods and services. The quality of life reflects the process of urbanization. Urban inequality and conflict reflect quality of life.	• Issues facing poor and elite urban areas, and squatter settlements (e.g. Chicago, Bombay, Bangkok, Surabaya)
7 Managing and planning cities	Cities need to be managed by public and private agencies.	• Managing change in cities, e.g. Berlin, London, Bangkok, Kobe
	Management may take the form of renewal or redevelopment of different areas.	• Contrasting different approaches, e.g. changes to the City of London, and Berlin
	Planning manageable urban areas for the 21st century is a major challenge.	• Sustainable cities and planning issues in London, São Paulo, Surabaya, Kobe

2

The impact of changing economic activities

The Sydney Olympics

Early in the morning of 24 September 1993 local time, the announcement reached the east coast of Australia that Sydney would host the Olympic Games in the year 2000. A celebration of over 1 million people, which had already begun in the city centre of Sydney, around the Harbour Bridge, and throughout the suburbs where Sydney's 4 million people live, continued until people left to go to work. The celebrations followed years of presentations, promotions, and competition between some of the world's major cities to host the event.

Why was there such competition? Although becoming host to the Olympics is a huge boost to civic and national pride, it is a costly exercise, and the promotion budget alone ran to several million Australian dollars. Many people see that the Olympics will have important social, economic, and environmental effects on Sydney, and the most immediate of these is likely to be economic. The cost of hosting them has to be matched against the economic benefits that can be gained.

In the last section you learned about urbanization and some of the challenges posed by it. This section is about economic activities. It considers how the changing world economy is affecting economic patterns of work, and the resulting impacts upon people's lives. What effect does hosting the Olympics have on a city and on a country? Who stands to gain? Who stands to lose? You will see that many of the issues which you investigated in cities such as Chicago, Berlin, and Bangkok are in fact economic issues as well as urban ones. The Sydney Olympics, as we shall see, is very much about economics.

▼ **Figure 1** Aerial view of Homebush, site of the proposed Olympic Park.

Siting the Olympic village

The Olympics will be centred around one Olympic village, situated in Homebush Bay about 14km west of the city centre, close to the suburb of Strathfield. The location, shown in the aerial photo in Figure 1 and on the map in Figure 2, is close to the harbour and to Sydney's arterial routeways linking the city centre with Burwood, Ryde, Parramatta, Fairfield, Bankstown, and Liverpool. The Olympic Park will be the venue for 15 of the 27 Olympic sports; all other sports will be held within the metropolitan area of Sydney – 8 of the remaining 12 sports will be in the central harbour zone.

1 Using Figures 1, 2, and 3, outline the geographical reasons that seem to have been important in siting the Olympic Games at Homebush Bay.

2 What particular features do you think Sydney had to present to the Olympic Committee to convince them of its suitability as a venue, and in order to win the vote?

What does hosting the Olympics involve?

It is clear that the sheer cost of developing an Olympic Park makes sport an economic activity, because it involves so much investment. Is it just a matter of finding the best location for an Olympic Park, or are there other considerations? Siting the Olympics in the past appears to have been based on a fairly logical process. Geographers study locations because some places are better than others for siting a feature such as the Olympic Park. Some aspects of the geography of economic activities deal with the question 'Which is the best location?' However, there is much more to the study of economic activities than location.

Study Figure 3. It shows some of the tasks that face the Sydney 2000 Organizing Committee between 1993 and 2000. It reads rather like a promotion brochure. Why is this? Why should Sydney's Olympic

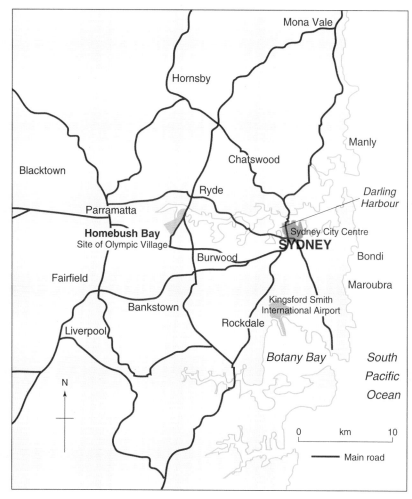

▲ **Figure 2** The location of Homebush, site of the Olympic Park.

Committee feel the need to promote the Games in the same way as a company might want to promote its products? In fact there is much similarity between running a company and organizing the Games, and the Olympic Games can be seen as an economic enterprise. A business looks at ways of raising maximum income in order to cover all costs and produce a profit. Its costs are reduced where possible and its income increased through sales, licensing, and marketing.

Read the details in Figure 3.

1 Which aspects of the Games is the Committee keen to emphasize? Why?

2 In pairs, consider all the similarities between managing a business and organizing the Olympic Games.
   a) What costs have to be met by the Olympic Organizing Committee?
   b) Suggest and list different sources of income that are available to the Committee, which might cover costs.

(a) 'The Olympic village will provide accommodation for 10 000 athletes and 5000 team officials. Other facilities include an International Broadcast Centre, a Main Press Centre, and a media village.'

(b) 'The Olympic village will be a model for future urban consolidation in Sydney, comprising primarily low-rise, medium-density housing. It incorporates major environmental design features which have evolved in consultation with Greenpeace. After the Games, the dwellings will be renovated for rental and sale to meet Sydney's housing demand.'

(c) 'Olympic spectators and other visitors to Sydney will have a wide range of accommodation alternatives available. These range from elegant five-star inner-city hotels with magnificent harbour views, to single campsites in bushland setting or adjacent to Sydney's famous beaches.'

(d) 'Homebush Bay is a magnificent 760ha waterfront site in the demographic heart of Sydney. The site, which includes major natural environments of significance as well as former industrial sites, is the subject of major Government-directed renewal and regeneration which will continue over the next decade.'

(e) 'More than two-thirds of Sydney's Olympic venues already exist. Most of the new facilities required for the Games will be constructed as part of the redevelopment program being undertaken at Homebush Bay.'

▲ **Figure 3** Extracts from the *Sydney Games Overview*, published by the Sydney Organizing Committee for the Olympic Games.

The economic impact of the Olympics on Australia

The details given in Figure 3 show you that the costs of the Olympic Games will be enormous. Unless the Olympic organizers can show benefits for Sydney and for Australia, they will be held to account for spending millions of Australian dollars with little apparent gain. Some of the benefits are immediately obvious. Figure 4d shows how the annual number of visitors to Australia – currently about 2.3 million per year – is expected to rise to over 7 million for the Olympic year. Australia's geographical location alone will tell you that Qantas, Australia's premier airline, and other international airlines, will gain from increased traffic. More traffic will almost certainly mean increased employment.

(a) 'Australia's economy will be boosted by about A\$7.3 billion (£3.2 billion) . . . an independent source claimed yesterday. It said that 156 000 full- or part-time jobs would be created.' From *The Guardian*, 23 July 1993

(b) 'Sydney has 140 ethnic groups. One in four Sydneysiders has at least one parent born overseas, while one in five speaks a language other than English at home. This means that every country competing at the 2000 Games will have its own ready-made cheer-squad – and on top of that we will be providing "hometown" cuisine, religion, language and culture.' Rod McGeoch, leading the Sydney bid for the 2000 Games, reported in *The Guardian*, 7 September 1993

(c) 'The one big minus Sydney had to address was its distance from anywhere else. Would poor countries be able to send a team halfway round the world? Such, by all accounts, stymied the recent Olympic bids of Melbourne (for 1996) and Brisbane (1992). Says the President of the Sydney Olympic Committee, John Coates, "No messing around, we're paying every fare, the lot. We have budgeted \$37 million to pay for every team's transportation as well as freight on any airline of their choice."' *The Guardian*, 7 September 1993

(d) Number of international visitors to Australia

1982–83	1.1 million
1987–88	2.25 million
1992–93	2.8 million
2000 (estimate)	7.5 million

(e) 'In 1993, the government-funded Bureau of Tourism Research estimated that in 1992 tourism provided 5.6% of Australia's gross domestic product (one measure of its wealth) and 10% of its overseas earnings, and accounted for 465 000 jobs. Domestic tourism was reckoned to be worth A\$22 billion to the economy, and international tourists worth A\$8.6 billion. Japan, the Asia/Pacific region, the USA, and Europe were the main contributors to the international tourist industry.'

(f) Sydney's housing market 1993. Graph A shows the average property price of properties sold in Sydney, 1989–93. Graph B shows the percentage of properties available for sale which sold during each year 1989–93. 1993 was a significant year – before the result of the Olympic bid was known, both the sale price and the proportion of properties selling was levelling off or even falling.

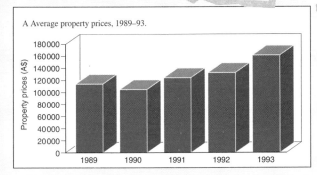

A Average property prices, 1989–93.

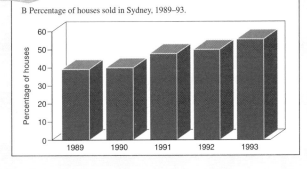

B Percentage of houses sold in Sydney, 1989–93.

▲ **Figure 4** The economics of hosting the Olympics.

▼ **Figure 5** A futures wheel. This is a means of brainstorming or trying to predict what might happen if something takes place. For example, 'increased employment' is a likely prediction as a result of Sydney hosting the Olympics. You can predict other effects as a result of this increased employment and add it to the wheel as a series of spokes radiating out. The result usually looks like a complex web.

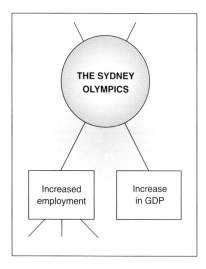

1 Study Figures 4 and 5 carefully. With a partner, construct a 'futures wheel' which predicts the increased economic growth that you expect Australia to gain from hosting the Olympics.

2 Do any problems occur to you? Which groups of people are affected, and why?

Can Sydney deliver?

In fact, there has been some opposition to the campaign to win the Games for Sydney. Nobody is doubting that it will provide economic growth in some sectors of the economy. The debate centres largely on costs, on whether the promises can be delivered, and on government priorities.

Costs

The economic costs of the Olympic proposals have not been published in full. Several changes are proposed to the transport infrastructure of Sydney, and its transport links

Ansett pilot praised after near-miss on runway

An Ansett Airbus with 108 people on board aborted a landing at Sydney Airport yesterday to avoid a possible crash with a Thai Airways DC-10 carrying 200 people. The Bureau of Air Safety Investigation is looking into the incident, which occurred after the Thai Airways aircraft reportedly failed to stop sufficiently short of an intersecting runway. The Ansett A320 was landing on the intersecting runway and is believed to have come within 30m of the Thai aircraft. It is believed that if the Airbus had not aborted its landing, its wing would have clipped the nose of the Thai aircraft. The Airbus landed without incident a few minutes later.

A Thai Airways spokesperson denied the Thai pilot had encroached on the other runway and said the aircraft had been cleared to land in line with normal procedures. But the Civil Aviation Authority's air traffic services general manager, Mr Buck Brooksbank, disagreed. 'The thing that has to be emphasized here is that the aircraft did not comply with its landing clearance, and the landing clearance is quite specific,' he said.

Mr Brooksbank praised the actions of the Ansett pilot in aborting the landing but said all pilots were trained to deal with this type of situation.

Air traffic controllers started simultaneous operations at Sydney Airport earlier this year in an attempt to reduce congestion at the airport. The procedure allows aircraft to land simultaneously from both Botany Bay and on the intersecting east–west runway, and involves one aircraft pulling up short after landing.

A CAA spokesperson, Mr Derek Roylance, said that in yesterday's case, the Thai Airways aircraft coming in from Botany Bay had been told to land and pull up short of the other runway. But it is believed air traffic controllers noticed that the aircraft was travelling too fast after landing to pull up in time. Controllers contacted the pilot and he apparently applied the brakes hard, causing the wheels to smoke.

A spokesperson for Ansett, Mr Peter Young, said the Airbus, which was arriving from Brisbane, was 'exactly where it should have been at all times'. He said the pilot had decided to abort the landing after he was not happy with the position of the Thai Airways jet. The aircraft began to climb again when it was only 6m off the ground.

Mr Young defended simultaneous operation procedures.

▲ **Figure 6** 'Near-miss' at Kingsford Smith Airport. Extract from *The Sydney Morning Herald*, 13 August 1991.

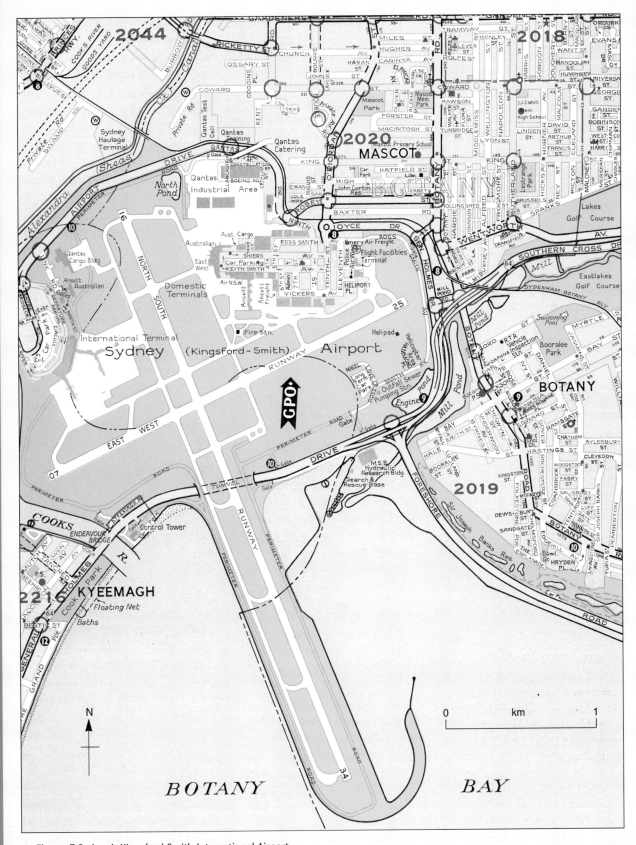

▲ **Figure 7** Sydney's Kingsford Smith International Airport.

are faced with several schemes designed to accommodate increased traffic. They will need them. Spain invested heavily in transport links, including improved motorway access to Barcelona, only to find that on occasions it was totally inadequate for the volume of road traffic created.

Sydney's airport weighs heavily in people's minds as the kind of facility which may not be able to cope. Figure 7 shows a plan of Sydney's Kingsford Smith International Airport. Notice how it is shaped like a cross, with two runways intersecting each other. This is to allow planes to land and take off irrespective of wind direction. In fact, a fairly tight balance is maintained during busy periods, with long-haul 747s using the north–south runway in almost all conditions, as it is the only runway long enough for fully-laden 'jumbo' aircraft to take off. Meanwhile, smaller aircraft use the shorter east–west runway. The question is whether Sydney's airport – the main gateway into Australia – can cope with any increase in traffic at all. Figure 6 shows how in August 1991 there was a near-miss on the ground as air traffic control gave clearance for a Thai Airways aircraft to land on the north–south runway at the same time as a domestic Ansett Airlines aircraft was permitted onto the east–west runway. Some people in Sydney regard the airport as 'a disaster waiting to happen'. With three times the number of overseas tourists expected into Australia in 2000, pressure on the airport can only increase.

Some people also feel that were it not for the Olympics, some of the changes already necessary would not have been made. Sydney's airport currently has no rail link with the city. In August 1994, an extension to the city's rail system from nearby Marrickville into the airport was announced.

The question in the minds of many people in Sydney is whether promises can be met. The Organizing Committee was unable to appoint a figurehead to lead it until August 1994. This was in spite of several attempts to head-hunt suitable people, following a series of job advertisements where no appointment was made. Even the appointment made in August 1994 only runs until the 1996 Atlanta Olympics.

Government priorities

Most of all, some people in Australia see the Olympics as a means of promoting Australia at a time when the Prime Minister, Paul Keating, is seeking to turn Australia from a monarchy under the rule of the British royal family, into a republic.

Explore all the evidence in this section so far. Divide a sheet of paper into two columns: 'Costs' and 'Benefits'. Summarize every cost or benefit – social, environmental, or economic – that you can think of. Where does the balance lie?

The Olympics and a changing global economy

Geographers study economic activities because they occur in different spatial patterns, and because they affect people. Some of those effects are beneficial and others are not. Some benefits are only benefits for certain people; for others they may create problems. To what extent will Sydney's and Australia's poorest members of society benefit? On 30 September 1993, *The Guardian* in the UK reported that, only six days after Sydney's successful bid for the Olympics was announced, Aboriginal groups were threatening to boycott the Games. To what extent will the Olympic Games reinforce the wealth or poverty of certain countries? Even though Figure 4c shows that the Olympic organizers have budgeted for travel costs for all participants, will competitors from some of the world's poorest nations be able to take part?

Economic activities raise questions about who gets what. As you read the four chapters in this section you will see that economic benefits and problems require decisions to be made. You will see that the decision-makers often represent certain sectors of society, and that increasingly they operate at a global level. It is no coincidence that the Olympics in 2000 will be transmitted and reported to every country in the world, in almost all cases as events happen. The Olympics is a truly global event; so too are many of the economic activities described in this book.

4 Introducing economic activities

The introduction to Section 2 has looked at the potential impact of the Olympics on Sydney in the year 2000. The chief impact, as we have seen, is on the economy of Sydney, and the ways in which the benefits that Sydney will gain through increased employment can be measured against other impacts. Section 2 explores the ways in which broader economic activities can be studied. This chapter provides the background and some basic ideas about economic activity which you can then apply to different case studies in Chapters 5, 6, and 7. Economic activity includes employment, manufacturing industries, service industries, new economic growth, economic decline, and environmental issues. The case studies are from different parts of the world; each emphasizes aspects of economic activity and change in different parts of the world including the UK, Ireland, Ghana, the USA, Taiwan, and the former Soviet Union. The differences between the wealthier and poorer countries are referred to frequently. The term 'EMDCs' (economically more developed countries) is used to refer to the wealthier countries. Because these are generally found in the northern hemisphere, they are often referred to as 'The North'. The term 'ELDCs' (economically less developed countries) is used to refer to poorer countries. These are generally found to the south of the world's wealthier nations, and are often referred to as 'The South'.

This chapter explores the following questions:

- What are economic activities?
- How are economic activities changing, and for whom are they changing most?
- How are economic processes managed globally?
- Where are economic activities located?

What are economic activities?

In many Social Sciences, such as Economics or Geography, most descriptions of economic activity and work are about those parts of the economy that are measured in terms of money. Newspapers and television describe changes to the value of the pound, or to house prices, or to the number of people unemployed and how much this costs the government in Social Security payments. The value of the Olympics has already been assessed in terms of the number of jobs that they will bring to Sydney.

This is only part of the story, however. Look at Figure 4.1. It shows how a country's economic activity includes various forms of production which do not involve money, as well as those that do. Some paid work is formal: people are paid wages, which they spend, and from which the government collects taxes. A great deal of work that people do is informal, however. Washing cars for payment at weekends, is informal economic activity, as is child rearing or gardening.

'Economic activity' includes all the processes of extraction, production, distribution, consumption, servicing, and conservation of resources that take place – whether they are paid or unpaid, formal or informal – which help to produce wealth for people and maintain for them a quality of life. Figure 4.1 shows that 'non-money' production actually makes up over half of a country's economic activity!

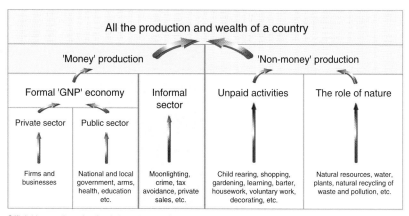

Official 'money' production is less than half the total of a country's economic activity

▶ **Figure 4.1** A country's economic activity.

Who is involved in economic activity in the UK?

If we take the national economy of the UK there are 24 million people working in the formal economy, over 4 million of whom work part-time. There are also 9 million in full-time education, many of whom are active in the informal economy working on deliveries, in shops, and in family businesses part-time. In addition, they are taking part in the unpaid economy. Another 3.5 million are aged between 0 and 5 years and need continuous care and attendance by adults who are usually unpaid. Then, besides the 2–3 million in Britain who are officially unemployed, there are 8 million 'retired' and 5 million 'others', mainly women without formal employment. Many of these people, and some of those in formal employment, take part in the informal economy doing a few hours' paid work each week. Almost all make a very big contribution to the unpaid economy, caring for children and looking after the home, doing voluntary work, and so on. In official terms, however, they are 'economically inactive'! You might like to think about the values that this implies, where only paid work counts as 'work' or 'economic activity'. There are issues to consider here – for example, is learning at school or college 'work'?

The position of women in the economy is bound up with issues of justice and the use by men of economic power, such as land ownership. Traditionally in most cultures all over the world men have worked in the paid economy, and women, most of whom work in the unpaid economy, have found themselves economically

1 Present the information in the section 'Who is involved in economic activity in the UK?' in a suitable way.

2 The population of the UK is about 58 million. Who might not be included in the statistics, and why not?

dependent on others in spite of the work that they do and the skills which they possess. This situation has been challenged in the 20th century, with more women joining the formal economy, and the gradual acceptance of the justice of sharing unpaid work between men and women. But even in more 'liberated' EMDCs, many women in full-time formal employment are expected to shoulder most of the domestic responsibility at home.

The role of Nature

The total economy also includes the work of Nature. Nature makes a complex contribution to national production, some of which is not immediately obvious. Some of it can be given monetary value. Suppose, for example, that a family with a garden puts all its domestic vegetable waste into compost which is eventually used to fertilize the soil. If Nature didn't break down the waste, much more waste would need to be transported to a dump and burnt – costing the family at least £20 a year in real terms. There are many more such hidden costs absorbed by Nature. On a different scale, and more difficult to measure, are contributions from Nature such as the growing of crops that are dependent on rainfall and natural fertility. What would it cost if this had to be done by artificial irrigation, chemical fertilizers, and artificial soil? At another level contributions of air, water, energy, and minerals are major natural resources, but are not always given economic values.

Dealing with very large numbers

Any discussion on national economies and populations involves very large numbers, and this happens all through the work on economic activity – most of the figures are in thousands of millions. It is as well to stop and think about the magnitude of these figures. If the 5 million people in the UK who work mainly in the home were to line up in single file with one metre between each person, the line would reach from London to New York or from London to Lagos. If they started walking past you at one-second intervals continuously night and day, they would still be going two months later!

It is difficult to imagine millions or billions, whether the figures refer to money, people, or tonnes of goods. In this book, the American unit of a billion is used – that is, one thousand million, or 1 000 000 000.

▼ **Figure 4.2** A main commercial street in Kumasi. Kumasi is the capital of Ashanti State in Ghana.

1 a) Look at Figures 4.2 and 4.3. In pairs, identify evidence of economic activity, past and present.

   b) Divide a sheet of paper into four quarters labelled 'Unpaid', Informal', 'Private formal', and 'Public formal'. Write each activity in the appropriate sector.

2 Compare your results with those of another pair. Try to explain any differences between the activities. How much do
   a) the environment
   b) who controls and owns resources
   c) social and economic conditions
   explain the differences you have noted?

3 What is the contribution of Nature in each of the activities?

Classifying economic activities

Classification is important. The way in which things are classified to a large extent controls how we think about them. Often hidden values lie behind the criteria chosen for classification. A system that chooses 'social class' as a criterion implies that one group of people is worth more than another, by using words such as 'upper' and 'lower'. A system that has no place for unpaid work suggests that such work counts for nothing. The term 'socio-economic groups' is often used to classify people by their (or their parents') main occupation, or whether or not they own a house, or how much they spend each week on different foods. Figures 4.4–4.7 show how different classifications can have different meanings and be used in different ways.

◀ **Figure 4.3** Preparing harvested cocoa beans, Combu Island, Amazon, Brazil.

Classifications

Formal	Informal or Non-formal	Unpaid

◀ **Figure 4.4** General divisions of economic activity.

▲ **Figure 4.5** Classification of households. W. Runciman's classification is based on control, ownership, and marketability of occupational skills.

▼ **Figure 4.6** Categories of labour: a new classification by Robert Reich, based on recent experience in the USA.

PRIMARY	Collecting or making available material provided by nature, e.g. farming, fishing, forestry, mining, etc.
SECONDARY	Manufacturing industry
TERTIARY	Service industry, the provision of services for primary and secondary industry and the community
QUATERNARY (sometimes differentiated from tertiary)	Services for primary, secondary, and tertiary sectors, concerned with specialist research, information, legal and medical specialist services, and administration

I Upper class: owners, executives, the wealthy

II Middle classes:

(a) the new upper service class: professionals, administrators, officials, managers

(b) middle service class: lower grade, smaller businesses than in (a)

(c) deskilled white-collar workers: clerical, technical, and sales workers

III Working classes:

(a) skilled working class: in decline with loss of manufacturing industry

(b) semi- and unskilled working class: many new jobs in consumer and producer services – insecurity and low pay

IV The underclass: long-term welfare-dependent households

A Routine Production Services (process workers)
Repetitive tasks typical of high volume enterprises – production line, most new technological jobs (data input, etc.). Pay declining/global location choice.
In the USA, these make up 25% of the workforce; this proportion is decreasing.
B In-person Services
Similar to **A** but the service must be given in person to the consumer – retail, hotels, taxis, etc. Pay in decline, competition with redundant A workers for jobs.
In the USA, these make up 30% of the workforce; this proportion is rising.
C Symbolic-Analytic Services
Problem identification, solving, manipulating symbols – teamwork essential, e.g. advertising, PR, investment bankers, consultants, actors, writers, journalists, etc. Pay rising, skills traded on international market.
In the USA, these make up 20% of the workforce; this proportion is rising.
D The Rest
Primary producers (<5%) and government employees, teachers, etc. similar to C.
In the USA, these make up 25% of the workforce; this proportion is steady, as it is less subject to global competition.

▼ **Figure 4.7** Official classifications of the UK 1991 Census. All these classifications are based on and apply only to the workforce in the formal economy.

(a) Occupation.

	% workforce	% male
1 Managers and administrators	15	68
2 Professional	8	61
3 Associate professional and technical	8	51
4 Clerical and secretarial	15	24
5 Craft related	15	89
6 Personal and protective service	9	38
7 Sales	7	36
8 Plant and machine operative	10	78
9 Other	9	53
All occupations	100	57

(b) Industry.

	% workforce	% male
0 Agriculture, forestry, fisheries	2	80
1 Energy and water supplies	2	81
2 Extraction and manufacture of minerals and chemicals	3	75
3 Metal goods, engineering, and vehicles	9	79
4 Other manufacturing	9	60
5 Construction	7	91
6 Distribution, hotels, catering, repairs	20	47
7 Transport and communications	6	77
8 Banking, finance, insurance, business services, and leasing	12	51
9 Other services	28	36

(c) Social class. This is used by a variety of UK government statistical departments to record people's backgrounds. It indicates the kind of work done by the main wage earners in order to classify them and their households. For instance, occupations are used to record and classify deaths in the UK; the data show marked differences in cause of death between people of different backgrounds.

		% workforce	% male
I	Professional etc. occupations	 5	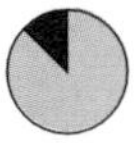 82
II	Managerial and technical	 28	 56
III(N)	Skilled occupations – non-manual	 23	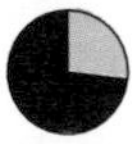 27
III(M)	Skilled occupations – manual	 21	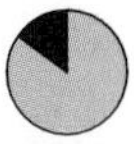 85
IV	Partly skilled	 15	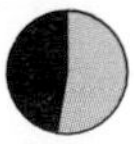 53
V	Unskilled	 6	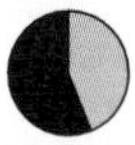 44
	Armed forces and others	 2	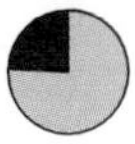 76

(d) Socio-economic groups. This is used to classify people by work done in the formal economy.

	% workforce	% male
1 Employers and managers in central and local government, industry, commerce, etc. – large establishments	5	71
2 Ditto – small establishments	10	68
3 Professional workers – self employed	1	91
4 – employees	4	81
5 Intermediate non-manual	14	41
6 Junior non-manual	21	24
7 Personal service workers	5	18
8 Foremen and supervisors	2	83
9 Skilled manual workers	13	91
10 Semi-skilled manual workers	11	61
11 Unskilled manual workers	5	41
12 Own account workers (non-professional)	6	80
13 Farmers – employers and managers	<1	89
14 – own account	<1	90
15 Agricultural workers	1	71
16 Armed forces	1	90
17 Others	1	64

The formal economy – bar graphs and divided bar graphs

The divisions within the formal economy of the UK can be represented visually using bar graphs. The following guidelines can be used with Figure 4.7a and b.
You should use centimetre graph paper for this.

Simple bar graph

A suitable scale for the data in Figure 4.7a is 2cm to 10%, and each bar drawn to 1cm wide. The bars may be vertical or horizontal.

1 Draw a base line 9cm (there are nine occupations).

2 At right-angles to the base line, draw a scale line 4cm long. At 2cm along this line mark a point to represent 10%. (The highest value here is 15%.)

3 Draw a bar 1cm wide for each occupation to the appropriate length, e.g. 3cm for 'Managers and administrators' (15%).

Divided bar graph

The same data can be represented by drawing a single bar 1cm wide and 10cm long, with a scale of 1cm = 10%. A divided bar graph shows all the components on a single bar up to 100%. It presents percentage figures rather than numbers.

1 Draw a base line 10cm long. Mark 1cm intervals (each = 10%) along one edge of the bar.

2 Mark off the bar in sections for each occupation, e.g. 1.5cm for 'Managers and administrators'.

3 Begin the next category at the point where you finished drawing the section for 'Managers and administrators'.

4 Continue until all categories are shown, up to 100%.

Make sure all parts are properly labelled, and that there is a key to the occupations shown.

1 Which graphical method gives the most useful diagram?

2 Draw similar diagrams for the other classification in Figure 4.7b, and compare results.

3 How might you draw a diagram to show all of the data in Figure 4.7a and b?

Reich's classification

Although it was worked out for the USA, Reich's classification (Figure 4.6) applies to all countries of the North. It presents a new, exciting way of understanding recent patterns of economic change in the world. During the 1980s and 1990s there has been a growing gap in the industrialized world between rich and poor, with the top fifth getting richer while the rest get poorer, especially the bottom fifth. This is due mainly to growing gaps in pay rather than to rising unemployment. Higher pay is closely linked with higher levels of educational qualifications.

Reich's suggested explanation for this trend makes three points:

1 The location of the process worker (category A) can now be anywhere in the world. Therefore workers compete with those in low-pay peripheral areas. The idea that English workers can compete with Chinese or even Brazilian workers in terms of pay-level is ridiculous. However, either levels of pay are driven down in the North, or jobs in the North disappear to the South. Thus workers in car plants in the UK and France face considerable competition with companies who are able to pay lower wage rates

in the newly industrializing countries (NICs). This applies more and more, even to skilled process workers, who find that technology replaces people in the production line.

2 In-person services (category B) cannot be exported overseas. But though the number of jobs is rising in this sector, it is kept in check as machines replace people for at least some of their functions. Pay is driven down with increasing competition for jobs from the redundant workers from category A.

3 Pay for the symbolic analysts (category C) is rising fast, and they are in short supply. Their market is global, and there is no alternative cheap supply from peripheral areas. The explosion in information and communications technology means that they can be available to a large number of customers almost instantaneously, and when they work in teams, they become a powerful force in shaping the world economy.

▲ **Figure 4.9** Elizabeth.

▼ **Figure 4.8** Peter.

Peter is 35 years old, and lives with his wife and three children in a suburb of Birmingham. He worked for twelve years as a maintenance worker in a local factory. He looked after machinery on the shop floor. 'Most of the machines were fairly old and there was plenty of work and overtime. As a result the wages were good, so over the years we were able to enjoy some luxuries including a car, holidays abroad and some new furniture.' Now the multinational company owning the factory has decided to sell it off, and the new owner, another multinational company, is only interested in office development on the site. Peter has been made redundant, and there is little alternative work in the area. Prospects for his family are suddenly bleak.

Elizabeth, who is 13 years old, is a water-girl in Kumasi, central southern Ghana. After helping her aunt with household chores for four hours she goes to the giant central market area. She carries iced water around in a basket on her head and sells it to traders. She can earn about 30p in a day – enough to pay for her food and give a little to her aunt. She cannot afford to go to school.

1 Study Figures 4.4–4.7. Use each of the different classifications to classify and describe the activities of:
a) Elizabeth (Figure 4.8)
b) Peter (Figure 4.9)
c) a friend or someone in your own family.

2 a) What values about the worth of people, money, goods, and services are implied by each system of classification?
b) Which people might select each system? Which people might reject it? Why?

3 a) In what ways is Reich's classification (Figure 4.6) helpful in understanding global and international influences on economic activity?

b) How far does Reich's classification help to explain what you have seen about:
i) Elizabeth (Figure 4.9)
ii) Peter (Figure 4.8)
iii) a friend or someone in your own family?

4 Look at the data for the UK in Figure 4.7. Do any of the figures surprise you? In what ways do the tables complement or duplicate each other?

5 Use Figure 4.7 to write a brief description of employment in the UK's formal economy.

How are economic activities changing?

Changes in economic activities do not just happen and they do not happen in a vacuum. They occur because certain people have decided that they should. Economic activities are part of the wider system of human activity. Changes in one part affect people and systems in another part.

Figure 4.10 shows some of the interrelationships involved. People on the receiving end of changes in economic activities, such as those who become unemployed, often seem removed from the causes of change and feel unable to influence them. The amount of control that an individual has over her or his fate varies enormously, and issues of justice in economic affairs are often bound up with this. The examples on these pages illustrate different ways in which changes can affect people for better and for worse.

1 Study Figure 4.10. With a partner, explain how the following can directly affect people's lives, and give examples:
   a) global trends
   b) power and control
   c) the world economy.

2 What does 'manifestations' mean in Figure 4.10? Give examples of how 'manifestations' of the world economy can affect people in the UK.

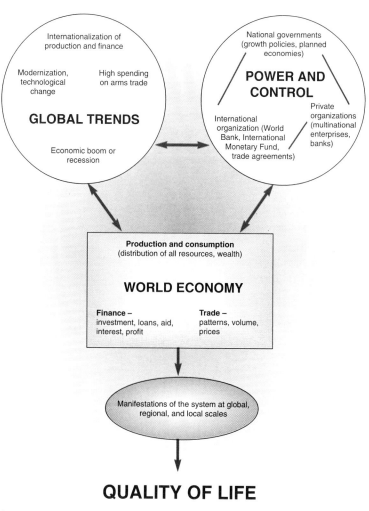

▶ **Figure 4.10** Global and national interrelationships.

1 Consider each of the changes presented in Figure 4.11(a)–(d). Decide for whom each change might be
   a) good news
   b) bad news.

2 Copy Figure 4.10. Select one of the changes (a)–(d) in Figure 4.11 to put as 'manifestations' on the diagram in Figure 4.10. Discuss some of the ways in which the 'world economy', 'global trends', and 'power and control' have influenced the quality of life of the people involved. Label your version of Figure 4.10 to record your comments.

▼ **Figure 4.11** Changing economic activity around the world.

A mother of three, Anju lives in a village near Chittagong. She earns about £1.50 a day during the harvest season by renting out her tractor to local farmers. She invests her earnings in her home and family.

But things were very different a few years ago. The family was poor and landless. Their only income was from Anju's occasional rice-husking and her husband's work as a travelling labourer.

Anju joined a new income-generating scheme with the Grameen Bank of Bangladesh, which offers small loans to landless women, and is supported by UNICEF. With an initial loan of £25 Anju bought a milking cow. Income from this enabled her to pay back the loan and its low interest, and borrow more to lease land. Eventually she saved £350, which was enough to buy her a small hand-tractor.

'It has changed my life completely', she said.

(a) Anju Dev, Bangladesh.

One of the UK Overseas Development Agency's largest ever projects was its £117 million investment in the Victoria Dam, part of the giant Mahaweli HEP and irrigation project in Sri Lanka. The aim of the project was to transform the country's economy within one generation.

The proposal planned to uproot 1300 families to make way for the reservoir, but by completion 5200 families had been moved and became refugees. These refugees, who had once been independent farmers, were thrown into dependency, and even four years after resettlement, in some areas 80% of the people remained dependent on food subsidies.

Electricity is being generated by the Victoria Dam, but is 40% below the original estimate in dry years. Meanwhile its second function, irrigation, has yet to be fulfilled since the irrigation works have not yet been developed.

(b) From the *New Scientist*, 23 May 1992.

(c) The ever-worsening gap between rich and poor.

	World income	
Richest 20%	World income – 82.7 / World trade – 81.2 / Commercial lending – 94.6 / Domestic saving – 80.6 / Domestic investment – 80.5	82.7%
Second 20%		11.7%
Third 20%	Global income and economic disparities	2.3%
Fourth 20%		1.9%
Poorest 20%	World income – 1.4 / World trade – 1.0 / Commercial lending – 0.2 / Commercial saving – 1.0 / Domestic investment – 1.3	1.4%

(d) Earnings and spending in the UK in the 1990s.

	Average earnings 1992 £'000 per year		Household spending 1992 £'000 per week		
	Men	Women	Food	Housing	Transport/ Vehicles
Scotland	<10K	5.1K	56	20	25
Wales	<10K	5.1K	55	23	25
England					
A	<10K	4.9K	54	20	25
B	<10K	4.9K	54	20	25
C	<10K	4.9K	54	20	25
D	<10K	5.1K	54	20	27
E	>10.3K	5.2K	55	27	27
F	<10K	4.9K	54	23	25
G	<10K	4.9K	56	23	27
H	<10K	5.1K	55	23	27
Greater London	n.a.	n.a.	56	30	30
n.a. not available					

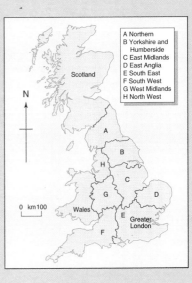

A Northern
B Yorkshire and Humberside
C East Midlands
D East Anglia
E South East
F South West
G West Midlands
H North West

Global processes

Core and periphery systems

The concept of 'core and periphery' is useful in Geography. It helps to portray easily how some parts of the world or of a country become more developed than others and why some people and regions are wealthier than others. The idea of core and periphery patterns, shown in the theory box and in Figure 4.12, is a useful aid to understanding changing economic patterns. This process is happening at all scales, from the local to the global.

Changes in technology are beginning to alter core and periphery systems and make new patterns of economic activity possible. This is summarized in Figure 4.13. New technologies have produced wide-ranging effects on people, the way they work, the way in which they live their daily lives, and on societies. Remember that these changes have been planned.

Core and periphery

Figure 4.12 shows how useful the idea of core and periphery can be. The South East of England is usually taken as the 'core' region of the UK. In this region, employment uses relatively high technology, offers higher pay than elsewhere, and promotes high capital investment. The wealth of the region attracts high densities of services designed to provide for the population. The relative wealth of the region means that house prices are higher here than elsewhere.

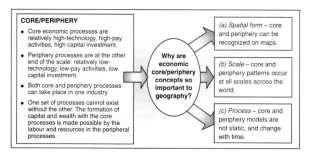

▲ **Figure 4.12** The concept of core and periphery.

Now consider the opposite scenario. Periphery processes occur at the other end of the scale: regions on the 'periphery' attract employment using lower technology, offering lower pay, and attracting low capital investment. However, such regions are often cheaper for people to live in. Northern Ireland and Scotland are examples of peripheral regions of the UK. However, this should not detract from any economic growth that does occur in these regions.

Figure 4.12 also shows how one set of processes cannot exist without the other. The formation of capital and wealth within the core processes is made possible by the labour and resources in the periphery.

Why are core/periphery concepts important?

- They present different patterns over space. It is usually easy to recognize core and peripheral regions using simple economic data. Economic processes tend to be separated geographically. For instance, companies may decide to locate in a particular place because a resource is there. This attracts investment, and offers job opportunities. As a result, core processes concentrate in areas which become affluent and gain political and economic control. Peripheral processes occur within areas which become relatively poorer with higher unemployment. Both core and peripheral processes can occur at the same place. Declining employment in one activity can be balanced by increasing employment in another.

- Core and periphery patterns occur at different scales. Global core regions such as North America and Western Europe contain many smaller-scale cores, for example southern California, or Berkshire. Other areas within global cores are in fact smaller-scale peripheral areas, such as western Ireland, or Labrador. In the same way, global peripheral areas such as Latin America and Africa contain smaller-scale cores like Accra or São Paulo.

- Core and periphery models are constantly changing. What is 'high-tech' today is 'low-tech' tomorrow. These concepts help geographers to remain aware of constant change, and not to assume that the world must be is as it is.

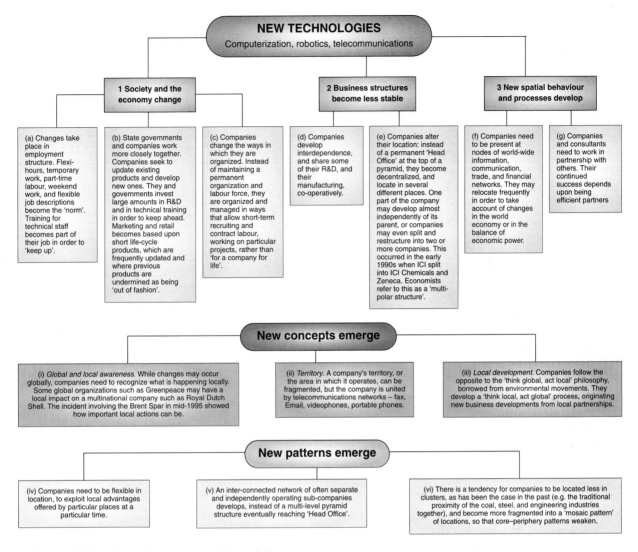

▲ **Figure 4.13** The effects of the technological revolution.

All this may be complex, theoretical, and not easy to understand, not least because change is happening so quickly. However, the environmentalist slogan 'Think global, act local' is certainly being turned on its head for business enterprise, to 'Think local, act global'.

Global control

The stage has been reached where huge wealth and giant economic enterprises are in the hands of a very few nations and institutions – and therefore a very few people, most of whom are men. Figure 4.14 shows that multinational enterprises (MNEs) have not suddenly appeared, but have developed steadily with the market economy.

1 With a partner, visit your local library and ask to see company reports for a multinational company of your choice. Write to the company and ask for information about the range of activities in which the company is involved, and where these take place in the world. The company's annual report to shareholders will often set out the details on what you want to know.

2 When you have information about the company, decide to what extent the changes shown in Figure 4.13 are true for the company you selected.

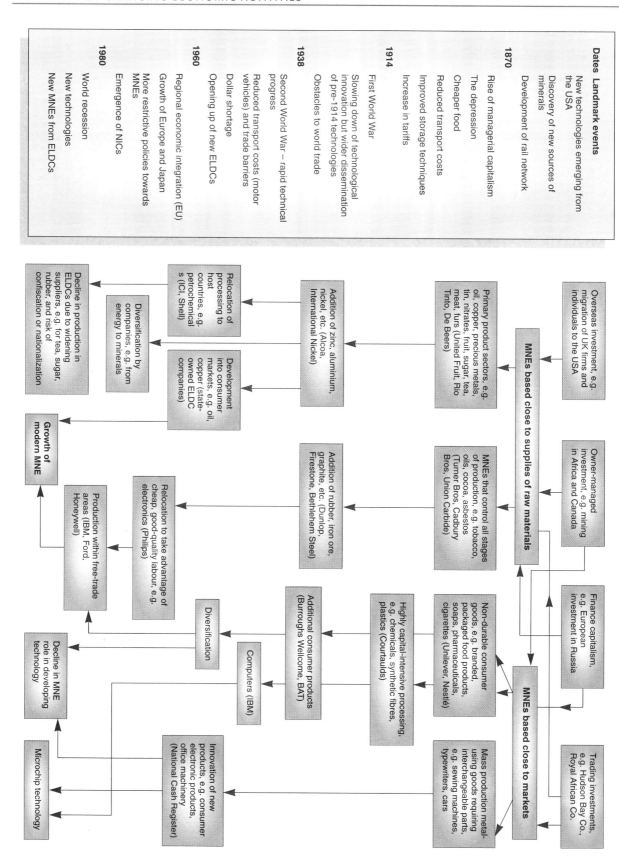

▲ **Figure 4.14** The evolution of modern multinational enterprises (MNEs).

The largest of these enterprises now challenge small nations in wealth, power, and trading. Figure 4.15 shows the world's largest companies in terms of their annual sales, their annual profits, and their market value. All are liable to change from year to year. Market value, for instance, depends on the company's share price on the Stock Exchange; a fall in the price can reduce the market value of the company. Figure 4.16 shows that these companies are generally located in the richer North, and in the NICs of South-East Asia.

a) Sales		b) Profits		c) Market value	
Itachu	180	Philip Morris	4.9	Nippon T&T	140
Sumitomo	168	Exxon	4.8	American T&T	82
Mitsubishi	166	Royal Dutch/Shell	4.8	Royal Dutch/Shell	82
Marubeni	162	General Electric	4.3	Exxon	81
Mitsui	160	AT&T	3.9	General Electric	79
Exxon	117	Dupont	2.7	Mitsubishi Bank	74
General Motors	113	Merck	2.5	Sumitomo Bank	66
Nissho Iwai	106	Unilever	2.2	Wal-Mart Stores	64
Ford Motor	100	Toyota Motor	2.2	Ind. Bank Japan	63
Toyota Motor	95	Chevron	2.2	Sanwa Bank	61

▶ **Figure 4.15** The world's top ten performers in 1993, based on (a) sales, (b) profits, and (c) market value of companies in terms of their share price (all figures in billion dollars).

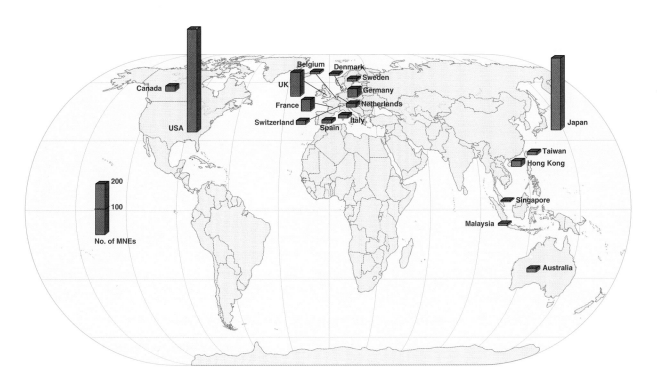

▲ **Figure 4.16** The global distribution of multinational enterprises (MNEs). This map shows the number of MNEs with a market value of over US $3 billion.

1 a) What are the differences between sales, profits, and market value?

   b) Why would the top ten companies in Figure 4.15 be different in terms of sales, profits, and market value?

2 Choose a range of diagrams to represent the data in Figure 4.15, and construct them. If you have access to a spreadsheet program, use appropriate styles of graph. Be prepared to justify your choice of diagram.

Even smaller MNEs have networks of global links. Figure 4.17 is based on a typical small textile firm in eastern Asia. Notice how it has markets in Australia, North America, and Europe. Though the location of production may be in eastern Asia, the company has to maintain its competitiveness by managing sales and distribution overseas.

▶ **Figure 4.17** Network for a small global corporation.

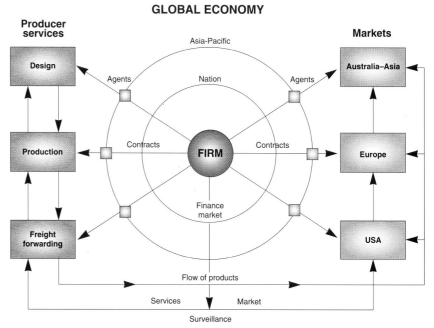

GLOBAL ECONOMY

Company X = brand-name textiles: subcontracts manufacturing

1 **a)** Assume that the rates of growth shown in Figure 4.18 are maintained for five years. Using your calculator or a spreadsheet, calculate the market value of each of the ten sectors by the end of the five-year period.
   b) Does the rank order change much in five years?

2 Where does economic power transfer to over the five-year period? Which sectors lose influence? Which ones gain?

3 What are the possible consequences of these changes?

Because MNEs are such an important part of the world economy, any changes which occur to or within them provide a good indication of what is happening globally. The changes in the market value of the top 1000 firms from 1992 to 1993, shown in Figure 4.18, provide a dramatic picture of a world economy in a state of change.

▼ **Figure 4.18** The top economic sectors by market value 1993.

	Market value $ billion	% change 1992 to 1993
1 Banking	1192	+42
2 Telecommunications	583	+36
3 Health & personal care	515	−11
4 Utilities	511	+26
5 Energy sources	488	+5
6 Merchandising	382	+9
7 Insurance	335	+22
8 Food and household	294	+6
9 Chemicals	281	+4
10 Electrical and electronics	279	+14

A major part of MNEs' activity is in trade, and the results create important geographical patterns. The main 'players' in world trade are governments and firms – see Figure 4.19.

An important feature of world trade has been the development of the trading blocks shown in Figure 4.20. These are countries that choose to trade together as a block, such as the European Union. However, this should not obscure the fact that most trade is between nations of the North, and only about 10 per cent of world trade involves countries of the South that are not oil producers. The development of trading blocks after 1945 was on a relatively small scale globally, but has accelerated rapidly during the 1980s and 1990s.

1 How far do the trade blocks in Figure 4.20 show a world North–South divide?

2 Do you think it matters whether or not a country belongs to a trade block? What might the consequences be for a country of:
   a) joining a block
   b) not joining a block?

3 In pairs, select one trading block from Figure 4.20. Using CD-ROM, newspapers in the library, and other sources such as *The Economist* and *Geographical Magazine*, find out whether the following are true:
   a) 'Most trade is *between* and not *within* blocks.'
   b) 'Trade benefits richer rather than poorer members of the blocks.'

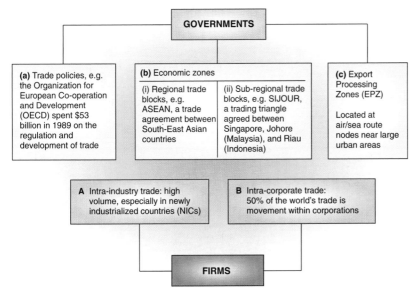

▲ **Figure 4.19** Players in international trade.

▼ **Figure 4.20** World trade blocks.

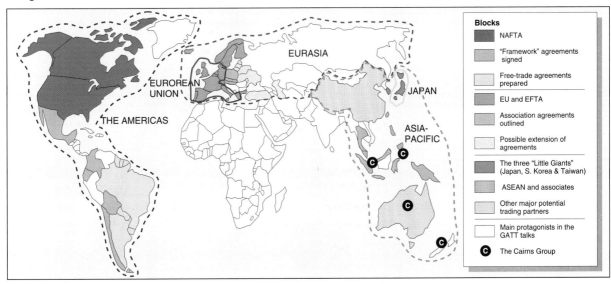

4 In 500 words outline your views on whether or not the UK should remain in the EU.

Most of the trade between countries of the North is now on the basis of differing quality and style rather than cost differences. People are likely to choose a product because of its quality as well as its cost. This is particularly true of the motor trade, where people choose a price band and then select within it, rather than opt for the cheapest. Even so, costs between different countries, and the quality produced, can vary significantly, as is shown in Figure 4.21.

The control of trade is one way in which the so-called 'free-market' economy is managed by powerful nations. At a global level the core areas of wealth – Japan, the USA, the EU, and now the West Pacific Rim – exercise enormous power. This is not only through their governments and MNEs based in those countries, but also through their power to influence the decisions of the World Bank and the International Monetary Fund (IMF). These two institutions and the global financial community have used the 'carrot' of loans and the 'stick' of interest rates to force almost every country in Africa into monetarist economic policies (Figure 4.22). Monetarism seeks to return wealth to private individuals rather than to maintain it within the control of governments.

▼ **Figure 4.21** Costs and quality in the car industry.

	DM per hour		
	1980	1985	1990
Germany	27	34	42
France	20	24	25
UK	15	23	24
Spain	13	23	28
USA	25	34	37
Japan	15	32	33

(a) Labour costs.

Firm/Region	Average no.of hours taken to produce one car	Defects per 100 cars
Japanese/ Japan	17	52
Japanese/ North America	21	55
USA/ North America	25	78
European/ Europe	36	76
NIC/NIC	41	72

(b) Productivity and quality.

▶ **Figure 4.22** One view of who runs the world.

The Structural Adjustment Plans (SAPs) of, for example, Ghana and Zimbabwe – which are considered to be IMF 'success' stories – have created some stability, wealth for exporters, and opportunities for investors, but have increased the cost of basic necessities and reduced government subsidies for health, education, transport, and food. Thus life for the poor has become even more precarious and difficult.

Attempts to manage economic change are made in many other ways by individual governments. Economic measures include taxation, interest rate and exchange rate adjustments, subsidies, import/export control, tariffs, quotas, and price control. Social control is attempted through benefit rules, training and retraining, and education.

How much do Figures 4.18–4.22 help you to understand what you see in the following aspects of the UK:

a) unemployment
b) changing technology
c) social changes, especially in health and education
d) any other changes you can think of?

Where are economic activities located?

Finally, this chapter introduces some of the important factors in locating businesses in specific locations. Companies select locations on the basis of what land or site is available for sale. Rarely is only one plot of land for sale – usually several are available. How do companies make the choice of which is best for them?

Industrial location theories

The case studies in Chapters 5–7 present a variety of different economic activities through which you will be able to understand how changes are occurring. You will use different theories which will help to explain why decisions are made in particular ways. These theories can broadly be divided into three groups.

1 Theories with a strong economic emphasis based on the idea of 'least-cost' locations. These emphasize the costs of labour, land, energy, raw materials, and marketing at alternative locations, and often identify transport costs as a vital discriminating factor.

2 Theories that focus on decision-making and the participants in the process. This approach is very useful for the study of a specific location decision where the actors in the decision-making can be identified. For example, the British government's attitude to overseas investment, and its willingness to support Toyota, was vital to that company's decision to open a car plant in Britain. On a local scale the Japanese directors' love of golf seemed significant. The site chosen at Burnaston near Derby not only had the appropriate existing infrastructure, but the package included the offer of 18th-century Allestree Hall, with 25 hectares of land and its own golf course, rent-free for five years.

3 A third group of theories might be called 'pragmatic'. These look in detail at what has happened, and try to identify the important location factors which may then be used to create some kind of model of the process. Sometimes specific locations cannot be explained other than by the fact that person X lived at place Y. For example, there is no reason why computer software should be produced by the Microsoft Corporation in Seattle rather than anywhere else – its founder, Bill Gates, just happens to live there.

Geographers study the location of economic activity at different scales – global, national, regional, and local – and the interrelationships between these. Chapters 5–7 use some of the theories which underlie decisions about specific economic activities described in the case studies.

Ideas for further study

1 Form groups of three or four. Select a factory in your area. Investigate how it functions, and its location. If possible arrange an interview there. Try to establish the following.

   a) What takes place at the factory – what goes in, what comes out?

   b) What buildings, machinery, and services are needed to do this?

   c) What management is needed? What labour, with what skills, is needed?

   d) What is there about (a), (b), and (c) that makes this location suitable?

   e) Was the decision to site there influenced by other factors than these?

2 Refer to different theories of 'least-cost location' (page 138), 'agglomeration' (page 114), 'inertia' and 'the influence of technology, research, and development', and from the 'References and further reading' suggested below. How do your findings about the factory relate to the ideas described there?

3 Carry out an investigation into economic change in your local region. You can obtain data from HMSO's *Regional Trends* and *Social Trends*, which are published yearly. How does your region compare with other regions of the UK?

Summary

- 'Economic activity' includes a wide range of processes which are linked to the production and consumption of resources that take place. These help to produce wealth for people and maintain for them a quality of life.
- Economic activities vary – they may be paid and unpaid, formal and informal. Unpaid informal work may contribute a very significant proportion to a country's economic activity

- Economic activities are important for people because they provide work. Changes to economic circumstances lead to changes in activities, and therefore changing patterns of employment.
- Economic change is usually due to processes beyond the control or influence of individual people, and lies with larger political or economic organizations.
- Most economic activities gain from their association with others. The close association of similar activities in an area leads to the development of core regions.
- The effects produced by the emergence of core regions tend to create more negative effects in peripheral regions, away from the core region.
- Core–periphery patterns have become dominant at a global scale, and can be seen at national and regional scales as well.
- Theories of location help in the understanding of both established patterns and in making decisions for the future.

References and further reading

The *New Internationalist* is published monthly and is excellent reading for gaining insight into global economic processes and the effects that these have on people.

The Economist contains useful reports, including specific reports on particular countries.

Good case studies of 'core and periphery' are Mick Dunford's 'Italy's uneven development' in *Geography Review*, May 1989, and Charles Pattie and Ron Johnston's 'The divide widens' in *Geography Review*, January 1990.

5 Changing employment patterns and their impacts

This chapter looks at changes in patterns of employment in Birmingham and on Tory Island, off the northern coast of Ireland. Changing work patterns affect people's lives, and have causes that are often a long way removed from where people live. Birmingham and the West Midlands have traditionally been part of the UK's major 'core' region of economic development which spans the area from the north Midlands to the South East of England. In recent years, Birmingham's economy has changed; some sectors of employment have fallen rapidly while others have increased. Meanwhile Tory Island has undergone changes which are typical of peripheral regions.

Patterns of employment

Some of the structural changes in economic activity are seen in global trends in GDP (gross domestic product). In Figure 5.1, 'Industrial market economies' are those that have traditionally included the industrialized countries of Japan, western Europe, and North America (the economically more developed countries, or EMDCs), and now also include the industrialized nations of South-East Asia. 'Developing market economies' include virtually all economically less developed countries (ELDCs) where industrial and service sectors are growing.

Industrial market economies have seen a decline in manufacturing employment and a rise in service employment. National employment figures reflect this. By 1993, 73 per cent of UK employment was in service, and 20 per cent in manufacturing. Some nations in this group, like Greece, are still developing their industries (Figure 5.2).

In recent decades changes in employment patterns have been massive and rapid. In industrialized nations these reflect changes in the structure of economic activity (referred to in Chapter 4). In many market economies these have led to high levels of unemployment, so that high unemployment is almost assumed to be part of society and affects the decisions that people make about society. This is known as structural unemployment, and it poses several challenges for society. A major issue for the 21st century is how to meet this challenge.

In industrialized nations, relatively few people are needed to produce all the goods that can be consumed or sold elsewhere, and the number of people needed to provide necessary services is falling. Thus more people are without work, or any formal economic activity. At the same time more people have retired or taken early retirement. In the future, will 'rewards' be limited to those in full-time employment in the formal economy? Will there be a change in the value placed on different kinds of 'work', such as unpaid work and that in the informal sector?

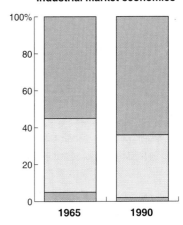

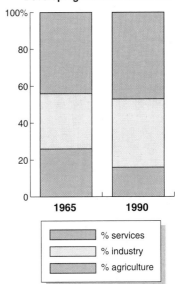

▲ Figure 5.1 Global GDP: proportions from each sector of the economy.

	Agriculture	Industry	Services	Total
Greece	−100 000	+800 000	+250 000	3.8m
France	−300 000	−1 100 000	+1 200 000	21.5m
UK	−150 000	−1 900 000	+1 700 000	25.0m

▲ Figure 5.2 Changes in the number of people employed in each sector, 1980–87.

Defining economic change

The UK Government and media provide a great deal of information about the economy. Rising or falling unemployment, the value of currencies, and share prices are all reported frequently, using official figures. It is assumed that in some way these are relevant to our lives. However, the concepts of growth and of decline are complex.

Geographers are interested in the spatial effects of growth and decline. Over the past 20 years Taiwan has been an area of growth, and by some indicators Central Scotland one of decline, but we need to be sure what we are talking about. This theory box suggests some questions that could be asked.

- *What time scale is used?* Growth and decline can be long or short-term. Almost the whole world was in economic recession during 1991, and in 1993 even Japan suffered. But by 1994, the UK and the West Midlands were classified by economists as areas of growth.

- *What is 'growth'?* Growth is usually defined as increase in production in every kind of economic activity. During the 1980s some parts of Birmingham's economy grew, such as services, while others declined, such as manufacturing.

- *What does growth mean to people and their lives?* Growth includes increasing production of goods and/or services, and may lead to increased employment opportunities. However, it can result from improved productivity (i.e. production per person) and investment with no increase in jobs. Increased production also means increased consumption. However, consumption may be increasing elsewhere in the world, away from areas of increased production.

- *How are growth data compiled?* Only the formal economy is included in statistics such as Gross Domestic Product (GDP). GDP is the sum total of the market value of all goods and services produced in a country over a year, less any income from overseas. However, should GDP be taken in *total*, or *per capita*, where total GDP is divided by the population in that country? Should it be taken as per person in employment, or per household? Though sometimes difficult to interpret, employment data, productivity, investment, and consumption may also be used alongside GDP. The distribution of GDP amongst the population is crucial. If a country allows a high proportion of its wealth to remain in the hands of a few people, any growth in GDP is likely only to affect those people.

- *Is the area growing or declining?* It may be too simplistic to state that an area is growing or declining. On the present pattern of alternate world recession and growth cycles, it seems that for periods of about five years at a time, groups of countries may be either in growth or decline at the same time. Within the UK, some economic activities have declined, such as shipbuilding, while other areas have grown, such as banking. Even in an area with a declining activity there is likely to be new activity growing at the same time.

- On a local scale another question arises: *Should growth in an area be defined on the basis of where people live or where they work?* Central London's economy owes as much to people who visit or who work there daily as it does to those who live there.

Over the long term the whole world is an area of economic growth, but in the short term, it can decline. In any area there will be growth and decline at the same time, and only some of it may be measured and recognized by official statistics.

Changing employment patterns in the West Midlands

At a regional scale in the UK, changes are also more marked in some regions than others, as is shown in Figure 5.3. Traditional centres of manufacturing industry like the West Midlands have experienced dramatic falls in employment and production in manufacturing (Figure 5.4). By 1993, 51 per cent of working men and 81 per cent of women in this region were employed in service industries.

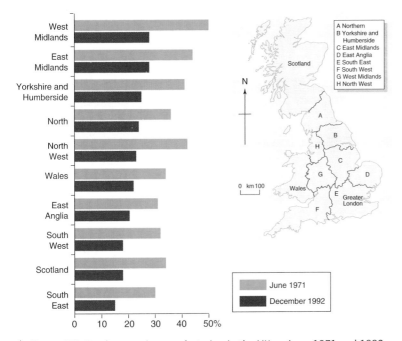

▲ **Figure 5.3** Employment in manufacturing in the UK regions, 1971 and 1992.

These changes have real effects on people and on their quality of life at the local scale. Local conditions can affect changes – some areas offer improved employment prospects, whilst others suffer near-devastation. Official unemployment statistics (Figure 5.5) have to be treated with care, and unemployment data are notoriously difficult to interpret. This is discussed in the theory box 'Dangerous statistics', on the next page.

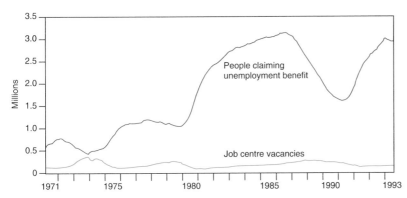

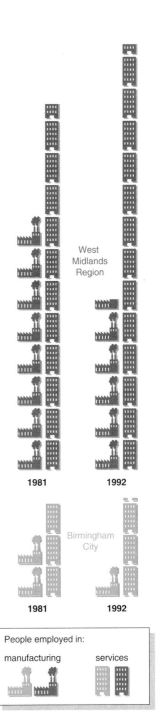

▲ **Figure 5.4** Employment trends in the West Midlands.

◀ **Figure 5.5** Unemployment in the UK, 1971–93.

113

Dangerous statistics

Never take statistics at their face value: always question. For example, there are problems of interpretation for data on employment in the UK.

- *Are the counts reliable or consistent? What is the basis for the classification used?*

Young people under 18, many older people, and many partnered women, cannot be included in the 'unemployed' category. There have been more than 30 changes to the ways in which unemployed people are 'counted' since 1979, and each change removed people from the official registers. For example, 16 to 18-year-olds are not included as they once were – they are either classified as being in full-time education, in work, or on a training scheme.

- *What information is omitted that affects the meaning of the data?*

Part-time employment is not differentiated from full-time employment. Many newly created jobs in the UK in the period since 1985 have been part-time, particularly in retailing.

- *Where trends are shown, what were the circumstances at the time shown at the start of the graph?*

Long periods of recession or recovery can disguise long-term structural trends. Partial recovery in the late 1980s shown in Figure 5.5 had a strong impact on UK employment. However, this still left unemployment well above average levels since 1945.

- *How significant are the data?*

Employment statistics must be judged against changes in the total population available for work (aged 16 to 65) and in the economically 'dependent' population (under 16 and over 65). The link is an important one, since wealth generated by the population available for work generates incomes from parents for their children, and government benefits for those who are dependent, such as the unemployed and the elderly.

Birmingham: location and economic change

Figure 5.3 shows the location and boundaries of the West Midlands Economic Region, in the centre of which is Birmingham. The West Midlands has been one of the UK's premier industrial regions for nearly three centuries. As one industry has developed – such as engineering – it has spawned others related to it, and which depend on it. This is known as the 'agglomeration' or 'multiplier effect' – see the theory box below.

Birmingham is the second largest city in the UK, and its accessibility helps to explain why it has become – and remains – a major economic unit. Look at an atlas map of England and see the way in which the motorway and rail networks, whilst

Agglomeration and multiplier effects

Existing patterns of industries, settlements, and infrastructure affect location decisions. Existing industries of a particular kind tend to attract others of that type, exchanging components, sharing services, and so on. They may also grow in ways that link them to other industries. Engineering in the West Midlands grew as a result of demand from coal mines for pumping and drilling equipment, and from railway companies. Thus a whole network of interrelated industries grew, forming a major industrial area. This is an **agglomeration effect**.

The opening, or closing, of an enterprise has enormous spin-off effects. A large manufacturing plant leads to the creation of jobs and new establishments as its needs for raw materials, energy, and so on are met. The new workforce needs housing and services, which leads to further employment opportunities. This is the **multiplier effect**. Eventually, employment diversifies so that the working population is employed in a variety of economic activities, from manufacturing to services, such as social services and retailing.

focusing primarily on London and the South East, make Birmingham a very accessible 'second city'. The theory box below helps to explain why this is important.

Accessibility and economic location

Transport costs are an important location factor for many companies. However, a number of changes have altered this. Costs of labour, land, buildings, plant, borrowing and marketing, sales and management are now high, and government intervention with grants or tax breaks is common. Many industries now use very light materials or produce high-value, low-weight consumer goods. In these circumstances, transport costs have become a relatively small part of total costs and are rarely a deciding factor. Indeed time is often a more important factor than other costs relating to distance. Thus accessible sites, like motorway access points in Birmingham, are favoured for rapid response to supplier and customer needs. City-centre locations may be close to people, but slow travel means that producers move away from urban centres, leaving the urban centres to deal with retail, property, and finance.

Accessibility models, based on time and the number of people within reach, are also helpful in analysing and understanding the location of service industries. Most service industries, and especially the retail trade, need to be within easy reach of a sufficient number of people to fulfil their customer requirements. 'Time' distance would always be part of the data analysed during the selection of a site for a hypermarket, and the number of people within each time zone would be calculated. Other services, like air transport, look at similar factors.

1 On a map of the UK, mark the location of Birmingham and UK motorways. Using an atlas, show how far along motorways you could travel in 1, 2, and 3 hours, assuming an average speed of 90km/h. This will produce a 'time–distance' map, and give some indication of what geographers call the 'centrality' of Birmingham.

2 Which other cities in the UK have similar good access, or poor access?

3 Which other transport network maps would provide insight into good economic locations?

In the early 19th century, Birmingham became the focal point of the English canal system – there are more miles of canal in Birmingham than in Venice – and from the mid-19th century it was an important rail centre. Both forms of transport have declined during the 20th century, but the canals and canal-bank locations are now being revitalized for tourism, and the city is still the centre of the busy Midlands rail network and an important InterCity node. Late 20th-century Birmingham (Figure 5.6) is well served by motorways: the M42 now provides an orbital motorway to the south and east, with access to the M6/M1 to the North, the M40 to the South East, and the M5 to the South West.

Good transport links helped to keep Birmingham's industry flourishing. It became the 'city of a thousand trades' during the period of the industrial revolution in the 19th century, and it had a close association with the nearby Black Country and with the south Staffordshire coalfield. Its small workshops and versatile entrepreneurs, with a skilled workforce, backed by well-funded research, led the way in world engineering. Business families, some enlightened philanthropists like the Cadbury family, and other local politicians like the Chamberlain family, made sure that Birmingham became a centre for major factories and developments, and eventually famous as the 'workshop of the world' (Figure 5.7).

▶ **Figure 5.6** The City of Birmingham, 1995.

▼ **Figure 5.7** The Birmingham centre of employment.

(a) Cadbury–Schweppes factory at Bournville, a famous Birmingham factory established in the 19th century and still flourishing.

(b) A newly developed square in the city centre, with the International Convention Centre, and Symphony Hall in the background – location for new service employment opportunities.

Economic success continued through the 20th century up until the 1960s. However, social and environmental success was not so evident. Although some of the city benefited from excellent workers' housing like those of Cadbury's in Bournville, and the Chamberlain's efforts helped to keep some suburbs green with parks and tree-lined roads

(Figure 5.8a), much of the inner city was begrimed, unhealthy, and overcrowded, with very poor housing and facilities. Anyone who could afford to do so moved out to the suburbs or surrounding countryside as soon as possible. Immediately after the Second World War, great efforts were made to remedy this situation, and there was large-scale redevelopment of the inner city. Communities were split up and moved to new high-rise and maisonette estates, some at the edge of the city, some replacing demolished slums near the centre. There is still plenty of housing near the centre that is more than a hundred years old, and the redevelopments of the 1950s have now degenerated, compounding the well-known problems of high-rise life.

Since 1950, many immigrants from the Caribbean, India, Pakistan, Bangladesh, and East Asia have settled in Birmingham. Now, nearly 50 years on, many of the people from ethnic minorities are not immigrants but are Birmingham born and bred. Most ethnic minority communities live in the inner city. Of the 240 000 people who live in the inner city, 135 000 are from ethnic

Much of Birmingham's engineering industry is related to the motor industry. Not only are car sales a barometer of affluence, and therefore strongly hit by any recession, car manufacture is also one of the most 'globalized' economic activities. Japanese sales and investment in the UK are a clear indication of this globalization. Birmingham's car industry has survived, with the Longbridge Works going through several ownership changes (Austin, British Leyland, Rover) and now owned by the German firm BMW (Figure 5.9). Its partner Land Rover plant is nearby, in Solihull. Now, with subsidy from the City Council, the American Ford Company is developing the Jaguar plant in east Birmingham, just adjacent to the old Fort Dunlop building (see Figure 5.8b).

▼ **Figure 5.8** Contrasting cityscapes in Birmingham.

(a) A view across leafy surburbia, a few kilometres south of the city centre.

(b) The now vacant Fort Dunlop, and part of the site for the expansion of the Jaguar car factory. This is part of the City Council's Heartlands Project (see Figure 5.6) and will be linked to the city centre by a new dual carriageway.

minority groups, while in the rest of the city only 11 per cent are from ethnic minorities. The inner city has become an exciting place of lively and colourful cultural diversity.

After the 1960s the economy of the city went into structural decline as large numbers of jobs were lost in the manufacturing industries – first with the rise in oil prices in the 1970s, then in the global recession of 1980–82, and finally in the recession since 1990. The consequent poverty is concentrated in the inner city, where reliance on welfare benefits is high and the urban and housing quality is poor. Urban regeneration projects, as opposed to the redevelopment policy of the 1950s, are making improvements, but the crux of the problem is still the lack of employment opportunities.

Competition in car manufacture took its toll. Fort Dunlop used to be a production centre for tyres – now its imposing building is used for cultural activities. BSA once made motorcycles in Sparkbrook – now the site of its large factory is a greenfield recreation area. Lucas, which manufactures electrical car components and batteries (and which has been blamed for causing lead pollution in the local area) has been forced to reduce its workforce, but has expanded successfully into the aerospace industry.

▶ **Figure 5.9** The Rover-BMW Longbridge Works, sited on the edge of the city to accommodate its huge space requirements. The new owners (BMW) hope to improve profitability with the appointment of a German manager.

▼ **Figure 5.10** The Jewellery Quarter 'Discovery Centre', now a tourist attraction as well as a centre of manufacturing.

▼ **Figure 5.11** Medium- and short-term employment changes in inner and outer Birmingham.

Inner City	Medium term % change 1984–91	Short term % change 1989–91
Energy and water	−8.1	+10.9
Manufacturing	−26.0	−10.6
Construction	−12.0	−6.7
Services	+3.1	−1.6
Total employment	−7.4	−4.3
Outer City		
Energy and water	−0.6	−7.3
Manufacturing	−15.2	−7.6
Construction	−0.9	−2.6
Services	+15.3	+7.4
Total employment	+4.2	+2.3

Other large firms have been forced to increase productivity, reduce local workforce, and use overseas factories with cheaper labour. Smaller enterprises, providing services and components for giant multinationals, survive by cutting their workforce, finding new outlets, and being flexible in their products. In some areas, 40 per cent of small businesses have gone bankrupt in one year of recession. However, concentrations of small factories, like the Jewellery Quarter (Figure 5.10), continue to flourish.

What is happening to employment in Birmingham?

The City of Birmingham is not a 'geographical' city. Some of the more affluent outlying areas Sutton Coldfield are part of the city, whilst Solihull is not. Economic changes during the 1980s and 1990s have varied in their spatial impact. Structural changes in employment show the increasing disadvantage of the inner city – see Figures 5.11 and 5.12. The technique box below will help you to analyse some of the data.

Choropleth shading

Choropleth shading uses grades of shading to represent densities. The paler the colour, the lower the density, and vice versa. Certain categories of data have to be decided upon, and then given colours. Use a copy of the outline map in Figure 5.12a and the data in Figure 5.12b. Follow these steps.

1 Draw a dispersion diagram for the data in Figure 5.12b (see page 41).
2 Find the median (mid-point) of the scatter, and the upper and lower quartiles.

3 You now have four categories by which to shade in your copy of Figure 5.12a. For most maps, four or five categories is enough, as any more than this tends to confuse. To obtain five categories, divide the dispersion graph into 'quintiles' – five divisions – by dividing the data into five sections, each with an equal number of wards.
4 Decide on a colour scheme. Select a colour which has variations from light to dark. Draw a set of boxes for the key, and shade each with its appropriate colour.
5 Shade in each ward according to your categories.

▼ **Figure 5.12** Plotting male unemployment in Birmingham.

(a) The wards of Birmingham.

Unemployment and ethnic groups

In British cities, high unemployment is concentrated in the inner zones regardless of the ethnic make-up of the population. Unemployment is just as high in the centres of 'predominantly white' cities like Plymouth or those on Tyneside as it is in Birmingham. But where black and white people compete for jobs in the same area, discrimination – both personal and institutional – works against ethnic minorities. The average unemployment for different ethnic groups in Birmingham is shown in Figure 5.13. The data were collected in the 1991 Census, just as the recession was starting.

(b) Male unemployment in Birmingham City, March 1995.

Ward	Male unemployment (%)
Acock's Green	18.4
Aston	44.5
Bartley Green	22.0
Billesley	17.3
Bournville	12.8
Brandwood	17.0
Edgbaston	26.2
Erdington	15.2
Fox Hollies	19.3
Hall Green	11.0
Handsworth	40.6
Harborne	15.7
Hodge Hill	19.8
Kingsbury	22.6
King's Norton	20.5
Kingstanding	21.9
Ladywood	36.7
Longbridge	17.9
Moseley	21.9
Nechells	34.9
Northfield	11.3
Oscott	11.6
Perry Barr	9.5
Quinton	13.3
Sandwell	21.4
Selly Oak	14.0
Shard End	23.0
Sheldon	12.8
Small Heath	30.8
Soho	33.4
Sparkbrook	42.1
Sparkhill	30.7
Stockland Green	19.6
Sutton Four Oaks	6.6
Sutton New Hall	7.7
Sutton Vesey	7.4
Washwood Heath	27.0
Weoley	22.1
Yardley	16.5

▼ **Figure 5.13** Unemployment and ethnic groups in Birmingham, 1991.

(a) City of Birmingham as a whole, percentage unemployed.

	Males	Females
White	14.9	8.2
Afro-Caribbean	27.2	15.9
Indian	18.3	16.6
Pakistani	35.3	44.8
Bangladeshi	41.5	44.0

(b) Inner-city Birmingham, percentage unemployed.

	Males	Females
Economically active	57 253	36 200
Unemployed total	17 074	7 600
Unemployed White	7 425 (26%)	3 200 (16%)
Unemployed ethnic minorities	9 649 (33%)	4 400 (27%)

Study the information in Figure 5.13. Suggest explanations for the differences in the percentages of unemployed in the city as a whole compared with the percentage of unemployed in the inner city.

		1984	1993
Males:	full-time	13 240 000	12 769 000
	part-time	570 000	886 000
Females:	full-time	5 422 000	6 165 000
	part-time	4 343 000	5 045 000

▲ **Figure 5.14** Full and part-time work in the UK in 1984 and 1993.

	Top 10%	Bottom 10%
Males	570	175
Females	400	140
Figures in £ per week		

▲ **Figure 5.15** UK average real weekly earnings per person in 1993.

1 In pairs, consider the evidence in Figures 5.14–5.16 and decide whether the following statements are likely to be true or not.

a) Women have benefited from employment changes in recent years.

b) The greatest increase in employment has been in the highest-paid occupations.

c) There has been an increase in employment in Britain since 1984.

d) People must be better off because there are more jobs, and earnings have increased.

2 Consider any statements for which you feel you did not have sufficient information to make a decision. Which information would it have been useful for you to have?

Unemployment, age, and gender

Unemployment is not only ethnically and spatially different but also varies in the ways in which different groups are affected. Older men who were in manufacturing find it difficult to get another job – 40 per cent of the jobless aged over 45 in 1993 had been unemployed for more than two years. Both young men and young women are also badly affected. Although half of the under-25s are now staying in education, a third of those looking for work are unemployed. The situation for women is unclear, because many do not appear in the employment statistics. However, many women have been forced to accept low pay and part-time work without security (Figures 5.14 and 5.15).

Changes in the number of jobs available in certain sectors of the economy, like manufacturing, have been accompanied by changes in the kind of job available (Figure 5.16).

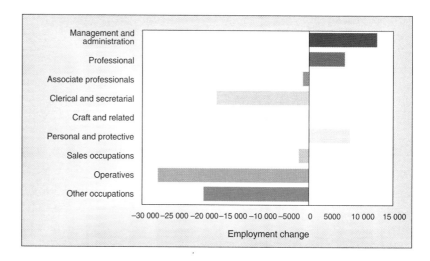

▲ **Figure 5.16** Occupational changes in the city of Birmingham, 1981–91.

Which employment sectors have been affected?

This chapter has already shown how large industrial cities like Birmingham have taken the brunt of job losses, and that the residents of the inner city have been particularly hard-hit. Job gains have nowhere near compensated for jobs lost. Birmingham's major job losses between 1981 and 1991 were in the automotive industries (–29 000) and engineering industries (–21 000). Major gains were in the public and caring services (+15 000) and financial and professional services (+16 000).

Birmingham is typical of many manufacturing cities in the industrialized world. Other areas outside the large manufacturing towns of the West Midlands have expanded service employment and modern manufacturing (often on 'greenfield' sites) to improve employment at a regional scale. Often this leaves people in inner-city areas further removed from employment opportunities and least able to afford increased travel.

What has caused employment change in Birmingham and the West Midlands?

Over time, economic activities and the employment which they generate may change. Geographers explore the causes of such change in order to understand the processes behind it. Figure 5.17 shows some of the global, national/regional, and local causes of change. Both economic activity and subsequent employment are symptoms rather than causes, and need to be investigated at different scales. At a national scale, industrial regions like the West Midlands are balanced by regions with higher proportions of employment in services. The South East, for example, with the global city of London at its heart, has been able to increase employment in services, especially in financial and professional areas.

It is important to look at employment changes at different scales. Each scale is within the context of those above it. It is impossible to understand patterns at the local scale without studying processes at the global, national, and regional scales. On the other hand global, national, and regional patterns mean very little without looking at what they mean for people at the local level. Globally there are at least four important long-term causes of change and two shorter-term causes.

Global long-term causes

Major scientific and technological innovation
Each successive major innovation leads to a surge in production and increase in global GDP. These surges are called Kondratiev waves. Electricity brought a rapid increase in production, while micro-electronics and robotics have brought the most recent wave. Now this will slow down until the next major innovation. What do you think this is likely to be? Will it be unlimited safe cheap energy from nuclear fusion?

The growth of consumer and service markets
This has followed the increase in GDP. As wealth increases, measured by GDP, so demand for goods and services increases.

Spatial separation
This process has been made possible by technological developments in production, distribution, and communication. So manufacturing, marketing, research, and management for a product can each take place in different locations almost anywhere in the world.

Internationalization
Internationalization (or 'globalization') is concentrating ownership and power in the hands of a few nations and multinational enterprises.

Global shorter-term causes

Waves of recession and recovery
'Slumps' and 'booms' affect all market economies, though the recession troughs hit different countries at slightly different times.

Mechanization and computerization
These processes have reduced the labour needed in manufacturing, and now in services as well, leading to 'increased productivity' (see Figure 5.18).

▼ **Figure 5.17** Influences on economic activity and employment.

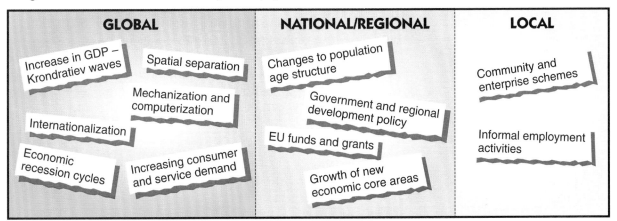

121

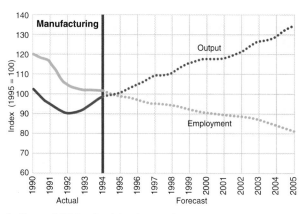

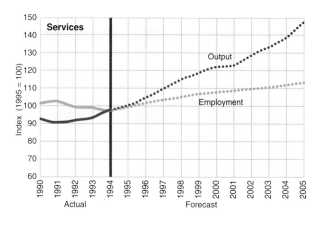

▲ **Figure 5.18** Productivity changes in manufacturing and services, actual and forecast.

National and regional-scale causes

Several influences can be identified. Some may be social, while others are economic.

- Changes in the age structure of the population are very significant. Most EMDCs, for instance, now have an ageing population.
- Changes in relationships between a nation or region and other areas of the world may affect economic development. The effect on the UK of the emergence of the West Pacific Rim as a rival economic 'core' area has upset traditional trading links. The UK has departed from its traditional economic links with Commonwealth countries such as Australia and New Zealand in order to forge stronger links with the EU. In doing so, the UK has lost markets for some of its products, as those countries now seek to forge links with nations closer to home.
- Government development policy can be important. Incentives may be offered to encourage new employment in certain regions or places, and outside funding (from the World Bank or the European Union) can provide capital and incentives for development in particular regions or towns. The UK, for example, received £2810 million in grants from European funds in 1992–93 (£1603m for agriculture, £685m from the Social Fund, £501m from the Regional Fund, and £21m from other funds). The UK also received a further £1993m from EU funds, making a total of over £4.8 billion.

It is interesting to compare these figures with UK aid to ELDCs (£2.3 billion in 1993) and total Official Development Assistance received by countries around the world. For instance, in 1991 Ghana received £483 million, India £1.8 billion, and by far the highest recipient of world aid was Egypt, with £3.5 billion. Food for thought. You could consider why the amount varies so much.

Local-scale causes

Influences on employment include community and enterprise schemes and activity in the informal sector of the local economy.

Fear Of No-Go Zone In Brum

by Ben Taylor

Birmingham's city centre risks turning into an American-style no-go zone if steps are not taken to halt the decline of people coming into the city centre.

Since the turn of the decade the number of people entering inner Brum has plummeted by 30 000 a day.

Re-location of industry, out-of-town leisure attractions, and the flight of families to the suburbs are blamed for the trend.

Birmingham Metro News, 3 November 1994

Rover Sell-Off Irks Japanese

by Simon Beavis, Patrick Wintour and Roger Cowe

British Aerospace triggered a furious political row when it announced it was to shut the door on nearly 100 years of independent car production in the UK by selling its Rover subsidiary to BMW, the German quality car manufacturer, for £800 million.

The deal also provoked an unusually sharp response from Honda, the Japanese car maker which has a 20% stake in Rover, and stirred fears that trading relations between Britain and Japan could be damaged.

BMW's takeover will create Europe's second largest car maker with 6.4% of the European market, and means that BMW's share of the British market will rise from 2.3% to 15.7%.

The Guardian, 1 February 1994

A Quiet Word Is No Longer Sufficient

by Lisa Buckingham and Ben Laurance

Fewer than a dozen besuited men settled down to dinner in one of the executive suites at the head office of insurance group Legal & General.

Beyond the confines of the City few people knew their names, but the small group around the dinner table controlled about £200 000 million worth of investments.

The Guardian, 28 November 1992

These men were the elite fund managers from Britain's insurance and financial companies. Working together, they can influence decisions even in multinationals. Compare the funds they control (for example Prudential £51 billion, Mercury Asset Management £40 billion, Invesco MIM £32 billion, and Schroders, Flemings, Standard Life, and Norwich Union, all with well over £24 billion each) with the annual GDP of some smaller countries!

▲ **Figure 5.19** Some impacts of economic change on Birmingham.

1 Form groups of three or four. Consider each of the influences shown in Figure 5.17 and explained in the text.
   a) Write out each influence on a separate card. Decide who, or what, is able to exert control on each influence. Write the influences on the space left around each card.
   b) Arrange the cards in a rank order, with the most difficult to control at the top and the easiest at the bottom.
   c) Why are some influences on economic activity and employment easy to control? What is it that makes them easy to control?
   d) Why are some influences on economic activity and employment difficult to control? What is it that makes them difficult?

2 Choose one of the reports in Figure 5.19. Place it at the centre of a large piece of paper and arrange the 'influence' cards around it, with the most important nearest and the least important furthest away. Annotate your arrangement to explain it.

3 Now take a similar event either from your local paper, or from a national news report, which has grabbed your interest. Repeat activity 2.

4 Write an evaluation of the part played by each influencing factor in employment changes in your home area. Do the same factors influence what happens in your area compared with events you have seen elsewhere, or in activities 1 and 2?

What impact has employment change had on Birmingham and the West Midlands?

In Birmingham as elsewhere, change in employment patterns is one of the most obvious results of change in economic activity. Such changes are part of a long series of cause and effect. This is explained further in the theory box below.

Every change has its causes and its symptoms, and is responded to in different ways by different people.

Employment changes have attracted a greater number of commuters into the city. In 1991 the proportion of jobs taken in the city by non-residents had increased to 35 per cent, part of a long-term trend since 1961 when only 18 per cent

Impacts of changes on employment, and responses to them

Primary impacts

- Unemployment for workers in declining industries
- Redundancy for the over–50s
- Few jobs for school leavers, especially the unskilled
- Low pay for jobs with surplus labour
- More part-time jobs without security, often low pay
- Opportunity for investment in growth sectors
- High pay for jobs in growth sectors
- High pay for people with special skills

Secondary impacts
For some:

- Deprivation
- Relative poverty
- Loss of self-esteem
- Rising crime, drugs
- Poor health
- Homelessness
- A concentration of poverty within cities into ghettos
- Greater divisions between rich and poor
- Poorer housing for some groups, especially single-parent families

- Poverty trap for the unemployed

For others:

- Affluence
- Need for new and improved housing
- Higher material standard of living – more cars
- Reliance on private means for education, health, etc.

Responses

- Voluntary and charity work
- Much more activity in the informal economy
- Government action: inner-city schemes, grants, planning, training and education policies
- Local government action: housing, health centres, social services, investments
- EU grants
- Migration to better job prospects
- New journey-to-work patterns
- Investment by national, foreign, and private organizations
- New images, new jobs, new functions
- New factories, distribution, consumer demands

1 What are the differences between 'primary' and 'secondary' impacts?

2 Draw a Venn diagram consisting of four overlapping circles. Label one circle 'economic', one 'environmental', one 'social', and one 'political'. Classify the impacts of the changes described in the theory box above. Does each belong just in one circle or in places where the circles overlap?

3 **a)** Construct a flow diagram, based on the theory box, to show how primary impacts are linked to secondary impacts, and how responses occur.

   b) Include 'feedback' loops on your diagram to show the effects of some of the responses.

were taken by outsiders. The total number of jobs in the city has continued to decrease, from 513 000 in 1981 to 466 000 in 1991. One reaction from Birmingham residents is to look elsewhere for work. The South East region is the most attractive because of the higher wage levels and increased job availability there. In many cases, this has resulted in long-distance commuting to the South East.

Figure 5.20 gives some idea of impacts that unemployment can have on individuals. Figure 5.21 shows some of the impacts on different parts of the city.

▼ **Figure 5.20** Views at a personal level.

'When you're homeless it's almost impossible to escape the pollution. You're on ground level and it washes over you. You can taste it and feel it in your eyes. You're dirty within an hour standing on the street.'

Bernard McGee, aged 44, became an asthma sufferer

The Big Issue, Number 108, 5–11 December 1994

'Sue rushes round all the time, organizes hundreds of different things, working in an adventure playground and doing shifts at a women's centre. Last week a man asked her what her job was. She mumbled, "I don't do anything really, I'm unemployed". Because she isn't paid for the things she does, she won't count them as a proper job.'

J. Seabrook, The Leisure Society, Blackwell 1988

'I was brought up in the south of England, did my A-levels in 1983, graduated with a first class degree in Business Studies in 1987, and hit the boom time of the late eighties. I lived for work then, doing professional exams at night school. I kept my job in spite of redundancies in the 1989–91 slump, got married in 1993 and now I'm 27 and a company accountant living in Birmingham. The economic recovery seems on and maybe I'll become Financial Director somewhere. But now I feel neighbours, leisure, sport, and open countryside are more important.'

Laura Jones

'When things are easy, it isn't a tragedy to be out of work. There are all kinds of little jobs you can do; but as unemployment rises these avenues close down, you can't get little jobs like window cleaning, car repairing. On my estate, in the road where I live, there were 8 to 14 households with cars – there's one now.'

J. Burnett, Idle Hands, Routledge 1994

1 Read the extracts in Figure 5.20. In pairs, identify where in Birmingham each person is likely to be (see Figure 5.21).

2 a) What factors may have contributed to the situation of each of these individuals?

b) Look back at the theory box on page 124. Construct a flow diagram to show 'impacts' for two of the extracts in Figure 5.20.

3 Using information from your local area, town, or city (e.g. census data, former employment directories, city guides), assess the impact of changing employment patterns.

4 How far does Birmingham conform to John Major's statement in 1990 that he wishes to see a 'classless society'?

5 At what level – global, European, national, local – do the causes of Birmingham's unemployment seem to lie? How should these be resolved? How effective can initiatives such as The Big Issue (see page 126) be?

▼ **Figure 5.21** The City of Birmingham – a city of contrasting economic opportunity.

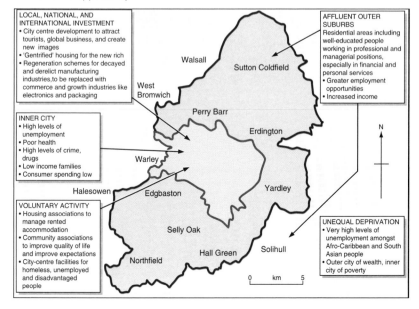

LOCAL, NATIONAL, AND INTERNATIONAL INVESTMENT
• City centre development to attract tourists, global business, and create new images
• 'Gentrified' housing for the new rich
• Regeneration schemes for decayed and derelict manufacturing industries, to be replaced with commerce and growth industries like electronics and packaging

INNER CITY
• High levels of unemployment
• Poor health
• High levels of crime, drugs
• Low income families
• Consumer spending low

VOLUNTARY ACTIVITY
• Housing associations to manage rented accommodation
• Community associations to improve quality of life and improve expectations
• City-centre facilities for homeless, unemployed and disadvantaged people

AFFLUENT OUTER SUBURBS
Residential areas including well-educated people working in professional and managerial positions, especially in financial and personal services
• Greater employment opportunities
• Increased income

UNEQUAL DEPRIVATION
• Very high levels of unemployment amongst Afro-Caribbean and South Asian people
• Outer city of wealth, inner city of poverty

Walsall
Sutton Coldfield
West Bromwich
Perry Barr
Erdington
Warley
Halesowen
Edgbaston
Yardley
Selly Oak
Solihull
Northfield
Hall Green

N

0   km   5

High unemployment has put increasing strain on individuals and families. Social services are at full stretch, and financial resources are swallowed up in income support, benefits, and extra health care. In fact there has been increased employment in these services, and some communities have responded with social and economic initiatives in housing and welfare, whilst others have started small businesses in either the formal or informal economies. The least fortunate and the young have sometimes looked to crime and drugs. Meanwhile, some members of the homeless underclass have become involved in national initiatives such as *The Big Issue*, a co-operative retailing venture in which homeless people sell the magazine and retain about 50 per cent of the selling price as a profit. Selling 200 copies per week can provide a wage of £140 per week for the seller, but only a few manage that kind of sales level.

Economic decline in EMDCs

It is difficult to specify areas in the 'economically developed world' that are suffering long-term economic decline. If GDP is taken as an indicator then certainly at national or regional scales waves of decline and growth follow one another in most countries of Europe, North America, and the West Pacific Rim. Relative decline is common, with poorer areas being left further behind, like the northern regions of England, but absolute decline in GDP usually only lasts for a few years.

It can be misleading to take rising unemployment as an indicator of economic decline, since increased productivity can make up for the fact that fewer people are at work. On the other hand, in some industrialized areas, like the cities of Latin America, the recent economic slump has been accompanied by a decrease in unemployment, with children and women going out into the informal economy and working for a very low income.

Long-term decline of both production and employment has however been experienced at a local scale in the industrialized world. Derelict areas may be found in certain parts of cities and towns which used to specialize in activities that have closed down – typically mining and heavy engineering in the UK.

The following case study describes another kind of long-term economic decline in a peripheral area of the industrialized world.

A case study of economic decline: Tory Island, Donegal

The context

Peripheral areas of EMDCs usually experience relatively slow economic growth and are harder hit by recessions than core areas. Some more isolated and remote areas have experienced long-term decline. Most small islands off the west coast of Ireland are 'Gaeltacht' areas – that is, Irish-speaking and with a strong traditional culture. These islands have experienced long-term demographic, economic, and social decline since the mid-19th century (Figure 5.22).

Emigration could lead to a redistribution of resources and improvements for those who are left, but this is seldom a long-term situation. Investment from outside, usually from county councils or the national government, sometimes gives islanders an economic fillip (see Figure 5.23). Self-help co-operatives can boost incomes. But generally such initiatives fail to stem the drift of population away from the area, and the long-term economic decline.

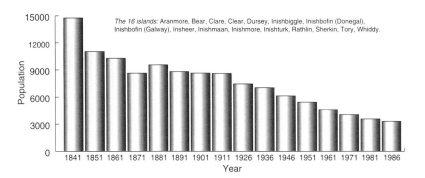

▶ **Figure 5.22** Population change on sixteen Irish islands.

Island	Service	Year	Grant (IR£)
Aranmore	Bakery	1987	38 223
	Fishing	1988	537
Clear	Cheese	1984	3 484
	Carpets	1987	2 340
Inishbofin (Co. Galway)	Fishing	1988	700
Inisheer	Café	1983	15 680
	Design	1987	9 203
	Tourism	1987	3 793
Inishmaan	Café	1987	11 580
Inishmore	Fishing	1985	39 875
Tory	Café	1985	13 571

▲ **Figure 5.23** Grant aid to small industries on the Gaeltacht islands, 1983–88.

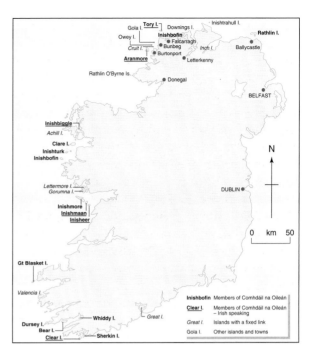

▲ **Figure 5.24** The islands of Ireland, including Tory Island.

Constructing line graphs

Population trends through time can be shown using a line graph with time along the horizontal (*x*) axis and population on the vertical (*y*) axis. To do this, use the data for the Irish islands in Figure 5.22, and follow these steps.

1. Decide on the size of the diagram you wish to create.

2. Choose a scale for the *y* axis that will fit into the space and be large enough to plot the data. To select a scale, look at the range of data from the lowest to highest. There is no need to start the axis from 0 in every case, though in this instance it would make sense to have the *y* axis ranging from 0 to 15 000.

3. Allocate equal spacing on the *y* axis. For example, 10cm to cover values from 0 to 15 000 would mean 1cm = 1500.

4. Choose a scale for the *x* axis. The time line is from 1841 to 1986 (145 years). Again, allocate equal spacing to the range, for example 1cm = 10 years.

5. Label each axis clearly.

6. Plot each figure and join up the points with a ruler.

▼ **Figure 5.25** Aerial view of Tory Island.

127

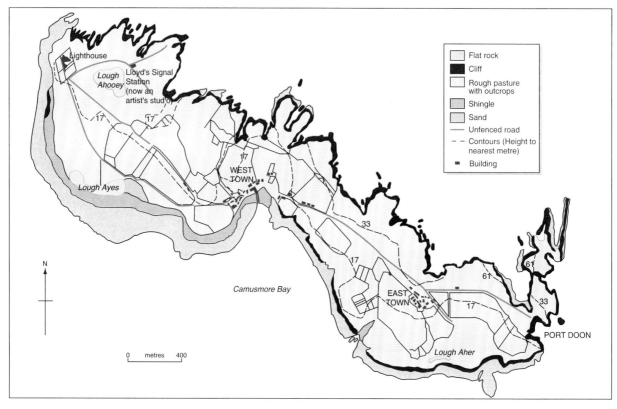

▲ **Figure 5.26** Tory Island. West Town has 31 households, a church, school, community centre, café, two shops, a dispensary, public lavatories, and the main pier. East Town has 14 households and no amenities.

The people of Tory Island – about 120 in winter, more in summer – call the Irish mainland 'the country'. Thirteen kilometres out from the Bloody Foreland in north-west Donegal and cut off by storms for weeks on end, their bare, rocky island is as separate a place as it is possible to imagine.

It takes its name from the high cliffs, or tors, eroded by the swells of the Atlantic. The lighthouse offshore is one of Ireland's oldest, and Tory cliffs have been a graveyard for shipping. But however harsh and remote the island may seem, it has been populated since the age of Neolithic farmers four thousand years ago. In legend which may date to the Bronze Age, the island was occupied by a race of pirates whose god-chief was Balor of the Evil Eye. In the 6th century, St Columbcille founded a monastery on Tory, and its round tower and Tau cross still survive.

Today, with government support, the islanders preserve their Gaelic culture, in which social life revolves around the music and dance of the Sunday night ceilidh and visits between friends and neighbours in the clustered houses of the two main villages. Many villagers have moved to the mainland, but return in summer for the salmon and mackerel fishing. In summer, too, the teenage children come home from school in Falcarragh, the nearest port on the Donegal coast. Tory has always been difficult to reach. The power of the sea is a constant theme in the islanders' 'primitive' painting. The island is served by a trawler from Bunbeg, but all journeys to and from Tory are subject to weather and the state of the sea.

▲ **Figure 5.27** from *Islands of Ireland*, Bord Failte [Irish Tourist Board] 1995

In 1992 a detailed account of the decline of Tory Island was published in the *Irish Geographer*. Information from this account is presented here, updated to 1995, to provide an example of economic decline in the 'economically developed world'.

The background

Tory Island is on the periphery of a periphery of a periphery in the economically developed world! It is a small island and a peripheral area of County Donegal, which is itself a peripheral region of Ireland whose core area centres on Dublin. Ireland is a peripheral nation within Europe. The island lies 14km from the coast of Donegal, and there is no proper harbour. Winters are particularly difficult, with only the irregular mailboat service and a fortnightly helicopter service (fare IR £18 in 1990) run by the local health authority, to link with the mainland.

The population declined from 400 in the mid-19th century to 250 in 1926 and just over 100 in 1993. Generally there has been a pattern of people going away in the winter to work or stay with friends or relatives on the mainland. Each summer some fail to return.

In 1974 'a seemingly never-ending storm severed the island from the mainland for eight weeks – even the helicopter couldn't fly' (Prom, *Donegal Democrat*, December). As a result about 60 people left the island, finding the hardships too much. In 1990, 30 per cent of the whole population, especially the younger element, said they would like to leave (Figure 5.28).

The situation

Of the population of 135 in 1990, 8 were employed, 40 were unemployed, 27 retired, 21 housewives, and 23 at primary school.

There were only two two-person inshore fishing boats working, catching lobster, crab, and salmon, but with poor landing facilities their skippers found it difficult to compete with mainland crews. Some smallholdings were worked, as part of an informal subsistence economy, but there were only 4 cows, 15 sheep, and 5 donkeys.

An investment of IR£50 000 had opened a small textile factory in 1983, but it closed in 1984. Factory closures have been common in peripheral Ireland, particularly subsidiaries of foreign companies. Between 1979 and 1986, 67 out of 162 overseas subsidiaries in western Ireland closed for a variety of reasons – see Figure 5.29. More than half the textile plants closed, so perhaps the Tory Island venture was ill-conceived.

(a) Motives for closure	
Lack of business/market turn-down	20
Company not competitive/loss of market share	16
Consolidation or merging with other plant	6
Change in organizational structure	5
Poor company management	4
Rationalization after take-over	4
Company in receivership	2

(b) Reasons for closure	
Cessation closures	
Unprofitable plant	7
Abandoned old or peripheral product	5
Abandoned new or risky product	3
Selective closures	
(i) Plant-related characteristics:	
Nature of product or process	8
Branch plant status	7
Size of plant	6
Poor plant management	5
Lack of investment	5
New plant	4
Rented premises	4
Quality of output	1
(ii) Area-related characteristics:	
Labour costs	6
Too far from market	5
Investment elsewhere	4
Poor location	3
Irish market dried up	2
Energy costs	1
(iii) Other characteristics:	
Difficult labour relations	3

Based on responses from 35 companies – more than one motive or reason from many companies

▲ **Figure 5.29** Motives and reasons given for branch plant closures in western Ireland, 1979–86.

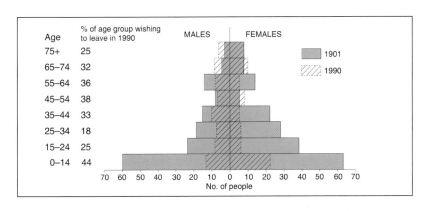

◄ **Figure 5.28** Population pyramid for Tory Island, 1901 and 1990.

The island is healthy.

There is a lack of facilities for the young.

Council housing can be made available on the mainland.

The island is quiet and peaceful.

Unemployment runs at 80 per cent.

Tourism can create jobs.

Many people would like to leave.

Frequent reliable connections with the mainland are expensive to run.

The island exists on subsidies and grants.

There is a strong cultural life, with music, drama, literature, and art alive in the community.

Tourism will destroy the isolated character of the island.

There are too many dangers getting to and from the mainland.

The soil is thin and infertile.

The winters are wet and stormy.

Community spirit is strong and moulded by isolation.

Half the households are unhappy with the educational provision.

Investments already made would be lost if the island became depopulated.

Secondary education and health care are difficult to provide.

Isolated peripheral areas are vulnerable to recessions.

The Irish language spoken here is an important cultural heritage.

The hardships of island life are getting too much.

More employment is available on the mainland.

Town life will always entice young people away.

Health, education, and retailing are all better elsewhere.

▲ **Figure 5.30** Twenty-four 'cards' – What future for Tory Island?

1 a) Using all the information on Tory Island, identify the features of the island and all that has happened to it. Classify them as 'natural', 'economic', 'social', or 'political' features. For each category use a different colour pen, and write the features onto cards.

b) Now get a large sheet of paper and make a copy of Figure 5.31. Form groups of 3–4 people. Decide where your cards should be placed on the copy you have drawn.

2 Do the main influences on Tory Island seem to be local, regional, national, or international?

3 Figure 5.30 suggests some points to be considered for the future of Tory Island. Make a card for each point, and, working with a group, rank these points in order of significance. Equal ranks are possible, and you may find a diamond-shape pattern appropriate.

▼ **Figure 5.31** Grid for activity.

	Natural features	Economic features	Social features	Political features
Local influences on Tory Island				
Regional influences on Tory Island				
National influences on Tory Island				
International influences on Tory Island				

Development initiatives

In the last few years attempts have been made to stop the depopulation of Tory Island. Investments have been made in its infrastructure. The road has been tarred, a public water scheme installed, a public toilet built, and a grant for a café made. Electricity is provided, a generator costing IR £50 000 installed, and the system runs at an annual loss after income from charges of IR £40 000. Links with the mainland are being improved. A new ferry company set up in 1992 is running a subsidized service which cost IR £440 000 to set up, and the helicopter service is subsidized at IR £30 000 a year. A feasibility study for a new harbour is being made at a cost of IR £60 000, and a site for an airstrip has been identified near to the lighthouse.

Investment in self-help included IR £75 745 in the late 1980s in the local co-operative. Recently, for the first time, Donegal County Council has built council houses on the island. People leaving have not sold their properties, but keep them for holidays or investment in the future. Seven houses, costing in total IR £260 000, have been built to cope with a housing shortage. Older houses have been renovated.

Economic development is being encouraged. The ferry service runs twice a day in the summer and tourism is growing. In 1991, 2000 visitors reached the island, and a potential of 12 000 per season is envisaged. A 14-bedroom two-star hotel, built at a cost of IR £1 million, has now been opened.

All these developments have been funded by grants and subsidized by county and national government.

1 In groups of 2–3 people, imagine you have been sent to evaluate recent developments on Tory Island. You have access to residents and visitors and to public accounts (but not to private finances and wages for individuals).
   a) Assess the criteria you will use to decide if recent developments were successful.
   b) What data will help you decide?
   c) Who would you interview, and what would you ask?
   d) Discuss how you would then analyse data, including interviews from people on the island. How would this help you to make a decision about whether developments had been worthwhile?

2 As a group, decide whether or not 'islands such as Tory Island should be left to market forces and not require government assistance'.

Ideas for further study

Study of changing economic activities can involve first-hand fieldwork and secondary sources. Work in your local area will be most appropriate. Topics for investigation include the following.

1 *Family economic change*
   From your family history and interviews with your family, trace the changes in economic circumstances over the past 20–30 years. Consider income, employment opportunities, paid and unpaid work, work in the informal economy, women at work, journey-to-work patterns, quality of life, etc. Relate these changes to local, regional, national, and global influences.

2 *Economic change in a locality*
   Statistical data for small areas are available in census returns and local government publications – your library or council could help you on this. Select an area that you know personally, for which employment data are available. Compare the present with the situation ten or more years ago, describing the changes suggested by the statistics. Visit the area selected for activity 2 and make an assessment of the effect of the changes on the buildings, environment, and lives of the people living and/or working there.

Summary

- Changes in economic activity lead to changes in the balance of employment.
- The number of people employed and the kind of work they do can change dramatically in a few years.
- There are conscious reasons why economic growth takes place. These are rarely spatial, but the result of political and cultural decisions which make business attractive to investors seeking to maximize profits. The effects are spatial, however, with variations in economic growth and quality of life between different places.
- Employment patterns vary at all scales, from the global to the local.
- Variations in employment between and within countries or regions can lead to inequalities in quality of life, and have profound socio-economic, political, and environmental consequences.
- Economic change can improve life for some people whilst causing deterioration for others.
- Data, particularly official data, are subject to the constraints placed on those who collect them, and are always suspect.

References and further reading

R. Holmes, 'Deprivation and the 1991 census', *Geography Review*, January 1995.

6 The structure, location, and impact of industry

Chapters 4 and 5 have shown how people's lives are affected by wider processes, some of which are international and over which they have little direct control. This chapter provides case studies of the structure of a manufacturing industry (based on a timber works in Ghana) and of a service industry, looking at some of the processes and issues that affect air travel. These studies can be used with the other chapters in this section to explore aspects of the location and impacts of industry.

Case study of a manufacturing industry: Log and Lumber Ltd

Log and Lumber Ltd is a hardwood timber manufacturer in Kumasi, Ghana. Although by international standards it is a small company, it is not divorced from issues that affect industry as a whole, and the timber industry in particular. The world hardwood timber trade and industry is surrounded by controversy and issues. For instance, most hardwood timber is produced in the 'South' but consumed in the wealthier 'North'. Much of the trade is in the hands of multinational enterprises (MNEs) or corporations controlled from the North. There are issues about the hardwood trade generally. Most hardwoods come from the world's tropical forests, and as Chapter 8 of *The Physical Environment* (the first book in this series) has shown, depletion of tree species and destruction of tropical forests are accelerating at an alarming rate.

Figure 6.1 lists major participants in the hardwood trade. Most tropical hardwood is used in furniture manufacture and the construction industry. Main products include veneer – thin 'slivers' of wood used to give the impression of solid wood over a cheaper wood or processed board beneath – and plywood, which is a series of thin layers of cheap wood capped by a more expensive layer to give the appearance of solid (and expensive) wood products.

Figure 6.1 also shows the chief timber suppliers to the key markets of the UK, the USA, and Japan. Timber is subdivided into veneer and plywood on one hand, and timber including logs on the other. Each country has its own rank order of key suppliers.

Figures are shown:			
Veneer and plywood/Timber including logs			
	UK	USA	Japan
South Africa	8.3/9.9	1.2/0.1	5.4/42.8
Congo	–/0.6	1.0/–	–/2.7
Ghana	6.9/23.5	0.6/2.9	–/0.1
Côte d'Ivoire	0.4/18.0	6.6/1.9	0.4/0.3
Cameroon	2.6/4.8	– /1.3	–/8.9
Zaire	0.2/4.2	– /0.2	–/3.5
Nigeria	– /1.6	– /0.7	–/–
Gabon	–/–	–/–	–/23.7
Total African hardwoods	18.4/62.6	9.4/7.1	5.8/45.9
Indonesia	105/24	391/27	989/269
Malaysia	50/96	28/38	126/1749
Philippines	38/17	–/11	–/52
Singapore	23/21	–/13	–/26
Thailand	–/–	–/–	–/43
Total tropical hardwoods	266/296	517/142	1121/2185
All non–coniferous wood imports:	1120/2513	1251/3413	1323/8803

▲ **Figure 6.1** UK, USA, and Japan: imports of tropical hardwoods in 1992. Values are in US$ millions.

Identifying the key players

1 On three blank world map outlines, construct flow-line maps to identify the key suppliers for each of the UK, the USA, and Japan. You will need to refer to the techniques box below to help you do this.

2 Identify the key players in:
   a) veneer and plywood supply, world-wide
   b) hardwood supply, world-wide.

3 Why should each of the three countries appear to have its own unique pattern of suppliers, compared with the other two?

4 In recent years, Friends of the Earth have been persuading consumers and timber retailers to avoid purchasing hardwoods. Form groups of 3–4 people and consider the following.
   a) In which of the three countries does this campaign seem to be most necessary?
   b) How would you organize such a campaign? What arguments would you use?
   c) How are the key suppliers most likely to react to these arguments? Why? How would you deal with these arguments?

Flow line diagrams and maps

A flow line diagram can show flows to or from a single location (like Figure 6.5 for Ghana) or flows between a number of locations (such as airline routes). They show volumes by changing the thickness of the flow line according to the number represented. For this exercise you should use Figure 6.1 and follow these steps.

1 Using the figures for the UK in Figure 6.1, it is possible to draw lines showing imports from Africa, Indonesia, Malaysia, and the combined other three South-East Asian countries. You will need to use a world map.

2 Decide on a suitable width for the flow arrows. For the figures in Figure 6.1, 1cm = US$200 million would be suitable. Any greater, the flow lines would be too thick.

3 On your map, draw a base line for the UK on or close to the UK, to represent total imports from the four areas: US$453 million, or 2.26cm wide. Divide this into sections for each exporting area, for example from the three combined South-East Asian countries 0.5cm to represent US$99 million.

4 Draw lines of appropriate thickness from each country of import. Label them with the exporting country's name. Draw a direction arrow.

5 Add flow lines for the USA and Japan, or for each of the exporting areas to the UK.

The timber industry, like most industries, is complex, with suppliers, markets, financial concerns, and people's interests at its heart, and can best be understood as a system. Systems have already been discussed in *The Physical Environment*. Systems are useful in Geography as they help to simplify processes which at first appear to be complex. Most manufacturing industry can be best understood using a simple input–process–output model – see the theory box and Figure 6.2 overleaf. The timber industry is no exception, and this model can be applied to Log and Lumbering Ltd and to the hardwood industry.

Hardwood timber manufacture in Ghana

Ghana is in West Africa – see Figure 6.3. You should use this map to find the places that are referred to in this study. Like all countries that have a significant area of rainforest, Ghana has suffered from deforestation, but there are still some densely wooded areas in the south of the country. The export of timber makes a significant contribution to Ghana's export earnings – £102 million out of a total of £650 million in 1993.

A systems approach to understanding manufacturing industry

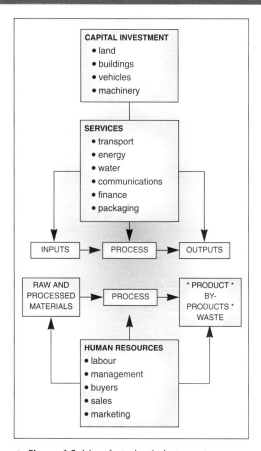

▲ **Figure 6.2** Manufacturing industry systems.

Figure 6.2 illustrates how a system works. It shows how industry can be seen as an 'input–process–output' model. Inputs are those things that need to be provided, both to establish the company in the first place, and to provide its raw materials for manufacture. Processes are those things that manage the development and production of a finished article for sale, including the ways in which people are managed. Outputs include all those things produced by the company, from the final product, to waste, and any by-products.

1 Copy Figure 6.2. In pairs, identify features that you think a timber works would need or the processes that would take place.

2 Can you modify the diagram?

3 In a search for increased profit margins, companies try to:
   ● reduce the cost of inputs
   ● maintain as high a level of income from products as possible
   ● reduce waste or recycle whatever is possible.

   In pairs, develop strategies to use within the company to maintain high profits. Who would gain and lose from this?

Since independence in 1957 there has been a large increase in the number of timber companies in Ghana and a rapid depletion of forests, especially of the better-quality hardwood species, such as mahogany. The impact of this on Ghana's forest reserves has been considerable, as Figure 6.4 shows. This study looks at the timber industry in Ghana as an economic activity. You should read Chapter 8 of *The Physical Environment* in order to gain insight into the environmental effects of logging.

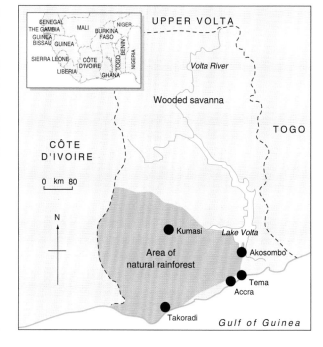

▶ **Figure 6.3** The location and features of Ghana.

▼ **Figure 6.4** Forest areas of Ghana.

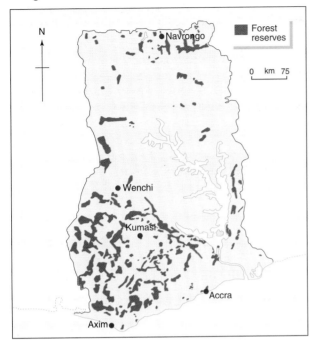

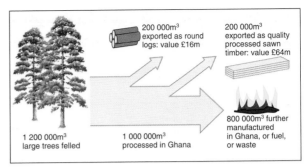

▲ **Figure 6.5** Ghana's timber production, 1993.

Areas of forest in Ghana have declined from 42 000km² in 1950 to only 15 000km² in 1990. Most of the forest clearance was to provide land for agriculture – just as in Western Europe forests have been depleted over the centuries to make way for farmland. Much of Ghana is still forested – 85 per cent of the remaining forests are in reserves (Figure 6.4). These were set up by the colonial administration in the 1920s and '30s.

Between 1983 and 1988, production of timber grew and the export trade increased from £10 million to £65 million. At that time accounting and financial systems were not reliable and fraud was common. It is estimated that the actual trade was as much as a third higher, some £31 million probably being siphoned off by malpractices in invoicing and accounts – a figure to compare with the £6 billion fraud losses each year from the EU agricultural budget.

Figure 6.5 shows Ghana's annual timber production. By comparison, fuelwood accounts for a further 10 000m³ each year, though this is often in the form of fallen wood or young saplings. The hardwood timber industry takes some 1.2 million m³ a year, but all in large mature trees. The timber industry has changed in the past 25 years. In 1970, 2.4 million m³ of logs were felled, of which 1 million m³ were exported as round logs and 200 000 m³ as sawn timber. Sawn timber is much more valuable than logs, volume for volume, and it is government policy to encourage more to be exported as 'value added' products – that is, as sawn timber rather than round logs. In 1992 just 26 000m³ of veneer, flooring, furniture parts, and plywood sold for £18 million.

Although efficiency is improving in the sawmills, about 65 per cent of logs going into a sawmill end up as low-grade timber, fuel, sawdust, and waste. The forest is destroyed for access roads and working areas – see Figure 6.6.

Many decisions about timber production and trade are not made in Ghana, however. Overseas, Ghana is faced with taxes on its manufactured wood. These are known as 'tariffs', and are payments of duty to a government. They are designed to make imported manufactured goods more expensive than those produced at home. Payments are calculated as percentages of value (see Figure 6.7). Countries such as Ghana have to balance tariff payments with increased earnings, possible by increasing sawn timber production. There are many similar examples of the 'market economy' being manipulated to the advantage of powerful nations.

▼ **Figure 6.6** Logging station, Supumo Forest Reserve, Ghana. A ceiba tree, felled by chainsaw in ten minutes, is loaded onto a lorry.

1 Using the data in Figure 6.5 and the information in this part of the chapter, draw two divided bar graphs to show the composition of Ghana's timber production and trade for 1970 and 1993.

2 How should Ghana attempt to increase its earnings from its timber production without increasing the amount of timber felled?

3 In whose interests are the tariffs shown in Figure 6.7 added? Who would make decisions to add such tariffs? Who would encourage tariffs to be added?

4 To what extent does either the addition or removal of tariffs:
   a) support conservation of rainforests
   b) support the interests of Log and Lumber Ltd
   c) support the timber industry in the EMDCs?

▼ **Figure 6.7** Tariffs on imported tropical wood, percentage value.

	EU	USA	Japan
Round logs	1.2	0.4	0.4
Simply worked	3.0	1.5	2.6
Veneers, plywood	4.0	4.4	8.9

▶ **Figure 6.9** The view of Anloga district, Kumasi, from the main road. Furniture, doors, windows, and household requirements are produced here by carpenters in small workshops.

Kumasi and Log and Lumbering Ltd

There are 30 integrated factories in Ghana which process logs. One important concentration of the industry is at Kumasi (Figure 6.8). Find Kumasi on Figure 6.3. Here several large sawmills cluster along the main road to the south of the town. Nearby the carpentry district of Anloga flourishes (Figure 6.9). Carpenters work in small workshops producing furniture, doors, windows, and household requirements.

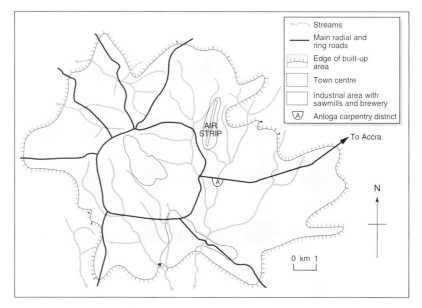

▲ **Figure 6.8** Location of sawmills in Kumasi.

The location seems to have been attractive originally because of the relatively good road transport into nearby productive forests, cheap open space for the extensive mills and storage needed, labour from Kumasi town, and water and thermal electricity from the municipality. Now Kumasi is still at the node of the regional road network, electricity is supplied from the HEP station at Akasombo, and more companies seem to have been attracted by an agglomeration effect (see Chapter 5). In fact this must be partly psychological, since the sawmills have little to do with each other.

Years ago many of the skilled jobs were filled by expatriates from Europe, but now the workforce is almost entirely Ghanaian. Ghanaians also own much of the industry, though several companies are Lebanese-owned. Most of the finance is from Ghanaian banks.

Log and Lumbering Ltd

Figure 6.10 shows three aspects of a sawmill owned by Log and Lumbering Ltd (LLL). The company has a long-established sawmill in Kumasi which is owned and managed by Lebanese businessmen. Although foreigners cannot own forest concessions, LLL is able to work other people's concessions and so has its own cutting teams and a fleet of 35 lorries to transport logs. LLL employs 1000 workers. Water is provided by the municipality and electricity by the National Grid – though LLL has its own standby generator in case of cuts.

Some reasons for the location of sawmills in Ghana have been explored. Like most businesses in the capitalist world, LLL exists to make a profit. It does this by seeking a 'least-cost location', shown in the theory box on the next page.

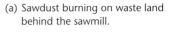

◀ **Figure 6.10** Log and Lumbering Ltd.

(a) Sawdust burning on waste land behind the sawmill.

(b) The boilers in LLL, recycling sawdust and waste as fuel, and generating steam and heat for timber processing.

(c) Modern machinery and skilled workers in the sawmill.

137

Least-cost location

An economic activity usually requires resources, energy, and people to be brought together at one place. Many theories about location, and especially industrial location, have been based on the idea that for each activity there is a 'best' location where the costs of bringing together what is needed, and the costs of distributing the product, are at a minimum. This assumes a capitalist economy (described in Chapter 7), where costs are kept to a minimum in order to maintain or increase profits. In the 1950s theories were developed assuming that transport costs would be the main factor in choosing between alternative locations. These theories were based on some fairly simple principles.

- Some raw materials are found extensively, for example water. Others are only found at certain locations, such as oil or bauxite. Attraction to a location will depend on which is the more important of all the materials used.
- Some industries use materials from several sources. If the materials do not lose any weight during manufacture – such as the car industry which assembles different components – then the weight of the final product is always heaviest when manufacture is complete. In this case, it is usually cheapest to locate manufacture of such a product close to markets where it will be sold.

- Other industries use materials from a number of sources, which lose weight during manufacturing. Examples include high energy-consuming industries, where coal or oil has to be brought to a location, only to disappear in volume as it is used for heat. Metal industries, or those using any materials that produce bulky waste, fall into this category. Weight of the final product is always lowest after manufacture. It is usually cheapest to locate manufacture close to the source of raw materials. If more than one material is used from more than one place, the most economic location is that of the heaviest material used in largest volumes which produces most waste.

Figure 6.11 shows how the cost of transporting two raw materials, and then the product to market, can be used to construct a 'transport cost surface' (with lines of equal cost, like contours) for that activity. R_1 and R_2 are two different places producing two different raw materials needed for a product. M is the market at which the final product will be sold. Lines radiate from each point. One set are known as 'isotims' – lines that show costs of transporting raw materials or finished products. The others are 'isodapanes', which are lines showing combined transport costs of all raw materials and finished products. The least-cost location is the lowest transport cost point.

▼ **Figure 6.11** Least-cost transport model.

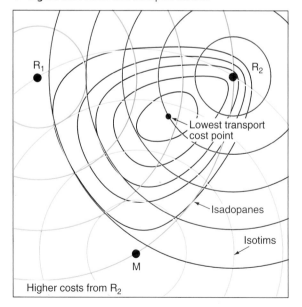

Higher costs from R_2

1 Explain the location of LLL in Kumasi rather than in an EMDC.

2 In pairs, brainstorm other examples of industries that locate close to markets or sources of raw materials. Explain their location. Share your results with those of other pairs.

Many forests near to Kumasi have been exploited and much is now farmland, so LLL goes all over southern Ghana for trees. Veneers need high-quality wood which is difficult to find as more timber is depleted.

Logging in tropical forests involves driving roads into the forest but, as only certain species are chosen, the whole forest need not be felled. The Ghanaian government has introduced strict regulations about felling, including replanting, but regrowth cycles are long, between 40 and 70 years. Lumber companies have to contribute to conservation. Extraction is limited by law, and some 14 species have been protected since 1980. However, illegal chain-saw gangs still supply local markets.

LLL processes about 1000 logs a month (7000m^3), mainly of high-quality mahogany, odum, kyen kyen, and onyina, and lower-quality wa wa. The logs are first stripped of bark, then cut into appropriate sizes. Some are then cut into planks and pieces of timber which are exported via Tema; some go through a process involving steaming and drying, then slicing for high-grade veneer, or rotary slicing for lower-grade veneer. Other wood is sawn and glued into plywood, and poorer material is made into blockboard. Waste and offcuts are sold locally as firewood.

Local carpenters are supplied with lower-grade lumber, plywood, and blockboard. High-grade lumber and veneer are exported to Europe.

Eighty per cent of the workers in LLL are local Asante people, and the rest are migrants mainly from northern Ghana. Wages are low by European standards – about £25 per month basic for eight-hour shifts six days a week, and perhaps another £25 paid in bonuses. A higher-paid union official might earn £120 a month. Conditions of service are negotiated collectively with union representatives. A clinic with a doctor and three nurses is provided for workers and their families, the canteen is subsidized, and allowances are given for travel and for rent. Insurance and compensation are available for accidents. There are no ear-muffs, nose-masks, goggles, or protective clothing, though hand gloves and some hard hats are supplied.

Much of the waste and sawdust in LLL is recycled to fuel the new boilers but, at the back of the factory, are piles of burning sawdust. Local residents suffer dust and smoke in their houses and live for days with the windows closed in a tropical rainforest climate. The sawdust piles are choking a stream and the land is becoming waterlogged and stagnant. LLL is involved with an initiative to make sawdust into blockboard.

Look at the system diagram you copied from Figure 6.2. Read through the information on LLL and annotate your diagram with details about the company, and issues that affect its inputs, processes, and outputs.

The next stages

LLL and sawmills like it do not produce a finished product. Locally, wood goes to carpenters like those at Anloga for furniture, doors, windows, and the like. Overseas, exported materials continue as a sequence of inputs to outputs until a finished product emerges for the consumer. Veneers, for example, are imported into England by wholesalers, and passed on to manufacturers for glueing to softwood or blockboard, and are eventually used in furniture, buildings, or car interiors. Wood Conversions Ltd in Surrey, for instance, sells imported veneers to Caberboard in Devon where they are used to face blockboard. These panels are sold mainly in UK DIY stores.

1 Use the photographs and information in the text to assess LLL and its activities from the following viewpoints:
   - a local resident
   - a worker from northern Ghana
   - the manager of the veneer plant
   - the Lebanese owner of the company
   - an official from the government Forestry Department.

2 Review this part of the chapter. Summarize all the information about the timber industry on a) a global scale, b) a national scale (Ghana), and c) a local scale (Kumasi). Consider the location of supplies and demand, and the key issues at each scale.

Case study of a service industry: air transport

The world scene

Study Figures 6.13 and 6.14. Figure 6.13 shows the airstrip at Chainpur in the far west of Nepal. Each week one civilian plane and one military plane (usually carrying cigarettes and drinks for the local army camp and prison guards) come from Kathmandu. Chainpur is a town of some importance and a District Headquarters, but there are no roads. It is three days' walk to the nearest roadhead. Compare Figure 6.13 with Figure 6.14, which shows Schipol International Airport, about 20 minutes from the centre of Amsterdam, and serving as the major airport for the Netherlands. Schipol lies at the hub not only of the Dutch motorway network, but of a network of road and rail routes that extend into the busiest industrial region of Europe, consisting of the Ruhr in Germany, Randstadt–Holland in the Netherlands, and the industrial regions of Belgium and northern France.

Air transport is one of the fastest-growing industries. Chainpur and Schipol (Figures 6.13 and 6.14) are at two extremes of the service, but both are very important to the people who use them.

Figure 6.12 shows the growth trends in air travel since 1945. Passenger traffic continues to grow rapidly and is expected to continue to grow in this way for the foreseeable future. Much of this growth has been concentrated in highly productive affluent areas of the world (Figure 6.15), and on routes between certain 'global' cities (Figure 6.16). Thus North America has reached an average of 2800km travelled for each member of the population, whilst for Europe the figure is 764km, the Asia-Pacific Region 121km, and for Africa, Latin America, and South Asia much less.

▼ **Figure 6.12** Traffic growth and safety improvements, 1945–93.

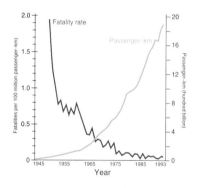

▼ **Figure 6.13** The airstrip at Chainpur in the far west of Nepal.

▼ **Figure 6.14** Schipol International Airport, Amsterdam, the starting point for KLM flights all over the world.

	Tonne-km (millions)		Passenger-km (millions)	
	Total	International	Total	International
United States	89 845	29 725	765 183	223 900
UK	17 427	17 026	126 240	121 510
Japan	14 679	10 103	110 770	54 340
Russian Federation	10 870	1 102	104 400	9 460
Germany	10 116	9 545	52 990	47 810
France	9 612	7 573	60 100	40 170
Australia	7 806	4 881	66 010	36 800
South Korea	7 191	6 660	35 270	29 940
Singapore	6 714	6 714	41 120	41 120
Netherlands	6 388	6 383	38 160	38 110
Canada	5 138	3 353	40 290	24 910
China	4 760	1 870	45 000	12 000
Brazil	4 152	2 523	29 560	16 130
Italy	4 030	3 395	29 560	22 790
Thailand	3 164	2 945	22 850	20 660

▲ **Figure 6.15** World air traffic 1993 – the top fifteen countries.

Rank	City-pair	Distance (km)	Passengers (thousands)
1	London–Paris	346	3402
2	London–New York	5539	2276
3	Hong Kong–Taipei	777	2223
4	Honolulu–Tokyo	6134	2131
5	Kuala Lumpur–Singapore	335	2109
6	Seoul–Tokyo	1227	2023
7	Hong Kong–Tokyo	2938	2019
8	Amsterdam–London	369	1775
9	Dublin–London	449	1720
10	Bangkok–Hong Kong	1711	1649
11	Jakarta–Singapore	906	1381
12	Singapore–Tokyo	5356	1256
13	Frankfurt–London	654	1222
14	New York–Paris	5833	1218
15	Los Angeles–Tokyo	8752	1094
16	Taipei–Tokyo	2182	1090
17	London–Los Angeles	8759	1015
18	Brussels–London	349	1015
19	Hong Kong–Manila	1126	998
20	Hong Kong–Singapore	2578	997
21	Bangkok–Singapore	1444	982
22	London–Tokyo	9590	951
23	London–Zurich	787	908
24	Bangkok–Tokyo	4644	901
25	Guam Island–Tokyo	2516	858

▲ **Figure 6.16** Passenger traffic between pairs of cities in 1992. The table shows some of the densest levels of traffic in the world.

1 Either manually or using a spreadsheet, construct a series of divided bar graphs, two for each of the countries listed in Figure 6.15.
   a) Identify the countries in the world where domestic freight and passenger travel account for over 30 per cent of the total. Explain why this is.
   b) Identify the countries of the world where domestic freight and passenger travel are insignificant – that is, 5 per cent or less of the total. Explain why this is.
   You should be able to give a variety of reasons in each case.

2 On a blank world map, locate the cities named in Figure 6.16. Using flow lines, show the density of passenger traffic between them.

3 Which are the world's most significant air 'hubs'? What does this mean for people living in those places: a) socially, b) economically, c) environmentally?

The first ever decline in world air traffic was in 1991, and relates to the slowing in the world formal economy, and to the Gulf War. Figure 6.17 shows the close relationship between world economic growth as measured by GDP, and the growth of air transport. Figure 6.18 shows how recessions have affected the profitability of the air transport business.

▼ **Figure 6.17** The effect of economic growth (GDP) on air travel.

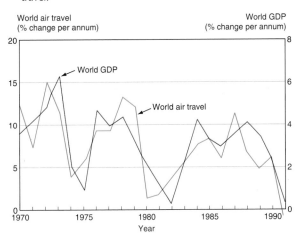

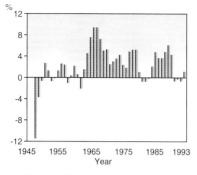

▲ **Figure 6.18** Operating results as a percentage of total operating revenues of scheduled airlines, 1947–93.

- 1250 million passengers per year
- 20 million tonnes of freight, including a quarter of the world's manufactured exports
- 21 million people employed
- International air transport
- 300 airlines, 14 000 airports, 15 000 aircraft

▲ **Figure 6.19** World air transport today.

		Passengers	Freight (tonnes)
New York	(JFK, LGA, EWR)	74 800 000	1 865 000
London	(LHR, LGW, STN)	64 800 000	950 800
Amsterdam	(AMS)	16 178 000	602 500
Frankfurt	(FRA)	28 862 000	1 105 700
Paris	(CDG, ORY)	45 761 000	872 400
Chicago	(ORD)	60 000 000	748 000
Los Angeles	(LAX)	45 800 000	1 124 000
Atlanta		48 015 000	432 000
Miami		25 837 000	827 000
San Francisco		31 034 000	563 000

▲ **Figure 6.20** Airport traffic 1990 – the world's major 'hubs'.

1 Using Figure 6.20, locate the world's major air 'hubs' on your map of flows of passenger traffic.

2 Draw scaled single bars at each location, one per city, to show the volume of passengers using each of the main hubs.

The impact of this growth in air transport has been enormous (Figures 6.19 and 6.20). The reasons for the growth are complex. Economic growth generates business travel. The link between air traffic levels and GDP suggests that economic activity is fundamental to the air travel industry. However, leisure travel is a significant by-product of economic growth. It is the balance between business and leisure travel which has led to many of the world's major 'hubs' developing more than one airport. Add to this the fact that a significant part of airport traffic is 'transit' – that is, people use the airport to change planes for a secondary flight rather than as a final destination – and the link between the world's 'hubs' of air travel and high population density centres is clear.

Global communications have been revolutionized. Not only has international tourism become the norm, but opportunities for the global organization of business have been created. There is now an increased focus on certain global cities for business, banking, conferences, and so on. The 'jet set' of international executives flitting from one hotel to another for face-to-face meetings is now a reality, as are the almost immediate transfer of materials, the immediate transfer of information by fax, telephone, and computer link. Global communication has also increased military capabilities worldwide. People and goods, especially perishables and valuables, flow easily and quickly around the world. Air transport is a vital element in the globalization process. But there are other effects too.

Competition and expansion

Speed, and to a lesser extent comfort, gives air transport the advantage over other forms of transport for long journeys. On shorter journeys, good road routes provide competition, and in Japan, the USA, and Europe high-speed trains are an increasingly competitive form of transport. For distances up to 400km these are at least as fast 'door to door' as air transport.

The concentration of air traffic onto certain major routes causes bottlenecks on flight paths, and congestion and delays at the few major gateway airports. In Europe, London's Heathrow and Frankfurt airports now have no excess capacity; in Japan, Tokyo's Narita Airport is near full capacity, as is Osaka at peak times. In the USA, 21 airports are near capacity and experience difficulties, especially those at New York (JFK), Boston, Atlanta, Chicago, Denver, San Francisco, and Los Angeles. On short journeys (say under 1000km) the actual flying time may only be two-thirds of the time spent travelling from door to door. For passengers, this means:

- increased check-in times before flights, in order to deal with increased baggage flows
- delays, caused by Air Traffic Control who, at Heathrow, have to deal with flights landing every 50–80 seconds and take-offs that are almost as frequent

- discomfort, when they are 'off-loaded' on to a bus and have to embark using a gantry, instead of the telescopic gangways, because terminal capacity is exceeded.

These problems are difficult to overcome. Much space is needed for expansion and it may not be available. For those who live near to a major airport, noise pollution is a major issue (Figure 6.21). At London Heathrow, the number of people who are affected by aircraft noise at a level of more than 35 NNI (noise and number index) has been reduced from 1.5 million in 1978 to 500 000 in 1988. This change has been largely as a result of older aircraft being phased out. However, an increase in the number of flights can offset this improvement. In the late 1990s, issues regarding increased space, capacity, and runways have become important. A fifth terminal and possibly a third runway are major issues.

Railway stations use a fraction of the space to turn round many more passengers than an airport. For example, the Gare St-Lazare in Paris handles 120 million passengers a year, compared with 60 million at O'Hare, Chicago – the busiest single airport in the world. In Japan, near Osaka, space has been created off-shore to build the new Kansai International Airport and relieve some of Japan's airport congestion. A similar plan was once suggested for London off Essex at Maplin Sands.

If air travel is to maintain its growth, which, after all, is the result of demand from consumers, then environmental issues will have to be balanced against arguments in favour of providing people with what they want.

Patterns in the air

'Hub-and-spoke' patterns (Figure 6.22) have become the basic feature of the structure of air transport networks. In Europe, major national airlines have tended to use their country's main airport as a hub for long-haul international flights. Thus British Airways (to Heathrow), KLM (to Schipol), and Lufthansa (to Frankfurt) provide spoke links to one centre where passengers board intercontinental flights.

▼ **Figure 6.21** Airport noise at London Heathrow Airport.

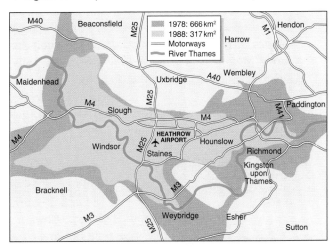

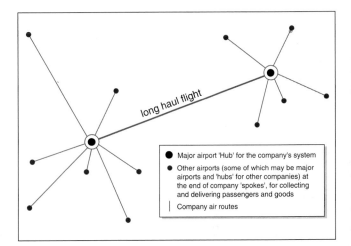

▲ **Figure 6.22** 'Hub-and-spoke' patterns of air traffic.

The airlines like this system. On the spokes they bring together passengers from one place wanting to go to a variety of destinations, then at the hub they combine passengers from a variety of places wanting to go to one long-haul destination. They can use larger and more economical aircraft, provide computer reservation systems, and plan for the most frequent economic service. If they can dominate a hub they can create a stable market for themselves. Increasingly, airlines are co-operating and sharing hub-and-spoke patterns. Qantas and British Airways already code-share – provide flights between them – between London and Auckland, and further code-sharing is developing between London and Australia, based around the hubs of Bangkok and Singapore.

However, airlines still compete, and spokes from different hubs can overlap. Within Europe many of the journeys are too short for hubbing – the change of planes and the wait at the hub would lengthen the journey time – but the system has been fully developed for flights within the USA.

Obtain an airline timetable for an international airline such as Qantas, British Airways, or Singapore Airlines.

1 Select the home country of the airline.

2 Identify from the timetable between three and five major overseas routes from that country.

3 Identify different 'hubs' and 'spokes' on these routes. Hubs are at the major international cities, and spokes feed off or into these from smaller towns or cities.

USA – the battle of the hubs

Deregulation – the removal of many of the restrictions on who runs which international flights at what prices – has opened up the international market to much greater competition between airlines. At the same time domestic flights in the USA have been the scene of tremendous competition between the dozen or so US airlines. The recession in the early 1990s made this competition all the more fierce, and takeovers and bankruptcies were not uncommon. The battle for dominance and control of a suitable pattern of hubs is vital in this competition.

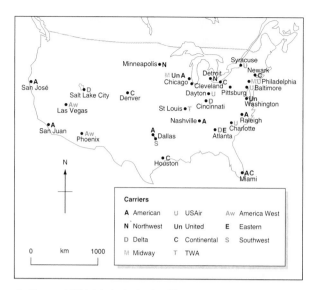

▲ **Figure 6.23** Main hubs in the USA.

Figure 6.23 shows the hubs used by the main carriers in the USA, and Figure 6.24 lists the location factors which are seen by airlines as important when selecting an airport as one of their hubs.

In the USA there are several very successful and well-located hubs where one company dominates. These include Dallas/Fort Worth, where American Airlines dominates with 61 per cent of traffic, Atlanta (Delta 61 per cent), Pittsburgh (USAir 88 per cent), St Louis (TWA 80 per cent), and Salt Lake City (Delta 65 per cent).

The lack of hubs in the western USA is partly due to the overwhelming north–south traffic along the 'Californian Corridor'. Traffic between three airports near San Francisco and five around Los Angeles accounts for 7 million passengers a year, 2 million of them between San Francisco International and Los Angeles International, about 20 per cent of whom are international passengers.

▶ **Figure 6.24** Location factors influencing the choice of hubs for domestic airlines in the USA.

Heavy population nearby	360° field Emphasis on all four quadrants: NE, SE, W, NW	Limited interference from foreign competitors
Potential for rapid growth, e.g. a high proportion of domestic capacity – Chicago has 26% of US domestic passengers, Washington only 5%	Finance available for a world-class terminal, the attitude of the local community is vital	Tax breaks
Well trained but unemployed workforce	Location relative to other hubs – multiple hub system needs well-dispersed hubs to avoid self-competition	Competition with other company's hubs – 500–1000km is 'close', so can Cleveland, Cincinnati and Dayton all survive in Ohio?

Competition between airlines is intense for traffic and for landing 'slots' at the world's major hubs. Airlines compete vigorously to obtain landing slots at London's Heathrow Airport, for example. Figure 6.25 shows some of the theory about how competition may develop between two fictional airlines. In the upper part of the diagram, each airline has a 'hub', from which routes radiate to places A–F. Along some routes, each airline is the dominant carrier, for example Utopia Airways' routes to A and D. Along others, the airlines compete, for example to places B and E, but one airline is dominant over the other. In the lower part of the diagram, Utopia has managed to divert traffic, by competitive pricing or by espionage, from Air Ecstatic along the route to B, making Air Ecstatic weaker. Weakening the airline forces it to cut the number of flights along other routes, such as the one to E, so Utopia becomes the dominant airline.

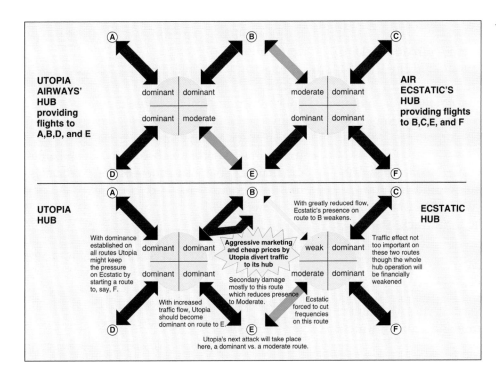

◀ **Figure 6.25** The battle of the hubs. The diagram shows how competition can change the patterns of traffic when two airlines have hubs within a competing distance. See the text for a full explanation.

1 In groups, discuss Figure 6.24.
   a) Are all factors equally important in their weighting? Add any other factors you think are important.
   b) Do the major hubs of the USA meet the 'ideal' factors suggested by Figure 6.24?

2 Form groups of three to four people. Decide on a ranking pattern of the factors, with the most important at the top. Compare your group's rank order with that of other groups.

3 a) On a blank map of the USA, and with reference to an atlas, mark and name cities with a population over 2 million, and those between 500 000 and 2 million.
   b) Compare the location and distribution of hubs in the USA (Figure 6.23) with this map. Assess the importance of city distribution as a location factor.

4 a) Study Figure 6.25, and suggest which hubs in the USA you would expect to be under threat of closure by competition in times of recession.
   b) How many hubs, and which ones, would you recommend to a company trying to establish itself as a US domestic carrier?

5 Are there any other industries you can think of where there is similar aggressive competition between rivals (see Figure 6.25)?

Ideas for further study

1 Investigate a manufacturing industry close to your locality.
   a) Assess the extent to which it can be seen as a system.
   b) Compare its operation with LLL in Ghana.
   c) To what extent are there similarities with LLL? How fundamental are the differences?
2 Compare the timber industry in Ghana with that of an EMDC producer such as Sweden or Canada. In what way are circumstances similar/different?
3 London's Heathrow Airport is currently seeking ways of maintaining its position as the UK and Europe's premier airport, in spite of traffic congestion at the point of entry for motor traffic, for flight paths into Heathrow, and terminal space. Other UK airports are seeking runway extensions.
   a) Monitor the progress of arguments for a fifth terminal and a third runway at Heathrow.
   b) Assess the extent to which Heathrow could lose some of its traffic to Gatwick, Stansted, or Manchester.
4 Monitor the co-operative arrangements between partner airlines that seek to provide increasing network coverage across the world. To what extent is this acting against the consumer, by providing fewer competing airlines which can boost fares?

Summary

- Manufacturing and service activities have evolved – and are continuously evolving – structures and patterns.
- The forces behind the patterns which produce economic change are becoming increasingly global.
- Economic changes, whilst themselves partly created by forces of globalization, cause global shifts in manufacturing and service industries.
- Much of the world's trade is in the hands of multinational enterprises (MNEs) or corporations.
- Most manufacturing industry can be best understood using a simple systems model, consisting of inputs–processes–outputs.
- Many economic activities bring environmental as well as social and economic impacts.
- Intense competition between rival companies can have spatial consequences for companies, for the people who work for them, and for consumers.

References and further reading

The Backbone of Development, Development Education Centre, Birmingham, 1994.

Developing Geography: Ghana, Development Education Centre, Birmingham, 1995.

B. Henry, 'Change in China', in *Geography Review*, November 1994.

The *New Internationalist* monthly magazine explores development issues and case studies of ELDCs.

7 Issues arising from economic change

Economic change, whether it is growth, decline, or re-organization, creates stress in societies – cultural, social, and environmental. Some of the issues are exemplified here with case studies of two nations where very rapid economic change has been experienced – Taiwan, and the former Soviet Union, most of which is now the Commonwealth of Independent States (CIS).

The Western Pacific Rim

Since 1950 the Western Pacific Rim of Asia (Figure 7.1) has become a major global economic core area, and now ranks alongside North America and Western Europe. Since 1985 the centre of gravity of this core area has shifted south from Japan to the four 'dragons' (Taiwan, South Korea, Hong Kong, and Singapore). Now Malaysia, Thailand, and Indonesia are experiencing rapid economic growth and they too will soon be a part of the core. Figures 7.2 and 7.3 show how already the symbols of economic growth and consumption are apparent. At the same time, parts of China are developing even more quickly and look set to take over a core role in the 21st century.

Taiwan – a fast-growing centre

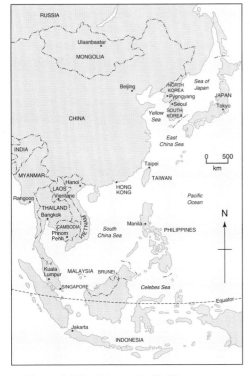

▲ **Figure 7.1** The Western Pacific Rim.

▼ **Figure 7.2** Economic activity in Taiwan.

635 000 machine tools
3.4 million sewing machines
19 million electric fans
2.1 million TV sets
400 000 motor vehicles
1.5 million motorcycles
8.9 million telephones
3.8 million radios
6.2 million sound recorders
12.9 million calculators
7.2 million integrated circuits
3.2 million electronic watches
17.9 million tonnes steel bars
1 million tonnes of shipping
24 million tonnes of cement
1.8 million tonnes of fertilizer
2.3 million tonnes of artificial fibre
1 million tonnes of cotton

(a) Production in Taiwan, 1993.

(b) An alleyway market in Taichung, Central Taiwan.

	Primary			Secondary			Tertiary		
	1965	1989	1993	1965	1989	1993	1965	1989	1993
China	44	32	19	39	48	48	17	20	33
Hong Kong	2	0	0	40	28	21	58	72	79
Indonesia	56	23	19	13	37	38	31	39	42
Japan	10	3	2	44	41	41	46	56	57
Malaysia	28	29	n.a.	25	21	n.a.	47	58	n.a.
Philippines	26	24	22	28	33	33	46	43	45
Singapore	3	0	0	24	37	37	74	63	63
South Korea	38	10	7	25	44	43	37	46	50
Taiwan	27	6	4	29	51	40	44	43	56

▲ **Figure 7.3** Growth in economic activity along the Western Pacific Rim (percentage of GDP).

1 What evidence is there in the UK of the global importance of the Western Pacific Rim?

2 Work with a partner. Select one of the 'Four Dragons'.

   a) Research the impact on the UK of the 'dragon' you have chosen. Find out names of products from your chosen country, and companies that produce them. Investigate a number of consumer products for this activity, such as electrical goods, cars, and clothing.

   b) Consider the pros and cons of this influence from different points of view. What are the benefits of the country's influence on your home country? What are the problems?

   c) Compare your statements with those prepared by other groups. How beneficial or detrimental does the influence of the 'Four Dragons' appear to be in the UK?

Taiwan and the NICs

Taiwan has become a very important part of the core and is now a global economic force to be reckoned with. It is grouped with the newly industrializing countries (NICs), which are mainly in the developing South.

The 'breakthrough' for industrialization in most

NICs has been due to overseas investment by multinational enterprises (MNEs), which take advantage of low wage rates and tax incentives to produce manufactured goods to be sold mainly in the richer North. Processing of primary products, again for export, is part of this. In many countries, coastal zones have been designated to encourage the location of industries owned by overseas companies (Figure 7.4). These have become known as Free Trade Zones (FTZs) or Export Processing Zones (EPZs), and are highly attractive to companies seeking high profit margins. They are free of tax to investors and industrialists. This compares favourably with the UK. In the UK, corporation tax of between 25 and 33 per cent is placed on company profits by the government. Profits made on, for instance, the sale of property or on shares are subject to capital gains tax of 25 per cent. Imports of some products are subject to EU tariffs, as described in Chapter 6. In the FTZs and EPZs this is not the case. Imports are cheaper, so profit margins are higher.

FTZs and EPZs work very simply. The host country provides land, buildings, services, and labour. The overseas company brings in raw materials, part-finished goods, management, technology, and capital. The host country receives rent and payment for services, wages, and experience. The overseas company exports goods and makes profits.

The attractions for the industrialist are cheap labour, no unions to enforce wage rates or monitor working conditions, no customs import or export

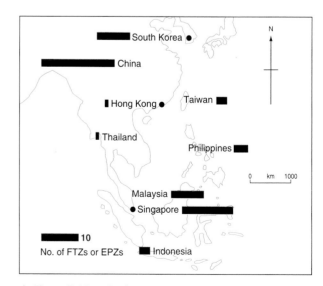

▲ **Figure 7.4** Free Trade Zones (FTZs) and Export Processing Zones (EPZs) in the Western Pacific.

duties, no local taxes, long periods between tax payments (known as 'tax holidays'), subsidized services, cheap loans, and unlimited profits which can be taken out of the country without restriction. (Compare this with Australia where all withdrawals of capital out of the country of more than A $5000 have to be notified.) Workers can find the situation less attractive, as Figure 7.5 shows, but conditions improve when better-paid work becomes available elsewhere in the country, as is now happening in Taiwan.

In Kaohsiung Export Processing Zone in southern Taiwan, as in most Asian FTZs, 85 per cent of the labour force are young women whose wages are lower than those of men doing similar work. The employers are exploiting the cultural training of the girls and say that they are 'obedient and pay attention to orders'. Beside causing 'less trouble' than boys, they say, their 'nimble fingers' are better for work in electronic assembly and textiles.

Low wages are backed by insecurity of job tenure and poor working conditions. Eye ailments are common in electronics assembly workshops, and near sweat-shop conditions exist in many factories. Near to the EPZ the women live in bare dormitories, one with a thousand girls, with very basic amenities. Sexual exploitation is common, but many of the girls are encouraged to continue to work there as their income is vital to their family's economy. And this is in a country which has managed the distribution of wealth more equitably than most.

▲ **Figure 7.5** Working in a Free Trade Zone, from *Dragons in Distress.*

1 Form three separate groups. Select one of the following people:

- a potential investor,
- a local person looking for work
- a human rights activist

Discuss the description of FTZs and EPZs in the text and in Figure 7.5 from the point of view of the person you have selected.

2 Present your group's findings to members of other groups and discuss different viewpoints which are expressed. Can the viewpoints and priorities be reconciled?

Taiwan's history has been very complex. In 1895 Taiwan was passed to Japanese rule after a war between China and Japan. In 1945, after nearly 50 years of Japanese occupation, Taiwan once again became part of China. Then in 1950 the Communists under Mao Tse-tung drove the Nationalist Chinese out of mainland China. Their leader, Chang Kai-shek, and a million of his followers, occupied Taiwan. Chang Kai-shek's political party (the Kuomintang or KMT) kept Taiwan under military law until July 1987.

During the 1950s and '60s the USA poured arms and aid into Taiwan to create a bastion against the further expansion of communist China. Much of the money was used for arms and to maintain a large military force, but the KMT also invested imaginatively in transport, education, energy, agriculture, health, water, and housing to build on the basics left by the Japanese. Chinese traditions of hard work and commitment to learning enabled the Taiwanese to develop industry and commerce rapidly, and improve most people's standard of living.

Since 1987 a 'democratic' movement has grown, supported by the Taiwanese people as opposed to the 'Mainlanders' who came with Chang Kai-shek. Taiwan now has free elections and more attention is paid by the government to human rights.

Taiwan has passed through the phase of low wages and exploitation from overseas, though this has often been replaced by similar conditions in local companies. Home-grown companies like Tatung, described in Figure 7.6, are as important as overseas 'transplants'. Taiwan is no longer a 'low wage-cost' location when compared with many other regions of South-East Asia. In fact Taiwanese companies are themselves now investing overseas in textiles and electronics in countries like mainland China whose economies are less industrialized, and peripheral to the new core countries. Research and development is as much a feature of Taiwanese industry as it is elsewhere in EMDCs.

Taiwan has moved 'from the bargain basement to the luxury goods department'. However, many issues remain, and the next sections look at some of these under the broad headings of economic, social, and environmental issues.

▼ **Figure 7.6** A message from Mr Lin, based on an interview in Taipei in 1992 with the Chairman of Tatung, the massive Taiwanese electrical manufacturer, by Keith King and David Stanton.

- *Tatung* shares the opportunities and concerns of Taiwan, and believes in its future prosperity.

- *Tatung* has an active policy of diversifying production and extending global links.

- *Tatung* has a loyal workforce, exemplifying the Confucian work ethic and its family values.

- *Tatung* will expand production in the Pacific Rim area as well as in Europe, the USA, and Sino-Russian regions.

- *Tatung* believes that the focus for the 21st-century commercial market lies in the Pacific Rim where a new economic superstate will emerge.

- *Tatung* realizes that this future is clouded by concerns for the environment.

- *Tatung* believes that its policy supporting education in the whole country can influence social problems and raise environmental awareness. Education is vital to economic success.

- *Tatung* realizes that Taiwan is a high-income country with a dense population. This necessitates a high volume of economic activity to create commercial success, but in the long term it must move to a high-income/lower population density situation if growth is not to become strangled by congestion and pollution costs.

1 Take each of Mr Lin's statements in Figure 7.6. How far does each one confirm the suggestions in the text about Taiwan's recent development?

2 How would you monitor the truth of his statements over the next ten years?

Economic issues: how will the rest of the world compete?

Taiwan has twelve MNEs each with a market value of over US $2.5 billion, and many smaller ones. These are now investing in factories in peripheral areas of East Asia to provide low-wage labour for their manufacturing (Figure 7.7).

The financial and management success of Taiwanese firms is exemplified by Delta Electronics and its worldwide links, shown in Figure 7.8. In order to establish itself inside the large markets of the EU and North America, Taiwan, like Japan before it, is also investing in higher-income areas. Now peripheral areas of the EU, like Telford (Taiwan's Tatung) and Teesside (South Korea's Samsung), are attractive sites for factories for South-East Asian MNEs, especially with grants and tax incentives from the host government. The UK government has tried to entice companies using EPZ strategies, in order to stimulate similar growth.

	Average cost per operator hour in 1989 (US$)
Japan	13.98
USA	9.71
Taiwan	3.56
China	0.40
Sri Lanka	0.26
Indonesia	0.23

▲ **Figure 7.7** Comparative labour costs in the textile industry in selected countries.

Financial markets

All the theories which have been developed in this section assume that costs remain similar over time. In fact this is rarely the case. In the 1980s and 1990s, financial markets and currency traders have dictated much of what happens in industrial location. Consider two scenarios, one relating to the cost of raw materials, the other to the cost of finished products.

Cost of raw materials

Oil is a widely used raw material for energy production or manufacture. It is usually priced internationally in US$ per barrel (36 gallons, or 164 litres). Its price depends on supply and demand. Supply depends on a regular supply from dependable sources. Interruptions to that supply will affect the price. Prices vary daily, and over several days rising or falling trends may affect a company's costs.

International currency markets affect prices of raw materials, even when the cost remains constant. Consider the following situation.

	Month 1	Month 2	Month 3
Oil price per barrel	$18	$18	$18
Exchange rate: £1 =	$1.65	$1.55	$1.45
Cost per barrel in the UK (£)	£10.90	£11.61	£12.41

The dollar price holds steady, but in fact is costing a British company more by month 3. Over time, a company using more oil may decide that it is cheaper to move to a country where currency moves less often.

Cost of finished products

Again, financial currency changes can affect locations where goods are produced. Consider the following example from Japan.

	Year 1	Year 2	Year 3
Cost of car made in Japan (yen)	Y18 million	Y18 million	Y18 million
Exchange rate: £1 =	Y250	Y200	Y150
Cost of Japanese car in the UK	£7200	£9000	£12 000

Unless the Japanese company moves to the UK, its cars will be out-priced by other manufacturers. This is exactly what happened during the 1980s, as the Japanese yen gained strength and the UK pound weakened. Companies such as Toyota and Nissan opened factories in the UK in order to avoid price increases caused by the strength of the yen.

▼ **Figure 7.8** From *The Global Money Machine*, 1994.

Delta Electronics Inc.

Delta Electronics was founded with less than £1500 by Bruce Cheng in April 1971. The firm is one of Taiwan's many industrial success stories – now worth £40 million.

From a small Taipei workshop, the company has grown into a truly international concern. The Head Office is still in Taipei but there are now factories in Taiwan, Japan, Singapore, China, Thailand, and Mexico; Research & Development establishments in Taiwan and the USA; and Sales Offices in Switzerland, the USA, and Scotland. Many of their 3000 workers and managers were educated in the UK or USA and they buy materials from many countries, principally Japan, South Africa, Australia, and Germany.

Delta works on the development, design, and manufacture of electronic components and equipment and its current products include switches, power supplies, fans, monitors, and modems. Its customers include major computer companies from around the world, including such famous names as Amstrad, Apple, Canon, Compaq, Epsom, Hewlett-Packard, IBM, Phillips, Tandy, Toshiba, and Zenith.

Growth has been phenomenal, with sales increasing from £5 million to the current £120 million in the last ten years. So how has this been done?

Investment

The company was floated on the Taiwan Stock Exchange in 1987. Three-quarters of the investors in Delta are individuals investing their savings – fewer than one in ten British investors are ordinary people. They have been rewarded by seeing the value of their savings grow, but not by receiving any share of the profits as a dividend. In Britain or the USA, any company not issuing a dividend every year would soon see investors selling their shares, but Delta re-invests all its profits in improvement and expansion – so shareholders see the value of their shares grow even more and are content. Of course, if the share price were to fall, people would soon sell and invest in one of the many other growing companies instead! This is what helps keep Delta on its toes.

Government support

The Taiwanese government is very supportive of high-tech firms such as Delta. There is government support for research and development through the giving of grants for specific projects. Products made for export, as most of Delta's products are, are more profitable for the company than goods made for the Taiwanese market – profits on export goods are allowed a 25% tax reduction.

Innovations

In Britain, our scientists and technologists are very good at designing new products. Companies invest in new ideas and then wonder how to sell them and who to sell them to. This sometimes has disastrous results – money invested in making goods that no-one wants to buy. (Remember the Sinclair C5?) Delta and other Taiwanese companies are market-driven – they find out what people want to buy, then concentrate their efforts on producing it more effectively. This means few original ideas, rather refinements of existing ideas, but it does mean they can usually sell what they make.

▶ **Figure 7.9** From *The Independent*, 18 October 1994.

1 Identify from Figure 7.8 all the places with whom Delta Electronics have links. Select a suitable way of representing these links on a world map.

2 What main points would you pick out about Delta Electronics, shown in Figure 7.8, to encourage someone who might be **a)** a supplier, **b)** a customer, and **c)** an investor for the company?

3 Who could lose out during this Delta success story, and in what ways?

4 Should the UK welcome Pacific Rim investment? What measures, if any, should be taken to control it?

Samsung Venture Means 3000 Jobs For Teesside

Samsung, the Korean electronics group, is to create 3000 jobs by the end of the decade on Teesside, with a £600 million investment in a five-factory complex at Wynyard Park.

Samsung also considered sites in Ireland, Hungary, and Spain. The company has been lured by £58 million in government grants under the regional selective assistance programme.

The investment is part of Samsung's plan to create five main production bases serving markets in Europe, Japan, South America, the USA, and China.

Major economic issues are involved in the potential host countries' responses to these initiatives. Should the UK 'compete' with other European countries to welcome the kind of Pacific Rim investment shown in Figure 7.9? Will this lead to a take-over by overseas firms and erode the nation's control of its own economy and way of life?

Social and cultural issues: Where do you begin?

Taiwan faces huge issues that are bound up with its cultural and social transformation. Values systems and cultural norms from the USA and Japan are making a tremendous impact on the younger people. Westernization is an established fact – American comics in Taiwanese translations, McDonald's, Burger King, and Kentucky Fried Chicken in the cities, fast foods competing with traditional Chinese dishes, clothes displayed on Western dress models in shops, electronic games arcades, consumerism, Western rock and dance music, computerization, and so on. Taipei (Figure 7.10) is indeed a 'global' city, where someone from the wealthy North would not feel out of place. Sometimes, as the case study of Bangkok in Chapter 2 has shown, there is a startling contrast between the buildings of the retail and commercial sectors and those of the traditional cultures of East Asia.

A crisis in family structure looms. At present the women of the older generation are willing to mind their grandchildren while their daughters go out to work, which enables many young Taiwanese women to be successful in business. But will *they* be willing to mind *their* grandchildren? The traditional family structure is holding so far, but its values are under stress. Already there is evidence that the values of the younger generation, its aspirations and ambitions, are markedly different from those of the generation before. In extended family households, where traditionally three or more generations live under one roof and the elderly and young are cared for, three or more sets of values sit side by side, sometimes uncomfortably.

As well as cultural issues, there are social issues, one of which is the fate of illegal migrant workers.

Illegal migrant workers in Taiwan

In the back streets and outer suburbs of Taipei conurbation (Figure 7.12), there are hundreds of small independently owned factories. They often produce partly finished goods and components for the bigger companies from which much eventually finds its way to Europe and North America. The economic boom has created a labour shortage – unemployment in Taiwan has been under 1 per cent for many years – and although some overseas labour is recruited legally, it has not been government policy to attract large numbers of immigrants. Thus agents operate in countries in South Asia which have low-wage economies, recruiting workers and

▲ **Figure 7.10** Part of central Taipei. Taipei is a growing modern industrial and commercial city. It is now becoming congested with people and traffic (mainly taxis, buses, and scooters – there are relatively few private cars), and an American-style Rapid Transit System is being constructed.

arranging their illegal entry into Taiwan, where they are actually hidden in the factory where they work. In small and medium-sized factories of Taipei and central Taiwan, there are about 10 000 legal immigrants and 50 000 illegal workers. Their status means they are outside the protection of the law, and Kanishka's story shows what happens (Figure 7.11).

An interview with Kanishka, a Sri Lankan migrant worker

Q How much did you pay your Sri Lankan agent in order to come here?

A I gave 35 000 in my country's currency.

Q What is that in UK pounds?

A About £600. After I came to Taiwan they also deducted £700 from my salary.

Q How many foreigners were working at this company when you arrived?

A Maybe 23.

Q From what countries?

A Bangladeshis are the majority. At that time there were five Sri Lankans and four Thailand people.

Q Can you describe an incident you remember well?

A I remember one incident. There were four Indonesians in the factory. Three of them had come to the end of their one-year agreement. They went to the office to ask for their passports back. The boss was very angry. He gave them their passports and told them to leave the company immediately. Then there

was only one Indonesian. The boss took revenge on him. He shouted at this guy and took him into the room. He used the electric gun on him, the Indonesian man told me he used it on him in the room. I heard him screaming in the room. We were very afraid. Then I saw him come out and near the elevator I saw the boss kick him. Then one Malaysian stopped the boss. On the day he mistreated the Indonesian guy I went to the office because the boss deducted £50 from our salaries per month. I don't like because my agent didn't tell me about that. The boss was very angry and he shout loudly. Anyway the boss was very angry and he called the Malaysian to come and translate, also he called a Filipino. I asked him why he deduct £50 from our salaries. The Malaysian guy told me the boss is very angry, that he takes this from all the salaries of foreigners and he will return it after 6 months. I said he cannot do that. The boss got very angry. He shout very loud at me: 'Any question? Any question?' He is a big man, maybe a six-footer.

Q Is there anything else you would like to say?

A I like Taiwan. But I don't like to work any more in that factory. Very hard. If people are kind OK. We can work hard. We can work very hard for them that's OK. But we must not always be afraid, we must have our human rights.

▲ **Figure 7.11** Kanishka's story. Kanishka is 28, one of about 3000 Sri Lankans in Taiwan.
He is interviewed here by Eamonn Sheridan, a Catholic priest who works with immigrants.

▶ **Figure 7.12** Taipei conurbation and northern Taiwan.

1 Work with a partner.
 a) List the issues arising from Kanishka's story in Figure 7.11.
 b) What can be done about each issue, and who should do it?
 c) What are the possible remedies for human rights violations in such circumstances?

2 In a group, discuss:
 a) how far people in the UK face similar cultural and social issues to those in Taiwan
 b) what you feel can or should be done about these.

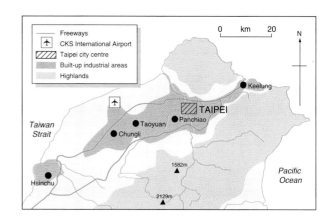

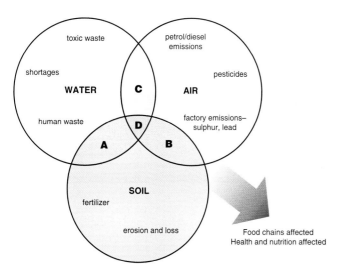

▲ **Figure 7.13** Venn diagram showing aspects of environmental pollution in Taiwan.

1 Copy Figure 7.13. Identify some of the effects of pollution in sections A, B, C, and D.

2 Do the environmental problems illustrated in Figure 7.13 require different or similar solutions?

Environmental issues: must growth cause pain?

Rapid industrialization and urbanization as experienced in Taiwan seem to be almost impossible without some environmental cost, particularly that of pollution. In capitalist free-market economies and in the former communist countries (discussed later in this chapter), infrastructure and legal controls inevitably lag behind developments in agriculture and industry. Profit and the immediate improvements in personal and family circumstances are the priorities for most people. Environmental issues are lower on their list.

There are all kinds of environmental issues, at all scales. Many arise in Taiwan – polluted rivers, air unfit to breathe in Taipei for an average of 62 days a year, and crops contaminated with pesticides and heavy metals. Taiwan is becoming an environmental nightmare. Figure 7.13 suggests one way of looking at these problems.

Agricultural as well as industrial development have caused this situation. Agriculture is highly mechanized and intensive, and the 'green revolution' has arrived, involving the increased and extensive use of pesticides, fertilizers, irrigation, and intensive animal-rearing methods (Figure 7.14). The demand for high yields from farmers in order to meet demand from consumers in the towns and cities means that water which has been polluted by industrial waste and untreated sewage is used for irrigation without testing or treatment. The extent of Taiwan's polluted rivers is shown in Figure 7.17. Many pollutants, particularly those that are soluble, transfer easily into the food chain. In addition, farming methods themselves create problems, as Figure 7.16 shows. Even the recently developed and highly productive aquaculture is in deep difficulties.

It is clear that rapid and in many ways very successful economic development faces a real challenge in environmental terms. The truth is that the polluters do not face the consequences of their own pollution, and improvements cost money. Future generations seem a long way off when your family is reaching for its first taste of wealth.

▲ **Figure 7.15** A Taiwanese millionaire farmer. It is not uncommon for Taiwanese farmers to be very rich these days. Mr Wu, on his farm near Nantou in central Taiwan, specializes in the intensive rearing of pigs and chickens for meat.

High crop yields in the lowlands of Taiwan have been obtained by the liberal use of fertilizers and pesticides. Taiwan is among the top users of chemical fertilizers in the world (1.3 million tonnes per year). The heavy use contributes to soil acidification, zinc losses, and reduced soil fertility. Nitrogen and phosphorus runoff stimulates the growth of algae in rivers and lakes, and contaminates groundwater. Pesticides are another source of contamination of freshwater resources. Farmers apply an average of 4 kilos per hectare per annum and now use almost 1% of the world's pesticide. Pesticide abuse is encouraged by aggressive marketing of some 280 brands by private companies, with no effective government regulation of the trade.

▲ **Figure 7.14** Agriculture – a toxic growth?

Hailed as the success story which 'every country in the business is scrambling to emulate', Taiwanese aquaculture has achieved fantastic growth rates, with prawn production, for example, increasing 45 times in just 10 years. Like other industries in Taiwan, aquaculture is made up of thousands of small specialized producers throughout the country, most of them in coastal areas. These producers are dependent on rivers and wells for clean fresh water, something that is fast becoming a scarce commodity. Thus mass deaths of shrimps and fish regularly occur as a result of toxic chemical waste from upstream industries.

In the infamous green oysters incident, millions of dollars' worth of cultivated oysters had to be destroyed after they turned green. Local newspapers traced the pollution upstream to scrap cable and wire-processing factories which did not have wastewater treating equipment.

But aquaculture is both a victim and a victimizer. Intensive exploitation of groundwater has already caused severe land subsidence. Rice farmers near the coast complain that saltwater seepage into their land from nearby aquaculture farms (where they mix seawater and fresh water) reduces their yields, while other farmers complain there is just not enough water left for their crops.

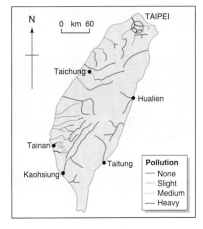

▲ **Figure 7.17** River pollution in Taiwan.

▲ **Figure 7.16** Aquaculture – the lethal loop?

Redressing the balance

1 a) Identify from Figures 7.14–7.17 the key environmental problems facing agriculture in Taiwan.
   b) Identify for each what you feel is the cause of the problem.

2 a) What are your own reactions to the agricultural situation in Taiwan?
   b) Are your reactions or concerns social, economic, or environmental?

3 In your group, consider what can be done to address environmental problems in farming in Taiwan by:

a) farmers
b) wholesalers and shopkeepers
c) consumers
d) exporters
e) local and national government
f) people outside Taiwan.

4 Present a collective report, written by the members of your group, which identifies key actions that you feel should be undertaken in the next five years:

a) to address the environmental problems you identified
b) to monitor how effective your actions would be.

Legacies of the past: the issues facing the former Soviet Union

Glasnost

After 70 years of totalitarian rule, the will to change became clear in the USSR under President Gorbachov, with 'glasnost' in 1986. 'Glasnost' involved some relaxation of communist control of society and the economy, for instance leaving more Russian farmers free to sell produce at a market rather than for the state. By 1991 the USSR had broken up into different states and most, including the largest, Russia, joined to become the Commonwealth of Independent States (CIS). Economic reforms, designed to transform the economy from centrally planned communism to free-market capitalism, were implemented in 1992. This resulted in a tremendous inflation and recession and greatly increased differences between rich and poor both by region and by occupation – see Figures 7.18 and 7.19. In order to understand the differences between economic policies before and after the reforms, read the theory box below.

The reasons for the inflation and recession suffered by the members of the CIS are complex, but result mainly from the removal of central government control. The communist economy of the USSR was self-contained: much of what was consumed within the USSR was produced there, and the inflation cycles of the 1970s and 1980s which so affected developing and developed economies elsewhere, left the USSR largely unaffected. The USSR had its own sources of energy, which was a major cause of inflation in Western economies, and it traded relatively little for its size. Prices in the USSR even in the mid-1980s were at a similar level to those of the 1930s, so that, for example, it cost little more than 1p to travel by train within Moscow. Food was grown strictly according to planned limits, and prices paid to farmers were fixed. Once the protection of government was removed, the countries of the CIS were exposed to higher prices from overseas trade. Farmers too, now that they were free of price restrictions, took advantage of the market prices for the food they produced.

Free market or state control?

Most countries of the world are involved in both market economies and state control. The **market economy**, or **free market**, is an economic system that operates according to free market forces. This means there is free enterprise and competition, private ownership of business, and prices determined by supply and demand. Sometimes such systems are referred to as **capitalism**. People under such systems work for whoever will employ them for a wage or salary. They compete with each other for jobs, and competition between people tends to drive down wage levels. In turn, this increases profit levels for the employer. It is in the employer's interest to keep wage levels down. In simple terms, the poor may become poorer, while increasing profit levels means that wealthy people increase their riches. Employers argue that by keeping wage levels down, they keep the costs of their product down, which encourages sales. This, they maintain, protects jobs in the long term.

State control of the economy can take many forms. In extreme it has been mainly associated with countries at war and with communist countries. **Communism** since the time of Karl Marx has been based on theories which advocate a classless society and the common ownership of property and business of all kinds, with an emphasis on the equal distribution of wealth. Nations following this theory have found it necessary to control the economy completely, thus often stifling imagination and enterprise. Uncontrolled capitalism leads to gross inequalities of wealth at all levels – local, national, international – and in practice a combination of free market and state control – **state capitalism** – avoids some of the pitfalls of each system.

Communist nations like China are now encouraging individual economic enterprise, and the countries of the old 'Eastern bloc' have moved dramatically towards free market systems, and become part of the global market economy. Free market nations like the UK and Germany emphasize private enterprise at a local level, but are committed to state (government) intervention and control at national and international levels. Thus they try to control their economies by taxation, planning restrictions, subsidies, and investment, and at international level are involved in complex financial and trade regulations.

1992 as a percentage of 1991	
GDP	−20
Retail trade	−37
Production:	
Industry	−18
Agriculture	−10
Real income	−36
Real outlays	−40
Retail prices	+1800
(now about +20% per annum)	

Note, however, that there is under-reporting of activity, and a huge informal economy.

▲ **Figure 7.18** Changes in the CIS following economic reform.

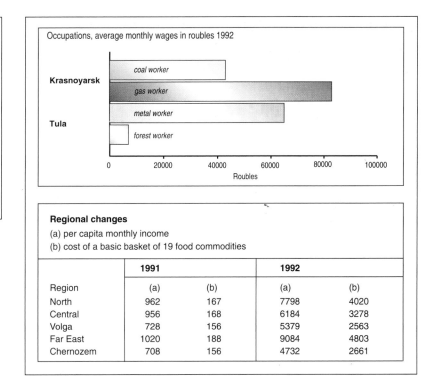

Occupations, average monthly wages in roubles 1992

Krasnoyarsk
- coal worker
- gas worker

Tula
- metal worker
- forest worker

Roubles

Regional changes
(a) per capita monthly income
(b) cost of a basic basket of 19 food commodities

	1991		1992	
Region	(a)	(b)	(a)	(b)
North	962	167	7798	4020
Central	956	168	6184	3278
Volga	728	156	5379	2563
Far East	1020	188	9084	4803
Chernozem	708	156	4732	2661

▶ **Figure 7.19** Differences in the CIS between the rich and the poor.

1 What were the immediate outcomes of economic reform for people in the CIS?

2 Form groups of 2–3 people. Brainstorm the different results that could be expected as a result of glasnost and economic reform:
   a) ways in which the people of the CIS could hope to gain in the long term
   b) ways in which the USA and the EU would benefit.

An environmental heritage

Secrecy and restrictions on free speech made it possible for the government of the USSR between 1917 and 1992 to concentrate on industrial and agricultural production with very little regard for the environmental consequences. Some of the results for this disregard of the environment are shown in Figure 7.20.

Figure 7.21 shows the location of the sixteen regions worst hit by environmental problems. The best known region is Chernobyl, damaged by fall-out following the 1986 nuclear accident, but there are other regions in almost as bad a condition. The Urals industrial region suffers from several environmental problems, some of which are discussed later in this section. The Moscow urban area itself, at the heart of Russia, suffers from bad air pollution and low-level radioactive waste sites which are unmonitored.

▶ **Figure 7.20** Attempt fo filter polluted water after Usinsk oilspill.

1 a) Using an atlas and its index, find each of the sixteen regions shown on Figure 7.21, and mark each on a copy of that map.

b) Annotate your map with details of why each area is 'critical'.

2 a) Write each kind of problem you have identified on separate cards. Use the cards with a partner to find a rank order, with those with the worst effects on people at the top. You may decide that you want to group some, thus producing a diamond shape.

b) Compare your rank order with those of other pairs. Justify your reasons for selecting your own order, and reach an agreed order if possible.

c) Are the environmental problems which give the worst results also the most difficult to eradicate?

Coalmining and steel-producing areas of the Kuznets Basin and the Dnepropetrovsk–Donets Basin suffer air and water pollution. Mining and processing around Semipalatinsk (now called Semey) and Ust-Kamenogorsk (Oskemen) in East Kazakhstan, and on the Kola Peninsula, cause air pollution and toxic metal poisoning.

The Aral Sea is severely depleted by the extraction of irrigation water. Soil erosion and chemical contamination as well as industrial pollution occur in Moldavia, the Kamlyk Republic, and the Fergana Valley. Water pollution from both agricultural and industrial sources is the main problem for the Black Sea, the Caspian Sea, and the Azov Sea coasts. Lake Baikal and the Volga river are similarly polluted.

Details of some of the problems experienced, presented in Figure 7.22, highlight the human element and express the awful dimensions of the issues.

▼ **Figure 7.21** Critical environmental areas in the former USSR.

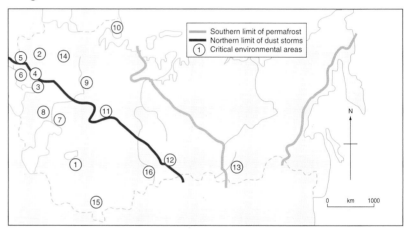

▼ **Figure 7.22** Living in Seitovka. Seitovka is 40km from Astrakhan near the shores of the Caspian Sea, in Ukraine.

'It looks like a yellow plastic football. Snap it open and out falls a gas mask.'
Rumiya's family has five footballs, one for each person.
'When I see Luisa's nose bleeding, I know it's the gas again.' She nods towards her 4-year-old. 'She's the first to be affected. Then I smell it. It's like bad eggs. We all feel sick; the kids get dizzy.'
Seitovka, 40km from Astrakhan, 3km from the largest sulphur production plant in the world.

Industrial cities – how do you prove causal relationships?

Magnitogorsk: 435 000 people; 50 000 steelworkers, 12m tonnes of steel each year, no gas or dust filters on smoke stacks – 140 000 people with respiratory ailments.
Monchegorsk near Murmansk: high sulphur content ores smelted for nickel, copper, and cobalt; SO2 is given off, forests polluted, acid rain to Scandinavia; cancer and respiratory problems common.
Oskemen: 300 000 people; half of ex-USSR's lead and zinc smelted here; titanium and magnesium smelting; plant to turn uranium into reactor fuel rods; high infant mortality rate; 40% of children chronically ill; age expectancy 55 (USSR average in 1991 was 65); high blood lead levels; lead, zinc, arsenic, mercury, and cadmium in excess levels in local soil; 58% children affected by immune system deficiencies; chromosome damage widespread; nosebleeds common.

The southern Urals – a disaster zone

Study Figure 7.23. The Institute of Geography at the Russian Academy of Sciences has now mapped in detail the worst ecological situations. For example, the area around Sverdlovsk in the southern Urals (see Figure 7.23) is in a desperate state. The areas with 'Most severe ecological situations' almost all suffer from air pollution, depletion of water resources, water pollution, loss of productive land, and soil erosion. The soil erosion, by water in the north of the area and by wind in the south, also affects much of the surrounding land. Perhaps the most devastating sequence of events took place 70km north of the city of Chelyabinsk, which has a population of more than one million. The time-line, in Figure 7.24, summarizes recent history.

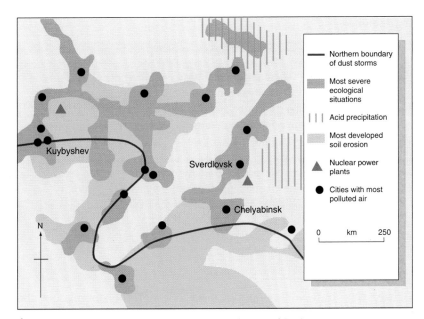

▲ **Figure 7.23** Environmental survey in the southern Ural Region.

Many of these events took place in 'secret cities', and were unmapped until recently because of their sensitive status. The USSR was probably encouraged in its waste dumping in the river by the knowledge that the Americans were successfully disposing of nuclear waste from their Hanford plant into the fast-flowing Columbia river. But the river Techa is slow-flowing and the highly radioactive waste formed a multicoloured slime on the surface before sinking into sediment on the bottom. Work on the river by prisoners from local camps went on until 1963, and 20 riverside villages were evacuated and demolished.

The secret cities did not appear on maps (rather as UK weapons plants do not appear on OS maps), and the Kyshtym explosion was not officially admitted until 1989, even though it had resulted in 20 000 km² of wasteland and 'nature reserve'. Many people have suffered, for example from radiation sickness and deformed births. The combined effects of these disasters have exposed 400 000 people to contamination by radiation, and even official figures reveal that 1000 people have suffered severe radiation sickness.

1945
USSR plans to produce its own atomic bomb.

1948
Six nuclear reactors and a plutonium extraction plant are completed at Chelyabinsk-40 – the Mayak association. Nearby the closed secret city of Chelyabinsk-65 (population 80 000) is built.

1947–52
Radioactive nuclear waste is dumped in the Techa river – health problems and radiation poisoning all along the river and down to the river Ob. 124 000 people are exposed to radiation.

1953
Underground waste storage tanks built. River Techa dammed to give reservoirs which are used with Lake Karachay for dumping of low-level nuclear waste.

1957
Kyshtym accident – a storage tank explodes, a radiation cloud of Strontium-90 travels east and north-east for 1000km and exposes 250 000 people to radiation.

1967 and 1972
Droughts – radioactive dust is blown from the dried-up margins of Lake Karachay, and deposited on 63 settlements.

1984
Construction of three fast-breeder nuclear reactors begun north of Chelyabinsk city.

1988
Work on the new power plant stopped because of anti-nuclear sentiment after Chernobyl disaster.

1991
Local referendum rejects the completion of the new reactors.

▲ **Figure 7.24** A time-line for Chelyabinsk-40 and Chelyabinsk-65.

Concerns now are that the contaminated silt at the bottom of the reservoirs on the river Techa will be washed out in times of flood, and will contaminate local land. Groundwater used for domestic supplies is becoming radioactive with natural seepage into the water table.

Five of Mayak's six reactors have been shut down. The three new reactors which were rejected by the local people were meant to provide a safe supply of energy to enable the Chelyabinsk region to recover. Now high unemployment and continuing environmental damage is making the situation worse – see Figure 7.25.

The trouble is that it costs millions of roubles to put right such a long-term series of disasters. The CIS is in a dire economic state and there is virtually no government money for the kind of clean-up that is necessary. The desire is there, but the new 'green' politics is challenged by economic needs.

▼ **Figure 7.25** Chelyabinsk – problems beside radiation.

The smoke emitted from Chelyabinsk's metallurgical factories and power plants contains quantities of sulphur dioxide, formaldehyde, and other pollutants far exceeding the limits allowable in the West. Local residents joke that some days, as one flies into Chelyabinsk airport, separate parts of the city appear to be different colours depending on the industry located at each spot. But when smelting works are shut down for refurbishing, thousands of workers and miners become unemployed.

There are about 130 major enterprises in the city of Chelyabinsk, including the largest zinc processing plant in Russia and one of the largest paintworks. Though the metallurgical region is set apart from the residential, the workers still live near to the works. A small river called the Miass runs through the factory zone and is used as a dump for waste water. It is almost completely dead. In 1992 several workers caught typhoid when they accidentally drank water from the Miass.

What is being done?

Clearly very little will be accomplished until the economies of the former states of the USSR improve. While recession continues and people get poorer, national money and energy will go towards consolidation and industrial production in order to produce wealth, rather than to environmental improvements. In the short term the onus is on the world community to provide capital and resources specifically for environmental work. The World Bank has agreed a £33 million environmental loan to the Russian Federation (a large part of the CIS), to be followed by £165 million from certain countries led by Switzerland, but this is slow in coming. However, put in perspective this is not such a great deal. In 1993 Russia paid £8.6 billion to the EU for imports, and spending by Russian central government was £46 billion. £198 million is unlikely to go far.

How far will some of it go towards clearing up the October 1994 oil spill in the Arctic tundra near Pechora? This disaster is described, and its ecological impact assessed, in *The Physical Environment* (the first book in this series). The pipeline there had been leaking since 1988 and the spill was caught in an earth-dammed reservoir. In 1994, heavy rains breached the dam, oil flowed into the Kolva river, then to the Pechora and so to the Barents Sea. Work in the Arctic is tricky and expensive, and the ecology is delicately balanced. Nature is very slow to break down the oil, which will be disastrous to the local environment, to more distant salmon fisheries, and to the indigenous Nenet peoples.

This kind of event is nothing new. In 1992, to the east of the Urals, the equivalent of the annual oil consumption of Australia was spilled into the environment. The CIS is still a massive economic and political unit by any standards, and the resources needed to make an impact upon such problems are immense.

1 Draw a large diagram explaining the problems in the Chelyabinsk region. What seem to be the possible alternative futures for the region?

2 Review the environmental issues brought about by uncontrolled economic development in the former USSR. How far are the issues the same as or different from those in the UK?

3 Divide into two groups. One group should explore and support the idea that 'Polluters should pay for costs of all the damage in all cases'; the other that 'Pollution is an international issue and will require international strategies to resolve its causes and problems'. Hold a debate on the issue.

4 After the debate, summarize in about 750 words your own attitude towards the idea of 'the polluter pays', as applied to the CIS.

Researching a MNE

You will probably have looked at the 'enquiry' theory box in Chapter 1, on page 9. This end of section technique box will help you research into MNEs – and it can be adapted for studies of smaller firms. Remember that MNEs may also be known as TNCs (transnational corporations) or multinational companies. Follow this sequence of questions.

1 What kind of company is it? What does it produce? Are all its outputs 'products', or does it have other activities, such as services, financial management, etc.?

2 Where is it based, and where does it operate? Are its activities at the same level in all places?

3 Who owns the company, and in which country is its ownership registered?

4 Are there any changes going on, to the company or to different parts of it? Over what timescale? What rate of change, growth, or decline is there?

5 Why are changes taking place (economic, social, political, and environmental issues)? What are the causes behind growth and decline?

6 Who causes the change? Who are the decision-makers? What links does the company have with public or private sectors in different countries? What is its attitude towards protest groups, or developers?

7 What impact is the company having in different parts of the world (economic, environmental, political, social implications, development versus conservation, inequalities in access and opportunities, changes in the quality of life)?

8 How sustainable are the company activities?

9 What is the future for the company?

You will also need sources of information. You may find, if you request information or interviews with companies, that you receive well-produced materials which describe many of the company activities. However, many of your questions may remain unanswered. You should therefore try to find answers by consulting other sources. At least try to find names of all the company's subsidiaries. For instance, you may find little on General Motors in the UK, but you should find plenty on Vauxhall, its UK brand-name.

- Try newspapers, especially past years which are published on CD-ROM – search for your company and its subsidiary names.

- Look through New Internationalist, a monthly publication which frequently looks at the activities of MNEs.

- Ask your library to obtain company reports for you.

- Keep a file of relevant press-cuttings and articles.

Ideas for further study

1 Monitor the press for **a)** local and **b)** international environmental issues arising from economic activities. Describe the way in which these issues reflect different priorities, and suggest ways in which such issues may be resolved.

2 Carry out an enquiry into a MNE, and the extent of its economic, social, environmental, and political activity. You should read publications such as the *New Internationalist* in order to gain a balanced view, and compare such a view with those offered by companies themselves. Use the technique box on the previous page.

Summary

- There has been a shift of economic growth into East Asia, where political and cultural climates have promoted it.
- Across the world, economic expansion has in some cases been at the expense of human rights and dignity.
- Economic change may bring with it cultural change which can be irreversible.
- The influence of multinational enterprises on the management of economic activity is very strong.
- Even though 'global forces' and the 'free market' are fundamental to economic change, the importance of government policies at regional and local levels can be paramount.
- The shift to an increasingly global economy has had major impacts on the former communist countries.
- Economic growth has brought with it environmental damage which will prove costly to reverse. The decision whether to accept or reverse the damage will have to be taken at an international level.

References and further reading

Rapid economic development in the Far East is explored in:

W. Bello and S. Rosenfeld, *Dragons in Distress*, Food First, 1990.

R. Hodder, *The West Pacific Rim*, Belhaven Press, 1992.

'Easy reading' on economic activity, global economics, Taiwan, and Ghana is to be found in the publications from the Development Education Centre, Birmingham:
Beyond the Backyard, 1993
The Global Money Machine, 1994
The Backbone of Development, 1994
Can You Be Different? 1994.

S. Artobolevskiy, 'Environmental problems in the USSR', *Geography Review*, March 1991.

E. Baigent, 'Nationalism in the USSR', *Geography Review*, March 1991.

Changing economic activities: Summary

In this section, you have learned about different economic activities and how these are changing. The table below shows you how these studies are linked to the requirements of the syllabus you are studying. Your examiners who will be setting the examination papers on the topics in this book will use the summary points below.

Key ideas	Explanation	Examples
1 Employment changes over time	The causes of change to employment in primary, secondary, and service employment, and impacts of physical and built environments.	• Regions and employment growth and decline, e.g. growth and decline in the West Midlands and its links to employment change, and decline in Tory Island • Changing employment and quality of life in contrasting countries, e.g. Taiwan, CIS, UK
2 Manufacturing and service activities have evolved a structure and pattern	The concepts of – product cycles, and their links to the growth and decline of industrial regions – inertia – globalization – NICs – MNEs.	• Car industry in the West Midlands, industrial growth in Taiwan • Industrial inertia in the West Midlands • Effects of global investment and change on the UK, Taiwan, Ghana, and on the airline industry • Taiwan • Kader in Hong Kong
3 Theories of industrial location	Different theories of – growth and decline – industrial location and change	• Core and periphery – UK (West Midlands), Tory Island, Ghana • Least-cost location, accessibility, the importance of raw materials versus market locations, 'hub and spoke'
4 Governments may influence location and attempt to manage economic change	A critical examination of government policies at a variety of scales.	• West Midlands, Tory Island, CIS, Taiwan
5 Employment patterns vary within regions and/or countries and over time, with profound social, economic, environmental and political consequences.	Changing employment patterns – differences in age, gender, ethnicity, and the changing nature of work and employment.	• West Midlands, Taiwan
	The spatial consequences of change, including social and environmental impacts.	• West Midlands, Tory Island, Taiwan
6 Economic changes can have a major impact on global patterns of manufacturing and service industries	Global shift in manufacturing and service industries	• The impact of global shift on the timber and airline industries
	Recent industrialization of ELDCs including the emergence of NICs and of the Pacific Rim as a major force.	• The economic, social, and environmental impacts of change in Taiwan
	Deindustrialization in EMDCs.	• The economic, social, and environmental impacts of change in the West Midlands and the CIS

3

Resource management

Sewage disposal – what a waste!

Imagine the scene. It is a warm summer day. You have taken an annual holiday close to one of Britain's beaches. Holidays, including mini-breaks, are the second largest annual expense for many families, after paying for rent or the mortgage. You relax but you also expect to enjoy yourself, because you have paid for this holiday. Read Figure 1. One holidaymaker, Mrs Mary Jones, found rather more than she bargained for.

1 With a partner, list the issues that are mentioned in the article in Figure 1.

2 Identify the different viewpoints expressed in the article. Divide them on a large sheet of paper into those that are optimistic and those that are not.

3 Identify some of the reasons why you think people are saying the things they are. Whose interests do they represent? What evidence do they have for what they say?

4 What do these issues have to do with studying Geography?

'Crust of a Wave'

Mrs Mary Jones, sheltering from a stiffish sea breeze on Blackpool beach, is 62 and one of the town's eight million visitors a year. Blackpool has been condemned in the European courts for its bathing water. There are signs warning bathers on the front but, no, she doesn't appreciate that the town's arrangements are flushed straight into the sea which she has come all the way from Preston to enjoy. She was going to go in 'for a paddle. That should be all right, shouldn't it?' Now she's not even sure of that.

'It all goes in raw, does it? That's terrible, but I'm too old for proper bathing now,' she says. 'Sometimes it's best not to know everything.'

The Government might agree: back in 1975 when Europe was first proposing minimum standards for bathing water, Britain was asked to identify its 'traditional' beaches. It came up with just 27: landlocked Luxembourg declared 33.

Little changes: this week John Gummer, Environment Secretary, launched the third annual report on UK environmental progress. It stated blandly that 80 per cent of British beaches now met mandatory EU standards: what was not mentioned is that no tests are done even for viruses or many minor ailments caused by polluted sea water, and that 20 per cent of British beaches, even after 18 years' legislation, still fail to meet minimum safety and legal standards.

The official line is relentlessly cheery. The Water Services Association, which represents the water companies, this week claimed, in a letter to *The Guardian*, that 132 of our beaches were (to paraphrase) great, and the public really needn't worry about bathing water quality after 'billions of pounds' investment' had been made in sewage treatment over the past few years

The tourist industry, too, claims all is well: the EU 'Blue Flag' flutters over 20 British beaches (a small improvement on the last year); more than 100 have now won UK government 'Seaside Awards' (26 more than 1992), and 56 have 'Premier Awards'. On Wednesday the National Rivers Authority calmed the waters, too, stating that there had been a 0.6 per cent improvement in bathing waters in the last year and the public could expect to see 'dramatic improvements' after 1995.

Mrs Jones's companion Denis knows he shouldn't bathe at Blackpool ('I'm far too old anyway, but I used to') and is not at all impressed that the town's waste is dumped just below low-tide level with only the most elementary wire screen at the end to catch the condoms and panty-liners. 'Out of sight out of mind, isn't it?' he says. 'I dare say the pipe is Victorian, too.'

It is, and Blackpool beach is the norm, not the exception. Government figures show that 80 per cent of towns with over 10 000 people dump 'preliminary' (i.e. raw) sewage in the sea, and 1000 million litres of untreated sewage are now sent straight out to sea each day.

▲ **Figure 1** From *The Guardian*, 13 May 1994.

In Britain the main method of coastal sewage disposal has always been to flush it out to sea so that the sea will dilute and disperse it. Clearly this approach to sewage disposal can cause major problems for water quality, with a subsequent threat to health, although there are differing views on the severity of the problem.

However, some people might argue that these problems are caused in part by a failure in resource management. How many water companies see sewage as a resource?

When does a resource become a resource? Answer: When we need it!

Resources are defined by society, not by Nature. Something becomes a resource when we have the ability to make it available to be used, matched by a demand for the end product.

For example, until recently waste was regarded solely as a problem. Whilst it is still true that the volume of waste we produce is a problem for a number of reasons, it is now recognized that in some cases it can be regarded as a valuable resource, for example methane from landfill sites or heat from waste incinerators.

Sewage can similarly be seen as a resource. A number of sewage works around the country are extracting biogas (a mixture of methane and carbon dioxide) from the treatment process, for combustion within the generation of electricity. The electricity is then used during treatment and is exported to the national grid. Avonmouth sewage works near Bristol

▲ **Figure 2** Maple Lodge sewage treatment works.

generates a total of 3MW, whilst Maple Lodge sewage works near Rickmansworth sells 1.5MW to the national grid.

During the process the sewage sludge is separated and passed through a digester where the biogas is extracted to be burnt in

the generators. The electricity that is produced is used to provide constant heat to keep the digesters at 26–28 °C, and to provide compressed air to aerate the liquid effluent during its treatment. This is shown in Figure 3.

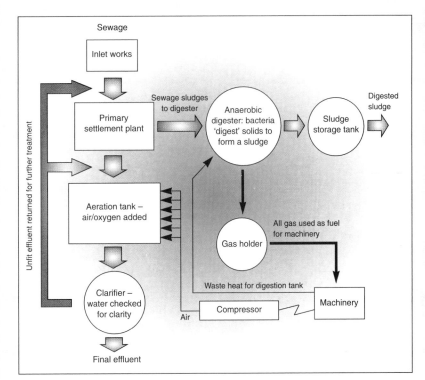

▲ **Figure 3** The sewage treatment process.

165

The digested sludge used to be dumped at sea. This will be phased out by 1998, and water companies are interested in finding other uses for the sludge. For example, the majority of the sludge produced by Wessex Water is used as an agricultural fertilizer. Experiments are also being carried out on the potential for using the treated sludge as a fuel.

The minimization of waste from any process, by finding alternative uses for the waste products, is an important part of resource management.

1 If a major programme for improving the quality of sewage treatment, including provision for methane extraction and energy production, was undertaken, which of the following do you think should pay for setting it up?

- The government, because a lack of past investment in the water treatment infrastructure is one of the major reasons why we are in this current position.
- The water industry, because since privatization water companies should be running a commercial business and making a profit. In any other industry you would expect the polluter to pay.
- The consumers through increased water bills, because we are the ones creating the demand and we should therefore take responsibility for our own actions. We, after all, want clean beaches.

2 Justify your response to question 1.

Why do we study resource management in Geography?

A clear understanding of resource management is funda-mental to our ability to develop our society on a sustainable basis, to meet our current needs without compromising the needs of future generations. This requires us to make the most efficient use of all the resources that we have available to us. We need to understand fully the economic, social, and environ-mental impacts of any resource use so that problematic effects can be minimized.

Studying resource use also enables us to understand more clearly the motivations behind many international political issues. The issue of who controls resource development and use is a vital question to consider. It has played a significant role historically in shaping major parts of the United States foreign policy, for example. This is not surprising when the level of resource use within the USA is considered. It cannot be self-sufficient and has to look further afield for the resources to maintain its consumption. This was an issue of major concern to many developing countries during the 1950s, '60s, and '70s, trying to retain control over resources they felt were indigenous to their countries.

It is still a major issue today, shaping many decisions that are made in the world. In 1990, the invasion of Kuwait – a major source of the world's oil – by Iraqi forces provoked support for Kuwait from Western industrialized countries. You should look at other conflicts in the world, and investigate whether resource issues lie at the heart of the disagreements over occupation and use of space.

1 Describe examples of materials that are now regarded as useful resources but were previously considered to be waste products.

2 In pairs, make a study of a current international conflict or disagreement. Use present and past newspapers, including CD-ROM, and follow this sequence of enquiry.
   a) What is the nature of the conflict? Between whom is the disagreement?
   b) Are there other players in the conflict, such as a world superpower?
   c) Are there resource issues behind the conflict?
   d) What are the motives behind each side of the conflict?
   e) How can the conflict be resolved? If it is resolved, who stands to gain? Who stands to lose?

Waste and resources

This section of the book deals with waste and resources almost as if they are one and the same topic. In fact, they are closely linked.

Good resource management involves the minimization of waste, not only for environmental reasons but also for economic ones. If you have ever watched the process of sausage-making, either on television or in real life, you will know that virtually nothing is left after the process of what is described as 'meat recovery'. Few industries operate on these lines, and many produce waste which is left as a residue from the production process.

One of the themes through this section is that of sustainability. Demand for and current use of resources throughout the world are increasing, so that many resources may not last. Sustainability is about maintaining resource use for future generations, so that resources are managed to last longer or even for ever. This section deals with three kinds of approach to resource management.

- Resources that are finite and may have a limited life. Here the issues are all about how we can make a little stretch a long way, and these are looked at in Chapter 8.

- Resources that are recyclable. The issues include the management of water in Chapter 9 and of waste in Chapter 10.

- Resources that are renewable, and in some senses 'infinite', and how we manage those. Developing an understanding of the implications of some of the decisions that have to be made is the focus for Chapter 11.

Suggest how using resources effectively can help sustainable development.

8 Resourcing our needs or needing our resources?

Introduction

Since the industrial revolution, the use of resources has increased hugely, providing people in the industrialized world with a quality of life never enjoyed by previous generations. The needs of Western societies have grown beyond what can be provided within their own borders. This has created political conflict, such as Suez in 1956 and Iraq's invasion of Kuwait in 1990. Energy and mineral resources are the lifeblood of our society, and their supply is willingly defended.

But who controls resource supply? Is it

- the country that owns it
- the country that seeks to gain and use it, or
- the multinational enterprises (MNEs) of the world?

Depending on the resource, all these answers are true!

There is an increasing desire within the Economically Less Developed Countries (ELDCs) to have greater access to the world's available energy and mineral resources, in order to develop their economies and to increase the standard of living for their people. As the world's population grows, will there be enough resources for everyone? Can we use resources in ways that are sustainable for future generations?

Answers to these questions depend largely on who you ask, and on what assumptions different people make. The following are a few of these viewpoints.

- For a long time the main sources of data on oil and gas reserves were the oil and gas industries themselves. Companies would find just enough oil and gas to ensure that the price stayed high. If too much oil was found, then the price of oil would crash, something the industry was keen to avoid.
- Many technologists would say that as one resource begins to run out, it will become more expensive, and an increase in price motivates companies to invest in research and development to find alternative sources. A comforting thought maybe, certainly one that allows us to keep on using our resources without worrying.
- Environmental groups believe that resources are finite, and also that using them has an impact on the environment. But whose environment? Is our concern proportional to the distance from the impact in question?
- People on low incomes are less likely to be concerned about which energy resources are left in the world, or the impact that their use might have on the environment. Their concern is how much the electricity or gas will cost, and whether they will be able to afford it.

1 With a partner, find an atlas that includes economic resource maps, and a data guide such as the *Geographical Digest*. List resources that are in common use, and find the main countries that produce them. Name resources that are controlled by
   a) countries that own the resource
   b) countries that own resources, but where in the past another overseas country has sought to gain them.

2 Using CD-ROMs of past issues of newspapers such as the *Financial Times*, investigate examples of resources that are managed by multinational enterprises (MNEs). You will find it helpful to search by referring to specific resources such as gold, tin, water, etc.

- The government of a developing country might be concerned with its access to resources and to the technology and finance to develop its own resources, but less concerned with whether development might make environmental problems worse.

Considering political, technical, economic, social, and environmental issues is part of managing the Earth's resources.

Identifying some of the issues – opencast mining

Resource use has implications for the environment. Figure 8.1 shows a large opencast coal mine. Opencast mining has been controversial in the UK during the 1990s. Its costs are lower than underground mining, as coal is more easily extracted, but it has major impacts on local environments, and the issues arising from this often find their way into news reports. Figure 8.2 shows some of the key issues.

▼ **Figure 8.1** An opencast coal mine.

▼ **Figure 8.2** Opencast mining in the news.

Hidden Agenda to Boost Opencast Coal

British Coal was accused yesterday of expanding opencast production at the expense of deep mines in an attempt to increase its value in the run-up to privatization. British Coal's highly profitable opencast subsidiary already provides a fifth of total coal production, and industry analysts believe there is a hidden agenda to build up a commercially attractive 'land bank' in Scotland, the North, and the Midlands . . .

'It seems that they are going for opencast to improve the balance sheet for privatization, building up sites which could be worth millions,' Dr Cox (editor of *UK Coal Review*) said.

He estimates the value of the opencast executive at between £250 million and £500 million.

Last year the executive made a profit of £171 million from 58 sites on a turnover of £718 million from 17 million tonnes [of coal].

By contrast the deep mines made only £153 million from 71 million tonnes [of coal] on a turnover of £2948 million.

Dr Cox says the huge opencast sites are more [attractive than deep mines] because they require little direct investment. By contrast, investment of £286 million last year in deep mines represented a 'major cash flow'.

(a) From *The Guardian*, 23 October 1992.

Imagine that a proposal is made to add a tax (e.g. VAT) to energy used in homes, which will be applied to each bill as it is used. How might each of the people or groups listed on page 168-9 react?

Compensation for Opencast Mining 'Needs Review'

Compensation paid to local residents whose lives are disrupted by large developments of national benefit, such as road building or mining, should be reviewed urgently, members of the Commons Select Committee on Wales said yesterday.

The Committee says in a report published yesterday that Welsh villagers affected by long-term opencast mining should be offered high-quality new homes.

British Coal spent about £500 000 a year on 'local benefits' out of an annual profit in South Wales of £20 million, but the MPs say they consider this to be 'a small sum to put back into communities. In future, a much greater share of the national surplus should be given back to the people affected by opencast.'

The MPs say, however, that they agree with British Coal that it should not be singled out for stricter treatment than other activities, such as road building, which exacted a high price from local residents for the national benefit.

The report says production of coal from opencast mines in Wales last year was 1.9 million tonnes out of a total for the whole of the UK of 18.6 million tonnes, and British Coal intends to increase production to about 3 million tonnes in 1993/94.

(b) From the *Daily Telegraph*, 24 April 1991.

Opencast mining – for and against

Increasingly, local councils in areas where there are coal-bearing rock strata are being asked by private companies for planning permission to extract coal by opencast methods.

Imagine that planning permission for an opencast mine is being sought by a private company owned and run by miners formerly employed by British Coal. You should look at Figures 8.7 and 8.11 later in this chapter for details of coal production and comparative costs for deep-mined coal and opencast coal.

1 List all the interest groups concerned with this development.

2 a) Briefly identify and describe whether their concerns are political, economic, environmental, technical, or social.
  b) What do you feel are the most important issues? Why?
  c) What else do you feel you would need to know before you could make a complete assessment of whether or not this development was justifiable?

Classifying resources

STOCK	
Those that are consumed during use	Those that are recyclable
Fossil fuels	Minerals
Coal	
Oil	
Gas	

FLOW	
Those that have reached critically low levels	Those that are not dependent on rate of use
Fish	Solar energy
Forests	Tides
Animals	Wind
Soil	Waves
Water in aquifers	Water
	Air

▲ **Figure 8.3** Classifying resources: 'stock' and 'flow'.

Resources can be split into

- **stock resources**, which are resources that are limited in quantity
- **flow resources**, which are replenished so that their overall volume does not diminish.

The important factor here is **time**. Technically, fossil fuels are flow resources, but because the time taken to replenish them is so great they are regarded as a finite resource. If the demand for flow resources exceeds a system's ability to renew reserves, then they too can be regarded as finite stock resources. For example, if an aquifer is drained faster than it is replenished it will run dry, or if an animal species is hunted beyond its ability to reproduce it will become extinct.

Resources can be further classified as follows:

- **Proven reserves** – those reserves that have a better than 90 per cent chance of being technically and economically extractable.
- **Probable reserves** – those reserves that have a better than 50 per cent chance of being technically and economically extractable.
- **Possible reserves** – those reserves that have a significant but less than 50 per cent chance of being technically and economically extractable.

Figure 8.4 outlines the relationship between the resource classifications.

	IDENTIFIED			UNDISCOVERED	
	Proven	Probable	Possible	In known districts	In undiscovered districts
Economic	RESERVES				
Sub-economic				RESOURCES	

▲ **Figure 8.4** Classifying resources.

Planning for the future?

Resources can be clearly defined as suggested in the theory box on page 170. Resource management involves making decisions about exploitation. As the example of opencast mining shows, demand for resources is affected by a range of sometimes controversial concerns. But how often is thought given to how *sustainable* our resource use is? The Brundtland Commission defined sustainable development in 1987 as:

'[meeting] the needs of the present without reducing the ability of future generations to meet their own needs'.

How far are we from this ideal in the UK? Figure 8.5 is an outline of the UK reserves of oil and gas.

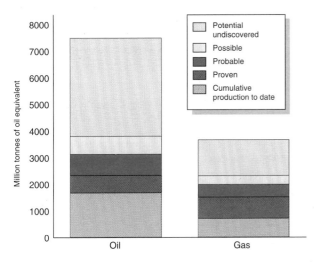

▲ **Figure 8.5** Estimated oil and gas reserves on the UK continental shelf, 1993.

At current rates of production, proven reserves of oil will be used up in six years and and gas in ten years. This figure is obtained by dividing the proven reserves by the current annual production. The Reserves/Production (R/P) ratio for the world's oil resources is currently 43 years. However, using this figure as a measure of the resource base can be misleading for two reasons.

1 Proven reserves are only a fraction of the total resources available. For example, the R/P ratio for all current reserves of oil on the UK continental shelf (see Figure 8.5) would be about 20 years, but if all potential resources are considered, then the figure becomes 55 years.

2 Reserves and production are not static. Figure 8.6 shows how much production of oil and gas has varied over a recent period of 28 years. Estimates of reserves also vary depending on the discovery rate of new deposits. Discovery rates are affected by economic and geological factors, and reflect the oil industry's wish to find enough oil to keep the prices at an economic level.

Figure 8.6 shows the rapid increase in oil production during the 1970s following discoveries in the North Sea, stimulated by price increases after the world's oil crises in 1973 and 1979.

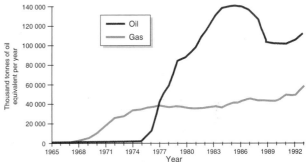

▲ **Figure 8.6** UK production of oil and gas, 1965–93.

Production fell in the early 1980s with a downturn in the economy, and again in the late 1980s following the major accident on the Piper Alpha oilrig, and during the introduction of safety improvements. Following an upturn in oil production after the Piper Alpha accident, there is now the possibility of new oil finds to the west of the Shetlands which could increase production further. These new finds have only become possible since improvements have been made in drilling technology, opening up deposits in the deeper waters of this area.

Gas production has developed more gradually, because the industry viewed the fuel as a limited resource for key uses such as central heating and processes requiring the use of heat within industry. This view has changed in the 1990s, creating a 'dash for gas'. As the coal industry has been run down, gas has been seen as an ideal substitute, being cheaper as a fuel for electricity generation, and less polluting. This change has been encouraged by the development of generating plant with energy efficiencies of up to 50 per cent – that is, only 50 per cent of heat is lost during generation. This compares with efficiencies of 35 per cent for conventional generation plant – that is, 65 per cent of heat is lost. This has created the increase in production in the 1990s shown on Figure 8.6.

Since 1967, oil and gas production from the UK continental shelf has varied as different factors have been considered by decision-makers within the industry and in government.

1 Which of the changes in oil and gas production have been due to:
   a) technical improvements
   b) resource considerations
   c) economic factors
   d) environmental factors
   e) other factors?

2 How far does the use of UK oil and gas resources fit the idea that 'sustainable development should meet the needs of the present without reducing the ability of future generations to meet their own needs'?

Coal in the UK and Europe

Coal has been the major fuel for the UK since the beginning of the industrial revolution. In the late 1970s and the early 1980s, it was overtaken in importance by oil, and now rates third behind oil and gas. The major coal strike in 1984 hit production severely. Although production increased in the years following the strike, coal production is again declining (see Figures 8.7 and 8.8).

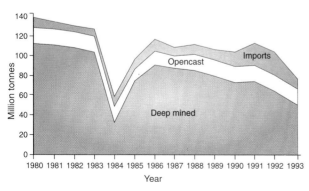

▲ **Figure 8.7** Sources of coal in the UK, 1980–93.

These changes have had major impacts in the UK, especially when it is compared with other coal-producing European countries.

Economic impacts

UK coal is amongst the cheapest in Europe; it requires the lowest subsidies and is being mined at an increasing productivity rate. However, the price of UK coal is still being undercut by cheaper coal imported from outside Europe.

	1984	1992	1994
Operating pits	170	51	16
Workforce	180 000	41 000	10 000

▲ **Figure 8.8** Changes in the UK coal industry, 1984–94.

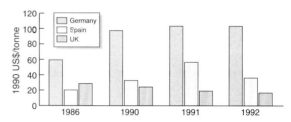

▲ **Figure 8.9** Trends in producer subsidies for hard coal in Europe, 1986–92.

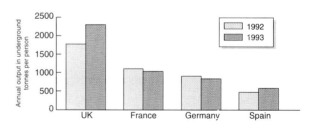

▲ **Figure 8.10** Changes in productivity of coal production, 1992/93.

		Output (million tonnes)	Average costs (ECU/GJ)*
Germany	Deep mined	71.8	4.88
France	Deep mined	8.3	3.42
UK	Deep mined	65.8	2.58
	Opencast	18.2	1.83
Spain	Deep mined	13.8	6.99
	Opencast	4.9	2.60
Imported coal from outside Europe			1.40

*ECU/GJ means *ECUs* (European currency units) *per gigajoule of energy.*

▲ **Figure 8.11** Volume and cost of coal production in Europe, 1992.

1 Look again at Figures 8.7 to 8.10. How can the number of
   pits fall to less than 10% of what they were in 1984 and yet
   the volume of deep mined coal is still over 50% of what it
   was before the strike in 1984?

2 Study Figures 8.8–8.11. In 200 words, outline the main
   changes within the UK coal industry, and state how it
   compares with the industry in other parts of Europe.

Social impacts

The run-down of the coal industry in the UK has had some major
social impacts. In some parts of the country whole communities used
to rely on the work provided by the pits. The workforce fell by 75 per
cent between 1992 and 1994, with a reduction in the number of
operating pits.

▼ **Figure 8.12** from *The Independent on Sunday*.

Vortex of Debt and Despair

The money soon goes. Two years after receiving large redundancy cheques, up to
three-quarters of former miners are still out of work. Those who have found jobs are
often back in the pits as private contractors in what can be insecure, poorly paid
work.

According to a study of 500 former miners in the Doncaster area by researchers
at Sheffield Hallam University, banks, once eager to offer advice on the investment
of large severance cheques, shy away from lending to those without a regular salary.
Loan sharks increase their business, while the community 'trades down' to lower-
quality shops. Communal amenities, supported directly or indirectly by British
Coal, fall into disuse.

The researcher found that very few miners had 'blown' their redundancy,
although most families had succumbed to a treat of some form. The majority opted
to pay off their mortgages on former pit and council houses. 'The closures were in
the late 1980s,' said Bella Dicks, a research assistant. 'Miners with redundancy
payments were advised to pay off their mortgages and quite a lot did just that or
improved the value of their home in other ways. They have got a secure roof over
their head but it is a trap, an unsaleable asset that prevents them from moving
away.'

Typical prices paid by sitting tenants for former council or British Coal houses
were about £12 000 for a three-bedroomed terrace or semi against a high market
value of £28 000. Hundreds are now for sale at about £16 000.

Ms Dicks said that families who had invested their redundancy money fell foul
of social security rules that prohibit claiming benefit while having more than £8000
in savings. 'Comfortable' working-class families slip into poverty with no family
holidays and few luxuries.

Women often find themselves as the sole breadwinner. Sixty per cent of wives
work, but their earnings are small compared with the average of more than £300 a
week in the pits. This also leads to disputes over who does what in the home. The
division of domestic labour was examined closely by the researchers in follow-up
interviews with men and women. 'Women still do more than three-quarters of all
domestic chores. Men may do a bit of washing-up and, if their wives are lucky, a bit
of hoovering. It causes many rows as wives believe their husbands should do more,'
Ms Dicks said.

Study Figure 8.12. Imagine
you work in the local
Citizens' Advice Bureau in
Dinnington. Consider the
options for a family of four
whose main earner has
been made redundant from
the pit. List the options,
and consider the advan-
tages and disadvantages of
each. On the basis of this
article, offer advice.

Environmental impacts

As the theory box below shows, coal is the most polluting fossil fuel. It produces the most sulphur and nitrogen oxides (linked with acid rain), and carbon dioxide (linked with global warming). There are targets for the reduction of sulphur dioxide and carbon dioxide (see Figure 8.17), and reducing the amount of coal combustion is one way of meeting them. However, clean coal technology does exist. If it is used, it offers another approach to emission reduction. Germany, for example, invested heavily in flue gas desulphurization, whereas the UK has tended to rely on a switch to gas and imports of lower-sulphur coal to replace more expensive and more polluting home-produced coal.

The 'dash for gas' has been significant. In November 1992, 0.68GW (gigawatts) capacity of gas-fired plant was operational with a further 7GW under construction. By March 1994 just over 6GW of plant was operational, meeting 11 per cent of the UK's maximum demand for electricity. A total capacity of between 10 and 14GW of gas-fired plant might be achieved, before changes in the economics of gas plants make them unattractive. Although the rapid increase in gas use has been encouraged by low prices for gas in the short term, the fact that gas combustion produces far less sulphur dioxide, nitrogen oxides, and carbon dioxide than coal has also been a factor.

Clean coal technology

Flue gas desulphurization (FGD)

In the most common form of FGD, lime or crushed limestone (the sorbent) is mixed with water and then brought into contact with flue gases (Figure 8.13). The sorbent reacts with sulphur in the flue gases and forms a residue of calcium sulphite and calcium sulphate. When dried and completely oxidized, it forms gypsum, a product with commercial uses in the manufacture of plasterboard.

The process has its own environmental impacts, such as quarrying limestone. The process also decreases the efficiency of the power station by about 5 per cent – note the slightly increased carbon dioxide emissions shown in Figure 8.16. FGD is generally expected to add between 0.35p and 0.55p per kilowatt-hour to the cost of generating electricity, although costs will fall as FGD technology is developed.

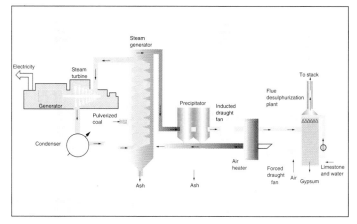

▲ **Figure 8.13** A typical coal-fired power station with flue gas desulphurization.

UK government plans have shrunk from fitting 34GW of plant with FGD in 1992, to fitting only 8GW, once it was realized that the sulphur dioxide emission limits could be met by switching to gas and to imported coal.

Nitrogen oxide control

Nitrogen oxides form during combustion, depending on temperature and the availability of oxygen. Low nitrogen oxide burners can be installed on either new or existing boilers. They work by controlling the initial mixing of air and fuel to maintain temperatures and oxygen levels at the minimum level necessary for effective combustion.

Fluidized bed combustion (FBC)

FBC uses a continuous stream of combustion air or oxygen to create turbulence within a bed of fine particles of coal. At a certain level, particles begin to behave like a liquid and become 'fluidized'. A fine stream of coal can be added and ignited at a lower temperature than normal combustion (Figure 8.14). This process is not as well developed in the UK as FGD, and the largest commercially operating plant is a 165MW plant in Canada. However, its future potential could be high if investment is made in research and development.

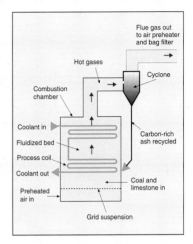

▲ **Figure 8.14** Fluidization of solids.

Combined heat and power (CHP)

The steam cycles within power stations mean that there will always be unavoidable heat loss. However, reflected heat can be used in providing heating for nearby homes, offices, and factories within district heating systems (Figure 8.15). Within power stations this heat is usually lost in the cooling towers. It can therefore increase the efficiency of the power station from 35 per cent to 80 per cent.

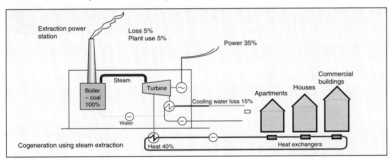

◀ **Figure 8.15** Combined heat and power.

The use of this system is restricted by economics. Laying heat pipes around a neighbourhood is costly. There needs to be nearby demand for heat in the first place. Some Scandinavian countries have used economic incentives like subsidies and taxation benefits to encourage development of CHP and district heating systems.

	Sulphur dioxide	Nitrogen oxides	Carbon dioxide
Coal (average UK)	1.0	1.0	1.0
Coal (typical imported)	0.5	1.0	1.0
Coal with FGD and low NO$_2$ burners	0.1	0.6	1.0
High-sulphur fuel oil without FGD	1.2	0.7	0.8
Gas (CCGT)	0.0	0.2	0.5
'Clean coal'	0.05–0.1	0.3–0.4	0.7–0.9
Nuclear	0	0	0
Renewables (excl. waste and landfill)	0	0	0

◀ **Figure 8.16** Relative emissions from different generating technologies (assumes average UK coal =1).

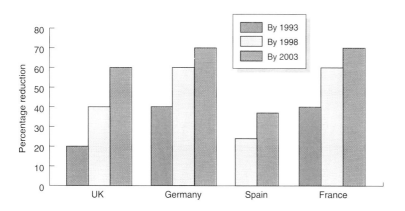

(a) Sulphur reduction targets, from 1980 levels.

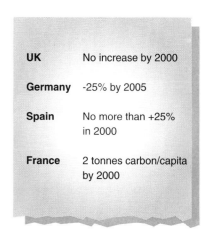

(b) Carbon dioxide targets, from a 1990 base.

▲ **Figure 8.17** Sulphur and carbon dioxide targets for selected European countries.

▼ **Figure 8.18** Using coal in Britain: outlook on the future.

Britain Still 'Dirty Man of Europe' Despite Clean Air Plant

Britain, long lampooned as the 'Dirty Man of Europe' for its pollution record, is building the world's biggest plant to curb acid rain. But the country, the largest producer of sulphur dioxide in Western Europe, will still be a laggard in the acid rain fight, environmentalists say.

The giant £700 million plant with ducts wider than the Channel Tunnel is being piggybacked onto Europe's largest coal-fired power station in north Yorkshire to remove its sulphur dioxide emissions which cause acid rain. By the time the plant is finished in 1996, it will cut 90 per cent of the more than 250 000 tonnes of sulphur dioxide emitted each year from the Drax power station, named after a nearby village.

But environmentalists say the plant is not enough to clean up Britain's poor image on environmental issues. Britain, whose coal has a higher sulphur content than many other countries, has resisted international pressure to curb its acid rain output to 80 per cent of 1980 levels by the year 2000.

'Britain will still be the dirty man of Europe', Friends of the Earth spokeswoman Fiona Weir said. 'Our clean-up plans are pitiful compared with other industrialized countries.' Britain has so far committed itself to cutting its sulphur dioxide emissions to 60 per cent of 1980 levels by 2003. Britain is mainly cutting its sulphur dioxide output by shutting down coal plants and switching to natural gas, which is cleaner.

'Britain has effectively said it will not put adequate sulphur dioxide prevention in place until most of its coal plants reach the end of their natural lives,' Weir said.

Coal imports are the most immediate threat [to the market for British Coal]. If the contracts between the generators and British Coal for 1993/94 and 1994/95 only reach 40 million tonnes and 30 million tonnes respectively, it is reasonable to suppose that the generators will contract for imports [to make up the shortfall – in 1993, 66 million tonnes of coal were used for electricity generation]. The delivered cost of British Coal remains higher than that of imported coal at most power stations, although the gap has been narrowing.

The sulphur content of British coal varies by coalfield, by pit, and even by individual seam, but the average is about 1.6 per cent, whereas the sulphur content of internationally traded steam coal is typically between 0.8 and 1.0 per cent. Many low-sulphur UK mines have closed, such as those in Kent. Thus the sulphur dioxide emissions limits could eventually force generators to use increasing quantities of imported coal.

(a) From Reuter's *Asia-Pacific Business Report*, 1 February 1994.

(b) From *British Energy Policy and the Market for Coal*, House of Commons Trade and Industry Select Committee 1993.

We have already considered the impact of opencast mining. Figure 8.7 outlines trends in opencast mining in the UK. The government plans to expand production, though the Department of the Environment is currently considering new planning laws governing applications for planning permission.

1 Summarize the main elements of coal policy in the UK.

2 Describe the main impacts of coal policy in the UK under three main headings: Economic, Social, and Environmental. You should refer both to how coal is produced and how it is used.

3 Critically evaluate UK coal policy, highlighting the major benefits and problems that it has produced.

4 How reversible are the changes in the coal industry? You might need to carry out further research using other secondary sources of information.

World overview of coal

Coal is the most abundant fossil fuel worldwide. At the end of 1993, proven reserves were estimated to last 236 years at current rates of production, compared with only 65 years for gas and 43 years for oil.

Figure 8.19 shows the distribution of the world's proven reserves of coal. There is a more even spread of coal reserves than oil, with massive concentrations of oil reserves within the Middle East, and gas reserves in the Middle East and Russia. Even so, Figure 8.20 shows that over half the world's coal reserves are concentrated in three countries, although these three cover a large area of the world's landmass. Estimates also vary in their accuracy. In 1987 China was believed to have over 45 per cent of the world's proven coal reserves but a more recent survey drastically downgraded this estimate as a high proportion is considered unrecoverable under current economic and technical conditions. However, some Chinese sources still emphasize the higher estimates.

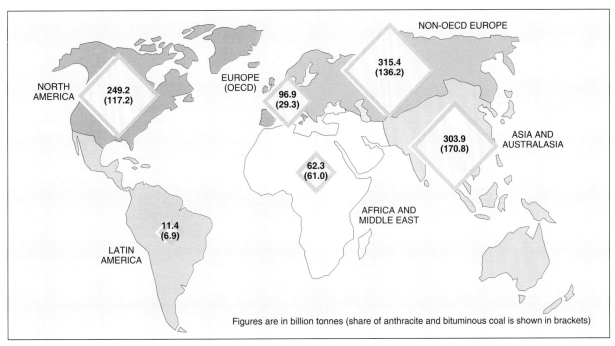

Figures are in billion tonnes (share of anthracite and bituminous coal is shown in brackets)

▲ **Figure 8.19** Proven world reserves of coal at the end of 1993.

	Anthracite and bituminous coal	Sub-bituminous coal and lignite	Total	Share of total	R/P ratio
	(million tonnes)			(%)	(yrs)
Former Soviet Union	104 000	137 000	241 000	23.2	446
USA	112 668	127 892	240 560	23.1	280
China	62 200	52 300	114 500	11.0	100
Australia	45 340	45 600	90 940	8.0	393
Germany	23 919	56 150	80 069	7.7	286
India	60 649	1 900	62 548	6.0	234

▲ **Figure 8.20** Estimated proven coal reserves for selected countries in 1993.

Figure 8.20 also emphasizes how long proven reserves are likely to last at current rates of production. Even without any future increase in the price of fuel or improvement in extraction technology, coal will be an important energy source for many decades.

Coal in China

Read the two extracts in Figure 8.21. They concern the growing emission of pollutant gases derived from burning fossil fuels in the ELDCs, as industrialization takes place.

▼ **Figure 8.21** Developing countries and the environmental dilemma.

Despite growing energy efficiency, developing countries will suffer from their growing energy needs. But economic growth is leading to greater public concern for pollution problems. Unfortunately, public concern and the development of advanced abatement technology will do little to affect the accumulation of heat-trapping gases in the atmosphere.

While many forms of pollution will be reduced in Asia, the International Energy Agency (IEA) and the World Energy Council (WEC) have forecast an alarming 50 per cent growth in carbon dioxide emissions by 2010. WEC further forecasts a 50–100 per cent growth by 2020. The key with global warming is 'not how fast stuffing is added to the greenhouse blanket, but how thick it is' – gas concentration rather than emission. WEC estimates that even if emissions are kept to 1990 levels through 2020 – an unlikely scenario – carbon dioxide concentrations would rise by about two-thirds as much as in the 200 previous years, or nearly double by 2100.

The IEA believes India and China will represent 25 per cent of the world's CO_2 emissions by 2010 because of their plan to rely on their coal reserves for increasing energy needs. By 2000, China will burn 1.4 billion tonnes of coal annually – one-third of 1992's global output.

(a) 'Growing Energy Needs in Developing Countries Add to Global Warming Woes', from *Network Online Today*, 20 June 1994.

Pollution-choked China will have a chance to demonstrate its concern for global green issues when it hosts a meeting on the restructuring of the Global Environment Facility (GEF) this week in Beijing. Delegates from at least 60 countries are expected to discuss the pilot phase of the GEF, which provides grants to developing countries for projects that will cut greenhouse gas emissions. The US$1.3 billion fund is being managed by the World Bank, the UN Development Programme (UNDP), and the UN Environment Programme (UNEP).

To participate in the GEF, however, developing countries need to post an 'entrance fee' of 4 million Special Drawing Rights, a form of international reserve currency. Asian activists have said this places too much of the burden on the South. They say the North, which is guilty of causing global warming because of its wasteful ways, is instead trying to shift the blame onto the Third World.

For instance, even with its population of 1.2 billion people, China is only the world's third largest producer of greenhouse gases, following the United States and the former Soviet bloc. The New Delhi-based Centre for Science and Environment notes that the United States and Canada, which have just 10 per cent of the world's estimated population of 5 billion, give off 40 per cent of the carbon dioxide and two-thirds of the net global emissions of methane.

Although Beijing has repeatedly said economic growth comes first before the environment, it has recognized that global warming may also harm its plans. Indeed, one of China's papers submitted to last year's Earth Summit noted that global warming has created drought, desertification, and alkalinization in the country itself, and has led to the spread of pests and diseases.

Last month, Beijing unveiled an ambitious programme aimed at phasing out the use of ozone-unfriendly chemicals by the year 2010. But China's environmental pollution problems come largely from its use of high-sulphur coal, which accounts for 74 per cent of the country's energy.

(b) 'China to lead South vs North in Global Environment Meet', from Inter Press Service, 24 May 1993.

Form groups of three or four people.

1 Write a short speech as if you were a Chinese politician presenting China's concerns regarding global warming to a meeting of the United Nations.

2 Briefly outline what your response to the speech would be if you were in a position of power as the UK or US representative at the same meeting.

Trends in coal trade, production, and consumption

A number of different factors affect the use of coal. High extraction costs and its relatively high environmental impact are significant. Coal is also difficult to transport, both within and between countries. See Figures 8.22 and 8.23.

> Write an extended essay entitled 'Coal – a changing resource'. Ensure that you:
> a) Explain, with reference to Figures 8.22, 8.23 and other resources, changes in coal production and consumption.
> b) Outline how you think trends in coal consumption and production will develop over the next ten years, and why.

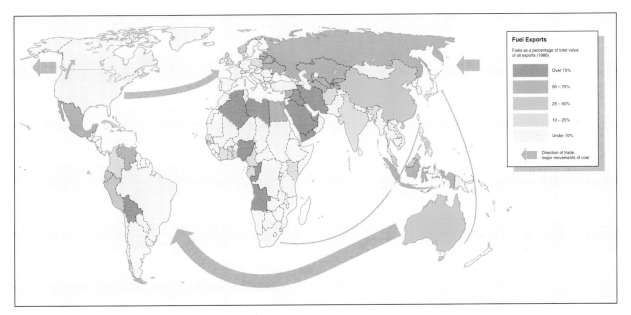

▲ **Figure 8.22** World coal trade movements.

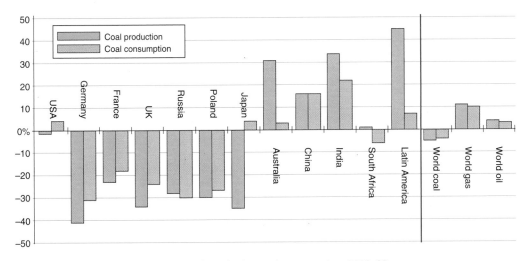

▲ **Figure 8.23** Percentage change in coal production and consumption, 1988–93.

Tin – a precarious resource

Read Figure 8.24. It tells a tale that is familiar to people living in Cornwall – that the future of their single surviving tin mine at South Crofty is in jeopardy. In Britain, such news is unfortunately frequent, as has been shown in the case study of coal in this chapter. What are the underlying issues that make the tin industry so susceptible to closure? This case study looks at the influence of production and market factors. If you have read Chapters 4–7, some of the processes that lie beneath the surface will be familiar to you.

Lee Williams, 17, stood at the pit-head in his bright new yellow work gear, proud to be following in his father's footsteps as a Cornish tin-miner.

The Friday before he clocked on for the first time, news broke that the South Crofty mine – the last in Cornwall – was to close. As in the past, the report was premature. But after a week of following his father Clevedon into the eight-man cages that take the miners underground, Lee's prospects remain uncertain.

'I was lucky to get the job and when I saw the news on telly I feared the worst,' he says. 'The older men say there's still plenty of tin down there, it's just whether we will be allowed to mine it.'

Kevin Ross, the mine's managing director, knows that, despite major savings which have seen the 500-strong workforce slashed by half and miners taking a pay cut, the company loses money on each tonne of tin it produces. The price needs to be £3750 a tonne to break even, and the current price is only £3370. He remembers halcyon days when the market broke the £10 000 barrier.

'We believe the price will rise, but we have to survive in the short term. We are walking closer to the cliff edge than we would like,' said Mr Ross.

▲ **Figure 8.24** From *The Observer*, 30 January 1994.

Where is tin found?

	1977	1982	1987	1991
		(thousand metric tonnes)		
China	20.0	15.0	20.0	43.0
Brazil	6.4	8.2	30.4	30.0
Indonesia	24.0	33.8	26.1	25.0
Bolivia	32.6	26.8	8.1	15.3
Thailand	24.2	26.1	14.9	15.0
Malaysia	58.7	52.3	30.4	14.3
Former Soviet Union	33.0	21.0	16.0	10.0
Portugal	0.5	0.4	0.1	6.5
Australia	10.0	12.1	7.7	6.4
Peru	0.3	1.7	5.3	6.0
Ten countries total	209.7	197.5	158.9	171.5
World total	231.4	219.5	181.3	179.5
World reserves 1992 (000 metric tonnes)				8000
World reserve base 1992 (000 metric tonnes)				10 000

▲ **Figure 8.25** World annual production of tin, 1977–91. (Some totals have been rounded).

Who produces tin?

1 On an outline map of the world, mark in the top ten tin producers.

2 Describe the location of tin production around the world.

3 For these ten countries choose a graphical way to display the figures for 1977 to 1991 to show the change over this period.

4 Describe what has happened during this time. In whose power does production *seem* to lie?

Tin – the nature of the resource

There are a number of tin-bearing ores but only one, cassiterite, is of economic importance, containing in its purest form 78 per cent tin. Cassiterite is found in two kinds of location.

- In thin, generally irregular veins (known as lodes) in granite. Lode deposits have a higher percentage of metal but there are fewer of them – they are found mainly in Bolivia and in Cornwall, England.
- In alluvial deposits of river beds and valleys. These are formed when granite is weathered, and sediment is carried away by water or wind. Rivers deposit mineral particles separately from other materials, because they are heavier, and they then

become concentrated as a reserve of ore known as a 'placer' deposit. Most of the world's tin comes from low-grade alluvial deposits – that is, they contain more waste material than usable tin. One of the features of tin mining is the enormous amount of waste produced.

Unlike deposits of other metals, tin deposits tend to be small, and few tin mines exceed an annual output of 2000 tonnes. This contrasts with copper mines which often have an output of over 40 000 tonnes. Much of the world's tin has come from a large number of small businesses – an annual output of 30 tonnes per site is common.

Selecting graphs

The skill in using graphs lies in knowing which kind of graph is most appropriate for your purpose. This technique box is designed to help you decide a purpose in presenting graphs: line graphs, bar graphs, divided bar graphs, pie charts, and scatter graphs. Graphs are used to show quantities, comparisons, trends, and relationships.

Quantities

Quantities are used in measuring amounts at a point in time – numbers of pedestrians, total coal produced, for example. They always express a unit of measurement – tonnes, kilometres, litres, etc. Graphs that show quantities at a point in time include bar graphs, divided bar graphs, and histograms.

Comparisons

Sometimes we wish to compare sets of data. For instance, in Figure 8.19, Europe has 96.9 billion tonnes of coal, of which 29.3 billion tonnes are anthracite and bituminous coal. Africa has less coal overall – 62.3 billion tonnes – but more anthracite and bituminous coal (61 billion tonnes). In percentages, 30.2 per cent of Europe's coal is anthracite and bituminous, whereas 97.9 per cent of Africa's coal is of these types. Although the data could be shown using bar graphs, pie charts and divided bar graphs showing percentages illustrate the quality of Africa's coal more effectively.

Trends

Sometimes, data are available over a period of time. Population, for example, is recorded during a census, held in the UK at ten-yearly intervals. Plotting each census point on a graph identifies changes and trends. Changes are specific – that is, by how much a population has increased or decreased between two census points. Trends show several points plotted together in order to see what is happening generally: Is population continuing to increase? Is it increasing more rapidly than it was? Line graphs show trends clearly.

Relationships

Data are often used to investigate relationships. For example, as GDP increases, so too does energy use. GDP and energy use are examples of **variables**. Variables are measurements of criteria that can be used to explore a relationship. For example, scatter graphs show two variables, one plotted on the vertical y axis, and the other on the horizontal x axis. The purpose of the graph is to show whether, when plotted, the data could be linked – that is, show a relationship. Detailed steps explaining how to draw a scatter graph are shown on pages 197–8.

Uses and users of tin

Tin has several special properties, and it is used in a variety of ways. It is soft and malleable, has a low melting point, and is resistant to corrosion. One of its most important uses has been as a coating for other metals that are prone to oxidation or corrosion.

	1977	1982	1987	1991
			(thousand metric tonnes)	
USA	47.6	46.3	37.0	37.1
Japan	29.7	28.7	32.6	34.9
China	14.0	12.5	16.5	23.2
Germany	17.6	16.8	19.8	19.2
Former Soviet Union	25.0	27.0	29.0	17.0
UK	14.9	10.4	9.8	10.3
France	9.8	8.2	7.4	8.2
Netherlands	6.2	5.4	4.9	6.2
Brazil	4.8	4.9	7.9	6.2
South Korea	0.8	2.1	5.8	5.9
Ten countries total	170.4	162.3	170.7	168.2
World total	232.5	215.4	229.1	218.2
World reserves life index (years)				45
World reserve base life index (years)				56

Who consumes ?

1 Add the top ten tin consumers to your map of tin production.

2 Describe and suggest reasons for the difference in patterns of production and consumption.

◄ **Figure 8.26** World annual consumption of tin.

181

Production methods

Tin is mined in three main ways: by dredging, both on- and offshore; by gravel pumping; and by opencast and underground mining.

Dredging

Dredgers are used for obtaining 'placer' deposits. They are ships which are used either at sea or on an artificial lake, and they scrape the bed for tin-bearing material using a chain of buckets. Some separation of tin ore from the waste is done on board and the waste is pumped overboard.

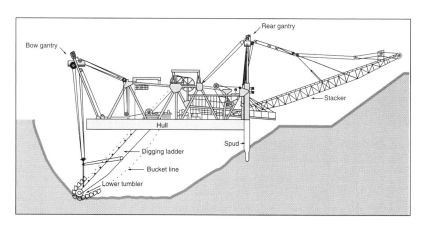

▶ **Figure 8.27** How a dredger works.

Gravel pumps

These deal with difficult alluvial deposits. In Malaysia, deposits of tin are found on an uneven bedrock of limestone with pinnacles which could damage a dredger. Powerful jets of water are used to break up alluvium which is then pumped into a sluice where heavier tin ore is tapped and lighter waste poured away.

Mining

Where veins or lode deposits are near the surface, they are reached by opencast extraction, using earth-movers. Deeper veins involve underground mining, sometimes at great depth. Mines vary considerably in size. Globally, mining is less important than it was in 1900, as a result of the development of dredging, particularly in South-East Asia.

The environmental impacts of tin production

Extraction can be the cause of two main environmental problems:

- *Water pollution* Both mining and the processing involve a great deal of water which, once used, carries a lot of suspended sediment. If discharged into rivers, sediment may cause difficulties further downstream. Underground mines often need water pumped out of them and this may cause pollution problems even after the mines are closed. Figure 8.28 describes an incident which happened in 1992 in Cornwall, where metals polluted local rivers.

● *Land disturbance* Where mining takes place onshore, surface disturbance and ecological damage are key issues. This may be tackled with land reclamation – land is re-contoured and attempts are made to return it to its former state. Underground mining creates problems of subsidence, which persists long after mines have been closed down. In Cornwall, 19th-century shafts still cause subsidence.

Toxic leak threatens shellfish

Concern was growing last night about the threat to Cornish shellfish beds and fish stocks from millions of litres of heavily contaminated water which has escaped from a disused tin mine.

In one of Britain's worst pollution incidents, water from the Wheal Jane mine, near Truro, containing high levels of toxic heavy metals including cadmium, zinc, and arsenic, has spread down the river Carnon and into the Carrick Roads estuary off Falmouth. The reddish-brown slick has passed over almost 1600 hectares of oyster beds in the river Fal and is moving into the sea.

Last night fishermen and oyster farmers were holding emergency talks with environmental health officers about a sales ban. Samples of water and shellfish are being analysed by scientists from the agriculture ministry and the National Rivers Authority. Although the results may take several days to come through, it is known that contamination levels are among the highest recorded in Britain.

Water began to build up in the mine after pumping stopped when it was closed down last March, and burst through a shaft in November. Carnon Consolidated, the mine owners, pumped the water away for treatment with NRA co-operation and financial help. The operation stopped on 4 January and on Monday night the water burst out through another shaft.

▲ **Figure 8.28** From *The Times*, 17 January 1992.

▲ **Figure 8.29** The effect of metal pollution on the River Fal. The slick affected local oyster beds.

World prices and production

1 **a)** Study Figure 8.30 and describe the trends in both production and price.

   b) Suggest why the two may be linked.

2 Suggest possible reasons for the collapse in price in 1985.

The global economy and tin production

The exploitation of tin, in common with other minerals, is not only affected by the availability of reserves and the technology to mine them. Demand and market price also affect whether or not the mineral is exploited. The effects of the global tin market on individual countries are illustrated in the following case studies.

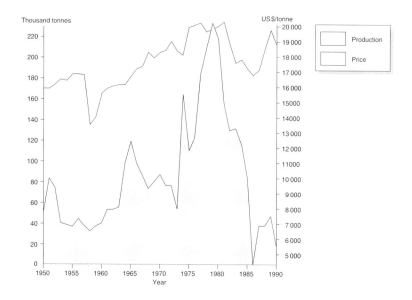

▶ **Figure 8.30** Tin prices and volumes produced.

Tin in Malaysia

Malaysia was once the world's leading tin producer but as Figure 8.31a shows, the industry has declined recently. As a newly industrializing country (NIC), Malaysia has been able to diversify into other economic activities so is not dependent on its tin industry. However, there are certain locations within the country which, like Cornwall, are experiencing problems of unemployment as decline sets in although, as costs are lower for dredging tin (Figure 8.31b), it could be resumed should the price of tin later increase.

▼ **Figure 8.31** Tin mining in Malaysia.

Production of tin (tonnes)	World price ($/kg)
1993 10 384	1993 13
1992 14 339	1981 32–34
1991 20 710	(production
1990 28 468	costs = 16)

Number of mines	Number of miners
1993 less than 70	1993 4000
1990 141	1980 39 000
	1913 200 000

(a) Selected statistics on Malaysia's tin-mining industry.

(b) Dredging tin in Malaysia.

Sungei Lembing tin mine

Some of Malaysia's tin is mined deep underground. Sungei Lembing is Malaysia's largest underground tin mine. It has over 700 000 tonnes of proven and probable ore reserves, containing nearly 10 000 tonnes of recoverable metal. Grade of ore varies from 1.5 per cent to 15 per cent. However, it is only partially open, employing only 55 miners compared with 5000 in the first half of the 19th century. At its peak, production was 4000 tonnes a year, but it only produced 744 tonnes in 1986, its last year of full production. The British owners went into liquidation after the sharp fall in tin prices in 1985, and the mine closed and was flooded in 1987.

The mine is currently owned by a local partnership which bought it in 1989 with a loan from the Commonwealth Development Corporation. It is the first lode tin mine to be re-opened since the 1985 price crash, but it is not yet fully opened. Output is still low while costs of pumping water out of the re-opened sections are high. However, the owners are optimistic, believing that tin is, and will remain, a vital part of many products. They are supported by the local community, which suffered from the closure of the mine.

The Cornish tin mining industry

Cornwall used to be one of the largest tin producers in the world, exploiting lode deposits by way of underground mines. However, only one mine is operating now, and that has been threatened on several occasions. The decline of the industry is due to the use of substitutes for tin. Aluminium has replaced tin cans for food and drink, and the collapse in world tin prices shattered confidence in 1985. Much effort has been put into saving South Crofty, the surviving mine, as is shown in Figures 8.24 and 8.32.

▼ **Figure 8.32** Can South Crofty survive?

The UK's last operating tin mine has won its fight for life.

Mr Kevin Ross, managing director of the South Crofty mine near Camborne, Cornwall, announced yesterday morning that applications for an offer of shares in the company had reached £1.15m, beating the minimum requirement under a survival package agreed with the government by £150 000 and the Thursday midnight deadline by a few hours.

The government will write off loans totalling £23.4m. Also, RTZ, the world's biggest mining company, which sold South Crofty and its sister mine Wheal Jane to management and employees in 1985, will forgive loans of £7.7m.

The survival of the 400-year-old mine and the jobs of its 260 employees are now assured for a year to 18 months. But Mr Ross believed the company's position was now actually stronger than that.

At about £3300 a tonne, the world tin price remains nearly £700 below the level that South Crofty needs to make a decent profit. But Mr Ross said the outlook was improving.

(a) From the *Financial Times*, 6 August 1994.

Read through the case studies of Malaysia and Cornwall.

1 Identify the similarities in the situations described.

2 What are the social and environmental implications of mine closures in the two places? How do these compare with the coal industry?

(b) South Crofty tin mine, Cornwall.

Bolivia and tin-mining

Bolivia is an ELDC which has traditionally been heavily dependent on its mineral resources. Until 1985 tin was the most important of these, earning 70 per cent of export earnings (US$266 million) in 1981, but with the collapse of the world market this had dwindled to US$83 million in 1986. Compare these earnings with the annual sales and profits of multinational enterprises (MNEs) shown in Chapter 4. As a result of the 1985 price collapse, half of the country's mines closed, 28 000 miners were made redundant, and efforts were put into exploiting other minerals. In 1993 nearly half of Bolivia's export earnings still came from minerals

Until recently the mining of tin and other deposits has been carried out by a mining corporation owned and run by the state called Corporacion Minera de Bolivia (Comibol). However, because it made a loss of US$662 million between 1981 and 1991, the government took the decision to privatize it and to encourage investment from overseas, and from other sectors of the economy. Overseas companies were invited to enter into joint ventures with Bolivians; in return they were offered tax incentives and opportunities to search for minerals in previously unexplored territory within the country. These and other incentives are described in Chapter 7, on pages 148–9. In 1991 only four overseas companies operated in Bolivia, but by 1993 this had risen to 40, and Comibol's control of tin mining enterprises had dropped to 35 per cent. Interest in mining operations in Bolivia has come from MNEs based in Australia, Canada, Brazil, Germany, and South Africa.

Because of the amount of investment required to open a mine, much development of minerals such as tin is carried out by MNEs. The involvement of MNEs is controversial. On the one hand, they possess huge reserves of capital for investment, but on the other they divert profits back to their home country, and are inclined to close down operations overseas when political or economic climates change. Not everyone agrees that the involvement of MNEs is a good thing: trade unions, which are strong in the mining sector, take the view that MNEs are only interested in profit, rather than in helping the country to develop.

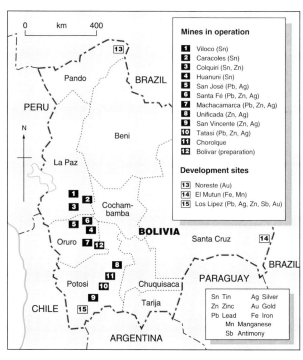

▲ **Figure 8.33** Location of the main mineral mines in Bolivia.

ELDCs and the role of multinational enterprises

1 How would the reduction in export earnings affect Bolivia? Explain what it means for the country socially, economically, politically, and environmentally.

2 What does this tell you about:
   a) the economy of ELDCs
   b) the economic stability of countries that depend heavily on mineral exports?

3 Could such issues be resolved by ELDCs alone? What actions might help them?

4 Suggest why RTZ sold South Crofty in Cornwall in 1985.

5 Sungei Lembing in Malaysia is run by a local independent partnership. Compare this form of ownership with joint ventures with overseas companies in Bolivia.

6 In pairs, consider the advantages and disadvantages of handing over control of mineral development to a number of MNEs, instead of to a single state company.

What future is there for tin mining?

Study Figure 8.34. It describes how in August 1994 there were concerns about the future of South Crofty mine because of the overseas competition posed by China and Brazil. Deposits which have recently been developed in China are entering the world market. The fall in price has so far been smaller than the 1985 price crash. However, the worries of Cornish tin producers are not all one-sided. Note in Figure 8.34 the concerns of the Tin Council, and how in order to hold up the price of tin, it had accumulated and stored over 40 000 tonnes of tin. Now the price is falling and the Tin Council is faced with the possibility of having to release some of its stocks onto a world market already flush with tin from China and Brazil.

How can this situation be resolved? Should producers control market supplies and prices? Should they be angry when ELDCs over-produce minerals in attempts to resolve debt burdens? If you have read Chapter 5, you will know how people's lives are often affected by international processes far removed from where they live and work. You might like to consider what has happened with tin and coal, and draw comparisons. Who is in control?

▼ **Figure 8.34** From the *Financial Times*, 12 August 1994.

Chinese tin exports rattle a fragile market

The possibility that Britain's last operating tin mine – South Crofty, near Redruth – might close down raised emotions in Cornwall but it created not a ripple of interest elsewhere in an industry decimated over the past ten years by mine and smelter closures.

Those left in the industry are obsessed by one question: when will the Chinese government gain tighter control over its recalcitrant tin miners and stop them pouring exports into the West? These exports, they claim, are destabilizing the market and prevent tin producers from benefiting from the improve-ment in world economic activity.

'We expected the tin price to reach about US$6000 a tonne by now,' says Mr Fidelis Madavo, tin specialist at the CRU International consultancy group. 'But here it is struggling along at US$5000 to US$5100.'

The tin market has been in turmoil since the sudden collapse in 1985 of a price support scheme operated by the producers' International Tin Council which was backed by the governments. The huge stocks accumulated by the ITC – more than 40 000 tonnes – have been a malign influence on prices ever since.

In an effort to whittle away the former ITC stocks, a group of producers formed the Association of Tin Producing Countries – its aim is to voluntarily restrict exports. The scheme has not worked well. Unexpected and unrestrained exports from Brazil – not a member of the ATPC – caused havoc in the early years.

Then China, now the world's biggest producer, continued to pump large quantities of the metal into export markets.

Assessing the future prospects of tin mining

1 Using information from Figure 8.34, assess the future prospects for the tin-mining enterprises in Cornwall, Malaysia, and Bolivia. What impact are producers in Brazil and China likely to have?

2 What similarities are there between what has happened recently in the tin and coal industries?

3 In groups of two or three, select one of the following arguments and defend it.

- 'Resource producers are entitled to take whatever action is necessary to protect prices.'
- 'There is no point in complaining about the production strategies adopted by ELDCs – they're only trying to pay off debt.'
- 'Production of any mineral should be left to market forces at all times, with no private or public controls.'
- 'The only solution to the alternate cycles of high and low prices is to plan globally.'
- 'The real sufferer under the present system of producing minerals is the environment.'

Ideas for further study

1 Choose one of the clean coal technologies discussed in this chapter. Write to your local electricity company and ask for information about its policies concerning this. Ask for technical, economic, and environmental information associated with such developments.

2 Investigate the debate about emission permits for greenhouse gases. You should consider:
a) EU and global agreements on emission targets
b) problems, and who stands to benefit from different approaches.

Summary

- Resource use is increasing in the EMDCs (economically more developed countries), and demand for a share in their use is rising sharply in ELDCs. This has implications for resource life.
- Resources may be seen as finite, recyclable, or infinite. Each requires different strategies for management. Finite resources have limited life, and their use needs to be controlled – these are known as stocks. Others are replenishable and are known as flows.
- Resource use has social, economic, and environmental consequences.
- Energy production requires management, both in terms of the resources that it uses and the effects that such uses may have. Both uses and effects depend largely on technology.
- Resource use depends on political decision-making. Sometimes, in market economies, few decisions are made, and resource use lies in the hands of individuals. This has implications for resource life. At other times, governments intervene directly, such as in the UK coal industry.
- Although many resources are located within ELDCs, their management and use lie largely within the control of EMDCs.

References and further reading

British Geological Survey, *World Mineral Statistics, 1986–90*.

J. Houghton, *Global Warming: the complete briefing*, Lion Publishing, 1994.

McGraw-Hill, *Encyclopedia of Science and Technology*, Vol.18, 1992.

N. Myers, *The Gaia Atlas of Planet Management*, Gaia Books Ltd, 1993.

W. Robertson, *Tin: Its Production and Marketing*, Croom Helm, 1982.

9 The use and misuse of water

Water: too much or not enough

This chapter looks at water, its supply, and its use in three countries. In Bangladesh, a country where flooding has been a major issue, managing water availability is explored. Water shortage is then investigated in Mexico. Both countries are primarily concerned with quantity of water. Finally, issues concerning quality of water in the UK, raised in the introduction to this section, are discussed.

Globally, there is a finite amount of water, which remains constant because of its recyclable nature. Of the Earth's total supply, about 3 per cent is fresh – that is, about $40000km^2$ of fresh water is potentially available for human use. Since present human consumption is the equivalent of $4000km^2$, only 10 per cent of the annual renewable supply is used. However, the supply of and demand for water are complex issues. Figure 9.1 shows how global demand for water is rising as populations grow and living standards rise. Figure 9.2 shows how all uses are increasing in demand. There is increasing likelihood of conflicts between different users. For example, $15000m^3$ of water could either be used to irrigate 1 hectare of rice, or supply 100 nomads and 450 head of livestock for three years, or provide house connections for 100 rural families for four years, or 100 urban families for two years, or 100 guests in a luxury hotel for 55 days.

Available fresh water is distributed unevenly over the Earth. About two-thirds runs off in floods, leaving $14000km^2$ as a relatively stable supply. Much of this is needed to safeguard wetlands, deltas, lakes, and rivers and will probably be left to follow its natural course. The management of environments does not always fit with human needs for water, as can be seen in the case study of Bangladesh.

Use of water

1 Five different uses for $15000m^3$ of water are given in the text.
   a) Are all five of equal priority? Justify your answer.
   b) Should all five uses be charged at the same rate by water companies?

2 Examine Figures 9.1 and 9.2 and comment on future trends in water consumption.

▼ **Figure 9.1** Water consumption by continent, 1900–2000.

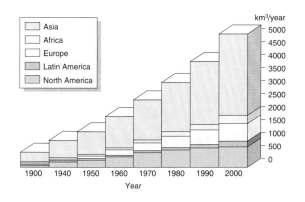

▼ **Figure 9.2** Global water uses, 1950–2000.

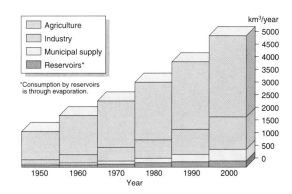

Water management in Bangladesh

The hydrological background

Water is central to the way of life in Bangladesh. As much as 80 per cent of the country consists of the floodplains of the Ganges, Brahmaputra (Jamuna), Meghna, and several smaller rivers which together form one of the world's largest delta systems. The climate is predominately tropical monsoon and the main rivers have a seasonal flow, reflecting the seasons of the monsoon. The rivers are huge – the average peak flow of the lower Meghna is about 2.5 times greater than that of the Mississippi. The three main rivers and their tributaries drain an area of more than 1.5 million km^2 (Figure 9.3). Water plays a dominant role throughout the year – in the monsoon season there is a huge amount of it, but frequently in the late winter there is a drought (Figure 9.4).

▶ **Figure 9.3** Catchment area of the major rivers of Bangladesh.

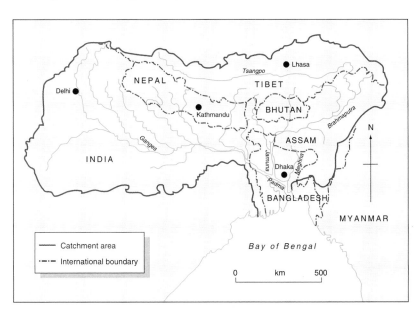

▼ **Figure 9.4** Seasonal rainfall.

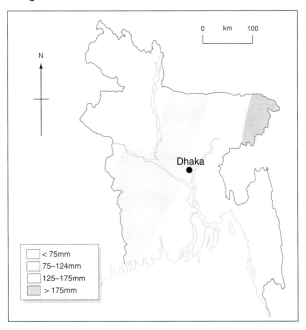

(a) Dry season, November–March.

(b) Rainy season, June–October.

Hydrological background

1 Use Figure 9.4 to describe the annual pattern of precipitation in Bangladesh.

2 a) Draw a large sketch map of Figure 9.3.
  b) Shade Bangladesh, and estimate the proportion of the river catchment that it occupies.

3 Use an atlas to annotate your map with the catchment area's relief, land use, and vegetation.

4 How are rivers in Bangladesh affected by precipitation patterns a) within Bangladesh, and b) elsewhere within the catchment area?

5 What difficulties do you think this presents for Bangladesh in trying to manage its water resources?

Life on the floodplains

News of catastrophic floods in Bangladesh brings that country to our attention from time to time. However, flooding is essential to the livelihood of most of the 120 million people who live there, and to the country's economy. The way of life is closely linked to the floodplain environment: settlements are on floodplain ridges, with individual houses on raised earth mounds; roads and railways are on embankments; and fish production and fishing are important activities, particularly in the monsoon. Agriculture is the main economic activity, with rice occupying 80 per cent of the cropped area. It is grown in three seasons: two crops (*aus* and *aman*) are mainly grown under rainfed, flooded conditions during the *kharif* (wet) season, while the other crop (*boro*) is irrigated during the *rabi* (dry) season. Farmers use thousands of rice varieties to suit local environments, including deepwater varieties for areas that may be flooded up to 5m deep. Individual farmers generally grow several

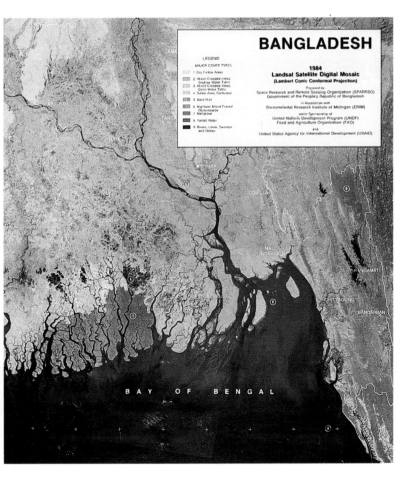

1 Study Figure 9.5 and estimate a) the total, and b) the individual percentages of land cover types – shown by different colours – that depend on the presence of water.

2 a) Draw a sketch map based on Figure 9.6.
  b) Using information in the text, annotate your sketch to show the influence of the rivers on land use.

◄ **Figure 9.5** Satellite image of land cover in central and southern Bangladesh.

varieties adapted to different depths and duration of flooding, which spreads the risks, makes the most of their labour use, and exploits market opportunities.

Floodwaters cover 35–55 per cent of the country during the monsoon period and are generally beneficial. They play a key role in supporting agriculture: groundwater aquifers are recharged, and floodplain soils are enriched so that crops can be grown without the use of expensive agrochemicals. Floodwaters also play an important role in the migration and breeding of fish caught by rural families. In Bangladesh 75 per cent of animal protein is supplied by fish, and fisheries contribute 12 per cent of annual export earnings.

▶ **Figure 9.6** Settlements on the floodplain.

Characteristics of flooding in Bangladesh

It is useful to distinguish between 'normal' flooding to which farmers' cropping practices are well adapted, and 'damaging' floods which occur when water rises earlier, higher, more rapidly, or later than farmers expect. High or sudden floods may also breach road, rail, and flood embankments, and submerge settlements and industrial sites.

Floods can be classified into four main types:

1 *Flash floods* result from exceptionally heavy rainfall over neighbouring mountains, and occur in upland areas where rivers from India enter the north and east of the country. Crops may be damaged, and large amounts of sediment deposited which silt up river channels.

2 *River floods* result from snowmelt in the Himalayas and heavy monsoon rainfall in river catchments. Generally these are beneficial, because they carry alluvial deposits, but they may cause damage when they occur early in June along the Brahmaputra and Meghna, or late after mid-August along all rivers, because then they damage crops at a critical stage of growth. Flooding is particularly serious when peak flows in the Ganges and the Brahmaputra coincide, as happened in 1988.

3 *Rainwater floods* are caused by heavy, prolonged rainfall within Bangladesh. Heavy pre-monsoon rainfall (April–May) may cause local runoff, which collects in depressions and is trapped on land by the rising river levels. In effect the water table rises above the ground surface. As with river floods, damage from rainwater floods depends on when the flood occurs. Unlike flash floods and river flooding, rainwater floods do not deposit new alluvium but may wash topsoil from ridges into adjoining depressions.

4 *Storm-surge floods* are associated with cyclones which move in from the Bay of Bengal. Incoming surges may only last for a few hours but the returning outflow may get trapped behind roads and embankments. The area affected is usually limited to within 4–8km of the coast, but the impact can be devastating, with great loss of life and huge areas of cropland damaged by saline water.

The 1987 and 1988 floods

Severe and damaging floods in 1987 and 1988 made headline news in the world's media. Each was reported as being the worst on record.

The 1987 floods

These were rainwater floods following periods of exceptionally heavy rainfall over northern Bangladesh and adjacent parts of India between June and September. Minor rivers in this area were unable to cope with the runoff, and the outflow from the raised water table. Silted channels, and constrictions caused by fish traps and inadequate bridges and culverts, contributed to the problem. High levels in the major rivers lasted for several weeks, preventing natural runoff from draining the land, and 40 per cent of the country was under water. Embankments which had been built in the region were deliberately cut, either to relieve rainwater flooding within them, or to reduce flood levels outside them. The Brahmaputra right-bank embankment was breached by erosion, causing severe flooding.

The 1988 floods

These were predominately river floods. Heavy early monsoon rainfall in the north-east brought the Meghna and Brahmaputra rivers temporarily above danger level in July. Heavy rainfall at the end of August brought the Brahmaputra to flood peak on 30 August, and the Ganges and Meghna to record levels on 2 and 7 September respectively. The sudden simultaneous rise of these rivers caused them to flood adjoining floodplains. Sixty per cent of the country was submerged, including two-thirds of the capital, Dhaka; 45 million people were affected, and over 2000 deaths were reported. Roads and railways were disrupted for several weeks, as a result of broken bridges and breached embankments.

The Bangladesh landscape

Bangladesh occupies the delta formed by three major rivers. Deposition of sediments by these rivers has produced an expanding delta, extending south into the Bay of Bengal. As rivers reach the sea, sediment is dropped to form fans. Often these deposits are re-suspended during floods and re-deposited elsewhere. Some are deposited on floodplains, contributing to the process of land formation. Where sediment is deposited on river beds, channels change shape and water has to find a new route, sometimes with the original channels drying up. The river channel is also significant: the Brahmaputra (Jamuna) is braided (Figure 9.7) from Assam downstream during the dry season, and as the river level rises the channels change position. This affects both bank erosion and the formation of sand bars and islands. In a country where there is a shortage of land, these areas are often settled, with frequently disastrous consequences when the next floods occur.

▼ **Figure 9.7** Braided channel of the Brahmaputra (Jamuna) river. Notice how sediment has choked the channel so that it has split into sections, a process known as 'braiding'.

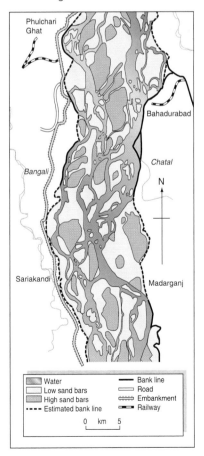

Item	Loss/damage 1987	1988
Area flooded	57 000km^2	2 82 000 km2
Houses totally/partially damaged	2.5m	7.2m
Human lives lost	1657	2379
Livestock lost:		
cattle, goats, etc.	64 700	172 000
poultry	206 000	410 000
Rice production lost	3.5m tonnes	2.0m tonnes
Roads: trunk	1523km	3000km
rural	15 107km	10 000km
bridges, culverts	1102	898
Railways: embankments	n/a	1300km
bridges	n/a	270
Flood embankments	1279km	1990km
Irrigation/drainage canals	222km	283km
Irrigation/drainage control structures	541	1465
Electric power:		
substations flooded	n/a	18
11KV powerlines de-energized	n/a	2000km
Industrial units flooded	n/a	>1000
Hospitals flooded	n/a	45
Health centres flooded	n/a	1400
Schools flooded	n/a	19 000
Rural hand tubewells flooded	n/a	240 000
n/a = not available		

▲ **Figure 9.8** Damage and losses due to the 1987 and 1988 floods.

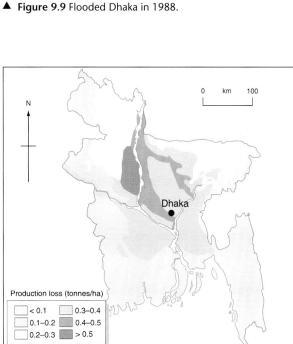

▲ **Figure 9.9** Flooded Dhaka in 1988.

▼ **Figure 9.10** Loss of monsoon season rice in 1987 and 1988.

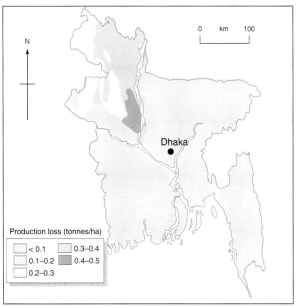

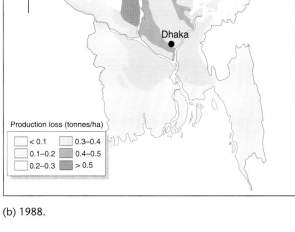

(a) 1987.

(b) 1988.

Coping with the floods

1 Using the information on each flood, construct an annotated diagram to compare the causes and effects of the 1987 and 1988 floods.

2 Using Figures 9.8–9.10, describe the problems that a) a rural farmer and b) an urban dweller in Dhaka would have had to cope with during these two severe floods.

3 Which was the worse flood? Justify your choice.

Flood control in Bangladesh

Four strategies are used in Bangladesh to manage flooding:

1 *Controlled flooding* – the spread of water over the floodplain is controlled with the help of mechanisms such as sluice gates which are built into embankments.

2 *Compartments* – areas that have been created by embankments being built around them, creating an environment where the amount of water within them may be controlled. See Figure 9.11.

3 *River training* – this attempts to direct the flow of the river in order to minimize bank erosion and scouring of river beds.

4 *Flood forecasting* – data are gathered about rainfall, runoff, and river levels upstream and are used with computer modelling to predict the impact on the river downstream.

The Flood Action Plan

Major flood control projects have been undertaken in Bangladesh since the 1960s, with varying degrees of success. In 1989, following the 1987 and 1988 floods, the World Bank organized an international conference to co-ordinate flood control efforts, and the Flood Action Plan (FAP – Figure 9.12) was drafted. It consisted of 26 projects with the aim of designing technically, economically, and environmentally sound flood prevention measures. The first phase (1990–95) involved pilot studies, costing US $150 million. Between 1995 and 2005, a range of projects will be undertaken, costing up to US $500 million. The FAP is funded by donor countries and work will be carried out by agencies of the Bangladeshi government, donor country governments, by international and local construction firms, university academics, and national and international non-governmental organizations.

The FAP's overall aim is to provide flood protection to the following flood frequency levels:

- Dhaka and other major cities: 500–1000 years
- district towns, trunk roads, and main railways: 100–500 years
- main river embankments: 100 years
- agricultural land: 10–100 years.

The main proposal is to construct new embankments along upstream sections of the Brahmaputra and the Ganges within Bangladesh.

▼ **Figure 9.12** The Flood Action Plan – location of some components.

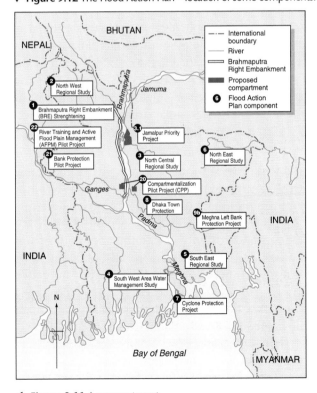

◀ **Figure 9.11** A compartment.

It will proceed downstream in stages to allow river channels to adjust to increased flows and sediment loads from the newly confined sections upstream. As embankments are completed, compartments will be created behind them using internal embankments, and making use of existing embankments where possible.

However, total flood control will not be attempted. Instead, controlled flooding will be allowed up to 'normal' levels with which farmers are familiar. The FAP will also investigate flood forecasting and disaster preparation, including provision of boats for escape and shelters on raised ground. Embankment construction is controversial.

Embankments – the Jamalpur Priority Project Study

The possible effects of embankment construction were investigated in one community – see Action Plan 3.1 on Figure 9.12. Project staff collected information from 500 households, and met representatives of the local council, co-operatives, and members of the public. Four project options were discussed with local people:

- *Option A*: floodproofing and drainage improvements
- *Option B*: controlled flooding for the entire area, with some compartmentalization
- *Option C*: controlled flooding of only half of the project area
- *Option D*: full-scale compartmentalization of the whole area to exclude all river flooding.

Options C and D were fairly quickly dropped on economic and social grounds. It seemed that Option A would benefit the landless, non-farming, and fishing households. Option B was expected to increase economic growth but would improve the living standards only of farming and land-owning households. Those who would lose out have threatened to breach embankments, an action known locally as 'public cuts'. These have been carried out elsewhere when embankments have prevented the flow of floodwater back into rivers.

There was also conflict between those who lived inside and those who lived outside the embankments. Flood modelling exercises carried out indicated that Option B was likely to increase flooding outside the project area and threaten more than half a million people along the river Brahamputra. The population within the project area is the same size. A decision has still to be made.

▼ **Figure 9.13** The impact of embankment construction on fisheries.

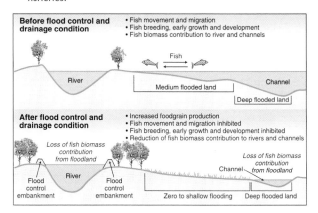

The Meghna–Dhonagoda Irrigation Project

This project was undertaken to examine the impact of one of the existing embankments, the Meghna–Dhonagoda embankment, on the health and well-being of the people living inside it. It is in Matlabthana, about 50km south-east of Dhaka. It was constructed between 1982 and 1987 and provides flood control and drainage to 17 000 hectares and irrigation to 13 800 hectares.

There is a widespread belief in Bangladesh that projects of this nature cause health problems associated with water quality inside the embankment. Traditional practices of sewage disposal and the selection of drinking water have developed which used the annual flood to flush the area, and it is not clear how well these practices have adapted to the changed regime. If water quality suffers, there are likely to be health problems, particularly amongst the children of the area. Figure 9.14 presents two indicators of the well-being of these children – it can be seen from these indicators that the situation is unclear. The relationship between these could be tested using the techniques described in the box on pages 197–8. You would need the figures represented by the graphs in order to do this.

▼ **Figure 9.14** Health indicators of children living inside and outside the Meghna–Dhonagoda embankment.

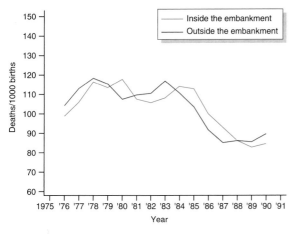

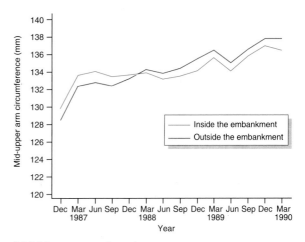

(a) Infant mortality rate.

(b) Mid-upper-arm circumference.

Relationships between sets of data

Relationships between sets of data are important and can be shown in several ways. The purpose is to show whether data may possibly be linked. In this way, a relationship can be investigated. For example, Figure 9.15a shows per capita data for the annual GDP of twelve countries, and the amount of energy consumed in million tonnes of coal or coal equivalent. Is there a relationship? Is it reasonable to assume that the higher the GDP, the higher the amount of energy consumed is likely to be?

Scatter graphs

Scatter graphs show two variables, one plotted on the vertical *y* axis, and the other on a horizontal *x* axis. In order to plot the data correctly, consider which variable needs to go where – at *x* or *y*? One will be the 'dependent variable' and the other the 'independent variable'.

▶ **Figure 9.15** (a) Per capita data for annual GDP of twelve countries, and the amount of energy consumed in million tonnes of coal or coal equivalent.

▼ (b) Scatter graphs.

Country	GNP per head (US$)	Energy consumption per head (tonnes of coal equivalent)
Australia	14 400	7.24
Bangladesh	180	0.07
Brazil	2550	0.80
Canada	19 020	10.91
China	360	0.81
France	17 830	3.95
Ghana	380	0.11
India	350	0.31
Japan	23 730	4.03
Mali	260	0.03
UK	14 570	5.03
Zambia	390	0.20

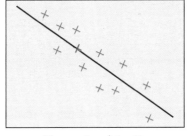

(i) a positive relationship

(ii) a negative relationship

(iii) no relationship

Continued on page 198

Continued from page 197

The **dependent variable** is the one you are seeking to explore, while the **independent variable** is the one you know is fixed. For example, in plotting population over time, 'population' is the dependent variable – the one you are seeking to explore over time. Time is the independent variable. In Figure 9.15a, energy is therefore the dependent variable, the one for which we seek a relationship.

Follow these steps.

1   Plot a frame for the graph, and a scale. Energy will be the dependent variable and is therefore on the vertical *y* axis, and GDP on the horizontal *x* axis.

2   Plot the data as a number of points, but do not join them.

3   The result is a scatter graph, where points are scattered, but probably show a trend or pattern. Next you can draw a best-fit line – see below.

Best-fit line

Having drawn scatter points, you can now investigate any relationship between them. Figure 9.15b will help you. Graph (i) shows that there is a **positive** relationship – as one variable increases, so does the other. Graph (ii) shows that there is a **negative** relationship – as one variable increases, so the other decreases. Graph (iii) shows that there is **no** relationship, only a random pattern.

To draw a best-fit line, follow these steps.

1   Find the average (mean) of each of the columns of data in Figure 9.15a.

2   Plot this as a separate 'mean point'.

3   Place a ruler on the graph, passing it through the mean. Rotate it until it is aligned with the trend of the points you have drawn. With twelve points plotted plus the mean, your ruler should ideally pass through about two, and leave five on either side. This is the 'best-fit' line.

4   When you are confident of a 'best fit', draw it as a line.

5   Interpret your result, using Figure 9.15b.

Other techniques can be used for testing relationships, including the Spearman rank correlation coefficient. This is described in Chapter 10, pages 214-5.

Additional issues concerning embankments

- *Positioning of embankments* There is strong pressure within Bangladesh to build the embankments as close to the rivers as possible to protect as many of the population and as much of the agricultural land as possible. However, this increases the incidence of erosion, because the rivers have unstable, braided, and actively meandering channels. Both the Ganges and the Brahmaputra have made major channel shifts in recent centuries. Some existing embankments have had to be rebuilt a considerable distance from the river several times. Confining floods between embankments increases river levels and speeds and channel instability.

  Again, building embankments close to rivers and defending them with groynes would cost twice as much – US $10 billion – as setting them back 5km, and annual operation and maintenance costs would be $180 million rather than $165 million. On the other hand, set-back embankments would leave 6.3 million people exposed to perhaps higher floods, compared with 1.3 million if they were built close to the river.

- *Timescale* Even with a comprehensive building of embankments, it may be 20–30 years before all the major floodplains are protected. In the meantime, many people will still be exposed to unregulated floods.

- *Impact on river processes* Where embankments have been constructed on major rivers, for example on the Mississippi in the USA and on the Yangtze in China, continued deposition has raised the level of the river bed above that of the adjoining land, so any breaching of the embankments would be catastrophic. Another effect is that increasing river flow in one place may transport more water and sediment to create difficulties further downstream.

- *Drainage* Existing embankments have at times trapped water and prevented it from returning to the river once its level has dropped. This can result in health problems and may affect crop production and fish movements. People so affected may be tempted to breach embankments deliberately, which can lead to conflict between communities, as a cut to drain one area may flood adjacent land.

- *Breaching embankments* The damage inflicted when embankments are overtopped or breached by floodwaters may be more severe than in unprotected areas, because flooding is more likely to be very sudden.

Critics of the FAP

The FAP has its strong critics. Figure 9.16 shows some of the arguments against it. It is criticized as being expensive, biased towards construction projects, and meeting the needs of those who are least affected by the most regular flooding.

▼ **Figure 9.16** From the *New Scientist*, 11 May 1991.

Human lives shrugged off in flood plan

Protection of human lives against floods caused by cyclones in the Bay of Bengal, such as the one which killed more than 100 000 people last week, has been a low priority for successive Bangladesh governments and aid agencies. A 26-project Flood Action Plan unveiled by the Bangladeshis and the World Bank in London 18 months ago included just one project aimed at protecting people from tidal waves whipped up by cyclones. The other projects were aimed at reducing the effects of river floods, which damage property rather than kill people.

Of the estimated US $500 million to be spent on the plan, coastal embankments are expected to cost around US $70 million. Most of the remainder will go on improving inland river embankments to protect cities and farms from floods on the rivers Ganges and Brahmaputra. These two great rivers inundated up to half the country in 1987 and 1988.

In an interview with *New Scientist* in Bangladesh last November, Wybrand van Ellen, a Dutch hydrologist, conceded that coastal flooding had a low priority. 'If one took human life as a yardstick for expenditure, this would be the problem to solve,' he said. 'Cyclones are regular and can kill hundreds of thousands of people, whereas the 1988 river flood was a once in 150 years event and still only killed a few hundred. The difference is that

cyclones don't hit the capital, and don't flood the lawns of foreign ambassadors.'

Ainun Nishat, professor of water resources at the Bangladesh University of Engineering and Technology in Dhaka and a member of a local overseeing panel, said: 'Yes, there is a priority for inland protection, where the risk to human life is much less. The reason is that the national priority is to increase agricultural production.' The government wants to protect its cities and its 'green revolution' farms which grow high-yield varieties of rice that are more vulnerable to flooding than traditional varieties.

Coastal embankments 'are not designed primarily to protect against cyclones, but to prevent salt water entering fields during normal high tides', Nishat said. Most embankments are 5 metres high, but last week's tidal wave was at least 7 metres high. Several heavily populated islands at the mouth of the wide coastal delta, such as Urichar Island, which bore the brunt of the death toll last week, have no banks.

A similar flood in 1970 killed between 150 000 and 500 000 people. No one knows the true figures because the inhabitants of these islands are landless migrants, the poorest of Bangladesh's 100 million poor. Cyclones also ravaged the coast four times in the 1960s and three times in the 1980s.

Evaluating embankments

Form groups of three or four. Imagine that you have been asked to produce a report and display for flood management workers in other parts of Bangladesh, to let them know the effects of what has happened so far. Your report should include spoken and written presentations.

1 Explain in two minutes the causes of flooding.

2 Summarize the arguments for and against embankments.

3 Evaluate the effectiveness of embankments based on the evidence so far.

4 Recommend the role that embankments should play (if any) in the FAP.

5 Suggest how future developments might be monitored.

6 Read Figure 9.16. List the different criticisms made of the Plan.

7 What measures are required in order to protect the people of Bangladesh more effectively?

8 What are the differences in values systems between the two sides of the argument?

The FAP has been criticized by some people for not including enough 'people's participation' in the whole process. The poorer people of Bangladesh, who make up the majority of the population, are not being listened to and are having to live with projects that they do not want in the first place.

1 VILLAGERS

'Give us the power and the resources that the Water and Power Development Authority has, and we would do things better than them economically and technically.'

'If I were to be consulted, what would I say? You see, I'm just an ordinary man. I don't know anything. All I know is that one has to have meals every day.'

'No, no. The Water and Power Development Authority-wallahs have never bothered about these things. They acquire the land first, start construction work for the embankments and then notify us that this land has been acquired. People give up the land whether they have food to eat or not . . . If anyone had said that I won't give my land, then the WAPDA officials would have brought in the police and roped him in . . . '

'If they had contacted the public before doing things then we would have stopped the Water and Power Development Authority from taking the trouble of building these embankments. We have said foremost that rather than building embankments you should try to do something about the river. Make it deeper. But they go on building embankments. Each one goes into the river, then they build another. They are making money out of this, while it's the public of the area who are being killed off.'

'Oh yes, the foreigners were here one day last month. But they only went to the school and spoke in English. We are not educated. We could not understand.'

2 MEMBERS OF NON-GOVERNMENT ORGANIZATIONS

'When I spoke to the FAP consultants in Dhaka I felt there was some scope for participation. But here in the field I see there is no scope.'

'What is significant by its omission in any debate is the fact that while the Flood Plan Co-ordination Organization receives its mandate from the donor consortium meeting held in London in 1989, the government of Bangladesh of that time had no such mandate to enter into such a monumental agreement from the people of Bangladesh.'

3 BANGLADESH WATER DEVELOPMENT BOARD

'With a low literacy rate and limited exposure to the outside world, rural people are not adequately equipped to find/suggest solutions to all of their problems. On the other hand, they may be suspicious of solutions given by experts.'

4 FAP CONSULTANTS

'If you want to consult everybody and wait for a solution agreed by all interested parties, we'll never finish.'

'Without people's participation you can't sell the project!'

'Another new idea from the social scientists. Only slogans! First, "poverty alleviation". Then "women" and "environment". Now "people's participation"! It's just a new fad!'

'Oh yes, but you have to consult my socio-economist, not me. I have not time for people's participation. I'm working 12 hours every day on the project.'

▲ **Figure 9.17** Comments on people's participation in the FAP.

'People's participation'

1 In pairs, carry out the following exercise.
   a) Read through the quotes in Figure 9.17, and identify the different points being made about 'people's participation'. Group them into categories of similar viewpoints.
   b) Within each group you have identified, what do the views of the individuals concerned have in common with each other?
   c) What does this suggest about the process of development and aid?
   Compare your findings and views with those of another pair.

2 Consider examples that you know of 'people's participation' in the UK. How effective is it? Why?

Are floods getting worse?

Deforestation in the Himalayas

It is widely thought that river flooding in Bangladesh has worsened in recent years as forests in the Himalayan areas of India and Nepal have been cleared. Increased runoff and sediment resulting from soil erosion are carried downstream by rivers and deposited on river beds, thus reducing the capacity of the river. However, some studies have challenged this view. Ives and Messerli, for example, show that:

- forest clearance in the Himalayas has been going on for centuries and could not account for any recent change
- more soil is lost from a forested slope than from a slope that is terraced for agriculture
- high erosion and runoff rates occur naturally as a result of climate and landscape
- there is no published evidence that flood magnitude and sediment load have increased recently.

Global warming

Will global warming create further problems for Bangladesh? There is no evidence yet that rainfall is increasing – a review of 150 years of rainfall records for Calcutta shows no change. There is no evidence either that sea-level is rising, which would aggravate inland flooding by raising river base levels. However, should sea-level begin to rise, even by a small amount, there would be a considerable impact on Bangladesh (Figure 9.18).

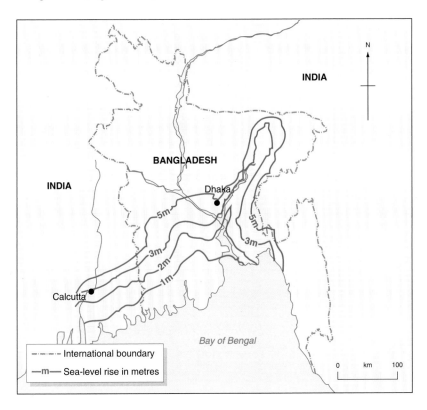

1 Consider the information in this part of the chapter on deforestation and global warming, and comment on the part played by the collection of data and scientific evidence.

2 How might a lack of clear scientific agreement affect policy development by the Bangladeshi government?

◀ **Figure 9.18** Potential impact of sea-level rises.

Water supply in Mexico

This case study illustrates the effects of unequal access to and misuse of the water supply in Mexico. Like many countries, scarcity is not a problem nationally, but there are serious shortages in certain regions. Water is also misused: it is not used in a sustainable way, so supplies will not be available for future generations.

Distribution of water

Although Mexico's per capita annual water availability of approximately 5000 cubic metres is twice the world average, and only 43 per cent of the country's renewable water is actually used, water distribution is very uneven within the country and the supply varies throughout the year. One of the results is severe shortages which affect several of the country's aquifers and rivers.

Of the annual rainfall of 750mm, the national average surface runoff rate is 47 per cent. However, more than a quarter of the country's people live at 2000m above sea-level, where runoff is only 4 per cent. By contrast, runoff at 500m is 50 per cent, in an area affecting another 25 per cent of the population.

1 a) Trace Figure 9.19, then identify and shade the areas of Mexico where water supply is likely to be a problem.
  b) Compare your map with Figure 9.21.

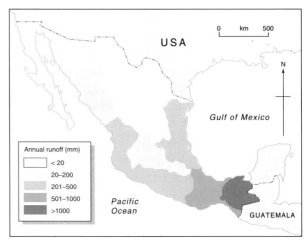

▲ **Figure 9.20** Distribution of annual runoff in Mexico.

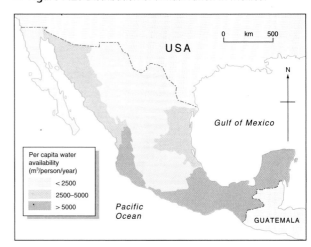

▲ **Figure 9.21** Per capita water availability in Mexico.

2 a) Use Figures 9.20 and 9.22 to help explain the differences between your map and Figure 9.21.
  b) Use an atlas to find out how water availability in Mexico compares with the distribution of population.

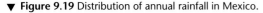
▼ **Figure 9.19** Distribution of annual rainfall in Mexico.

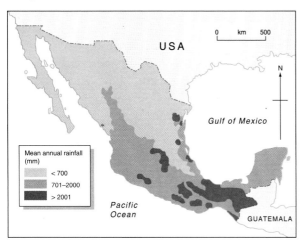

▼ **Figure 9.22** Annual rainfall in Mexico.

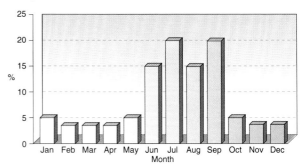

Issues of water management

The mismatch of water supply and demand leads to a variety of problems. In the highly populated central highlands, runoff and groundwater are insufficient to supply the economic activities there. Excessive use of aquifers (water-bearing rocks), costly transfers of water from other areas, water contamination, and conflict between users are all found in these areas.

At the same time, in areas with excess water, there are costly flood control and drainage projects. There has been conflict between neighbouring regions over water supplies, and there are increasing problems with inefficient use of water, poor water quality, inadequate maintenance of the water supply infrastructure, and lack of flood control. The government is making water management a high priority, with legislation covering the use of water based on the idea that water is national property.

Agriculture and water use

Agriculture is the main consumer of water in Mexico. Eighty-five per cent of the land is classified as arid or semi-arid, and only 16 per cent of the country is considered suitable for crop production. Only 3 per cent is irrigated, and much depends on small reservoirs and wells which are rapidly depleted in dry years. The development of irrigation is essential, and huge amounts have been spent on it since 1940. Eighty per cent of Mexico's public expenditure in agriculture has been on irrigation – irrigated crops produce 50 per cent of the national total of crops. Irrigation is still inefficient, however, and needs to be improved.

Irrigation management

There are 77 irrigation districts covering 60 per cent of Mexico's irrigated area. The state used to own all the irrigation facilities and was responsible for maintenance, with water users paying a fee. Gradually, local users' associations are taking over.

Using groundwater for irrigation

Groundwater moves very slowly, in some cases only a few metres a year. Aquifers may take thousands of years to accumulate but with modern pumps they can easily be used up faster than they can be recharged. Shallow wells dry up, increasing pumping costs; poorer-quality saline water may be introduced by pumping near coasts; and overlying ground may subside, damaging buildings or roads.

To sustain irrigated agriculture, water management schemes must be developed to balance groundwater recharge and use. In some areas of Mexico, water tables have been lowered by as much as 30m over the last 20 years. Agreements have to be reached about the volumes of water that can be extracted within each district. The following example of Altar Pitiquito explores how this might be done.

▲ **Figure 9.23** Location of Altar Pitiquito.

Irrigation system	Efficiency (%)
Gravity	
Conveyance:	
concrete-lined canal	90.0
earth canal	87.0
Irrigation method:	
furrows	59.2
borders	56.3
Pressurized	
Conveyance: pipe	95.0
Irrigation method:	
sprinkler	80.6
trickler	86.5
microsprinkler	90.6

▲ **Figure 9.24** Comparison of efficiencies of irrigation systems.

Study Figure 9.24. Why do different systems have different efficiencies?

Focus on Altar Pitiquito

Altar Pitiquito is an agricultural area in northern Mexico whose main output is fruit (grapes, melon, watermelon, and citrus), tree crops (olives), and arable crops (wheat, asparagus, cotton, alfalfa). Irrigation systems are of two types.

- *Gravity-fed systems*, which feed water from higher ground to lower ground. These vary in reliability, because flow rates vary according to season. Often when water is most needed, it is least available.
- *Pressurized systems*, which pump water through pipes from individual wells, and do not have to rely on gravity. These vary in efficiency because each system is individually owned by farmers. Some systems are reliable, and water can be fed through exactly when it is required, which makes it cheaper. Others are less efficient, or deplete water from their wells too quickly.

In common with many areas in the north of Mexico, Altar Pitiquito experiences the problem of groundwater depletion, and farmers are suffering serious economic losses with high water and electricity costs. The aquifer in this area has an annual natural recharge of 300 million m³, and an annual extraction of 800 million m³. Following a number of meetings, extraction rates are to be reduced from 798 million m³ in 1994, to 435 million m³ in 2001 and finally to 301 million m³ in 2004.

One benefit is that by reducing the amount of water extracted, the amount of electricity required for pumping it would also drop. In addition, a large reduction in water extraction could be achieved by improving the efficiency of irrigation systems. Different systems have different efficiencies (see Figure 9.24). This could be done by updating existing pumping equipment owned by individual farmers, which would reduce leaks and avoid wastage, and would provide more constant supplies. Incentives to make these changes are offered to farmers through the government's 'Programme for Efficient Use of Water and Electricity' in which they are able to choose one of three options. Clearly, making these changes is costly. Farmers can take advantage of government incentives to improve farming efficiency including incentives to invest in improving pumping equipment, canal lining, constructing pressurized irrigation systems, and land levelling.

1 Farmers whose pumps operate at less than 40 per cent efficiency receive half of the cost of upgrading their wells and equipment.
2 Those whose pumps operate at over 40 per cent efficiency receive half the cost of constructing storage reservoirs, land levelling, and upgrading to a pressurized irrigation system.
3 Those wishing to improve both pumps and irrigation systems can request government assistance for up to half of the costs.

A new programme has changed electricity tariffs by removing subsidies and making electricity more expensive. The aim is to cut back on the use of electric groundwater pumps, so decreasing the amount of groundwater being extracted. Money saved from the electricity subsidies is retargeted to schemes that help to improve the efficiency of irrigation systems, particularly drip and sprinkler systems.

In order to encourage the farmers of Altar Pitiquito to make changes, three models were put forward so that they could see where savings in running costs could be made.

- *Model 1* maintains cropped areas and types of crops for farms of 50 hectares. Irrigation water is brought under gravity. Current annual extraction of 800 000m³ requires 5900 hours of pump time, using 600 000kWh and costing US$25 000. By updating pumping equipment, the same volume of water could be extracted in 2800 hours, requiring 326 000kWh for a total cost of US$12 670.

- *Model 2* has the same farm size, cropped area, and types of crops, but the irrigation system is pressurized. An annual pumped volume of 570 000m³ is required, using 326 000kWh over 3600 hours and costing US$12 800. Improving pumping systems could result in reducing time further to 2000 hours, but because pumping would be over a wider area it would use 325 000kWh, costing US$12 600.

- *Model 3* is based on a smaller farm size of 40 hectares but assumes the same proportion of crops. The irrigation system is pressurized and pumping equipment is renewed. The amount of water required would be 460 000m³, taking 1600 hours to pump, using 260 000kWh and costing US$9200.

Conclusions

It is still too early to say how successful these types of schemes will be. Under the government programme, 251 pumps of the 831 in operation in Altar Pitiquito have been updated, but this has not solved the problem of severe depletion of the aquifer. Enforcing and monitoring the reduction in pumping, and the impact of reducing farmers' livelihoods, remain objectives for the future.

Making a choice

1 Devise and draw up a table to compare the three models described here.

2 Use your table to evaluate each of the models.

3 Which do you prefer? Would farmers agree with you?

Essay

'When no-one owns a resource, users have no incentive to conserve for the future and the self-interest of individual users leads them to over-exploitation' (*Water Policies and Agriculture*, FAO publication 1993). Discuss this statement in relation to the water and irrigation management policies of Mexico.

Explain:
- how and why water 'ownership' is a problem in Mexico
- how water supply and irrigation are managed
- how individuals are allowed to exploit water resources
- why there are no real incentives for people to conserve water
- how you see the future of water management in Mexico.

Water quality in the UK

Water quality in many of the world's rivers and seas is increasingly threatened by a range of human activities. If it is to be maintained at a level that enables water to be used with no risk to health, then management is necessary.

In the UK until recently, mainly raw sewage has been discharged into the sea through short outfall pipes, for the sea to disperse and absorb it. Sewage systems designed a hundred years or more ago have been unable to cope with the increase in population and the number of disposable items that are flushed down the toilet. However, in spite of recent improvements, water companies still discharge 1360 million litres of semi-treated sewage daily close to shore. Some scientists, and the group Surfers Against Sewage, believe that there is a more serious problem of increased risks for anyone who comes into contact with the sea, from bacteria, viruses, and pathogens. They maintain that steps taken by water companies to prevent the release of harmful bacteria are insufficient. They also maintain that claims made by water companies, the government, and the National Rivers Authority (NRA), that water quality is up to EU standards, mislead the public. They would like to see sewage treated in ways that would eliminate risks and enable effluent to be used productively.

Figure 9.25 shows how non-bathers at Ramsgate in August 1990 compared, in terms of symptoms suffered, with bathers, and the risks to each group. Notice that the non-bathers had some illnesses. Bathers, however, suffered more illnesses of every type. The right-hand column is based on an index of 1.00 or more, comparing bathers and non-bathers. Non-bathers are 1.00 in every case, and the risk to bathers is shown as 1.31, 1.25, etc. Notice how in every case the figure for bathers is greater than 1.00. This implies a risk of bathing in the sea.

Assessing the risks

Some scientists and the government have accused Surfers Against Sewage of being alarmist, and point to the findings of a four-year independent study carried out from 1989 to 1994. Study Figures 9.25 and 9.26. How far do they support the view put forward by Surfers Against Sewage outlined in the text?

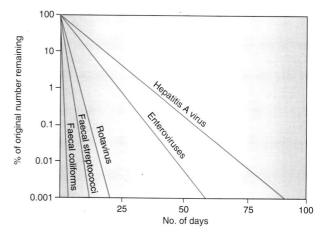

▲ **Figure 9.26** Life of viruses, bacteria, and pathogens in sea water.

	No. reporting symptoms (%)	Relative risk (95% confidence interval)
At least one reported symptom (total sampled)		
Non-bathers (839)	180 (21.5)	1.00
Bathers (1044)	275 (26.3)	1.31
Waders (561)	142 (25.3)	1.25
Swimmers (399)	105 (26.3)	1.31
Surfers or divers (84)	38 (33.3)	1.81
Gastro-intestinal symptoms		
Non-bathers	68 (8.1)	1.00
Bathers	116 (11.1)	1.47
Diarrhoea		
Non-bathers	30 (3.6)	1.00
Bathers	61 (5.8)	1.88
Eye symptoms		
Non-bathers	41 (4.9)	1.00
Bathers	62 (5.9)	1.24
Ear, nose, and throat symptoms		
Non-bathers	110 (13.1)	1.00
Bathers	148 (14.2)	1.08
Respiratory symptoms		
Non-bathers	47 (5.6)	1.00
Bathrs	77 (7.4)	1.40

▲ **Figure 9.25** Symptoms reported from visitors to a British beach in August 1990.

1 Read Figure 9.27.
   a) List facts that are made about the issue.
   b) Read the article again and identify statements that are value judgements.
   c) Compare your lists with someone else's.

2 How easy do you feel it is to assess the nature and extent of this problem?

3 How would you monitor which argument was likely to have truth on its side?

Britain's dirty beaches can make you sick

Bathing at Britain's beaches makes you ill, official government research will disclose tomorrow.

The report, the result of the most thorough survey ever carried out into the effects of dirty bathing water, shows that the greater the pollution, and the longer people stay in it, the more likely they are to get gastro-enteritis and other diseases. And it reveals that people get sick even from bathing at beaches that pass official EU cleanliness standards.

The results of the four-year research, which surveyed more than 16 000 people at 13 popular beaches, are embarrassing to ministers who are campaigning to weaken EU bathing-water standards and trying to delay measures to clean up sewage discharges to the sea.

The study – carried out by the Water Research Centre and funded by the Departments of Environment and Health, the Welsh Office, and the National Rivers Authority – examined Langland Bay, near Swansea, in 1989; Moreton in the Wirral, and Ramsgate in 1990; Rhyl, Morecambe, Lyme Regis, Paignton, and Southsea in 1991; and Cleethorpes, Skegness, Westward Ho! and Instow near Bideford, and Thorpe Bay in Essex, in 1992.

Bathers at dirty beaches such as Ramsgate and Morecambe suffered more gastro-intestinal and ear, eye, and upper respiratory tract infections than those at cleaner resorts such as Paignton and Lyme Regis, though people became sick there too. The longer they stayed in the water the more likely they were to become ill; surfers and divers were more at risk than swimmers, who in turn got sick more frequently than paddlers.

Young people aged between 15 and 24 reported the most illness; it is this age group that usually spends most time in the water.

Last summer, Britain's progress in cleaning up its beaches stagnated, and it is now unlikely to reach its target of meeting EU standards for virtually all its beaches by 1995 – ten years after the original deadline. In July, Britain was convicted by the European Court of failing to clean up bathing water at Blackpool and Southport.

▲ **Figure 9.27** From *The Independent on Sunday*, 30 January 1994.

Cleaning up the seas of west Cornwall

A major scheme to improve bathing water quality by tackling treatment and disposal of sewage in west Cornwall was completed in 1995. It caused considerable controversy and raised a number of questions.

Background to the scheme

Before the scheme, this stretch of the Cornish coast had 47 sewage outfalls. Many of them dated from Victorian times, and all discharged raw sewage into the sea. This created problems for tourist resorts in the area. Quality of bathing water was affected by sewage debris, and failed to meet requirements of the EU Bathing Water Directive, which had to be complied with by April 1995. In order to meet the

Sewage treatment

There are several ways of managing sewage disposal in this country.

- *No treatment*: whatever is flushed down toilets or drains ends up in the sea. At present this accounts for 37 per cent of coastal and 11 per cent of estuarine outfalls.
- *Preliminary treatment*: also known as screening, raw sewage is passed through a screen in order to remove sewage debris before it is discharged. This accounts for 50 per cent of coastal and 24 per cent of estuarine outfalls.
- *Primary treatment*: raw sewage is held in sedimentation tanks to allow gross solids to settle to form sludge which is then removed. The remaining liquid is then discharged. Sludge may be pumped directly into the sea or treated biologically or chemically to remove pathogens, excess water, and odour. It may then be dried before it is disposed of in the sea, on landfill sites, or in incinerators. After treatment to reduce pathogens it may be used on farmland. Disposal of sludge at sea is to be phased out by 1998.
- *Secondary treatment*: this involves biological digestion using the process of oxidation. It is intended to treat the liquid effluent from primary treatment and remove suspended solids.
- *Tertiary treatment*: this improves effluent quality after secondary treatment using rapid sand filtration (filtering through sand), micro-screening (being fed through a micro-mesh), or reedbed treatment (where final settlement of any solid is allowed in reedbeds). A clear liquid is produced which contains very little organic matter, but a large quantity of faecal and other bacteria, most of which die off quickly in seas and rivers. Disinfection can be carried out to kill them all using ultraviolet light.

A House of Commons Environment Select Committee in 1990 called for all sewage to receive tertiary treatment.

Directive, and to update the sewage disposal system, South West Water designed a system involving the intersection of the existing sewage outfalls of Penzance, Marazion, and St Ives, entitled 'The Clean Sweep'. It is one of the largest sewage schemes in the country, and has transformed the sewage systems of west Cornwall at a cost of £900 million. Instead of raw sewage disposal from each of the settlements, sewage from the whole of west Cornwall is now pumped to the new works at Hayle. Here it is given secondary treatment and discharged through an outfall 2.65km offshore.

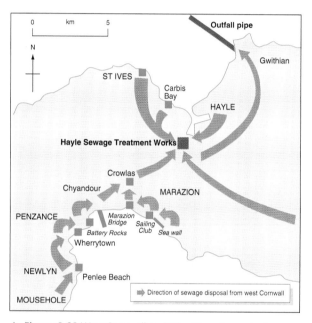

▲ **Figure 9.28** West Cornwall and 'The Clean Sweep' scheme.

The impact on St Ives

One of the resorts most likely to be affected by the new scheme is St Ives, which is located across the bay from a new long outfall. In St Ives there are EU designated bathing waters at Porthmeor and Porthminster beaches (Figure 9.29), as well as several other beaches in the area. Before, the area's sewage was discharged into a main sewer in the valley of the river Stennack, and to a holding tank beside the harbour. From there, it was pumped to a screening plant and, with further treatment, discharged through an outfall 75m beyond the low-water mark at Bamaluz Point. Several storm overflows also discharged onto the bathing beaches.

The scheme

Much of St Ives has been re-sewered, so existing overflows to the sea need no longer be used. Nearly all of it is now carried to a new pumping station via a new sewer which has been laid under the harbour and Porthminster Beach. At the pumping station the sewage is pumped up to the highest point on the road between St Ives and Carbis Bay and carried by gravity to the works at Hayle. At the pumping station the number of pumps in action at any one time depends on incoming flow. If this exceeds pump capacity, excess flow is screened and discharged via a new outfall off Bamaluz Point. Calculations indicate that such a flow could occur once every seven bathing seasons.

> Using Figures 9.28 and 9.29, draw an annotated sketch map to show the key features of the scheme as it affects St Ives.

Opposition to the scheme

Although there was a need for improvement, there has been opposition to this scheme. When it was first proposed in 1989, St Ives had just been awarded the Blue Flag (see page 210), and people felt that this would be threatened by the discharge of so much sewage from the north coast. Opposition was widespread, as Figure 9.30 shows.

The County Council opposed it because of the harmful effects of construction. They believed that a better alternative would be to build the pumping station in the form of a pier or jetty, situated just north of one of the existing piers. They were concerned that the tourist industry would suffer from disruption caused by such large-scale and long-term construction work. The County Council's refusal of permission for the pumping station was later overruled at a public enquiry.

As well as opposition to the construction process, there were other arguments which questioned the basic principles of the scheme. The view of some scientists and Surfers Against Sewage is that the discharge of secondary treated sewage through long outfall pipes is not the best option, and that the scheme is outdated.

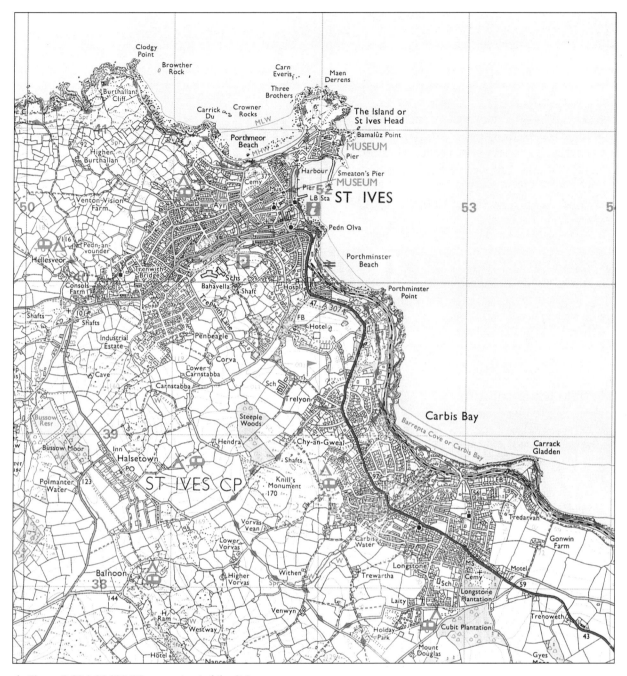

▲ **Figure 9.29** 1:25 000 OS map extract of the St Ives area.

The pumping station will be built in the teeth of intense local opposition: the people of St Ives have been fighting the plan for years. Prominent residents, such as the painter Patrick Heron and Labour MP Peter Shore, have thundered against it, Surfers Against Sewage, a pressure group, have campaigned against it, locally based engineers have drawn up cheaper and less destructive alternatives, and, in 1990, the town held a referendum on the subject in which 99 per cent of the population voted 'No'. Last year they had their first major success, when Cornwall County Council refused the water company planning permission to build the pumping station.

▲ **Figure 9.30** From *The Independent Magazine*, 26 March 1994.

Who's who in water management?

The National Rivers Authority (NRA)

The NRA is a quango – an unelected body consisting of people who are appointed directly by the government – set up under the Water Act 1989, which took over the management of rivers from water companies. It answers to Parliament through the Secretary of State for the Environment. It is responsible for the protection of rivers, groundwater, coastal waters, and estuaries. Its responsibilities are:

- monitoring water quality
- controlling pollution
- regulating discharges into rivers, streams, lakes, and the sea
- managing water supply resources by regulating extraction from rivers, lakes, and underground
- providing flood and sea defences
- maintaining and developing inland fisheries
- conserving and protecting water environments
- promoting recreational water activities.

Private water companies

There are over 30 private water companies in the UK, each originally based on river catchment boundaries. They were privatized in 1989 under the Water Act. Prior to 1989 authorities were responsible both for providing water and sewage services, and for pollution controls along rivers and coasts. The regulatory role has now been taken on by the NRA which can prosecute water companies if their activities threaten the quality of river and coastal waters. Privatization also meant that they were no longer financed or controlled by local councils. Their income now comes from charges, and they are owned by shareholders. The industry is regulated by Ofwat, an independent body which controls prices and reports to Parliament.

European Union influences

- *Bathing water directive* was introduced in 1975 to define standards for beaches where bathing is practised. All EU countries were allowed ten years to bring their beaches up to scratch. The UK only identified 27 beaches (Blackpool and Brighton were amongst those excluded) but in 1987 a further 350 were added. The directive sets physical, chemical, and microbiological standards, and beaches are tested, with fortnightly samples taken during April–September. In the UK tests are carried out by the NRA, which reports to the Department of the Environment.

- *The Blue Flag Award* This began in 1987 as part of the European Year of the Environment. In the UK it is supported by the Tidy Britain Group and the English Tourist Board, with help from the NRA, the Department of the Environment, and local authorities. The award is given annually and is valid for one year. It means that certain levels of water quality are met, that certain standards of facilities such as toilets and parking are provided, and that both these and the beach are clean.

- *Urban waste water treatment directive* This was passed in 1991 and states that a minimum level of primary treatment is required before sewage from settlements of over 10 000 is discharged into the sea. Outfalls serving settlements with populations of over 150 000 must have secondary, biological treatment. Governments have until the year 2000 to comply with its conditions. In addition by 2005 all discharges from communities with a population between 2000 and 10 000 must be primary treated.

The scientists and Surfers Against Sewage also believe the scheme is too large, and favour several small-scale sewage works, where sewage will receive tertiary treatment including UV treatment, as is done in Jersey, and which has recently been adopted by Welsh Water.

Other criticisms have been made by a local resident, an engineer, who claims that the outfall pipe is too short and has been put in the wrong place, where local currents – from the west into St Ives Bay – will wash liquid effluent onto the beaches. He also believes that sand movements caused by such currents will eventually block the pipe. Finally there is a financial argument: the scheme is expensive with 32 per cent of the cost being met by only 3 per cent of the population through increased water bills. South West Water already have the highest charges of any company in the UK. Critics claim that it has been developed by the local water company purely on the grounds that, as a 'grand scheme', it makes more profit for its shareholders.

Views of South West Water

South West Water manages water supply and waste disposal in West Cornwall. Its position is that this scheme is the best for dealing with the problems. It has put considerable effort into keeping local people informed by publishing brochures and posters, and opportunities have been provided for people to ask questions about the scheme through the staging of exhibitions and meetings in the main places affected.

▼ **Figure 9.31** South West Water puts forward the benefits of the scheme.

The problem

The enjoyment of some of the best beaches in West Cornwall has been spoiled for many years because of 47 outfalls discharging raw sewage into the sea. Many of these outfalls date back to Victorian times.

The solution

Providing the right solution for such an environmentally sensitive area is not something that can be achieved overnight.

Our professional engineers and scientists spent several years carrying out environmental studies and investigations, some taking whole seasons to complete, to find the best possible scheme to solve the local problems.

The scheme now under way provides the most practical and cost-effective solution, and will help local bathing waters to comply with the latest European standards. It has been approved by the Department of the Environment and has the backing and support of the independent National Rivers Authority.

Scheme benefits

When we have completed the scheme in 1995 it will:
- eliminate 47 crude sewage outfalls
- help to ensure local bathing waters meet European standards
- protect against inland sewage flooding
- replace or repair local unsound sewers
- cure the smell problem at Hayle
- have the flexibility to meet new future standards and allow capacity for growth in the local population
- allow restrictions on new developments to be lifted.

(a) Publicity brochures.

As stated in the brochures, treatment at Hayle Waste Water Treatment Works includes preliminary, primary, and full secondary treatment before the treated waste water is discharged through a tunnelled outfall, 2.65km off Gwithian Beach, St Ives Bay.

The secondary treatment process at Hayle includes the Biopur-C submerged aerated filter system. This process has been designed to treat all flows, taking into account the existing and projected populations to the year 2011.

Our discharge consent from the Secretary of State for the Environment granted in May 1990 requires us to provide only primary treatment such that no sample taken by the NRA shall contain more than 150 milligrams per litre of suspended solids. There was no requirement to meet criteria for biochemical oxygen demand (BOD). The secondary biological treatment process we are now installing at Hayle will mean we will far exceed the required standard by producing a treated waste water with approximately 30 milligrams per litre BOD and 50 milligrams per litre suspended solids.

(b) Extract from a letter from the water authority to the author.

How successful is the scheme?

Work in groups of two or three people, using Figures 9.28–9.31.

1 Carry out Environmental Impact Assessments on the water authority's scheme and the alternative posed by Surfers Against Sewage. Use the format suggested in Chapter 10 on page 227.

2 As a reporting team for BBC West, you have been sent to report the story, and to represent the views of the following:

- residents of St Ives
- residents of Penzance
- tourists
- engineers
- South West Water.

Present the variety of views in a report. One of the groups should act as a consultant and suggest how the issue should be resolved.

3 How should decisions like this be made? Who should have the final say?

4 Read the theory box on 'Who's who in water management?' (see page 210). How effectively do you consider Britain's water quality is monitored? Would you make any changes?

Ideas for further study

1 Extremes of water supply in Bangladesh and Mexico lead to an awareness of the importance of water. How aware are people in the UK? Consider the following questions as part of your enquiry:

a) What is the balance between supply and demand?

b) What is the pattern of water availability per capita?

c) How are supply and demand controlled?

d) What proportion of water consumed comes from groundwater, river extraction, and reservoirs?

e) Who makes decisions about the construction of new dams and reservoirs?

f) Is there a need to conserve water?

A starting point is to contact your local water company.

2 The quality of drinking water is an issue in many countries. Find out what problems exist in a) EMDCs and b) ELDCs. Compare problems and measures taken to tackle them. Sources of information include Friends of the Earth, Oxfam, water companies, and the Department of the Environment.

3 Investigate:

a) how your local water company treats sewage and what happens to effluent

b) awareness of sewage disposal issues and effects on bathing water quality.

4 Pollution of seas is reported in many areas of the world including the North Sea, the Mediterranean, and the Barrier Reef in Australia. Select one area to investigate sources of the pollution, its effects, and measures being taken.

Summary

- Global demand for water is increasing and placing pressures on supply, in terms of quantity and quality.
- The supply of water varies spatially, and this leads to management problems where there is either too much or too little.
- Water needs to be managed if the needs of current users, and those of the future, are to be met.
- The management of water has economic, social, and environmental implications.

References and further reading

J. D. Ives and B. Messerli, *The Himalayan dilemma: reconciling development and conservation*, Routledge, 1989.

N. N. Myers, *The Gaia Atlas of Planet Management*, Gaia Books Ltd, 1993.

F. Pearce, 'Human lives shrugged off in flood plan', *New Scientist*, 11 May 1991.

F. Pearce, 'Acts of God, acts of man', *New Scientist*, 18 May 1991.

J. Seymour and H. Girardet, *Blueprint for a Green Planet*, Dorling Kindersley, 1987.

F. Slater (ed.), *People and Environments*, Collins Educational, 1986.

F. Slater (ed.), *Societies, Choices and Environments*, Collins Educational, 1991.

Waste: a recyclable resource?

Where does waste come from?

Globally, over one billion tonnes of waste are produced every year as a result of our consumption habits, and of industrial processes. The very act of living, whereby food is eaten and digested in order to provide energy, produces human waste. Increasing amounts of all types of waste are being produced as the world's population grows, and as people's lifestyles are changing. In particular there has been a change in consumption patterns which have emerged in ELDCs since 1945. Increased affluence in these countries has enabled more people to buy consumer products, while at the same time there has been an increase in product marketing to promote consumption. This has given rise to the term 'consumer society'. Product sales and presentation have also changed, for example packaging for hygiene purposes or to enhance the visual appeal of a product. This, and the short lifespan of many products, has created another new term, the 'throwaway' society.

Economic wealth and waste

1 a) Test the relationship between economic wealth and the amount of waste produced by countries by calculating the Spearman rank correlation coefficient R for selected countries in Figure 10.1. The technique box on pages 214–5 explains the Spearman's rank correlation coefficient.
   b) Comment on what your result tells you.

2 Work in groups of two or three people.
   a) Survey the contents of kitchen and bathroom cupboards at home, and count how many items are packaged (i) for hygiene and (ii) for visual appeal. Are there any other reasons for packaging to be used?
   b) Find some examples of 'over-packaged' items.
   c) Collate your results, and report to another group.
   d) With other groups, consider to what extent you feel that packaging is necessary.

3 a) Using a graphical method, display the data in Figure 10.2. If possible use a spreadsheet.
   b) Describe what is shown by your graph.
   c) Why is it difficult to obtain this type of information for ELDCs?

4 Suggest what future global trends in waste generation are likely to be.

Country	GDP per capita (US$)	Waste produced per capita 1990 (kg)
Canada	19 020	601
Czech Republic	4000	251
Germany	16 500	350
Greece	5340	296
Hungary	2560	463
Japan	23 730	411
Poland	1760	338
Portugal	4260	257
Spain	9150	322
Sweden	21 710	374
Turkey	1360	353
UK	14 570	348
USA	21 100	721

▲ **Figure 10.1** Wealth and waste.

Country	1980	1990
	(kg/inhabitant)	
Austria	222[1]	320
Belgium	313	343
Canada	524	601
France	260	328
Germany	348[2]	318[3]
Greece	259	296
Italy	249	348
Japan	355	408
Luxembourg	351	448
The Netherlands	489[4]	497
Norway	416	472
Portugal	214	287
Spain	270[5]	322[6]
Sweden	302	374
Switzerland	351	441
United Kingdom	319	398
USA	723	803

[1] 1979   [2] before Oct 1990   [3] 1987
[4] 1982   [5] 1978   [6] 1988

▲ **Figure 10.2** Quantities of municipal waste, 1980/90.

Spearman's rank correlation coefficient

This is a statistical method used to test the strength of a relationship between two variables. It provides a single value between –1 and +1: +1 tells us that there is a positive relationship, –1 tells us that there is a negative relationship, and 0 tells us that there is no relationship.

▼ **Figure 10.3** Spearman's rank correlation coefficient.

(a) Using the data.

(c) Level of significance.

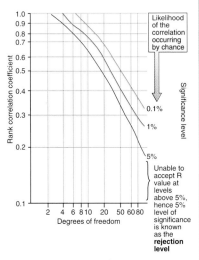

	Column 1	Column 2	Column 3	Column 4	Column 5	Column 6	Column 7
1	Canada	19 020		601			
2	Czech Republic	4000		251			
3	Germany	16 500		350			
4	Greece	5340		296			
5	Hungary	2560		463			
6	Japan	23 730		411			
7	Poland	1760		338			
8	Portugal	4260		257			
9	Spain	9150		322			
10	Sweden	21 710		374			
11	Turkey	1360		353			
12	UK	14 570		348			
13	USA	21 100		721			

(b) Assessing the correlation.

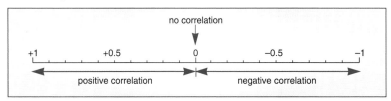

In order to test the relationship, follow these steps.

1 Copy Figure 10.3a, using the data in columns 2 and 4.

2 Rank each set of data from 1 (highest) to 13 (lowest) in each of columns 3 and 5.

3 Calculate the difference between the value for each country in columns 3 and 5, and write it in column 6, e.g. a rank of 2 in column 3, and of 4 in column 5 gives a difference of 2.

4 Square the values in column 6, write the answers in column 7, and add a total at the foot of column 7, known as a Σ value, for step 5.

5 Use the following formula to calculate the Spearman rank correlation coefficient value R by substituting the figures used:

$$R = \frac{1 - (6 \times \Sigma d^2)}{n (n^2 - 1)}$$

n is the number of values, which in this case is the number of countries (13).
Σd^2 is the sum of the squared differences, at the foot of column 7.

6 Interpret your result using Figure 10.3b.

The result should show a positive relationship, but not a strong one. The closer the final figure R is to +1 or –1, the stronger the relationship is. This is known as a **correlation**.

Significance

For greater precision, the result may be tested for significance. When a correlation is sought, techniques such as Spearman's rank are useful. However, a figure of +0.5 or –0.5 does not suggest a definite link. There is a possibility that a result may have been due to chance. Before it is considered statistically significant, it has to be tested against the probability that chance influenced it. This is done using significance tables, which give theoretical values against which results may be compared.

To test for confidence, follow these steps.

1 Note how many examples you had in your correlation. Data for thirteen countries means n is 13. This gives you the degrees of freedom.

2 Note your correlation figure. Ignore the + or – as only the figure is important.

3 On Figure 10.3c, find where the two meet. If they meet above the 5% line, you have found a low possibility (less than 5%) that your result was caused by chance. If it is above the 1% line, the likelihood of chance is less: 1% or less. Even better if it is above the 0.1% line!

Using significance tables, a result may be given as a percentage value, usually 95% or 99%. This means that 95 or 99 times out of 100, the relationship is unlikely to have been caused by chance, and is significant. Percentage values are referred to as **confidence limits** or **intervals**. The greater the n value the lower the likelihood that chance affected the relationship.

In the example used here, the result is outside the 99% confidence level. Consider why the relationship between waste production and GDP is not strong.

Methods of waste disposal

Every country in the world has to decide which methods of waste disposal it wishes to adopt. The EU Waste Directive 1991 sets out its preferred hierarchy of waste management:

- waste minimization
- re-use
- recycling of materials
- incineration with energy recovery
- incineration without energy recovery
- landfill.

Methods chosen depend on various factors including the nature of the waste, economic costs, and environmental impact.

Waste avoidance

One view is that not producing of waste is the only really environmentally sound option. However, it is generally accepted that we can only reduce waste, not eliminate it, in the foreseeable future. It needs a basic change in attitude by the public and by manufacturers, and this is only likely if governments are prepared to take action. In the USA, environmental groups talk of 'precycling', where consumers select products with less packaging and avoid disposable items. It is attractive to consumers on cost grounds, as about one-tenth of the average weekly shopping bill is spent on packaging. However, in EMDCs, highly packaged items are the norm, so waste avoidance is not easy. There are a few signs that governments are trying to tackle the problem – for example, the EU Packaging Directive 1993 sets a goal for 25 per cent of packaging to be recycled by the year 2000.

Changing our behaviour

As a group, collect packaging from things that you and your families have bought in one day.

1 Consider all the materials and what is likely to happen to them in your local area, using the EU Waste Directive 1991 classification (see page 215).

2 Reclassify them with reference to Figure 10.4, and consider what each person could do to alter his/her consumer behaviour.

▶ **Figure 10.4** How to cut down on plastic waste.

ECO PILLOWS AND DUVETS

Excellent-quality pillows and duvets filled with recycled plastic bottles. It's a good way of keeping plastic (otherwise known as PET) bottles out of landfill sites and incinerators until the time comes when we revert back to re-usable glass bottles. The PET bottles are shredded and respun to make a hollow polyester fibre that traps and retains heat, but which is as soft as cotton wool. Currently the fibre is spun using at least 50% recycled material but this will increase over time to 100%.

▲ **Figure 10.5** Recycling.
(a) Different uses of recycled materials.

POSITIVE ACTION

- **Don't buy fresh food pre-packed in plastic**

  In many supermarkets, meat and vegetables are pre-packed in plastic, to the ridiculous extent that four tomatoes may have their own plastic tray surrounded by plastic film. This is a quite unnecessary source of plastic pollution. Whenever possible avoid pre-packed food.

- **Refuse plastic containers for takeaway food**

  You don't need them. Most of these containers are thrown away within minutes. Paper bags are all that is required.

- **Choose natural materials for clothing**

  Avoid artificial fibres in clothing, even those present as mixtures with natural materials. Also, if you can, avoid the plastic that is disguised as leather in shoes.

- **Avoid disposable plastic in the kitchen**

  Plastic is long-lasting, so it makes no sense to use it in objects that are disposable. Use plastic food boxes instead of throwaway film and bags.

- **Ask for biodegradable packaging**

  Your local supermarket manager may not have heard about biodegradable plastic bags. Try suggesting that they are used instead of permanent plastic.

Recycling

Recycling is one of the most popular options to environmentalists. It involves either processing waste products to produce secondary raw materials which are then used to make a new but similar product, or using waste to generate new products or to generate energy. Figure 10.5b shows a recycling plant in London.

The first prototype Deja shoe was made in 1990, funded by a US$110,000 grant from Oregon State for innovative recycling projects. The grant enabled production of the first 5,000 pairs of recycled shoes, made from, among other things, plastic trimmings from the manufacture of disposable nappies, and used plastic milk containers. Shortly afterwards, supported by a management team of footwear industry specialists and financial backers, the Deja Shoe Company was formed, dedicated to the production of footwear made from recycled materials. This year's newest lines include as many as 15 different recycled materials.

"Footwear people feel comfortable in, and comfortable about."

Julie Lewis, founder of Deja Shoes

Deja shoes: one person's waste is another's raw material

◀ (b) A recycling plant in London.

Recycling involves a change of attitude towards waste, which is summed up here:

'There is rarely such a thing as "waste": rather there are materials that are sometimes in the wrong place.'

Gaia Atlas of Planet Management

However, recycling has its opponents. It is sometimes more expensive than other options, which may mean that ELDCs are less able to use it. Other arguments suggest that some recycling uses more energy than it saves, and is therefore not as environmentally sound as it seems: materials vary – recycling aluminium, for example, saves energy, whereas recycling plastics uses more. Finally, recycling plastics is chemically complex, though they make up an increasing proportion of waste.

◀ **Figure 10.6** One of the costs of recycling.

It is possible to build recycling potential into certain products. Germany, Sweden, Italy, and Japan are planning to introduce legislation requiring manufacturers of electrical goods to take them back at the end of their useful life, dismantle them, and re-use or reprocess as many component parts as possible before disposing of the remainder. This should encourage manufacturers to design goods with a high proportion of recyclable materials, and better-quality materials and design for the non-recyclable parts.

Composting

About 30 per cent of the average household's waste matter is organic. This can be dealt with by composting which can then be used for landscape work in road building, housing, and shopping developments, or then be bagged and sold as garden compost. If it is left to decompose anaerobically (without air) in landfills, organic waste produces a large amount of methane which is one of the main greenhouse gases, and which presents a fire/explosion risk. When organic matter is composted aerobically (with air present), there is no production of methane. Some local authorities in the UK either collect organic waste and compost it centrally (e.g. Dundee), or actively encourage residents to carry out their own composting by offering free or subsidized composters (e.g. Bristol).

Landfill

In most countries, the bulk of household waste ends up in landfill sites or on rubbish tips. In ELDCs, it may just be taken to a designated site and dumped. In EMDCs, waste is dumped on landfill sites rather than on rubbish dumps. A landfill site is managed and organized so that waste is spread as a layer, then covered by topsoil. This approach avoids the creation of heaps of rotting waste, but waste is still dumped, unsorted, having only been crushed into a foul-smelling mass.

▶ **Figure 10.7** Landfill.
(a) A landfill site, where household waste is disposed of by local authority waste collections.

(b) Decomposition – a matter of time.

WHAT HAPPENS TO DISCARDED RUBBISH?

In the last two decades litter from cans and bottles has become almost universal. What happens to this waste after it has been thrown away?

Will natural processes get rid of it? The answer depends on the material. Metal cans and glass bottles eventually break up fairly harmlessly, but plastic bottles, an ever larger part of packaging, are resistant to all forms of natural chemical decay and are practically indestructible.

ALUMINIUM

Aluminium in cans reacts with oxygen in the atmosphere, but forms a layer of oxide which protects it from decomposition. Aluminium rubbish takes many years to disintegrate.

After one year
Most of the paint has dissolved, but otherwise the can is intact.

After five years
The can has been flattened and has sunk into the soil.

After ten years
The can is very slowly being decomposed by contact with the soil.

GLASS

Glass is a harmless and wholly inert substance – it does not chemically decompose at all. However, it does disintegrate, although after burial this process more or less stops.

After one year
The bottle is still intact on the surface.

After five years
The glass has broken into large fragments.

After ten years
The glass, now in small fragments, lies buried harmlessly in the soil.

PLASTIC

Many plastics are broken down to some extent by ultraviolet light: this makes them brittle. However, once underground most buried plastics do not decompose at all. Much work is being done on developing a biodegradable plastic.

After one year
The bottle is in much the same state as when it was thrown away.

After five years
Sunlight has partially decomposed the plastic, but the bottle is intact.

After ten years
Once buried, the plastic will remain intact almost indefinitely.

The argument in favour of landfill is that it is cheap, and in countries that can afford to cover it with soil, the waste is hidden from view. After the site has been filled up, it may be landscaped and used for other purposes.

However, there are criticisms of this method:

- increasing land shortage
- opposition from those who live nearby, as sites tend to attract rats
- disturbance created by delivery lorries
- water percolating through the site becomes polluted with chemicals and may contaminate local watercourses
- generation of methane gas creates fire risks
- even though it may be hidden from view, waste smells and may take a long time to decompose (Figure 10.7b)
- any subsequent land use is threatened by possible subsidence.

Incineration

In response to difficulties associated with landfill, some countries have decided to burn some of their waste. By doing so, waste is reduced in bulk and may then be buried, thus taking up less land; at the same time, heat produced may be used for energy production. Although economically and ecologically sound, it has its problems. Unless they are burned at above 900 °C, plastics emit dioxins which are some of the most poisonous substances known: some incinerators are unable to maintain such a level of heat or are too costly. Other pollutants released in the smoke may cause problems of which we are not yet aware. Research is being carried out on this method of disposal and many believe that under carefully controlled circumstances it offers the best option environmentally. Both landfill and incineration offer opportunities for energy generation – see pages 225–7.

Dumping at sea

This is the cheapest option and is used by many countries, particularly for hazardous waste. However, it arouses opposition because the impact on the marine environment is largely unknown. Items of waste thrown into the sea off North America have been discovered on the western beaches of Scotland, highlighting the global implications of sea dumping. Campaigns by environmental groups have led to the practice being abandoned by some of countries: early in 1994, 70 countries agreed to a ban on sea dumping of radioactive material, and a similar treaty dealing with other industrial waste was signed by countries bordering the North Atlantic.

Comparing options

1 Draw up a table to illustrate the advantages and disadvantages of each of the waste disposal options detailed in the text.

2 *Role play:* Your local council plans to create a landfill site in your local community. A public meeting is to be held to give people a chance to voice their opinions. The following groups are to be represented:

- residents' associations
- local conservation groups
- local leisure groups, e.g. Ramblers, Friends of the Earth
- the council
- local businesses
- the Department of the Environment.

Divide into pairs with each pair taking a different role. Prepare a presentation of your views. If you reject the proposal you must be able to argue for alternative methods of disposal.

Each group has three minutes to give their presentation, and may then be questioned by the other groups. When everyone has had their say, the proposal and any alternatives that have been put forward must be voted on.

Evaluating the options

1 a) Use the figures for Canada and Switzerland in Figure 10.8 to draw a pie chart.

   b) Using an atlas, suggest reasons why these two countries have different solutions to waste disposal.

   c) What other factors may have influenced their choice?

2 With reference to Figure 10.8, and applying your knowledge of waste issues so far, suggest strategies for waste disposal which the UK could reasonably adopt within five years.

▶ **Figure 10.8** Waste disposal routes. (Some figures have been rounded.)

Which is the best option?

Local councils are often influenced in their decision-making:

- by national policies which may favour and subsidize particular waste disposal routes
- by international policies – since 1992, many local councils are working on the recommendations from the Earth Summit in Rio de Janeiro known as 'Agenda 21', which promoted local initiatives to improve environmental quality.

National waste is one of the hardest environmental problems for governments to tackle. There is no agreement on which disposal option is least harmful to the environment. Economic costs are important and may be influenced by regulations controlling certain options. For example, landfill costs vary according to the strictness of legislation. Costs are influenced by factors such as the physical geography of a country or region. In the Netherlands there are few landfills because it would be easy to pollute the water table there, whereas in Britain 90 per cent of waste is sent to landfill sites, using sites such as former quarries. Different countries adopt different strategies to tackle the problem (Figure 10.8), and these are examined in the following case studies.

Country	Amount (thousand tonnes/year)	Combustion	Landfill	Composting	Recycling
		(expressed as % of amount of material)			
Austria	2800	11	65	18	6
Belgium	3500	54	43	0	3
Canada	16 000	8	80	2	10
Denmark	2600	48	29	4	19
Finland	2500	2	83	0	15
France	20 000	42	45	10	3
Germany	25 000	36	46	2	16
Greece	3150	0	100	0	0
Ireland	1100	0	97	0	3
Italy	17 500	16	74	7	3
Japan	50 000	75	20	5	*
Luxembourg	180	75	22	1	2
The Netherlands	7700	35	45	5	16
Norway	2000	22	67	5	7
Portugal	2650	0	85	15	0
Spain	13 300	6	65	17	13
Sweden	3200	47	34	3	16
Switzerland	3700	59	12	7	22
United Kingdom	30 000	8	90	0	2
USA	177 500	16	67	2	15

* Figures for Japan are calculated after the removal of recyclables.

Using waste as a resource

Increasingly, countries adopt waste disposal routes which use waste as a resource. This reduces the impact on the environment, and produces a raw material of economic value. The following case studies of Germany, and Cairo in Egypt, highlight some of the issues that may be raised when adopting this approach.

Waste management in Germany

In common with all EMDCs, Germany deals with increasing amounts of waste from industry and households. Industrial waste includes hazardous substances, and problems associated with this are considered on pages 228–32. Waste is collected from 98 per cent of households connected to a regular collection service. Most of this is still taken to landfills or incineration plants. However, by the end of the 1980s, sites for landfills were limited and there was a growing awareness among the German people of environmental issues, including waste disposal, and the government responded to this. Waste avoidance was promoted as the first choice, followed by the development of returnable systems. It was acknowledged that these alone could not deal with the problem, and recycling was adopted as a policy for reducing the amount that would otherwise be disposed of in landfills and incinerators – described as 'one-way' waste. A law on the Avoidance of Packaging Waste was introduced in 1991, focusing on packaging, which makes up 30 per cent of all household waste.

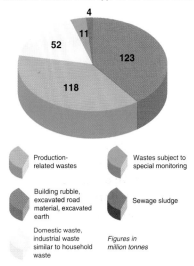

Amount of waste in 1990: approx. 300 million tonnes

4
11
52
123
118

Production-related wastes	Wastes subject to special monitoring
Building rubble, excavated road material, excavated earth	Sewage sludge
Domestic waste, industrial waste similar to household waste	*Figures in million tonnes*

▲ **Figure 10.9** Amount and type of waste generated in Germany.

▼ **Figure 10.10** A typical household's waste and its recycling potential.

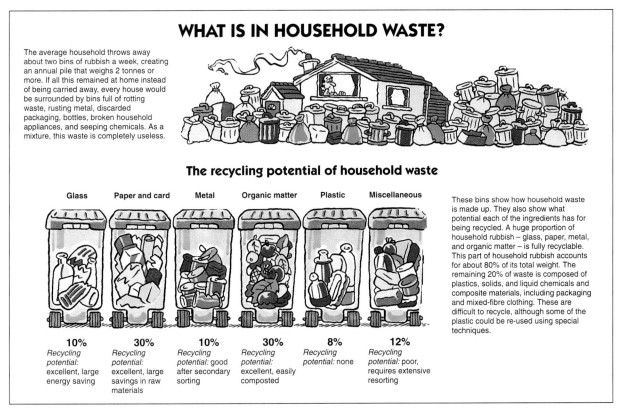

WHAT IS IN HOUSEHOLD WASTE?

The average household throws away about two bins of rubbish a week, creating an annual pile that weighs 2 tonnes or more. If all this remained at home instead of being carried away, every house would be surrounded by bins full of rotting waste, rusting metal, discarded packaging, bottles, broken household appliances, and seeping chemicals. As a mixture, this waste is completely useless.

The recycling potential of household waste

Glass	Paper and card	Metal	Organic matter	Plastic	Miscellaneous
10%	**30%**	**10%**	**30%**	**8%**	**12%**
Recycling potential: excellent, large energy saving	*Recycling potential:* excellent, large savings in raw materials	*Recycling potential:* good after secondary sorting	*Recycling potential:* excellent, easily composted	*Recycling potential:* none	*Recycling potential:* poor, requires extensive resorting

These bins show how household waste is made up. They also show what potential each of the ingredients has for being recycled. A huge proportion of household rubbish – glass, paper, metal, and organic matter – is fully recyclable. This part of household rubbish accounts for about 80% of its total weight. The remaining 20% of waste is composed of plastics, solids, and liquid chemicals and composite materials, including packaging and mixed-fibre clothing. These are difficult to recycle, although some of the plastic could be re-used using special techniques.

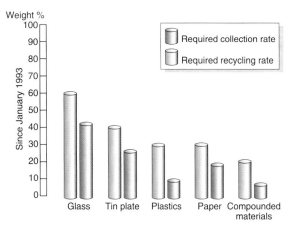

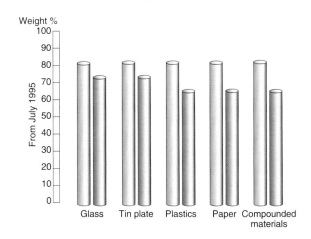

▲ **Figure 10.11** Targets for sales packaging.

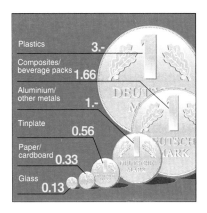

▲ **Figure 10.12** Licence fees for the 'Green Dot'.

Who should pay ?

1 Suggest reasons for the differences in fees shown in Figure 10.12.

2 Calculate the amount added to the price of a can of drink, and a television or other piece of electrical equipment. How significant is the increase?

3 Who is paying for the system? Do you think this is fair? What are the alternatives, and how feasible or popular might these be?

The Packaging Ordinance

This obliges manufacturers and distributors to take back a certain percentage of packaging for re-use and recycling. It distinguishes between three types of packaging:

- *transport packaging* – pallets and outer protective wrapping used for the journey between manufacturer and retailer
- *outer packaging* – extra packaging used in retailing for assembly or presentation, including gift packs and blister packs
- *sales packaging* – used by the final consumer for transportation or protection until the goods are consumed.

Targets were set for each of these types and for different materials used in packaging – some of them are shown in Figure 10.11.

The retail trade cannot take back all its packaging – it has a shortage of storage space and there are potential hygiene problems – so companies are exempt from having to accept packaging if they are members of a nationwide scheme for the collection, sorting, and recycling of packaging waste. Six hundred industries joined to organize the Duales System Deutschland (DSD), a non-profit-making organization financed by fees from companies which use a special Green Dot trademark. Only packaging with the Green Dot is collected by DSD.

How the Duales System works

Regional waste disposal firms both from the public and the private sectors collect used packaging and sort it into individual materials. Collection is either from households issued with special bins, or from containers set up near homes. Individuals play a crucial role in this first stage of sorting. After sorting the firms then forward packaging either to manufacturers of different packaging materials, or to companies established especially for the purpose of recycling and marketing secondary raw materials. Both guarantee to accept the waste from DSD.

How successful has it been?

Some data suggest that collection and sorting have been successful, with local authorities reporting a 20 per cent reduction in waste for landfill sites. However, when looking at re-use and recycling of the sorted materials the picture is less clear, and is causing controversy in Germany. For some of the waste material, the market is not big enough within Germany, and so some is exported. The various problems are examined in Figure 10.13.

Too much of a good thing

Every day for a year, Margot von Shad carefully picked her rubbish apart, setting aside the cans, cartons, packaging and other household products marked with a green dot to put in yellow rubbish bins in front of her house. But last Sunday she decided, along with some friends, that it was a waste of time. She is dismayed by reports that the country's waste collecting and recycling scheme is going bankrupt. Last week it announced that it needs DM500m (£200m) just to keep going.

Part of the problem is the scheme's success. For plastics alone, Duales System Deutschland (DSD) expects to collect this year four times the amount it was set up to deal with. At the weekend, Klaus Topfer, the federal Environment Minister who devised the scheme, proudly referred to his fellow Germans as the '(trash) collectors of the world'.

But Topfer's compliment is hardly soothing the worries of both an environment-conscious public and German industry. DSD's ability to recycle waste lags well behind its success in collecting it. With dumping sites filling up and scandals over waste exports increasingly surfacing, politicians and industrialists are now under pressure to rethink the entire system. In practice, the system contains a major flaw. In the case of plastic, the largest packaging product on the market, recycling may be economically less viable than 'down-cycling' – destroying the product through methods such as incineration.

Unlike glass, aluminium, and paper, which have been recycled for decades, plastic packaging such as yoghurt pots and beverage bottles are of little value to recyclers. They contain different colourings and are usually made of mixed elements.

In 1993, DSD expects to collect nearly 400 000 tonnes of the 1.2m tonnes of plastics produced annually in the country. But recycling capacity in Germany stands at just 124 000 tonnes.

However, a further 152 000 tonnes will be exported. In response to a scandal last year in France, where German waste was found sitting in the open air on a badly controlled landfill, DSD has set up a system to test the viability of recycling companies abroad.

Many cases slip through DSD's net, says Greenpeace, the environmental group. Only last March Greenpeace claimed to have found thousands of tonnes of DSD waste in Indonesia, despite an Indonesian government ban on waste imports brought in last November to curb the flow of waste entering the country. 'DSD even pays foreign firms to take back plastics, which are then put on empty ships returning to Asia from German ports,' a consultant says. Part of the solution lies in Germany developing its own recycling facilities. But investments in plastic recycling, which is costly and involves lengthy research, are dragging behind.

▲ **Figure 10.13** From the *Financial Times*, 23 June 1993.

Opinions of the Duales System

1 Read Figure 10.13 and identify the main groups and individuals affected by or involved with the System.

2 For each group or individual, summarize their views of the System.

3 Does Germany's experience seem to sound a death knell for recycling?

Modifying the System

Because of criticisms about the Packaging Ordinance, the Environment Minister announced modifications in February 1994. Collection targets have been replaced by minimum recycling rates, a percentage of the total 'Green Dot' packaging in a region. The time in which targets are to be met has been extended by three years; and incineration of secondary, transport, and packaging materials in excess of targets is allowed.

Discussion points

1 Do you think the modifications are likely to be sufficient? Explain your answer.

2 Other countries are aiming to increase their recycling rates. What lessons could they learn from the experience of Germany?

Recycling waste in Cairo, Egypt

One of the oldest and most extensive recycling operations in the world takes place in squatter settlements on the outskirts of Cairo. Here thousands of people make their living by collecting the city's waste, bringing it back and sorting it into piles of paper, plastic, bone, glass, and metal. Household waste varies: in wealthier areas where people shop at supermarkets, refuse is mostly packaging, whilst in poorer districts only rotting vegetables tend to be thrown away. Salvaged materials are then sold to the thousands of small industries and workshops in Cairo. This system, which manages to recycle 30 per cent of the city's waste, is run by people known as the Zabbaleen who have traditionally used donkey carts to collect waste from almost all of the city. Sixty per cent of Cairo's household waste is collected by the Zabbaleen; the remainder is either collected by 'official' refuse collectors or left to rot in the streets.

The city authorities tend to be embarrassed by the Zabbaleen system, which they feel is outdated and not suitable for a capital city. However, Cairo has a population of over 14 million which grows by approximately 1000 a day and produces over 10 000 tonnes of waste each day, so the Zabbaleen play a vital role. Although the authorities have encouraged new Western-style waste collection companies to compete with the Zabbaleen, they have had mixed success: modern compressor trucks used by these companies have made the rubbish collection far more efficient, but there is a huge problem with disposal. Disposal facilities have not grown with the city's population: Cairo has one composting site with a capacity of 600 tonnes a day, and landfill sites are 10km outside the city, which incurs considerable transport costs. As a result, the new companies have been selling refuse to the Zabbaleen who recycle most of it.

The Zabbaleen system was forced to change when donkey carts were banned from the city in 1990, and groups co-operated to buy pick-up trucks. Although the settlements give the impression of poverty and deprivation, many Zabbaleen are doing well in a city where there is a considerable market for recycled goods. There are also signs that some goods made of recycled materials are becoming popular with the wealthy in Cairo, and recycled glass jugs are even being exported for sale in fashionable department stores in Britain. The Zabbaleen are beginning to expand their interests in order to take advantage of such developments by setting up recycling industries of their own, thus making use of materials themselves rather than selling on.

▼ **Figure 10.14** Sorting through the rubbish.

Importance of the Zabbaleen

1 Compare the percentage of recycled waste in Cairo with waste recycled in other cities. Suggest reasons for the difference.

2 a) What problems may arise from the Zabbaleen way of life?

b) How might these problems be tackled without preventing the Zabbaleen from continuing with their valuable work?

c) How do you rate the system in Cairo compared with others you have studied? Is there potential for this type of system in the UK?

Energy from waste

As well as reduction, re-use, and recycling of waste, there are also opportunities for extracting energy from waste. Both waste incineration and landfill offer opportunities for energy extraction. However, both have environmental impacts that need to be assessed. One possibility is to develop landfill sites for the recovery of biogas, a mixture of methane and carbon dioxide; another is to build more waste incinerators that have a means of heat recovery.

Landfill or incineration?

Each of these two options has a major environmental impact – on global warming. A report by the Royal Commission on Environmental Pollution in 1993 entitled 'Incineration of Waste' concluded that incinerating domestic waste has a smaller impact on the greenhouse effect than landfill, even if it is assumed that some methane is extracted and burnt. This conclusion was based on the assumption that only 40 per cent of the methane could be collected and burnt, and the other 60 per cent would escape to the atmosphere. One kilogram of methane has a far greater greenhouse impact than one kilogram of carbon dioxide – the Report assumed that methane is 7.5 times more potent than carbon dioxide as a greenhouse gas. The overall impact of the landfill option was therefore considerably greater.

However, the data can be interpreted in other ways. Figure 10.15 shows a reworking of the same figures but with a different outcome. The main differences in assumptions made are:

- far more of the carbon than was assumed in the Royal Commission report remains trapped in the landfill site and never reaches the atmosphere
- only 50 per cent of the methane leaks to the atmosphere
- the reworked figures assume a lower power station efficiency, which reduces carbon dioxide emissions saved by the incineration route.

It is therefore possible to compare the environmental impact of energy options from waste, when the environmental impact is known. The problem comes when comparing different environmental impacts, for example, comparing the risk of accidental ignition of leaking methane with the increased lorry traffic to an incinerator.

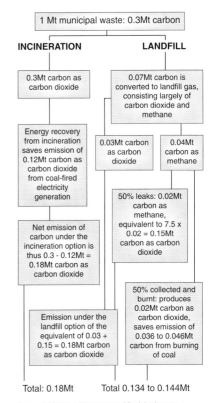

▼ **Figure 10.15** Incineration or landfill? Comparing emissions of greenhouse gases.

The unit Mt is 1 million tonnes. Municipal waste landfilled in the UK is around 30Mt/year, while methane emissions are around 2Mt/year.

225

1 Using the information provided in Figure 10.15, identify the quantity of carbon (in million tonnes) produced by:
   a) 1 million tonnes of municipal waste
   b) incinerating 1 million tonnes of municipal waste, allowing for carbon emissions saved from burning an equivalent amount of coal
   c) allowing the waste to decompose within a landfill site
   d) leakage of methane, taking into account the greenhouse impact of methane.

2 Using these figures, which option has the least greenhouse impact?

One area of dispute in the above calculation is the assumption that methane has a 7.5 times greater greenhouse impact than carbon dioxide. Other reports quote a figure of between 20 and 30 times. This will have a significant impact on the outcome of the calculations.

3 a) Carry out the calculation again, assuming that methane has a greenhouse impact that is 21 times that of carbon dioxide.
   b) What impact does this have on the outcome of the analysis?

The other area of dispute is the percentage of methane leakage.

4 If the technology for extracting methane from landfill sites could be improved so that only 15 per cent of the methane leaked into the atmosphere, what impact would this have on the outcome of the analysis?

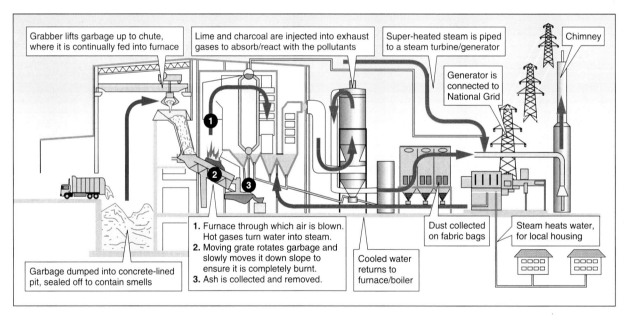

Grabber lifts garbage up to chute, where it is continually fed into furnace

Lime and charcoal are injected into exhaust gases to absorb/react with the pollutants

Super-heated steam is piped to a steam turbine/generator

Chimney

Generator is connected to National Grid

Dust collected on fabric bags

Steam heats water, for local housing

Cooled water returns to furnace/boiler

1. Furnace through which air is blown. Hot gases turn water into steam.
2. Moving grate rotates garbage and slowly moves it down slope to ensure it is completely burnt.
3. Ash is collected and removed.

Garbage dumped into concrete-lined pit, sealed off to contain smells

▲ **Figure 10.16** Waste incineration process.

The following exercise is an example of an Environmental Impact Assessment (EIA) using a Leopold matrix. If you have used the EIA in Chapter 3 of the other book in this series, *The Physical Environment*, you will be familiar with the purpose of EIAs. This example is for assessing an industrial site.

Use Figures 10.16–10.18, and the guidance within the technique box, to carry out an environmental impact assessment of the two waste management options.

▶ **Figure 10.17** Energy from landfill gas.

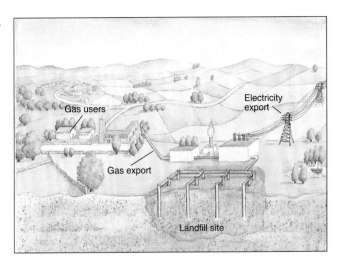

▼ **Figure 10.18** A Leopold matrix.

Characteristics of the development

| | Construction | | | | | | | | Operation | | | | | | | | |
Characteristics of the existing situation	Land requirements	Labour requirements	Raw material inputs	Transport of raw materials	Water demand	Energy demand	Noise and vibration	Emission of particles, dust, water	Waste disposal and discharge	Raw material inputs	Effects on transport	Transport of products	Water supply	Energy demands	Noise from plant	Emissions – gas, smells, particles, dust, water	Solid waste	Emergencies	Other criteria you can think of
Air																			
Land																			
Water																			
Climate																			
Land use																			
Landscape quality																			
Ecological characteristics																			
Resident population																			
Energy supply																			
Water supply																			
Sewerage																			
Solid waste disposal																			
Transportation																			

Using impact matrices

Many environmental impacts are subjective – that is, they represent opinions and reactions: someone else's view might be totally different. An impact matrix provides a framework for identifying all the impacts and their importance as you see them.

To use an impact matrix, follow these steps.

1 Identify the characteristics of the existing site.

2 Identify major impacts you feel the new development might have. These will vary according to the site.

3 Decide which impacts you will use to compare the existing site and the proposed new site. Make a list for each.

4 Construct these two lists in the form of a matrix similar to the one in Figure 10.18.

5 For each characteristic of the proposed development, consider the impact it will have on the existing site, and place a score in the appropriate square, using this scoring system:

+5 +4 +3 +2 +1 0 –1 –2 –3 –4 –5

very beneficial   no impact   very adverse

6 Score each characteristic. Remember that not all characteristics will have an impact.

7 When you have done this for both options, add up each column, and find a total score for each of the existing site and the proposed new site.

8 Compare the totals and use this to decide which option is best.

9 Evaluate your methodology. Have you identified any potential errors? How could your assessment be improved?

What happens to hazardous waste?

Some household waste, and a considerable proportion of industrial waste, is considered to be hazardous. This means that it poses particular disposal problems, with dangers of contamination to those who handle it and to the environment. As legislation for the disposal of hazardous and toxic waste becomes more strict in many countries, so the cost of dealing with it increases. One way of tackling the problem has been to export toxic waste to other countries with less stringent regulations, where it may be dumped or recycled more cheaply.

The new waste colonialists

About a year ago, customs officials in Argentina became alarmed about some of the applications crossing their desks. One businessman wanted to import 5000 tonnes of highly toxic industrial solvents. Another wanted to bring in soil with low levels of radioactivity. There were other requests to bring in tonnes of toxic waste from PVC plants and proposals to import hundreds of thousands of tonnes of waste plastics.

'In 20 years of working at customs I have never seen the quantities of industrial waste and trash coming into this country from the United States and Europe that we are seeing,' says Carlos Milstein, deputy director of the Office of Technology Imports.

By last October 200 tonnes a week of hazardous waste was coming into the country from Europe and the USA.

For Argentina, read Guatemala, Poland, Romania, Chile, or a dozen other countries that are now in the front line of a massive export drive by the most 'environmentally aware' countries in the world. The USA, Germany, Netherlands, Switzerland, and the Nordic countries, who are introducing ever tighter environmental legislation on the back of increasing consumer demands for clean industry, are now exporting millions of tonnes a year of hazardous wastes to countries with weak laws or administrations that are unable to monitor or tell the difference between raw materials and toxic waste.

'The rich countries' new standards of cleanliness are leading directly to waste colonialism,' says Andreas Bernstorff of Greenpeace Germany, who has been monitoring the trade for several years. 'The primary goal of the ecology movement – the avoidance of waste in both consumption and production – has not been achieved.' Indeed, it could be argued that environmental pressure in Europe and the USA has only shifted the problem on to the weakest.

No one doubts that Germany is the 'world champion', known to be shipping more than half a million tonnes to some 50 countries in 1991. It is no accident that Germany also has the toughest environmental laws.

Close behind in terms of tonnes per person come the Dutch, shipping more than 250 000 tonnes in 1988, the USA with 141 000 tonnes, and Switzerland and Austria with 200 000 tonnes between them. In what is increasingly a buyers' market, more than 175 million tonnes of hazardous waste was offered on the world market between 1986 and 1991, and 10 million tonnes was actually exported.

The worldwide trends of the last three years are becoming clear: an enormous increase in shipments to the Caribbean and Central and South America, an almost complete halt in wastes going to Africa where political initiatives have all but banned the trade except in South Africa and Morocco, a huge growth in eastern and central Europe, a potential explosion in the former Soviet states, and further developments in the Far East.

Critics retort that waste plants in developing countries are almost always poorly equipped, with low environmental health standards. 'In 99.99 per cent of cases', says Bernstorff, 'it is 100 times safer, ecologically, for the rich countries to treat hazardous waste "at home" where technological standards are much higher. No developing countries insist on the cleanest technologies. Very few have any idea of the long or short-term dangers of what they are handling.'

▲ **Figure 10.19** From *The Guardian*, 14 February 1992.

The Basle Convention

The Basle Convention is an international treaty that was drawn up under the UN Environment Programme in May 1992 to give importing countries the power to regulate which wastes they accept. Under the terms of the Convention, countries wishing to export hazardous waste have to request permission, and the importing country has 60 days in which to issue a permit.

However, many of those involved in the recycling business thought that this was too long to wait, as the value of many recyclables changes very frequently. As a result of this concern, the OECD (the Organization of Economic Co-operation and Development), a 'club' of 24 industrialized nations, adopted a set of rules to protect the recycling industry just before the Treaty came into force. For trade between members, the Organization drew up a graded list of hazardous wastes (Figure 10.21).

The red list in Figure 10.21 includes substances that everyone agrees are very dangerous, so it takes 60 days to obtain a permit for these. The amber list is for wastes that are slightly less dangerous and so only require a 30-day wait for a permit; and the green list covers wastes that can be recycled, are considered to be non-hazardous if they are being shipped for recycling, and do not need to wait 60 days for a permit. Although OECD categories apply initially to trade between member countries, they have since been included in the EU policy on waste regulation, and it is legally possible to extend this definition to waste exported to non-member countries.

There is debate about which substances are considered hazardous, with disagreement about those on the non-hazardous green list. The debate has intensified since the Treaty was tightened in March 1994, with:

- a complete ban on the export of hazardous materials for disposal
- a ban to take effect from 1997 on those destined for recycling.

The first part was agreed by all, and most African countries had already banned imports of toxic materials for dumping. However, the second is causing great controversy. It is being claimed that a number of ELDCs could suffer serious financial losses, as they have developed industries dependent on recyclable waste products. India, China, Pakistan, Brazil, and Hungary all import scrap metal, some of which is considered to be hazardous, as it yields toxic material when it is reprocessed.

EMDCs such as the UK, Germany, and the USA are also concerned about losing markets for their toxic materials. However, the proposed ban is supported by environmental groups who argue that unscrupulous waste dealers are exploiting the green list by labelling hazardous waste 'for recycling' and then dumping it. They also say that as long as opportunities exist to get rid of toxic materials cheaply, companies will not invest in cleaner technologies. Meanwhile cheaper but dangerous options in the ELDCs continue to cause damage both to the environment and to people.

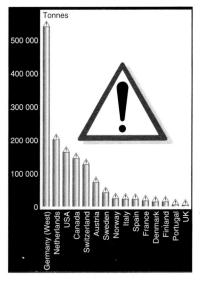

▲ **Figure 10.20** Exports of hazardous waste.

Wastes containing PCBs, polychlorinated terphenyl, polybrominated biphenyl, chlorinated dioxins, asbestos, leaded anti-knock compound sludge

Ash from iron and steel manufacture, petrol, coke and bitumen, lead acid batteries, waste oils and oil/water mixtures, phenols, thallium compounds, hydrogen peroxide solutions

Scrap metals: gold, platinum, silver, iron and steel, copper, nickel, lead, cadmium, indium, gallium, thallium

Plastics: PVC, polythene, polypropylene, styrene polymers, polyamides, Teflon, phenol-formaldehyde resins

Ceramics, mining wastes, glass, rubber wastes, textile and tannery wastes, gypsum, certain ashes from coal-fired power stations

▲ **Figure 10.21** OECD lists of hazardous waste.

It would be wrong to assume that all ELDCs are unconcerned about their people and their environment. Most African countries have introduced laws to prevent the import of toxic waste for dumping. Figures 10.22 and 10.23 show where steps are being taken in two countries to tackle the problem of hazardous waste, and highlight the dilemmas that these steps raise.

▼ **Figure 10.22** From the *Financial Times*, 30 March 1994.

An Indian tale of two extremes

The effluent from the Shriram chemical works on the outskirts of Delhi is so clean that samples are routinely passed through a fish tank. In seven years the plant has not killed a single goldfish and officials boast the waste is so pure they could drink it.

A few miles from Shriram· stand the smoky workshops of about 20 dyers, full of steaming vats of colours and bleaches. The untreated wastes are poured straight into a ditch. Sultan Ahmed, who inherited his workshop from his father, says he never checks his waste. Nor have his neighbours ever complained.

The Shriram works and Ahmed's workshop are the two extremes of the management of industrial waste in India. Shriram Foods and Fertilizer Industries, controlled by a Delhi-based diversified group, is a model plant producing vegetable oils, caustic soda, and chlorine. It was turned into a showpiece for the rest of Indian industry after a sulphuric acid leak in 1985 in which 500 people were injured. Today, it even has its own nature reserve. Ahmed, meanwhile, is just one of millions of self-employed craftsmen in India who have not heard of pollution control, know nothing of the law on waste, and have never seen an inspector.

Nobody knows how much industrial waste is poured into India's rivers. Data at the government's Pollution Control Board (PCB) are fragmentary and often out of date. The Board's work mainly covers the country's large and medium-sized factories, and barely touches the small workshops which account for about one-third of India's manufacturing output. Moreover, even large plants evade the law – some publicly owned enterprises secure protection from their ministries; some private companies pay bribes. A common trick is to install pollution control equipment, but leave it switched off because of power shortages, breakdowns, or deliberate evasions of the law. As Kapil Narula, a researcher at the Tata Energy Research Institute, a private think-tank, says: 'With an average of only one inspector for 50 factories, it is easy for a company to get away with breaking the rules by paying money.'

However, Indian pollution experts believe that standards of waste disposal – as of airborne emissions – are gradually getting higher, particularly in the large factories. In 1991, the PCB found that of 1551 large plants with potential pollution problems, only 112 had installed adequate control equipment. By the end of last year, 1119 of these factories had made the grade and 77 had closed.

Finding a dustbin for corruption

Behind Mexico City's international airport lies one of the capital's biggest waste disposal sites. A lorry enters the site every few minutes, the driver invariably tips the security guard at the entrance, and then dumps solid, and often hazardous, waste into a vast open-air pit that stretches far into the distance.

Hundreds of scavengers, from young children to old men, walk around the fly-infested pit picking up plastic containers, bottles, cardboard boxes and anything else that can be re-used or recycled. Some scavengers sell any re-usable waste they find directly to the union that runs the dump, others pay the union boss about US $20 a month for the right to sell it elsewhere. Either way, most appear to earn much more than the minimum wage.

The dumps are owned by the municipal government. The unions controlling them are powerful supporters of Mexico's governing party. Admirers point to the undeniable efficiency of the system at recycling waste; detractors attack the corruption that has made union bosses extraordinarily wealthy, and the appalling health conditions in which scavengers work.

With no commercial toxic incinerators, just one authorized toxic waste site, and few modern solid-waste facilities, almost all of Mexico's household waste and much of its industrial waste ends up in such pits. What does not make it to these sites is invariably dumped in rivers, the sewage system, or empty fields.

The government estimates that industry generates about 6m tonnes of toxic waste a year. But according to David Robinson, a consultant with Quimica Omega, an environmental services company in Mexico City, total installed capacity for treating toxic waste is about 200 000 tonnes. He says almost all of the 800m litres of lubricating oil used every year is dumped into the sewage system – equivalent, he calculates, to one *Exxon Valdez* spill a month.

▲ **Figure 10.23** From the *Financial Times*, 27 April 1994.

Managing radioactive waste

Waste disposal options

The disposal of radioactive waste is an issue not only for the nuclear industry but also for other parties such as hospitals. However, with nuclear power the issue is integral to the viability of the industry. Environmentalists state that as yet there is no acceptable method of disposing of nuclear waste. The industry itself feels that the waste it produces is smaller in volume than that produced by fossil fuels, and nuclear power stations do not produce any carbon dioxide. Although radioactive waste can be stored in containers, the question remains where to put the containers.

Disposal at sea
This was the preferred option for a long time. However, as a result of several amendments to international agreements on marine pollution, disposal at sea has ceased to be an option, for the moment at least.

Reprocessing
Reprocessing extracts uranium and plutonium from used nuclear fuel rods. The process produces much greater volumes of lower-level waste but does provide re-usable quantities of uranium. The process also provides plutonium for future use within fast-breeder reactors. The fast-breeder reactor is a technology that has not yet become commercially available, and while plutonium stocks mount up, concerns are raised about the possibility of plutonium being diverted to an increasing number of potential customers for making nuclear bombs. The price of uranium also fell sharply during the 1980s, which has made the economics of the reprocessing process potentially unattractive.

The UK and France have invested heavily in reprocessing. The reprocessing plant in Sellafield, Cumbria has recently been strengthened by the opening of Thorp, British Nuclear Fuel (BNFL)'s new reprocessing facility (Figure 10.24).

Deep storage
Storing waste underground provides a potentially permanent solution to the problem, reducing the need for surveillance and security. However, the

▲ **Figure 10.24** Thorp, BNFL's new reprocessing plant.

choice of the location of the site has always been a political problem. Few people are willing to accept a nuclear waste site on their doorstep. There are important technical questions that still need answers. It is hard to find sites that are guaranteed safe from geological fractures and water seepage for the next 10 000 years (the effective life of some of the radioactive materials).

Dry storage
Dry storage of high-level radioactive waste involves storing waste materials on the surface, surrounded by an inert gas. Some sources suggest that this provides an option for containing highly radioactive fuel rods for 50 years or more, reducing radioactivity and thereby making them easier to deal with.

Give it to someone else!
Dealing in radioactive waste is big business. Countries with tough environmental laws such as Germany, or with large nuclear programmes such as France, are keen to identify other countries that are prepared to accept their waste. British Nuclear Fuels is keen to sell the services of the new Thorp reprocessing plant at Sellafield to other countries seeking options for dealing with their nuclear waste. Increasing trade in nuclear waste has raised concerns for environmentalists who are worried about accidents involving shipments of radioactive waste, as well as from people who live where the waste is destined.

▼ **Figure 10.25** Disposing of the waste.

Radioactive Waste Rules May Tighten

The government is leaning towards tightening a key rule governing the shipment of nuclear waste sent by foreign customers for reprocessing in the UK.

The move on nuclear waste 'substitution' affects reprocessing contracts, which generally require clients to take back waste reprocessed by British Nuclear Fuels at its Sellafield plant.

By measuring the waste it returns in terms of radioactivity rather than volume, BNFL can 'substitute' a small volume of highly radioactive waste for a larger volume of lower-level waste.

The advantage of substitution is that it reduces the volume of waste to be returned, improving the economics of reprocessing. However, it leaves BNFL with a larger amount of waste to dispose of itself.

Intermediate and high-level waste is stored at present in special tanks and vitrification facilities at BNFL's Sellafield plant. Although much of the waste is from reprocessed fuel for British power stations, part is from foreign customers and should eventually be returned according to their contracts.

The government has so far kept an open mind on substitution while it considers technical reports. But ministers are believed to be increasingly opposed to the practice on environmental grounds. Although no decisions have yet been taken and officials say the subject is still 'fuzzy', a final conclusion is expected soon.

The issue of substitution has gained relevance this month, as BNFL's big new Thorp reprocessing plant at Sellafield has recently begun full operation.

Thorp, which will process large quantities of nuclear fuel for clients in Europe and Japan, will handle 7000 tonnes of nuclear waste in its first ten years, two-thirds of it from overseas.

(a) From the *Financial Times*, 28 February 1995.

Mixed Welcome Awaits Nuclear Cargo

For the past few months employees at Japan Nuclear Fuel, the operators of Japan's nuclear power facilities at the northern tip of the country's main island of Honshu, have been rehearsing for the arrival by ship today of a massive steel flask of nuclear waste and its transportation to the company's site.

The 112-tonne flask containing 400kg of high-level radioactive waste from Japanese fuel reprocessed at the La Hague nuclear reprocessing plant run by France's state-owned Cogema group, is due to be delivered at the port of Mutsu Ogawara by the British-owned ship *Pacific Pintail* which left the French port of Cherbourg in February.

On arrival the flask, radiating heat of up to 85° C, will be transported to the nuclear fuel cycle facilities at nearby Rokkasho where the waste will be lowered into underground storage pits.

'We are ready for it,' says Mr Takahisa Nemoto, general manager at JNFL, confidently.

However, the residents of Rokkasho, a former fishing and farming village, have mixed feelings. Some, including Mr Hiroshi Tsuchida, the mayor, point out the economic and social benefits of the construction of the Y1260bn (£9.46bn) nuclear facility, which – with its waste storage, uranium enrichment and plutonium reprocessing plants – is central to the country's nuclear programme.

With nuclear energy already accounting for 30 per cent of electricity generation – the country has nearly 50 nuclear power plants and more on the way – the scale of the nuclear commitment is set to rise.

Government subsidies to the region have totalled some Y40bn. Visitors to the village are struck by a large modern gymnasium and a new history museum. A golf course is being built near the nuclear site.

But the imminent arrival of the high-level waste shipment has fuelled cries from the environmentalists. The main concern is that of safety, which has become more pressing than ever since the Kobe earthquake in January.

The Aomori region was hit by an earthquake last December, and local opposition groups have published photographs of cracked roads and a damaged quay at a fishing port only a few miles away from the nuclear site.

The Aomori municipality has refused permission for permanent storage and since last December, when the government reached an agreement with Rokkasho and the municipal government to limit the length of storage to 50 years, the government has been forced to look for alternatives, including the northern island of Hokkaido.

The opposition camp has dubbed the country's nuclear programme a 'flat without a toilet', and some villagers are worried that the central government may eventually back-track on the agreement since the legality of the letter of intent signed at the end of last year remains vague.

Citizens' organizations and concerned geologists have taken the government to the district court, demanding a withdrawal of its construction permit for the facility's plants.

(b) From the *Financial Times*, 25 April 1995.

1 a) Explain in your own words 'substitution' as described within Figure 10.25a.

   b) What are the environmental consequences of 'substitution'?

2 a) In groups of three or four, identify issues concerning transport of waste to Rokkasho in Japan that are of interest to an organization like Greenpeace.

   b) In your group, write a press release of 200 words from Greenpeace highlighting concerns about this shipment of nuclear waste. Consider researching further, using sources of information about nuclear waste.

3 a) In your group, identify the issues concerning transport of waste to Rokkasho in Japan that are of interest to the Japanese government.

   b) In your group, write a press release of 200 words from the Japanese government highlighting their interest in this shipment of nuclear waste and the planned further development of the nuclear facilities. Consider researching further, using sources of information about nuclear waste.

Ideas for further study

1 Investigate how much waste your household disposes of in an average week. Consider the following:

   • the proportions of each type of waste (e.g. paper, plastic, organic matter, etc.)
   • the recycling potential of each type
   • possibilities for reducing the total amount of waste and/or increasing the recycling potential.

2 a) Find out which waste disposal method is used by your local council, and how the decision was reached to adopt that method.

   b) If recycling is carried out, investigate what happens to the materials.

3 Compare and contrast the development of the use of biogas in this country with the development of the use of biogas in India or China. You should consider different economic, social, environmental, and technical issues that shape the development of the technology in the two countries.

4 Investigate the debate surrounding *either* the development of nuclear power *or* the disposal of nuclear waste. You should consider the economic, technical, and environmental issues related to the development of the technology.

Summary

• The generation of waste, and the problems associated with its disposal, are increasing.

• There are various routes for waste disposal, each of which has different social, economic, and environmental impacts.

• Waste may be viewed as a resource, the exploitation of which will help to sustain primary raw materials and to reduce pollution.

• Countries of the 'North' are becoming stricter in pollution controls to satisfy an increasingly aware voting public, while at the same time exporting toxic waste to other countries.

• Waste export and import follow a North–South flow, raising issues of social, economic, and environmental justice.

References and further reading

J. McCarthy, *Reuse, Repair, Recycle*, Gaia Books Ltd, 1993.

N. Myers, *The Gaia Atlas of Planet Management*, Gaia Books Ltd, 1993.

J. Seymour, H. Girardet, *Blueprint for a Green Planet*, Dorling Kindersley, 1987.

K. Wallis, 'Changing perspectives in waste management and recycling', in *Geofile*, April 1994, no.241.

The Warmer Bulletin, a free periodical on recycling and energy from waste, is produced by the World Resource Foundation, UK Headquarters, Bridge House, High Street, Tonbridge, Kent TN9 1DP.

Renewable energy

Introduction

Chapter 8 highlighted a range of problems with the fossil fuels that most EMDCs currently depend on for most of their energy. Some people believe that the development of renewable energy offers the only route towards more sustainability. Others believe that renewable energy sources will never be able to provide enough energy to meet demand. This chapter considers this debate in more detail. Decisions made now about how demands are met will affect all our lives in the future.

Sources of renewable energy – defined as 'flow resources' in Chapter 8 – are energy sources that are replenished at the same rate or more quickly than they are used. The Sun is the major source of energy, either directly or indirectly. Figure 11.1 shows the relationship between the Sun and major natural energy flows. Tidal energy produced by gravitational pull of the Sun and the Moon, geothermal energy resulting from heat generated from within the Earth, and energy from waste, are also regarded as renewable energy sources. In Figure 11.1, the unit TW is used – this means trillions of watts of power. Read the theory box to find out what these units of power mean.

▶ **Figure 11.1** Renewable energy flows.

Discussion

Figure 11.1 illustrates the vast quantities of energy available from the Sun alone, compared with the amounts of energy currently used. So why can't renewable energy provide us with all the energy that we want? In groups of 3–4, discuss the question: 'What constraints reduce the amount of renewable energy that we can actually use?'

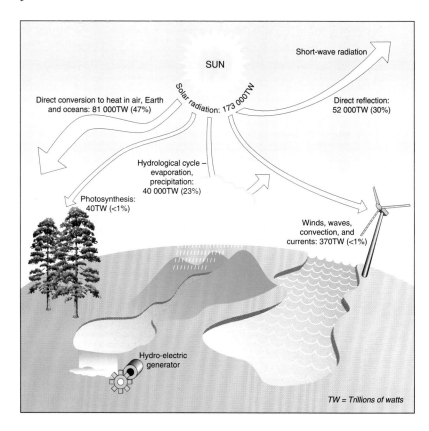

Understanding energy units

'Power' is the rate at which energy is delivered or used. It is measured in watts (W), and a watt is equal to one joule per second. Joules are the internationally recognized units for energy.

1000 watts = 1 kilowatt (1kW) = 10^3 watts = the power rating of a one-bar electric fire

1000kW = 1 megawatt (1MW) = 10^6 watts (300MW = the output of a small nuclear power station)

1000MW = 1 gigawatt (1GW) = 10^9 watts (55GW = the maximum electricity demand placed on the UK system during 1993/94)

1000GW = 1 terawatt (1TW) = 10^{12} watts

Energy consumption over time is measured in watt hours (W/h). For example:

- a one-bar electric fire with a power rating of 1 kW – on for one hour will use 1kWh, on for 5 hours will use 5kWh
- a typical household might use 2MWh – or 2000kWh – of electricity during one year
- a 500kW wind turbine might produce 1.7GWh of electricity during one year
- a 1GW power station might produce 5.5TWh of electricity during one year
- the total amount of electricity delivered in the UK during 1993 was 285TWh.

▼ **Figure 11.2** Views on renewable energy.

From the Toronto Statement, World Conference on the Changing Atmosphere, June 1988

'Humanity is conducting an uncontrolled, globally pervasive experiment whose ultimate consequences could be second only to a global nuclear war. The Earth's atmosphere is being changed at an unprecedented rate by pollutants resulting from human activities, inefficient and wasteful fossil fuel use, and the effects of rapid population growth in many regions. These changes represent a major threat to international security and are already having harmful consequences over many parts of the globe.'

Sir Bernard Ingham, former press secretary to Mrs Thatcher, adviser to the nuclear industry, and Vice-President of Country Guardians

'Forests of these infernal contraptions are springing up on our pristine Pennine moors. Yet . . . each [wind] turbine generates but a tiny fraction – one-thousandth or less – of the electricity of a small power station. It is unreliable, even in blowy Britain. It cannot cope with surges in demand when we boil kettles during natural TV breaks. But unless we blow up in revolt we shall find every mountain, hill, and cliff colonized by flailing pylons.'

Fiona Weightman, Friends of the Earth Renewable Energy Campaigner, August 1993

'This growth of interest in renewable projects demonstrates that the expertise and potential exists to develop a credible renewable energy industry, if only the government would increase its target to meet the renewable energy challenge. Friends of the Earth calls on the government to increase its renewable energy target to 3500MW.'

Ministerial Declaration on Sustainable Development in the Economic Commission for Europe (ECE) Region, signed by the UK government, Bergen, May 1990

'Taking into consideration that the ECE region presently accounts for about 70 per cent of global primary energy and fossil fuel use, we [Europe] assume a major responsibility to limit or reduce greenhouse gases and other emissions and to lead a global effort to address this matter by promoting energy efficiency, energy conservation, and the use of environmentally sound and renewable energy sources.'

British Nuclear Forum

'Along with the significant advantages offered by renewables, there are problems as well of course, and their main disadvantage is simply one of scale. Because there is so little energy involved in the wind or in water, compared with a chemical fuel like coal, or even more with a nuclear fuel like uranium, a considerable amount of machinery, spread out over quite a large chunk of the world, is needed to make meaningful amounts of energy . . . Furthermore, at present there is no large-scale way of storing electricity. To be able to keep hospitals and industries running, to be able to keep people alive in the winter months, we must be able to rely on a certain amount of our electricity being available come what may. However, many of the renewables are not so reliable. It is not possible to be certain that the output from wind power, tidal power, or solar power will necessarily come when it is needed. The difficulty is not too great if less than 25 per cent of electricity comes from such sources, but beyond that problems could arise.'

The Department of Trade and Industry in Renewable Energy Bulletin No 5

'The government's policy is to stimulate the development of renewable energy sources wherever they have prospects of being economically attractive and environmentally acceptable, in order to contribute to diverse and secure and sustainable energy supplies, reduction in the emission of pollutants, and encouragement of internationally competitive renewable industries.'

The Coal Review White Paper (Cm 2235), published in March 1993, announced the government's intention to work towards a figure of 1500MW of new renewable electricity generating capacity in the UK by the year 2000.

Energy Technology Support Unit in An Assessment of Renewable Energy for the UK

'In the 1970s the dramatic fluctuations in the price of oil caused governments to look for ways of increasing the diversity of their energy supplies. Attention was turned towards renewable energy since replacing imported fossil fuels with indigenous renewable resources would help to achieve a more balanced energy portfolio with less risk of interruptions in supply and destabilizing price rises.'

Data from Digest of UK Energy Statistics 1994

'By the end of March 1994 the total plant capacity in the UK was 69 117MW. During 1993/94 the simultaneous maximum load met by UK power producers was 54 848MW.'

Country	Production (TWh)	Installed capacity(MW)
Canada	308.6	59 381
USA	288.3	90 141
Former Soviet Union	235.0	14 100
Brazil	217.8	45 558
China	125.0	30 500
Norway	110.5	26 945
Japan	105.5	37 830
India	67.5	18 864
Sweden	63.7	16 331
France	61.9	24 747

▲ **Figure 11.3** Production of HEP.
(a) Countries with the largest HEP production in 1990.

(b) HEP station in the Snowy Mountains, northern Victoria, Australia.

1 Look at Figure 11.3 and an atlas showing physical features and precipitation. Find each of the ten largest HEP producers, and look at their physical features.

2 What conditions make HEP possible in the main producing countries of the world?

Read Figure 11.2.

1 In groups of three or four, identify the interests of the people quoted.

2 Summarize arguments for and against renewable energy. Rank each of these in importance.

3 Of the arguments against renewable energy, which ones can something be done about?

Renewable energy around the world

Globally, there is currently a very low level of renewable energy production from solar, wind, wave, water, and geothermal power. In EMDCs only hydro-electricity is significant, producing 6 per cent of the world's primary energy and 20 per cent of the world's electricity. Energy from biomass is also vital within ELDCs.

Hydro-electric power (HEP)

World-wide, river flows show that the potential of HEP is about 50 000TWh per year – five times the annual output from all the world's power stations. This figure is reduced after considering local conditions, and the need to match supply with demand. Rivers with seasonal flows may be of little use without expensive damming. Figures for *accessible* HEP resources range from 10 000 to 20 000TWh. Even the lower figures would give significant savings in CO_2 emissions and other pollutants.

Biomass

Renewable energy can be produced from finite resources, as long as resource stock is replenished more quickly than it is depleted. Biomass – that is, plant material produced through growth, using the Sun's energy – can in theory provide limitless raw material for energy production. It is difficult to estimate how much of the world's biomass is being used in a renewable way. Globally over 2 billion people depend on fuelwood for cooking, but 1.5 billion of these have daily difficulty in finding sufficient supply. Increasing populations have put pressures on the use of fuelwood to the point where its collection is destructive and unsustainable.

Currently, there is a need to find substitutes for:

- fuelwood in ELDCs, where depletion is unsustainable
- fossil fuels in EMDCs, because these are finite, and because of threats posed by pollution.

Can HEP reduce dependence on fuelwood and fossil fuels? This chapter investigates: the Three Gorges Project in China, the Tucurui dam in Brazil, and the use of renewable energy in the UK.

The Three Gorges Project, China

The Three Gorges Project on China's Yangtze river has been planned for over 60 years. When completed it will provide 18 200MW from 26 sets of 700MW turbine generators, and generate 85TWh a year, or 14 per cent of China's 1990 electricity supply. It will be the largest HEP project in the world. The dam will be 185 metres high and will produce a lake 600km long with a width of about 1.1km storing 39 billion cubic metres of water. The project will take about 17 years to complete with a cost in the region of US $10–12 billion. See Figure 11.4.

The level of water in the reservoir is altered during the year (Figure 11.5):

- to increase water flow to keep up electricity production
- to ensure maximum flow of water at times of high sediment transport to prevent sedimentation within the reservoir
- to provide capacity to control flood surges
- to provide maximum storage capacity, thus preventing uneven incoming flow rates which have an adverse impact on potential electricity production.

1 Referring to Figure 11.4, find the area of the Yangtze river in an atlas. Draw an outline sketch map of China to show the location of the Three Gorges Project.

2 Using your atlas, annotate your map with details of the climate of the river basin which leads into the upper Yangtze. What features of the climate suggest that a dam might be necessary for year-round water and energy supply?

▼ **Figure 11.4** Location of the Three Gorges reservoir.

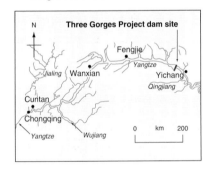

▼ **Figure 11.5** Planned water levels within the Three Gorges reservoir.

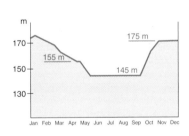

▶ **Figure 11.6** The expected effects of the Three Gorges Project on the flow of the Yangtze river downstream of the dam.

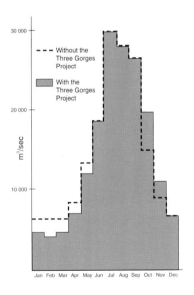

1 Annotate a copy of Figure 11.5, identifying on it seasonal changes in water levels.

2 a) How do you think sediment flows along the river will vary during the year in response to the river flow rates shown in

Figure 11.6? Annotate your diagram further.

b) Explain your answer

3 How important is it to prevent excess sedimentation taking place in the reservoir?

Read Figure 11.7.

1 Identify differences in the writers' values.

2 Divide into three groups. Each group should take one of the following roles:

- A government minister, announcing plans to develop the Three Gorges Project.
- A village elder destined for resettlement, on hearing plans for the development.
- An engineer, keen to show China's technical expertise.

In groups, produce a display to show how your group views the project. Prepare questions to ask the other groups, and discuss with them whether they will compromise.

3 Suggest criteria that could be used to assess the environmental impact of the Three Gorges and design an EIA – see Figure 10.18. Which is preferable environmentally: the Three Gorges Project, or the same amount of electricity generated from coal?

▼ **Figure 11.7** Views on the Three Gorges Project.

'Energy is needed to keep pace with China's economic growth. It is estimated that China's power output must rise by 8 per cent annually to keep pace with a 6 per cent annual increase in gross national product. In practical terms, that means the nation's total 1990 power capacity of 130 000GW must grow to 580 000GW by the year 2015.

Chinese officials note that the dam would relieve the danger of flooding in the flood-prone Chang Jiang river valley. In addition, because generating electricity equal to the dam's projected output requires burning about 40 million tonnes of coal, the dam would substantially reduce emissions of SO_2 and carbon dioxide.

By lowering demand for coal, the dam would also ease pressure on an overburdened rail transport network.

However, the river will partially or completely inundate 2 cities, 11 counties, 140 towns, 326 townships, and 1351 villages. About 23 800 hectares of cultivated land will be submerged. More than 1.1 million people will have to be resettled.'

(a) World Resources 1994–95, World Resources Institute.

'Flooding the Three Gorges would uproot more than 1 million people, whose resettlement would cost an additional US $4.8 billion. The reservoir would drown dozens of historical and archaeological sites. The single greatest loss would be the Three Gorges, one of China's most celebrated national sites. It is a popular attraction for Chinese and foreign tourists, many of whom fear great environmental and scenic losses if the dam is built.

According to the Institute of Water Resources Protection, people will be moved up the valley slope to raise cattle and grow oranges or work in newly built factories. Scientists at the Academy of Science are less confident. They say that the area is already overcrowded, heavily deforested, and over-cultivated, and that resettling such a huge populace in the area would be an environmental disaster. Since 1949, one third of all the people moved to make way for dams have failed to receive proper housing, land or due compensation.

The reservoir, which will be located on a major geological fault, will impound so much water it could trigger an earthquake that would devastate the nearby populations and damage the dam itself. Landslides, common to the Three Gorges area, could occur, causing a tidal wave to breach the dam and unleash terrible floods on the valley below.'

(b) 'Exposing the Secrets of the Three Gorges Dam' by Grainne Ryder in *World Rivers Review*, January/February 1989.

'With its navigation capacity amounting to 78 per cent of the total of China's inland rivers, the Yangtze is the artery for navigation in the Eastern and Western regions. The navigation conditions of its natural watercourse, however, cannot meet the requirements of national economic development. The river flows through an area of high mountains and deep valleys, with considerable turbulence and dangerous shoals, which have limited its development.

The navigation facilities of the Three Gorges Project consist of a double-lane, five-step ship-sized lock and a vertical shiplift, with 113m variation in water-level and 12 000 tonnes lifting capacity, capable of handling 3000-tonne ships passing through the dam.

Upon completion of the Three Gorges Project, the reservoir backwater will reach Chongqin and the annual transportation capacity for freight will be increased to 50 million tonnes with costs reduced by 35–37 per cent.

Considering the importance of the Three Gorges Project, its structure is designed to be protected against an earthquake of intensity 7. The possibility of reservoir-induced earthquakes is not ruled out, though the magnitude of any should not be high. In the light of such an earthquake, risk analysis shows that the maximum size of earthquake in the dam region should not exceed grade 6, so should not affect the safety of the dam.

(c) 'Three Gorges Project – A Progress Report' by Lu Youmei in *International Water Power and Dam Construction*, August 1994.

Tucurui dam, Brazil

Brazil's rapid economic growth has created a demand for energy which the country is fighting to provide. In 1988, one-quarter of Brazil's US $121 billion foreign debt, the largest among ELDCs, came from loans to finance its electrical sector. One-third of the system's annual revenues pay for interest on loans from overseas. To pay for them, the utility borrows more, as well as other loans required to finance new development.

There is a desperate need for overseas loans. This is not always in Brazil's best interest or on terms that favour Brazil. Money could be found from overseas sources, but comes with strings attached. For example, although companies in Brazil *could* supply high-quality HEP equipment, France only guaranteed loans for the Tucurui dam if some of the generation equipment came from French companies.

Figure 11.8 describes the effects of Brazil's energy policies and projects, originally intended to provide the infrastructure for economic growth and for sustainable energy supplies.

▼ **Figure 11.8** From 'The Last Frontier', in *The New Internationalist*, June 1988.

The Last Frontier

'Of course I chop trees. What else is there for me? My family is hungry and I must feed them.' There were four of us sitting round a rickety table in a shack restaurant, eating chicken, beans, and rice; Jose the migrant logger, the woman who owned the restaurant, my guide Ju, and me.

'We have come many miles from the south along the new roads,' said Jose. 'The logging company in Repartimento pay money for the logs I fell. And there is nothing else. I've tried farming. The soil is no good. My crops failed. This way I earn money. Maybe I'll have enough soon to buy land further up the road where people say the soil is good.'

Repartimento is a new settlement town 100km down the red-dirt Trans-Amazon Highway from Tucurui in eastern Amazonia. The old town has been destroyed by the flooding of the Tucurui dam, the fourth largest in the world. Repartimento (mark two) was supposed to be a model settlement, one of several promised by Brazil's northern power company Eletronorte to house thousands of people displaced by the reservoir.

In fact the town is little more than a refugee camp, as settlers quickly discover when they step off the buses which roar through daily. Crude shacks dominate except on the hillside covered by the rapidly deteriorating suburban-style bungalows which Eletronorte was finally persuaded to put up. There are no sewers, no paved roads, no proper schools, no shops, no facilities. There isn't even tapped water or electricity despite the great hydro-electric dam just down the road.

And yet Repartimento is smack in the middle of one of the largest development schemes ever conceived – the Program Grande Carajas, or Carajazao. This US $62 billion complex of mines, dams, towns, roads and railways, farms, and forestry plantations was designed to bring prosperity to the region and haul Brazil's economy out of debt and into the 21st century. In return for credit from the World Bank, the European Community (EC), and Japan, it was hoped that exports of minerals, agricultural products, and timber would repay the loans. Every year the EC is guaranteed 13 million tonnes of highest-quality iron ore at what one Brazilian politician calls 'banana prices'. Japan has a similar deal.

Tucurui is a larger version of Repartimento. Most of the 40 000 people who live there come from the neighbouring state of Maranhao or were displaced from their original homes by the reservoir.

Stretching across the Tocantins river, the dam was begun in the late 1970s. It was supposed to be finished in 1986. Its 8000MW of electricity are intended to power industrial developments central to Carajazao – including aluminium smelters and refineries outside Belém 300km to the north, and the railway which carries iron ore for export 880km from the Serra dos Carajas to a new deepwater port at São Luis to the north-east.

Today half the 3km-wide dam is an enormous earth-covered concrete wall. Only six of the 24 turbines are in place and just two usually work at any one time. Standing on a hillside overlooking the site it seems an impressive piece of engineering. But all around you can see the environmental and social price that has been paid.

The reservoir flooded over 2000 km^2 of rainforest, known to contain many rare and unique wild species. Apart from one well-publicized rescue attempt which saved some 15 000 of an estimated several million drowning animals when filling began, there was no attempt to survey the area to find out if there were potentially valuable medicinal or food plants that could be transplanted. Worse still, the lands of two Parakana Indian tribes were lost. One was completely flooded and the tribe forcibly moved to Marudgewara over 160km away. The other lost half its land to the water and is fighting to regain control of the unflooded part from settlers who have been illegally moved in by Eletronorte. Meanwhile there are more immediate problems. Ranchers have moved into the area, attracted by the new transport network. Their first priority is to remove the forest. Erosion rates increase over 100 times once the forest is gone. The Amazonian development agency SUDAM and Eletronorte are extremely worried about the reservoir silting up and making the dam useless.

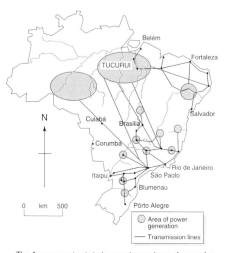

The Amazon region is to be a major producer of power for industrial and population centres in Brazil's Southeast and Northeast regions. More than 25GW are to be connected by the year 2010, when the heavily industrialized regions of São Paulo and Rio de Janeiro will get one-third of their power from the Amazon basin.

▲ **Figure 11.9** Where does the electricity go?

▲ **Figure 11.10** Tucurui dam.

Winners and losers

1 Examine Figures 11.8 and 11.9. Show in a table the social, economic, and environmental consequences of the Tucurui dam.

2 Identify all groups of people whose lives have in some way been involved in the dam at Tucurui. Classify, and justify, a list of people who benefit from the Tucurui dam development, and those who lose.

3 Might it have been possible to make the development more equitable? How?

4 Write a brief analysis of 500 words, saying to what extent the Tucurui dam provides a sustainable ELDC substitute for the use of fuelwood.

Renewable energy resources

As with the classification of fossil fuel resources, resource estimates change according to the criteria on which they are assessed. For example, as wind turbine technology improves, the cost of generating electricity decreases, thereby increasing its potential availability.

Total resource	Total energy content of any renewable energy source
Accessible resource	The resource available for exploitation by a defined technology when siting constraints have been considered, such as national parks, housing, roads, lakes, etc. Often a resource is defined as that which can be produced at a cost of less than 10p/kWh.
Maximum practicable resource	A realistic assessment of the available resource after full consideration of social, economic, and environmental constraints on its development.

▲ **Figure 11.11** Renewable energy resources.

Renewable energy in the UK

The UK is well endowed with potential sources for renewable energy, with one of the best wind resources in Europe, massive potential for wave energy, the world's second largest tidal range (in the river Severn), and closely linked, densely populated urban areas which provide significant potential for generating energy from waste.

Figure 11.12 shows the potential for generating electricity using renewable energy technology, based on a cost of production of 10p/kWh or less. Wind energy – both on and offshore – dominates but there are many other sources too. Figure 11.13 is complex, but shows how cost plays a vital role in assessing the potential of renewable sources of energy. At 10p/kWh, 400TWh of electricity can be produced using renewable technology; this saves 80 million tonnes of carbon emission from thermal power stations, emitted in the form of carbon dioxide.

The densely populated nature of the UK presents a major constraint for sustainable development of renewable energy. Because of the small-scale and local nature of most renewable energy sources, there would need to be an increase in the number of energy-producing sites compared with conventional large-scale centralized power sources. This may make it difficult for some new technologies to be accepted, since they are likely locally to be very visible.

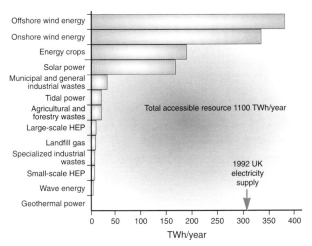

▲ **Figure 11.12** Accessible resource for electricity produced using renewable technology, assuming a cost of 10p/kWh or less (1992).

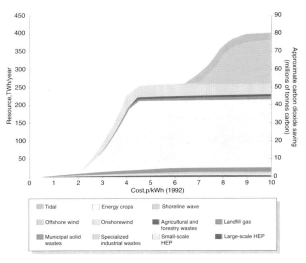

▲ **Figure 11.13** Maximum practicable resource for electricity production using renewable energy technology by 2025, assuming a cost of 10p/kWh or less (1992).

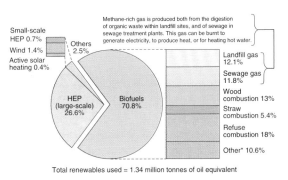

▲ **Figure 11.14** Renewable energy use, 1993.

Figures 11.12 and 11.13 provide two types of estimate of the renewable energy resource in the UK.

1 Outline the main points highlighted by the two graphs.

2 In Figure 11.13, how much energy is generated when generating costs reach the current average cost of about 3p per kWh? Which is the largest source of this energy?

3 Which source will be providing most of the UK's electricity by 2025? Why?

1 **a)** In 1993, a total of 302 TWh of
electricity was generated in the UK.
Using Figures 11.14 and 11.15,
calculate what percentage was supplied
from renewable energy sources (1TWh
= 1000GWh).

   b) Which renewable technologies are
growing fastest ?

   c) What is causing the marked increase in
use of renewable energy?

2 Using the information so far on current
use and available resources, which
technologies should be a priority for
research and development?

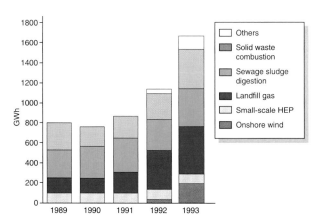

This graph excludes large-scale HEP, which in 1993 amounted to 4143GWh.
'Others' includes farm waste digestion, waste tyre combustion, and chicken
litter combustion.

▲ **Figure 11.15** Generation of electricity from renewable
energy sources in the UK, 1989–93.

Privatizing energy supply

The main recent structural change in the supply of
energy in the UK has been the privatization of
both the gas and the electricity industries. There
has been much debate over the benefits and
problems of privatization. However, there have
been some significant benefits to the renewable
energy industry as a result. Within the current
structure, a separate national grid and twelve
regional electricity companies (RECs) supply the
electricity to consumers. RECs are able to look
anywhere for their supplies, including small
generators. This improves the economic case for
developing small-scale electricity generation,
including renewable energy, and has resulted in a
large increase in the number of small-scale
generators.

During the privatisation on the electricity
industry, it became clear that the nuclear element
was a liability, and no-one would buy it, so the
government had to keep it in the public sector. To
make nuclear power competitive, the government
set up the Non-Fossil Fuel Obligation (NFFO) as
part of the 1989 Electricity Act. This requires all
RECs to take some of their electricity from non-
fossil fuel sources – mainly nuclear power, but also
including renewable energy. The extra cost paid by
the RECs is passed on to consumers of electricity
through a 10 per cent increase in fuel bills. This
levy produced a huge income, of which the nuclear
industry claimed 94.5 per cent (£1.236 billion) in
1993/94. Renewable energy sources claimed the
other 5.5 percent (£68 million).

The government has set a target of 1500MW
capacity of renewable energy in the UK by the year
2000. It sees the NFFO (see theory box) as the
principal mechanism for achieving this. Friends of
the Earth suggested that the target should be
3500MW, or 6–7 per cent of the current maximum
demand for electricity.

There are benefits of using technologies that do
not:

● require finite fuel
● produce emissions of greenhouse gases
● produce emissions linked to acid rain.

This raises an important issue. Can localized
environmental impacts of a wind farm, for example,
be compared with international impacts caused by
acid rain, global warming, or radiation
contamination? The following case study looks at
wind energy production in Wales.

Wind energy

To understand future wind energy developments,
it is useful to look at issues which have arisen in
existing wind farms. The exercise below is designed
to enable you to draw up criteria by which such
developments might be accepted or rejected, and
to develop your own viewpoints.

MPs back wind farms for Wales

More wind farms should be allowed in Wales, the Commons Welsh Affairs Committee said yesterday, Roland Adburgham writes.

The committee's report says: 'Within the framework of a robust, appropriate and locally accountable planning system we see no objection to the continuing development of wind farms in Wales, subject to their environmental acceptability.'

The Committee's support comes at a time when there has been increasing opposition to the turbines on grounds of visual intrusion, noise, and lack of economic justification.

The MPs stress: 'We believe that concerns over visual impact are the most deep-seated and firmly held objections to the development of wind energy.' There should be 'the strongest presumption' against turbines in national parks and areas of outstanding natural beauty.

(a) From the *Financial Times*, 21 July 1994.

Wind farms win public support

A survey of people living near three wind farms in Wales has found that nearly three-quarters would be prepared to see further development.

No fewer than 68 per cent of those interviewed said the wind farms had had little impact on their area – in spite of the turbines being visible for up to 15 km. A total of 457 people were interviewed.

The positive attitudes to wind farms come as planning objections to them have been increasing. Most interviewees felt the farms were neither intrusive nor noisy, and at least half thought they were in keeping with the countryside. Most hostility to wind farms was found among a 'control' sample near Brecon, Powys, where there are none.

The survey included the National Wind Power site at Llandinam in Powys, which is the largest in Wales with 103 turbines. The other two sites were at Rhyd-y-Groes on Anglesey, and Llangwyryfon near Aberystwyth.

(b) From the *Financial Times*, 21 July 1994.

Curb wind farms, says tourist board

Restrictions on wind farms are backed by the Wales Tourist Board today in a strategy for tourism in the principality.

Wind farms use turbines to harness the wind and provide an alternative source of energy. But opposition from local authorities and residents in Wales is increasing because of the visual intrusion and noise of the turbines.

The Board says in its Tourism 2000 strategy document – to be launched today by Mr John Redwood, Welsh Secretary: 'The quality of Wales's natural environment is one of the industry's greatest assets.

'Tourism 2000 recognises the need to conserve and enhance that environment and is concerned about threats which might impact upon the industry, for example wind farms.' It endorses the policies of the Countryside Council for Wales, which opposes wind farms in national parks and other designated areas.

Wales has eight wind farms, about a third of the UK total, and planning consent is being sought for many more. The strategy hopes to create 10 000 jobs in the principality and a growth in earnings of £700m in current prices by the year 2000. Tourism employs about 95 000 people in Wales, or 9 per cent of the workforce, and contributes £1.3 billion, or 6 per cent, to the principality's gross domestic product.

(c) From the *Financial Times*, 16 March 1994.

Sir – The impact of wind farms on landscape may be significant (letter, Oct. 8), but noise is more relevant to those of us living next to this new industry. My home nestles on the north-western slope of Mynach Bach, Ceredigion, below the 20-turbine Llangwyryfon wind farm owned by National Wind Power. We live about 350 metres from the nearest turbine and about 750 metres from six or seven others. The 'thwump' of the blades and grinding gears is driving us to distraction. My kitchen chimney amplifies these noises sickeningly. Earlier this year during wind turbine experimental stages, and since commissioning in July, the house has frequently vibrated with penetrating soundwaves. At night, these disrupt sleep even when all windows are closed. As I write, turbine droning is audible above the computer's hum. For my family and those in a similar plight on wind-farm sites in Wales and Cornwall, there is a distressing human cost for this supposedly 'environmentally friendly' electricity. For us, this is no brave, new, clean energy but a rapacious industrial giant. Regulation must be introduced immediately. First, to switch off all turbines at night. Secondly, to turn them off when prevailing and gusting winds cause them to be excessively noise and disruptive. Thirdly, for National Wind Power and other wind-farm companies to compensate those households affected by noise pollution, so that we might improve the quality of our insulation and make life more tolerable.
Caroline Kerkham, Llangwyryfon, Dyfed

(d) Letter to the *Daily Telegraph*, 21 October 1993.

▲ **Figure 11.16** Attitudes towards wind farms.

1 Read Figure 11.16. Copy and complete Figure 11.17.

Interested party	Pro or anti wind farms	Primary interest	Other interests

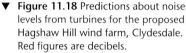

▲ **Figure 11.17** Table for attitude analysis.

2 Are concerns expressed local, regional, or global? Are they social, economic, or environmental?

3 Comment on the scale of the benefits and the disadvantages of wind energy.

4 In groups, suggest five criteria that should be applied to all wind-farm proposals before they are given planning permission, and rank them in order of priority.

5 Discuss your criteria with other groups. Try to establish a consensus on the most important criteria for the development of wind farms.

Wind energy for Hagshaw Hill, Clydesdale – a decision-making exercise

A new wind farm is being proposed at Hagshaw Hill in Clydesdale, Scotland (Figure 11.18). This exercise is designed to help you gain insight into some of the local issues, using information from other wind-farm developments elsewhere. Look at figures 11.18–11.21, then do the activities on page 246.

▼ **Figure 11.18** Predictions about noise levels from turbines for the proposed Hagshaw Hill wind farm, Clydesdale. Red figures are decibels.

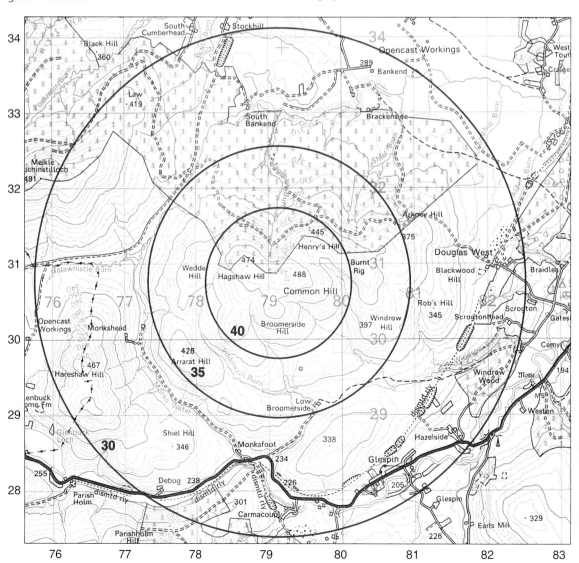

▲ **Figure 11.19** Two photographs taken from different points showing the visual impact of
▼ the proposed development at Hagshaw Hill.

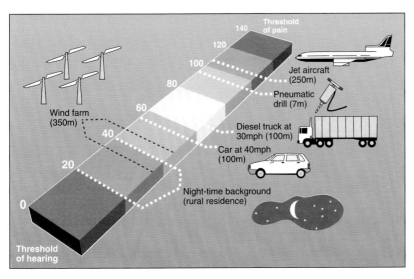

◄ **Figure 11.20** Common noise levels in decibels, for comparison with those of a wind farm.

◄ **Figure 11.21** Hagshaw Hill predicted noise levels at nearby residences.

Residence	OS grid reference	Predicted noise level at 5m/s (decibels)
Monkshead	770 301	33.5
Scrogton	826 305	29.5
Douglas West	821 310	31.0
Glespin	808 284	31.0
Monksfoot	786 286	33.0
Stockhill	788 340	29.5

5m/s (18km/h or 11mph) is seen as a crucial windspeed. If it is any stronger than this, the noise of the wind usually covers the sound of the turbines. Department of the Environment Planning Inspectors have indicated on several occasions that 40 decibels is felt to be an acceptable noise limit for wind farms. Where are these points on the site map?

Wind energy – Making your case

Either

You are a representative of the developers and you have organized a public meeting for local people. Develop your initial presentation to the meeting, outlining your proposals for the wind farm. Highlight how you will deal with the problems you feel the local people will raise concerning the development.

Or

You are a representative of a local residents group opposed to the new wind-farm development. You have been requested to voice your concerns at the initial public meeting about the new development. Outline your concerns about the development and highlight what you think the developers should do to meet your needs.

To do this:

- highlight local, national, and global concerns about energy production
- summarize your opinions about the proposed wind farm, using data provided in Figures 11.18–11.21
- show how wind farms elsewhere have confirmed either your acceptance or rejection of this proposal (Figure 11.16 is useful here)
- provide an analysis of why you do or do not favour wind energy as opposed to other renewable options
- outline a future strategy for energy production for this part of Scotland.

Reports may be in written form, as a display, or as a presentation to the rest of the group.

Willow set to become a power in the land

Robert Goodwin has a long association with willows. For many years his family has grown cricket-bat willows at Ashmans Farm, in the Blackwater Valley, near Colchester. So for him, taking six acres out of cereals, and growing instead a dense scrub of willows and poplars as a likely environment-friendly fuel of the future, was not a dramatic change.

For Britain as a whole, however, 'energy coppice'—the name for the new scrub crop—does indeed represent a radical shift. Clean, green, and soon to be planted on a farm near you, it looks ready to change the face of the landscape in some parts of the country.

It is rooted in the demand for 'clean energy'. First, it is a source of renewable power, unlike coal or oil. Secondly, willow and poplar contain very little sulphur and nitrogen, acid-rain causing pollutants produced in a vast quantities by burning coal and oil. Thirdly, the carbon dioxide it produces when it is burnt is no more than that taken in during its growth—so it cannot be accused of aiding global warming. Energy coppice also needs little man-made

energy in the form of fertilizers.

Small wonder, then, that government support for it is growing fast. The idea is that a sufficient area of energy coppice could fuel a small, new power station, and local industries could use it for heating. It could also replace gas, oil, or coal at a very local level—the farmer's central heating system, perhaps. It may even be practical to mix chipped wood and straw in eastern England, where a balance of cereal growing and wildlife-rich willows would be a much more environmentally friendly farming option.

Robert Goodwin is in the forefront of moves in this direction. His is one of six energy coppice demonstration farms, part of the Farm Wood Fuel and Energy Project funded by the Department of Trade and Industry. 'We've always grown cricket-bat willows,' says Goodwin. 'Then my mother got interested in basketry, so we planted other forms of willow for her. I went to an open day at the Long Ashton Research Station, near Bristol, back in 1987, and ordered a few hundred cuttings of

basketry willows.

'I looked at willows, poplars, beech, and other trees they were growing there as an experimental energy crop. That was it. I bought 2500 willow and poplar cuttings home and planted them on a half-acre I had spare.'

Now he has six acres across the farm planted with as many as 40 varieties of willow and about 15 poplar varieties.

The idea is catching on. South Western Power wants to construct two wood-burning power stations, one in Suffolk, the other in North Wiltshire. It has secured contracts to sell the electricity that they will produce at between 8p and 9p a kilowatt hour (twice the price of coal-generated power), subsidized by consumers to get the technology started.

'Each power station should produce 5.5 megawatts of electricity and require 1200 acres of energy coppice to keep it running year-round,' says Gerry Swarbrick, South Western Power's director. Subject to planning consent, he hopes to get started on the construction of these power stations this year.

▲ **Figure 11.22** From the *Daily Telegraph*, 21 January 1995.

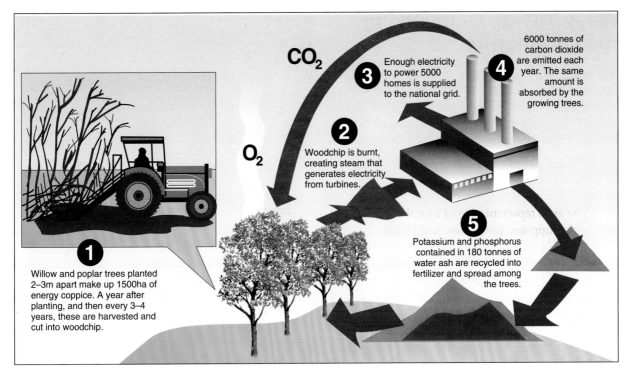

CO₂

O₂

1 Willow and poplar trees planted 2–3m apart make up 1500ha of energy coppice. A year after planting, and then every 3–4 years, these are harvested and cut into woodchip.

2 Woodchip is burnt, creating steam that generates electricity from turbines.

3 Enough electricity to power 5000 homes is supplied to the national grid.

4 6000 tonnes of carbon dioxide are emitted each year. The same amount is absorbed by the growing trees.

5 Potassium and phosphorus contained in 180 tonnes of water ash are recycled into fertilizer and spread among the trees.

▲ **Figure 11.23** Woodchip for electricity generation

Coppicing fuelwood

Study Figures 11.22 and 11.23. They show how the use of wood from coppicing – periodic pruning or cutting without destroying the tree – has potential for energy production. At a local level, it could become significant as an energy provider.

One of the major constraints on the wider use of coppice is the capital cost involved in setting up. Establishment costs can range between £600 and £1600 per hectare, the major outlay being the purchase of the saplings. This cost can be reduced from 20p to 8p each through co-operative buying. In Sweden the development of a market has brought the cost down to 3p each. This seemingly small price is significant when it is considered that 8000 saplings are needed per hectare. Costs can be further reduced by staggering the planting in blocks over 3–5 years. This enables free cuttings to be produced by cutting back the previous year's crop. 'Better Land Supplement' grants of £600/ha are available for land that is brought out of food production, and there are also various Forestry Commission planting grants.

Another constraint to the further development of fuelwood coppicing is the lack of a market for woodchip. This will take time to develop, and most schemes currently being developed are already linked to some end use, often electricity generation. Here one issue to consider is the transport needed to move a bulk fuel, and the subsequent need to locate the power station close to the source of the woodchip.

1 Explain how the generation of electricity from woodchip represents zero impact in terms of carbon dioxide emissions.

2 Highlight the major benefits of fuelwood coppicing.

3 Why might transport and storage of woodchip be more of a problem than the transport of coal to produce the same amount of energy?

Ways forward – involving the community

Many objections to renewable energy developments such as wind turbines come from local people who feel that they are getting all the local environmental impact without any benefits. This problem has been addressed by Sweden and Denmark, where community involvement in renewable energy development is encouraged. On the island of Gotland in Sweden, 1200 out of 20 000 households are associated with co-operatively owned wind power projects. By July 1994 there were 46 turbines on the island, with varying methods of ownership – see Figure 11.24.

The co-ops, or *Samfallighet*, on Gotland consist of residents from towns and villages from all parts of the island, not just those in the immediate vicinity of the wind turbines. Objections from the local population have been rare and those that have come are mainly from summer-house owners who are not permanent residents on the island.

No. of turbines	Ownership	Installed capacity (kW)
15	Community-owned	3525
20	Private company	4400
6	Utilities	3720
2	Private	75
3	Share-owned limited company	950
Total installed capacity: 12 670kW		

▲ **Figure 11.24** Ownership of wind turbines on Gotland, July 1994.

Goteborgsvind – a case study

On the Swedish mainland in Gothenburg harbour, two 225kW turbines were erected in 1993 by the Swedish Electricity Utility, Goteborg Energi. Domestic electricity consumers in the region were eligible to buy shares in the wind turbines up to an equivalent of their own electricity consumption. Through advertisements in the press, all customers of Goteborg Energi were invited to apply for shares in the project.

▲ **Figure 11.25** The position of Gothenburg in Sweden.

The estimated annual output of the wind turbines was 1 100 000kWh/year. In total, 1100 shares were issued, so each share was the equivalent to an output of approximately 1000kWh/year. The price for each share was 3000SEK (equivalent to about £250). Members of the association were eligible to buy 'green' electricity from the wind turbines, at a price lower than they would normally pay for their electricity from the utility. Figure 11.26 shows tax-free benefits to members for each share owned.

As the majority of Swedish homes are electrically heated, an average annual consumption can be up to 20 000kWh/year. The project was heavily oversubscribed and the utility had to erect a third turbine to meet the demand.

Normal cost to the consumer for 1000kWh	1000 x 48.2 ore = 482SEK
Cost of 1000kWh of wind-generated electricity	1000 x 24.8 ore = 248SEK
Reduction in electricity cost per share (tax free)	234SEK/year
This corresponds to a return of 7.8% after tax on the 3000SEK invested in a share.	

▲ **Figure 11.26** Financial benefits of membership.

Integrating Renewable Energy

Wind power in Sweden and the UK

In Sweden the process of obtaining power purchase contracts is a lot more straightforward and therefore cheaper to initiate. This is crucial to the success of small-scale community-based renewable projects with limited capital. All the checks and balances built into the UK NFFO procedure are appropriate for large-scale renewable projects, but are costly and discriminate heavily against the smaller-scale projects.

The level of technology development, particularly in Sweden and Denmark, provides a lot of confidence in wind power, both from financial institutions and from the general public.

Finally, it is worth noting the comments of Keith Boxer of Vindkompaniet, a leading wind energy development company based in Gotland, Sweden.

'We do not think that there is a significant cultural difference between the various countries which would inhibit community involvement in the UK. In Sweden people invested because they thought renewables were good for the environment, but primarily they invested because it was a long-term investment with a reasonable return.'

	Sweden	UK
Financial support for wind power	Until recently there has been a 35% grant to developers. This is changing to the introduction of a tax on fossil fuel generating plant, enabling wind developers to obtain a higher price for the electricity they produce.	The Non-Fossil Fuel Obligation (NFFO) enables developers to obtain a higher price for the electricity they produce.
Obtaining power purchase contracts with a favourable price for wind-generated electricity	Simple procedure for obtaining an environmental bonus for wind-generated electricity.	Limited number of power purchase contracts available through the NFFO. Procedure is lengthy and it is expensive to obtain them.
Wind-speed data collection	All turbines that receive a state subsidy have to publish all wind data from the site. On-site wind monitoring is not a prerequisite to obtaining a power purchase contract. The assumption is that it is in the best interests of the developer to ensure that the site is a good one.	There is an obligation to provide a minimum amount of measured and correlated wind-speed data before obtaining an NFFO contract.
Technology development	A lot of experience in Scandinavia of wind-turbine manufacture and operation.	Limited experience of wind-turbine manufacture and operation.

▲ **Figure 11.27** Comparison of wind power development in Sweden and the UK.

1 Imagine you are a domestic energy consumer in Gothenburg using an average amount of electricity annually.
   a) How much would you have to pay (in £) to buy shares equivalent to your electricity consumption?
   b) What would you save on an annual basis (in £) through purchasing 'green' electricity from the wind turbines?

2 Produce an advertisement for the local newspaper, aimed at encouraging domestic consumers to invest in the wind turbines.

3 Write a 250-word article for a national UK newspaper reporting your view of whether community development of renewable energy is a good idea and whether it is feasible within the UK.

Looking to the future

4 How do you think the trend in renewable energy will change in the next 30 years? Consider also what you learned in Chapter 10 about energy from waste. Form groups – which of the following do you think is most likely, and why?
   - There will be a huge increase in production of renewable energy.
   - There will be a slight increase in production of renewable energy.
   - Renewable energy will make little impact on the way we produce energy.

5 Consider fossil fuels, renewable energy, nuclear power, and energy efficiency in the UK. What would be the advantages and disadvantages of each of the following strategies for the future?
   a) Allow whatever energy supply happens to be cheapest and most plentiful at the time.
   b) Save stocks of any fossil fuel, reduce energy demand, and develop renewable energy sources.
   c) Develop a mix of fossil fuels and nuclear power and renewable sources.

6 Which of the strategies (a)–(c) in question 5 or another stategy of your choice do think the UK government should adopt? Why?

Ideas for further study

1 Form groups of three or four. Investigate the benefits and problems associated with the development of tidal power at a site like the river Severn. You should consider the following points.

- Its production potential – ability to match electricity supply with demand.
- Economic factors, including capital and electricity generating costs.
- Environmental impacts, such as impact on wildlife, water quality, and changes to dependence on fossil fuels or nuclear power.
- Social impacts of increased leisure facilities.

2 Using secondary sources of information, carry out more detailed research into the benefits and problems of nuclear power. Produce a report summarizing the main issues and highlighting your views.

3 Form groups of three or four. Carry out a feasibility study to consider the development of *either* wind *or* solar power to supply a small-scale energy need for your college or school. You will need to do the following.

   a) Carry out a site analysis, collecting wind speed and solar radiation data around your college or school to identify the best site.

   b) Identify a small-scale energy need that could be met, such as a 12V supply to the science labs, or hot water for the technicians' room.

   c) Find out from manufacturers' data if this need could be met, and its cost.

   d) Evaluate the environmental impact on your college or school, including any loss of amenity as a result of installation. Use a Leopold matrix as described in Chapter 10.

To help you, the Engineering Council produces a resource for A-level Geography students to help carry out this study – see 'References and further reading' below.

Summary

- Renewable sources of energy have a limited share of the world's energy production at present, though they have great potential.
- The development of renewable energy raises several questions about the use of land.
- As for other means of energy production, there are social, economic, and environmental impacts.
- HEP is seen by many ELDCs as a potential source of energy in a world that has finite fossil fuel reserves.
- Like virtually all economic activities, decisions made about the use of renewable energy can have an impact on those who are less advantaged.
- In the UK, it is almost impossible to separate energy production from political issues, such as privatization and government policies. However, there are few explicit energy policies, and energy production tends to develop in an uncoordinated way.

References and further reading

M. Flood, *Energy Without End*, Friends of the Earth, 1991.
Friends of the Earth, *Planning for Wind Power – Guidelines for Project Developers and Local Planners*, 1994.
Review, free periodical on renewable energy from the DTI, available from the Renewable Energy Enquiries Bureau, Energy Technology Support Unit, Harwell, Oxfordshire, OX11 0RA.
Engineering Council, Geography section of the Technology Enhancement Programme Post-16 Energy Module.

Resource management: Summary

In this section you have learned about resources and their management, and about the impact of using resources. The table below shows you how these studies are linked to the requirements of the syllabus you are studying. Your examiners who will be setting the examination papers on the topics in this book will use the summary points below.

Key ideas	Explanation	Examples
1 The nature of resources	The nature of resources depends on rates of usage and renewal in relation to stocks available: – Classification and definitions of resources – Physical formation of mineral resources – Uses of and demands for fossil fuels, minerals, water, and renewable energy sources – Current water or waste resource situation at a regional, national, or international scale.	• Finite (fossil fuels and minerals), recyclable (water and waste), sustainable (woodland) and renewable sources • Origins of tin • Finite and renewable energy supply and demand in the UK • Uses for and options for supplying and/or using waste or water. • Issues of water quality in Cornwall and the UK
2 There are limitations upon resource exploitation	Resources are limited by stock, flow, and carrying capacity. – Geological and fossil fuels are finite – Some resources are sustainable or renewable – Different resources are extracted and used in different ways – Recyclable resources require various processes and management methods.	• Coal in the UK, and tin in the UK and Malaysia • Renewable energy in the UK • Opencast coal mining, and extraction of tin • Water management and options in the UK and Bangladesh, and waste management, e.g. recycling, landfill
3 Resources vary spatially	Resources are distributed differently over space, and so lead to variations in human activity: – globally – nationally.	• A study of the global tin industry • Tin mining in the UK and Malaysia, coal in the UK.
	Renewable energy has great potential.	• Renewable energy in the UK
4 The potential exploitation of resources depends on a variety of factors	The decision to use resources depends on political thinking, availability of alternatives, technological capacity to exploit, and social, economic, and environmental consequences.	• The tin industry in the UK • Water management issues in the UK, Mexico, and Bangladesh. • Waste management in Germany • The potential for renewable energy resources in the UK – wind energy
5 Resource exploitation and use has significant impacts	Resource use has social, economic, and environmental consequences, which may vary according to how the resource is managed.	• Issues for the disposal of waste. • Toxic waste and sewerage • The impact of MNEs and individual water and mineral companies on local areas of EMDCs (Cornwall) and ELDCs (Malaysia) • Energy and waste water policies in different countries, e.g. the UK • The impact of HEP development

Glossary

Accessibility A measure of how easy it is to reach one place from another.

Agglomeration The process of accumulation, where services and employment grow together.

Aquaculture Farming based on water ecosystems, producing fish or seafood.

Aquifer A rock which holds water reserves as a result of its porosity or permeability.

Bid-rent theory A theory which states that different land users are willing to pay different amounts for land which, in turn, leads to zones of different land use.

Capitalism A theory based on private economic wealth, where individuals invest capital in order to maximize income from it.

Census A count of a country's population, normally held every 5–10 years.

Centrally Planned Economy An economy where central government plans investment, production and distribution of goods.

Communism A theory which is based upon communal, rather than private, wealth generation.

Concentric zones Zones of land use of similar age, growing outwards from a central urban core.

Conservation The policy of saving or preserving features or resources.

Conurbation An extensive built up area formed by the joining of once separate settlements. A large concentration of population, economic activities and services.

Core regions Regions of economic growth which attract investment and develop employment, services and income to a higher level than surrounding regions.

Correlation Comparing sets of data in order to investigate a relationship between them.

Cosmopolitan Belonging to all parts of the world; having international taste; unprejudiced.

Economic Activity Activity which is based on the generation of wealth, including the processes of extraction, production, distribution, consumption and conservation of resources in order to produce wealth.

ELDC Economically Less Developed Country; groups of these are also known as the 'Third World' or 'The South'.

EMDC Economically More Developed Country; groups of these are also known as the 'The Rich World' or 'The North'.

Environmental Impact Analysis A means of assessing the impact of a proposed or actual development upon a place.

Ethnic A group with its own distinct culture, introduced from another country.

Exploitation The use of resources by people.

Favela Also known as 'slums' or 'squatter settlements', this term is used to describe low quality housing in South American cities. In India, these are known as 'bustees'.

Finite A fixed, known amount.

Free market economy An economy in which central government plays no part, where all economic activity depends upon market prices for goods based upon supply, demand or what people are willing to pay.

Greenfield site Land which has not previously been subjected to significant building development (i.e. agricultural land) and is therefore relatively cheap to buy and easy to use. The increase in urban decentralization has increased the pressure on such sites.

Globalization The process by which something becomes world-wide; often used to describe how global factors influence national or local economies.

Gross Domestic Product A measure of national wealth, determined by the value of goods and services produced by a country.

Growth poles Locations where economic activities are planned to stimulate the economic health of a surrounding (often depressed) region or hinterland. Investment is concentrated into these 'poles' rather than being spread thinly throughout the region.

Human Development Index An index, or figure, which seeks to show human well-being as well as wealth generated.

Hydrology The processes by which water acts upon the landscape and within the atmosphere.

Infrastructure The services and amenities necessary to make organized economic and social activity possible. These include communications (e.g. road, rail) power and water supply, and sewerage disposal. Often these are provided through public funds raised by taxes.

Inward migration The movement of people into a place.

Irrigation The artificial introduction of water into a place by means of, for example, wells, dams, pipes or canals.

Least-cost location A theory which states that any economic activity will seek a location where its costs are lowest, thus increasing its profitability.

Lode deposits Mineral or metal-bearing rocks, such as tin 'veins' found in granite.

MNEs (Multi-National Enterprises) Companies which operate in more than one country.

Monsoon A rainy season, common to areas of South-East Asia.

Multiplier effect The process by which economic growth increases, by attracting additional economic activities and generating further wealth.

Natural increase (of population) The increase in population produced by an excess number of births over deaths.

NICs Newly-Industrializing Countries

Pathogens Agents which introduce disease, such as bacteria within sea water.

Peripheral regions Regions of economic growth which attract lower investment and develop less employment, fewer services and lower incomes compared to surrounding regions.

Placer deposits Weathered minerals or metal-bearing ores found in alluvial deposits of river and sea beds.

Population density The number of people in a given unit area, such as a square kilometre.

Primary activity Economic activity based upon the production of natural resources, through forestry, farming, fishing and mining.

Primary processing Economic activity which processes natural resources, e.g. timber.

Primate city A city, often the capital, which completely dominates a country through its size, and attracts a disproportionate amount of investment, employment, political power and influence, compared to the rest of the country.

Quango A government-appointed group which manages activities; because it is appointed it is undemocratic. Literally, a Quasi-Non-Governmental Organization.

Quaternary activity Economic activity based upon the provision of specialist advice, for which professional qualifications are required, e.g. legal, medical.

Radicalism Any idea or theory which promotes fundamental change.

Renewable energy Energy produced using resources which are infinite, and which do not deplete resource stock.

Resource Any material or substance of use to people.

Resource flow Resources which can be replenished so that their stock does not decrease.

Resource stock Resources which are limited in quantity.

Rural–urban migration The movement of people from rural to urban areas.

Satellite towns Towns close to a major centre, which are dependent upon it or have been built to reduce or control its growth.

Secondary activity Economic activity based upon the production of natural resources, through forestry, farming, fishing and mining.

Segregation The separation of people or groups within society or an area.

Semi-permanent housing Housing of medium quality in ELDC cities, where people pay taxes or rates in return for services, but which is not fixed, permanent housing stock.

Sociology The study of human societies.

Squatter settlement A settlement, usually temporary, in which people settle illegally, on property owned by someone else.

State capitalism The management of economic activity by a government designed to influence and modify free market economies.

Subsistence A lifestyle which produces little or no surplus for sale, producing goods for own consumption.

Suburbanization The process of urban expansion, by which outer urban areas or rural villages become 'engulfed' by urban development and growth.

Succession A sequence of vegetation communities in an area; also used to describe sequences of people living in a place.

Sustainable development Development which neither depletes resource stock nor reduces that capacity for future generations to enjoy an acceptable quality of life.

Systems A group of components consisting of inputs, stores and outputs, linked by processes or flows.

Tariffs Charges levied on imported goods by governments in order to protect home-produced goods.

Tertiary activity Economic activity based upon the production of natural resources, through forestry, farming, fishing and mining.

Toxic Poisonous or ecologically damaging.

Urban morphology The analysis of the evolving structure and land use within towns and cities concentrating particularly on their layout, land use, form and function.

Urban revelopment Demolition of all existing urban structures within an area and rebuilding from scratch.

Urban Built-up areas, such as towns or cities.

Urban infill The process by which urban growth occurs by using spaces between existing developments.

Urban models Theories designed to show how cities have grown and developed.

Urban sectors Separate areas of cities which have developed in unique ways.

Urban sprawl Uncontrolled growth of cities.

Urbanization The process by which both numbers of people, and the percentage of people, living in cities increases.

Variable A number which varies, or a component of a statistical relationship.

Westernization The process of adopting Western values and lifestyles.

Zone of transition An area of mixed commercial, industrial and residential land uses, found in inner cities; often as one decays another replaces it.

Index